The World of Count Basie

THE WORLD OF
COUNT BASIE

Stanley Dance

CHARLES SCRIBNER'S SONS · NEW YORK

Editor's note: The film *The Last of the Blue Devils,* which is discussed herein, opened in New York in June 1980.

Library of Congress Cataloging in Publication Data
Dance, Stanley.
   The world of Count Basie.
   Bibliography: p. 371
   "Selected discography":   p. 357
   Includes index.
   1.   Basie, Count, 1904-   2.   Jazz musicians—
United States—Biography.   3.   Jazz music.   4.   Big
bands.   I.   Title.
ML417.B2D3   785.42′092′4   [B]   80-15641
ISBN 684-17289-5 (paper)
ISBN 684-16604-6 (cloth)

To the Holy Main

Acknowledgments

Interviews with Harry Edison, Gus Johnson, and Gene Ramey were supported by the National Endowment for the Arts Jazz Oral History Project, and excerpts from these interviews appear by permission of the artists.

Part I of the Count Basie section originally appeared as *The Kid from Red Bank* in *This Is Jazz,* published by George Newnes Ltd., and is reproduced by permission of Syndication International Ltd.

The Dicky Wells chapter, originally entitled *Basie Days,* is from *The Night People* by Dicky Wells as told to Stanley Dance (Crescendo, 1971). Copyright 1971 by Stanley F. Dance. Reprinted by permission of Taplinger Publishing Co., Inc.

The interviews with Marshall Royal and Snooky Young first appeared in *Jazz Journal* in March and April 1962, respectively, and are reprinted with that magazine's permission.

Part II of the Lester Young section is reproduced by permission of *Melody Maker,* London.

Part II of the Lockjaw Davis section, originally entitled *Two-Career*

Man, the Frank Wess chapter, originally entitled *Wess Points,* and Part II of the Basie section, originally entitled *American Institution,* are reprinted by permission of *Down Beat* magazine.

The interviews with Sir Charles Thompson, Al Grey, and Lockjaw Davis (Part I) are reprinted by special permission of Robert Asen, publisher of *Metronome.*

The Buck Clayton and Eric Dixon interviews first appeared in *Jazz* and are reprinted by permission.

Permission to quote from *Living in a Land of Extremes: Melting Pot or Mosaic?* by Joe B. Frantz was granted by the Southwestern Library Association, Southwestern Mosaic Project, for whom it was written under a grant from the National Endowment for the Humanities.

CONTENTS

List of Illustrations

Introduction

Like *The World of Duke Ellington, The World of Swing,* and *The World of Earl Hines,* this book consists largely of interviews with musicians. It is not meant to stand as a biography of Count Basie, and I am presuming that the reader brings some knowledge of Basie and his world to the book. The oral historical method affords the reader many different views of Basie's career and lets aspects of his life emerge that might remain hidden in a straight, chronological account. While the musicians generally confirm each other in matters of fact (venues, recording session personnel, etc.), they sometimes contradict each other in matters of opinion (why, for instance, Basie is reluctant to take solos). Also, of course, the time at which a musician gave an interview affects his narration of the events. For example, when I interviewed Frank Foster in 1961, he was a virtual newcomer to Basie's world—and this fact no doubt colors his interpretation of that world. Now, almost twenty years later, this experienced, adventurous musician would probably recall that world differently. But Foster's early statements reveal a spontaneity that might be lost in an updated retrospective.

In the introduction to *The World of Earl Hines,* I wrote that interpretation was left to the reader. What I wanted then, as now, was to
have the musicians speak as directly as possible to the reader. A
running commentary from the interviewer, particularly if it conflicted
with the musicians' statements, would serve no useful purpose. There
are many interpretative histories of jazz and most of them suggest that
their authors' experience of the music is radically different from that
of the men and women who made the music. Generally, the musicians'
evaluations have an authority that their interpreters seem to lack. The
musician may sometimes be more impressed by technical virtuosity
than critics are, and he may, too, show a reluctance to fault or
condemn a colleague, but the *degree* or tone of his praise is usually a
reliable guide to quality.

The World of Count Basie is made up of two parts. Count Basie, to
my way of thinking, represented the First Wave from Kansas City and
Jay McShann the Second. Each brought with him an innovator
destined to exert an enormous influence on the whole course of jazz.
With Basie, it was Lester Young; with McShann, Charlie Parker. But
above and beyond this, the relationship of one to the other, and to a
common tradition, tells us much about both. In the course of *The Last
of the Blue Devils,* a documentary filmed in Kansas City, Basie says:
"I'm glad I got out of here as fast as I did, because he was breathing
down our backs so hard. We had to get out and move over and let this
cat in—Jay McShann."

This was a rather generous exaggeration, but a very few months
after Basie left for Chicago and New York, in 1936, McShann began
his important engagement at Martin's-on-the-Plaza.

The interview with Gene Ramey portrays the Kansas City scene at
that time with much clarity. The great popularity of Andy Kirk's band
is noted, but its style, with more emphasis on ensemble playing, was
closely related to that of bands in the East and contrasted sharply with
those of Basie and McShann, which were much more loose-knit, as was
Bennie Moten's in its last year.

The Basie and McShann "books," or repertoires, consisted mainly of
"head" arrangements, a large proportion of which were blues. Soloists,
backed by ensemble or section riffs, were extensively featured, and
particular attention was paid to the role of the rhythm section. So close
was the stylistic relationship of the two bands that three of McShann's
key musicians (Gene Ramey, Gus Johnson, and Paul Quinichette)
subsequently worked effectively and comfortably with Basie. The
shared roots and, for some years, the parallel courses of the two bands
explain the inclusion of the McShann section. Interviews with Eddie

Barefield, Sir Charles Thompson, Snub Mosely, and Melvin Moore further illustrate the music scene in the Southwest.

Jazz in that part of the country is a far larger subject than was originally recognized, and some knowledge of its history and landscape is essential to an understanding of the Basie band. Early jazz writers tended to focus their attention almost exclusively on New Orleans, Chicago, and New York, but first Dave Dexter and then Frank Driggs began to reveal the musical potential of the Southwest. While it is true that no really impressive records emanated from there prior to 1932, the work of talented individuals could certainly be heard on the relatively few records that were made. Bennie Moten's band, which recorded quite prolifically from 1923 onward, offers little of artistic significance on its Okeh and Victor records until its rhythm section is enhanced by the presence of Basie and bassist Walter Page. Even before their arrival, though, the band's personnel included musicians who made valuable contributions to Basie's band and to jazz in general, such as Eddie Durham, Ed Lewis, Joe Keyes, Lips Page, Jack Washington, Ben Webster, Eddie Barefield, and Harlan Leonard, not to mention singer Jimmy Rushing. Moten himself appears to have been an undistinguished pianist, but he was a capable leader and organizer. Basie referred to him in *The Last of the Blue Devils* with affection: "He was a very warm, very lovable man. . . . Bennie taught me an awful lot, by just watching him. I mean, I had no idea that I was watching him for any *reason* at all, but just that I was crazy about him. I had no thoughts of fronting any band while I was with Bennie."

Nevertheless, after Moten's tragic death, Basie soon found himself leading a group with a nucleus of musicians from that leader's band.

The joint interview with Basie and guitarist Freddie Green in *The World of Swing* revealed some of their beliefs regarding swing and tempos. Green joined Basie in 1937 and, apart from a brief interval in 1950, has been with him ever since—the longest tenure of any sideman in the band. His role in the rhythm section is of great significance. In Basie's view, "it holds things together." A reserved, dignified man, Green was born in Charleston, South Carolina, where his close friend, Lonnie Simmons (tenor saxophone and organ), got him his first professional job with the Nighthawks. Another friend, trumpet player Samuel Walker, whose father taught at Jenkin's Orphanage, helped Green to learn to read when he began to play banjo. Although he was not a member of the famous Jenkin's Orphanage Band, this friendship led to his first experience of "the road" when he toured with the band —along with Cat Anderson—as far as Maine. Green went to New York in 1930 and stayed with an aunt, in whose house he became familiar with rent parties and stride piano. He worked as an upholsterer by day, and at night in an after-hours club, the Yeah Man, where the manager advised him to switch to guitar. "Lonnie Johnson came in one night and upset me," he recalled. More invaluable experience came when he worked at the Exclusive Club with Willie Gant, a stride pianist. Gant had a huge repertoire and Green had to learn to accompany singers in all kinds of keys. Because there were no drums, maintaining a good beat was essential and, since there was room in the club for dancing, tempos were important too. When John Hammond heard him at the Black Cat in Greenwich Village in 1936, he was working with Kenny Clarke (drums), Lonnie Simmons (tenor saxophone), Fat Atkins (piano), and Frank Spearman (bass), Clarke's stepbrother. He auditioned for Basie at Roseland and got the job, thus determining the pattern of his life. Acoustic, rhythm guitar is seldom heard in the few remaining big bands, but Freddie Green's continues to be a vital part of the Basie band's pulse.

In their joint interview, Basie and Green were almost equally guarded in naming their favorites, but there are two bands that Basie consistently refers to with the greatest respect and admiration—Duke Ellington's and Jimmie Lunceford's. His liking for the latter is incomprehensible to many, for Lunceford's was a "show" band that emphasized arrangements and the ensemble. Lunceford's performances could be considered almost the antithesis of the loose, open kind that were Basie's original specialty, and its liking for "two-beat" rhythm, as opposed to the even four-four of Kansas City, was another major point of difference. Yet as Basie well knew, having encountered it in more than one ballroom, Lunceford's was a band with a flair for danceable tempos and a rare ability to swing, not so much, be it noted, on the flagwavers that excited white audiences, but on medium and slow tempos.

It is customary to divide Basie's career as a bandleader rather arbitrarily into two periods: one before he broke up his big band in 1950, the other after the brief period when he led a small group. The band's character changed considerably during the forties as a result of the departure of Lester Young, Jo Jones, and Walter Page, but the new band of 1951 closely resembled that of the late forties. The three individuals most responsible for a change of concept and direction later in the 1950s were Marshall Royal, Neal Hefti, and Joe Williams.

According to Hefti in a *Billboard* article (July 18, 1964), Basie wanted to get out of the "riff-raff rough" and develop a stage band that could appear on the Ed Sullivan Show! Although it never became a show band in the sense that Lunceford's was, it did become much more of an ensemble band, partly because soloists of marked individuality were less common than a quarter-century before. Hefti's neat, well-crafted arrangements, and the polished performances that Royal, as deputy music director, exacted from the band, all resulted in a new identity that has been maintained for more than twenty years, often in rather pale imitations of such Hefti originals as *Li'l Darlin'*.

Apart from Hefti's, successful arrangements were contributed from outside the band by Benny Carter and Quincy Jones, but, as in the early days, much of the best and most appropriate writing came from men in the band, such as Ernie Wilkins, Frank Wess, Frank Foster, Thad Jones, Eric Dixon, and Bobby Plater. Wilkins's and Foster's settings were of great significance in launching Joe Williams and his blues repertoire.

For many readers, especially those overseas, the Southwest may need defining geographically, culturally, and ethnically. The importance of its six states as background to the music and musicians discussed in this book will soon become evident, but the Southwest is not the entity casual references in jazz writings often suggest. It is well described in *Living in a Land of Extremes: Melting Pot or Mosaic?*—an essay written by Joe B. Frantz, Director of the Texas State Historical Association:

> Citizens in the eastern portion of the region descend from the Old South rather than the West, and the mixed culture is black-white rather than red-brown-white. Texas itself is split—an out-reach of the Old South in the eastern one-third of the state, a combination desert-mountain area in the western two-thirds. Or you can split Texas laterally (as well as horizontally). North Texas is WASP country, heavily white Anglo-Saxon Protestant. The farther south you go in Texas, the more it becomes Catholic and Mexican and brown. Like Texas, Arkansas is bifurcated—Old South in the east and hillbilly and western in the west. Oklahoma, the most Indian of the southwestern states, has a southeastern area it calls "Little Dixie," while its northwestern panhandle knows no cultural difference from the plains of the Texas Panhandle. New Mexico varies from the forested mountains with their isolated towns, still redolent of colonial Spanish days; to the Indian pueblos, mainly in the north; to the pervasive desert that offers little to the person who can't afford to irrigate or mine it. Arizona has natural wonders that suggest emptiness punctuated by spectacle, most notably in the north; relieved by the grass-lands and forests of the White Mountains and Oak Creek Canyon across the center; and the more genteel Patagonia rolling region in the south. Phoenix and Tucson sit in the middle of the state like twin hubs of a giant wheel, with the desert on all sides—

meccas for sunshine seekers. Here are two of the fastest-growing cities in the nation, with all of the pleasures and problems of people who represent extremes—wealth and poverty, youth and age—ethnic differences, and the political range.

In short, every subsection of the Southwest has its own cultural pattern, its own personality.

Basically, the region is tri-cultural though the components of that three-way culture vary. Arizona and New Mexico are Indian-Mexican-Anglo. Texas is Anglo-Black-Mexican, and Louisiana is French-Anglo-Black. Arkansas and Oklahoma tend to have only two principal cultural groups, but again the pattern varies. Arkansas is black-white, while Oklahoma is red-white, though each has elements of other cultural/ethnic groups.

This diversity means not only that the Southwest is enormously interesting culturally, but that stereotypes must be discarded to move from area to area within its six-state confines. Thus the notions of the Southerner's religion, black or white, as stemming from one of the more evangelical denominations loses its credibility in Louisiana and eastern Texas where both blacks and whites may be Roman Catholic. And the generalizations about the soft Southern speech lose authority in a region where French, Spanish, German, and many Indian dialects are commonly spoken.

Four of the six states have a cattle and cowboy heritage—Texas, Oklahoma, New Mexico and Arizona. But looking farther back, the American cowboy, that star of screen and penny dreadfuls, learned to ride from the Mexican, who learned from the Spanish, who learned from the Moors. The heritage is Moorish-Spanish, as are the original cattle and horses that stocked the grasslands of those future states. Even the terms are Spanish-derived—lariat for *la riata*, calaboose from the Spanish *calabozo* and the French *calabouse*, *cafecito* from the Mexican-Spanish diminutive for coffee, chaps from the Mexican *chaparreras*, canyon from the Spanish *cañon*, *cayuse* from the Cayuse Indians, and so on and on. That most typical Texan, the cowboy then, is a derivative of other cultures and so are his cattle and horses. He descends from the Spaniard and the Indian who handled cattle over vast stretches of land that had inadequate roads and few railroads.

Irrelevant as much of this may seem to jazz, it was through this huge, dusty region of plains, deserts, and mountains that the old cars and raggedy buses full of jazz musicians moved. The musicians who endured the hardships of those rough roads and their inadequate accommodations were a resilient breed and singularly free from self-pity. Weathering the Depression with hardy independence, they simultaneously shaped new, innovative forms of musical expression on the traditional framework of the blues. Their counterparts of today, whose experiences are considerably less harrowing, call this "paying their dues."

In conclusion, I wish to acknowledge the contribution made to this, and to my previous books, by my wife. Her constant help and, in particular, her familiarity with the Basie band's early days were especially valuable in the present case. She was also responsible for the interviews with Gus Johnson and Jimmy Witherspoon. I am, of course, greatly indebted to all the musicians whose voices are heard here, and I much appreciate the cooperation of my friends Chris Albertson, Frank Driggs, and J. R. Taylor. And as before, Mrs. W. J. Boone's customary skill and meticulous care in transcribing interviews have been very important in the realization of this book.

STANLEY DANCE
Vista, California

The World of Count Basie

PART 1

Count Basie

I

In 1936 the world of jazz was dominated by the "big band"—a term employed to describe a group usually consisting of five or six brass, three or four reeds, and four rhythm. Its success largely depended upon acceptance by the dancing public, and this for several years had been regularly forthcoming from black audiences. Now, leaders like Benny Goodman, Tommy Dorsey, and Bob Crosby were taking their versions of the same idiom to white audiences. The Swing Era was under way.

The best bands at that time were led by Duke Ellington, Jimmy Lunceford, Chick Webb, Fletcher Henderson, Earl Hines, Don Redman, and Claude Hopkins. These bands, their soloists, and their arrangements were the real pacesetters. There was plenty of variety in their work, yet out of the heat of competition, out of the "battles of swing," standards had been set and a general conception of the big-band sound and program developed. Although these were still unashamedly "dance" bands, they were often to be found playing from

3

theater stages and accompanying increasingly ostentatious floorshows in nightclubs. As a result of this, and because of the growing importance of radio as a means of publicity, there was a definite tendency in jazz toward elaboration and decoration.

Upon this world, and upon New York in particular, the band Count Basie brought from Kansas City at the end of 1936 made a startling impression.

It was, however, by no means an entirely favorable impression. The band's business, as Basie saw it, was to provide swinging dance music. Opening night at the Roseland dancehall—formerly the scene of Fletcher Henderson's triumphs—found Basie facing the band across the piano with his back to the audience! This was no studied slight of the kind fashionable among the boppers a decade later. Rather, it denoted a single-minded concentration upon the work in hand, and perhaps more than a little nervousness, for the magic-carpet transfer from Kansas City to Broadway, engineered by critic John Hammond, had a quality of dream about it. Would Basie wake up and find himself and the band on their way back to Kansas City? What would the cats from the bigtime bands have to say when they dropped by to dig the music?

Many years later, Basie recalled one of the band's first New York reviews. It went like this: "If you think the reed section is out of tune, listen to the brass, and if you think the brass section is out of tune, listen to the band."

Yet even before the problems of intonation and ragged section work were overcome, the band had become the rage among the better informed. Its success resulted not so much from what it did as the way in which it did it. Its formula was not a new one. It took the big-band mixture as before and shook it in a newly effective way. The riffs (figures that the reed and brass sections played behind soloists and in climactic ensembles) were no new discovery. They had been long known and practiced by the Eastern bands, as Basie, a native of Red Bank, New Jersey, well knew. What he brought to them was above all a new emphasis. His band's performances were rhythmically intoxicating—and lean. Fat, in the form of commercial concessions or exotic coloring, was conspicuously absent. The essence of the big-band idiom was presented unadulterated, without equivocation. And, miraculously, it was accepted.

It would have seemed incredible in 1936 that twenty-odd years later there should be only two big jazz bands in regular existence. Had that possibility been entertained, it would have seemed reasonable enough that one should be Duke Ellington's. But that the other should be Count Basie's—that, too, would have seemed incredible!

"My favorite band is Count Basie's all the way. He is direct. He keeps it simple and sincere, and swings at all times."

These views were expressed in 1958 by trombonist Eli Robinson, himself a member of Basie's band from 1941 to 1947. They sum up very aptly the qualities that account for Basie's enduring popularity.

The main source of inspiration in the band has always been the rhythm section. Much credit must be given to such other members as that great-hearted bassist, the late Walter Page, the inimitable guitarist, Freddie Green, and the peerless drummer, Jo Jones. "You may think you're the boss," Basie once said, "but the drummer is really the head man; when he isn't feeling right, nothing's going to sound good."

However that may be, it is an inescapable fact that Basie's piano is always the heart of his rhythm sections; he makes the drummer feel right, and does much more than set tempos and feed soloists. Even in the first demonstration of the potency of the new Kansas City brew, Basie's piano played an extremely significant part. This demonstration, overlooked in several otherwise painstaking studies of Basie, took place on December 13, 1932, when Bennie Moten's Kansas City Orchestra recorded ten titles for Victor, among them *Moten's Swing*, *Toby*, *Lafayette*, *Prince of Wales*, and a salacious *Two Times*. These performances gave record buyers a foretaste of what New York was to experience in 1936. They showed the kind of revitalization the Moten band had undergone, and they showed the Count striding and swinging with an abandon that was wonderfully contagious.

The continual stress on the rhythm section's role and the importance of swinging are fundamentals to which Basie remains steadfast, but this does not mean that he is unaware of superficial changes in jazz. His reactions to the bop onslaught were illustrative of this: "You got to bop for the kids," he said. "They're the ones who support you. I want to play a lot of things that start off with a little bop figure, build into a real shout and then come back into the bop theme. Of course, there'll be solos. I'm for bop solos so long as they show sense. But if a guy is gonna play good bop he has to have a sort of a bop soul."

Basie, of course, never had a bop soul.

Two years later, after referring to the need to provide "a little taste of bop," he was saying, "We still keep a beat in the back line, relaxed and solid, behind the horns. So it doesn't matter what they do up front; the audience gets the beat."

Six years later, he was recounting some of his greatest musical thrills: "My biggest thrill as a listener came one night back in, I think it was, 1951.

"The so-called progressive jazz was going big then, and here comes Duke Ellington on opening night at Birdland. He had just revamped his band, and no one knew just what he'd have. We all dropped in to catch him—and what we heard! What a thrill that was!

"The Duke was swinging. All this 'progressive' talk, and the Duke played the old swing. He scared a lot of people that night. It was just wonderful. Of course, the Duke has always had the greatest band at all times. There's never been another band for me, year in and year out."

Other thrills that he recalled at the same time, as provided by Art Tatum, Louis Armstrong, Fletcher Henderson, and Jimmie Lunceford, were consistent with the same viewpoint and clearly indicated in which direction his sympathies lay. To him, Duke was "The Master," Art Tatum "The Boss," and Louis Armstrong, affectionately, "Pops"—"I can listen to Louis play or sing or talk or anything. . . ."

Nevertheless, his attitude to past and present is essentially realistic. "You don't sit still anymore. You got to go. Are you gonna fight to stand still?" he asked in 1948. "Maybe you don't convert entirely. You have to retain your identity, but you get points for effort."

When Basie played in concert halls, for instance, he sometimes felt the need to include in the program show-stopping material of a kind unsuitable at dances. Playing in concert halls has similarly required a far greater degree of instrumental polish and precision, and this has often resulted in a reduction of that remarkable feeling of spontaneity the early bands conjured up when riffing as an ensemble or behind soloists.

In the beginning there was a tendency for the band's success to be credited to its two tenor stars, Lester Young and Herschel Evans. Since then, Basie has always featured a couple of tenor soloists, such as Buddy Tate, Don Byas, Lucky Thompson, Illinois Jacquet, Paul Gonsalves, Paul Quinichette, Lockjaw Davis, Frank Wess, Frank Foster, Jimmy Forrest, and Eric Dixon. "I've always been queer for tenor men," he says.

His ability to come up with "unknown" star talent time after time is a reflection of his alert listening habits. Listening to music, with him, is a major pleasure, not a duty. He remembers those who favorably impress him, and when the time comes he sends for them. The extremely popular singer Joe Williams, whose reputation has been made with Basie, is a case in point.

Yet it is perhaps in the way his music has retained its essential identity, despite occasional diplomatic and partial conversions, that his character is best revealed.

Underlying as unpretentiously relaxed and frankly hedonistic an exterior as any in jazz is Basie's rare and wholly admirable resolve, a holding fast to purposes. His own personal success is the consequence of this resolve, but far more important has been his influence upon the whole course of jazz. By keeping it "simple and sincere," and swinging "at all times," his music has provided a guiding light in the chaos of the past two decades.

It might even be argued that his influence was greater than Duke Ellington's during the postwar period. Ellington was a source of inspiration rather than an influence, evolving creatively out of himself, little affected by the change and decay around him. Basie reflects change more because, unlike Ellington's, his repertoire has consisted of the compositions and arrangements of many different writers, among them Buck Clayton, Eddie Durham, Jimmy Mundy, Buster Smith, Tab Smith, Don Redman, Sy Oliver, Andy Gibson, Buster Harding, Nat Pierce, Neal Hefti, Ernie Wilkins, Johnny Mandel, Manny Albam, and Frank Foster. But like Ellington's, his music acquired its truth and identity in performance.

Buddy Tate, who went on to lead one of the best small jazz combinations, was featured by Basie as tenor soloist for longer than any other musician. He was once asked how he liked his position. "I like playing in this band," he replied. "It's been a real pleasure ever since I joined Count."

Dicky Wells, who was with Basie for ten years, is one of the greatest trombone stylists and a veteran with experience in several of the finest big bands. Looking back over his career up to 1958, he said without any hesitation, "Count was my favorite big-band leader. I can't say one bad thing about him."

Arranger Ernie Wilkins, while a member of the band, said, "You know, sometimes we can't wait to get on the stand, and we hate to quit when the night is over."

Endorsements of this kind justify Basie's care in building his bands. "I think it's important to have a likeable guy, a happy sort of guy as well as one who is a nice musician. Those things," Basie said in 1952, "put together, make a happy band."

The enthusiasm of his men also stems very much from the fact that Basie, again like Duke Ellington, plays jazz for kicks, for his own pleasure. And, like Duke, he doesn't stand in front of the band waving a baton. He is in there, a part of it, contributing, prompting, suggesting, a playing member.

Offstage, too, there is no false dignity, no attitudinizing. Dressing-room exchanges are conducted on the men's own terms, whether angry, serious, or humorous. An argument may grow heated and involve such original and picaresque language that even Basie grows excited. Eventually, he will discharge a verbal barrage and then relapse, with almost disconcerting suddenness, into tranquillity. In a serious discussion, he will be considerate, sensitive to another's point of view, shrewd in judgment, and, above all, disarmingly modest.

The wit that finds expression in his stimulating piano interjections is a natural part of his conversation. It may be drily deflationary, a comment upon a pretentious or mistaken idea, or it may be provocatively intent on extracting the maximum pleasure from an amusing situation.

Before leaving London after his second successful British tour of 1957, he had some last-minute shopping to do. Having made a number of discerning purchases for his wife, he sought a particular kind of fur gloves for his daughter. Nowhere could they be found. Mitts were recommended as best for kids.

"Yeah?" Basie queried. "How're they going to count in the wintertime?"

In East Anglia one cold night, the band had hungrily descended upon a small and humble café. Lockjaw Davis regarded a dish of ill-shaped pastries on the counter. Several squadrons of flies were using them as emergency airstrips, landing and taking off with rapidity and agility.

"What are those?" Lockjaw asked the waitress, pointing at the dish.

"Flycakes, man," said Basie, long before the official reply was forthcoming.

Typical of his quietly effective comebacks to criticism was that made when he quitted Alan Freed's rock 'n' roll radio show. Basie and band were undoubtedly miscast in this series; the friction began, it is rumored, with his refusal to play Freed's conception of suitable arrangements. When the parting of the ways came, Freed announced magnanimously, "He has the greatest band in the country, but it isn't a dance band."

A statement of this kind could have had a damaging effect on the band's bookings for dances, and Basie mildly demurred.

"I think people were dancing before rock 'n' roll," he said.

Nevertheless, he was not blind to the worthwhile aspects of rock 'n' roll, and on another occasion he made this comment: "It's been good for the bands. It got the kids dancing again. Right after the war I thought everyone had forgotten how."

The shy, unassuming person that this world-famous band leader essentially is can also sometimes be seen in the novel role of host at the elegant bar that bears his name on 132nd Street in New York. Early in 1958, after extensive remodeling and redecoration, the bar opened with a trio led by his friend and former tenor soloist, Lockjaw Davis. A great attraction in this group was Shirley Scott, a brilliant young organist. Somewhere, unobtrusive in the background, was the benign figure of Basie. There was no piano in the house, so he was inevitably asked to play the organ.

"Not after her," he said, grinning, and pointing at Shirley.

The earliest part of Count Basie's professional career is not, unluckily, documented by records, but the evidence of it is clearly heard in his subsequent music. In New York in the mid-twenties, he had been influenced by the "stride" piano school, of which such men as James P. Johnson, Fats Waller, and Willie (The Lion) Smith were natural leaders. As recently as 1957, he made a record called *The Kid from Red Bank*, in which the exciting characteristics of the stride style were still rewardingly prominent. This style was a full, two-handed one, and Basie employed it at the 1932 session with Bennie Moten, mentioned earlier.

Between 1927 and 1936, Kansas City obviously exerted its special influence on Basie. He recalls it as "a good town for music with joints up and down 12th Street—all the way out to the Paseo—where folks could go and listen and dance. Bennie always played a foot-pattin' beat. Never anything you couldn't dance to."

Emerging as leader of his own band, he increasingly developed the personal style by which he is identified today. This style originated during choruses devoted to the band's rhythm section when Basie contributed isolated notes and chords, or short phrases, with electrifying effect. The success of these choruses was such that Basie came to build nearly all his solos in this idiom, playing very brief phrases in the right hand with occasional punctuations from the left, while bass and guitar provided the regular sustaining rhythm that was normally the left hand's function. It sounded casual and relaxed, but his timing was so wonderful that the rhythmic result was unusually stimulating. The apparent simplicity, and an ironic quality of understatement, made the style ideally suitable for the interpretation of the blues.

The blues have always been Basie's forte, slow and moody, rocking at an easy, dancing pace, or jumping at passionate up-tempos. Nearly all his greatest successes have been blues, from *One O'Clock Jump* to *Every Day*. It is through the blues that jazz communicates most warmly and surely, as he well knows.

Nowadays he does not take as many solos as his admirers wish. It is a matter of modesty again, not laziness. He has excuses, reasons, and suggests that his style is too familiar. Then he will come up with an intimate, moving performance like *After Supper*, full of the old mastery and magic. He is even more reluctant to feature himself on organ, although this one-time protégé of Fats Waller probably plays the

organ to better effect than any other musician in jazz. He was egged
into playing the instrument at a concert in Paris in 1954. Four years
later he was admitting he had not played it publicly since. Recordings
like his version of Buster Harding's *Paradise Squat* should, however,
be sufficient to convince anyone that the organ has its place in jazz.

But so long as Basie is at the piano, leading a band, we may be sure
that we shall hear a lot of blues, at good tempos, and swinging. For
that, in an era when basic jazz values are often forsaken, we should be
profoundly grateful.

(1960)

II

As his musicians took their places on the stand at the beginning of the
evening, Count Basie ran his hands over the keyboard. The treble
sounded reasonably true, the bass like a deranged guitar.

"You never heard a piano like that before in your life, did you?"

"No."

"Vietnam!"

He tossed the word over his right shoulder as he and the rhythm
section began to set the tempo for the opener. The brass came in
with a great, powerful exclamation that took the crowd's breath away
and left it bright-eyed with excitement.

Another night had begun. Another night in more than thirty years of
nights, back and forth across the land—across the world.

What does a life of that kind demand beyond talent and stamina? A
certain kind of temperament? Melancholic, sanguine, phlegmatic,
choleric? None of these is common to the enduring triumvirate of
Basie, Ellington, and Herman, but each leader is slow to anger, patient,
and able to put on a good face when things go wrong. More important,
each has an unfailing sense of humor.

Basie's humor is dry, unhurried, and terse, and it is delivered off-
hand, deadpan. If it goes unheard or is lost on the listener, he doesn't
seem to care. The satisfaction in a witticism, for the true wit, lies
more in the thought than in its expression, and certainly more than in
any laughter it may arouse.

Another night. The band was grouped compactly in the corner of a
large, almost empty club. The weather was bad and the house prices
were outrageous. The band was swinging softly and beautifully before
coming up into the climax.

"You gotta play *April in Paris!*" bawled a drunk at the bar.

"I know it," Basie answered, without turning around, without accent, the voice modulated, apparently genial, but full of irony to anyone who knew him. They played *April in Paris* next, and one-more-timed themselves into intermission.

Another night, backstage at Carnegie Hall, a story Basie's friend and confidant, Teddy Reig, tells with relish. It illustrates the kind of folksy repartee Basie enjoys, and it came at the end of some straight-faced ribbing.

"You're making my knife nervous!" Basie told Big Mama Thornton.

"And you've got my pistol shakin'!" the blues singer replied.

Yet another night, in 1968. "A man of very few words," in the phrase with which he comically introduced singer Richard Boone, Basie had gallantly accepted an invitation to address the New York chapter of the Duke Ellington Society. ("You know you're not going to get a speech.") Later he sat, like a Daniel among hungry lions, and answered questions.

"What is the attitude of younger guys coming into a band with players who are much older?"

"They're very eager and interested—and they get old, too."

"Was Charlie Christian known as a comer in those days? Most of us hadn't heard of him until he got to New York."

"Don't say 'most of us.' Say 'most of you.'"

"Will you tell us a little bit about your childhood?"

"No, I will not."

"How did you get your nickname?"

"Which you mean? Count or Bill?"

"Did you get a chance to hear Ethel Waters at the Cotton Club?"

"The Cotton Club! I couldn't get in!"

"Are you going to make any more albums like *Battle Royal?*"

"I'd certainly like the invitation. It was one of the greatest experiences of my life, apart from being scared to death. At first, you know, they had planned it quite differently. We were to make a side, and then Duke was to make a side. Now I've been knowing this guy for about seventy years, and I know what he can lay on you when he gets ready, so I thought it would be a lot better to augment the two bands. But he's a nice guy! Just because he can drop trouble all over you, he doesn't necessarily do it."

"How many Ellington compositions have you in the book?"

"Anytime we think we can get away with it, we play one. We play *All Heart* and a lot of others he doesn't play now, and I'm very happy about that!"

"When did you first hear Ellington?"

"Well, I remember my father taking me to hear my cousin Edward . . ."

(Tit for tat. "I remember when I was a little boy, I stood on the other side of Fifth Avenue," Ellington would claim, "and heard him playing in Edmond's.")

Behind the modest, almost shy manner, and the relaxed humorous twists of speech, there is, of course, a serious, sensitive person. No one can have said more fitting words at Art Tatum's passing than Basie.

"It's bad enough when a man and a friend dies," he said. "When a man dies with all that talent, it's a disgrace."

He listens to pianists, of course, with particular interest, as these comments on Newport, 1967, show: "Earl Hines had us all spellbound backstage. He hasn't lost anything and he hasn't got dated, because he's a real originator. Don Ewell was terrific with Willie The Lion, too. I was glad to hear him play *Handful of Keys*, because Nat Pierce has done an arrangement of it for us. Don didn't miss a note."

At record dates, he may delegate authority to the arranger and Marshall Royal, the straw boss, but when he intervenes he is decisive. After several takes at one session, dissatisfied with a passage for brass, he got up from the piano and addressed his trumpets forcefully: "Lean on that as hard as you can—and harder than that!"

As is well known, racing is among his preferred forms of recreation. One summer, he pretended a good deal of irritation with Willard Alexander for booking him into Atlantic City before racing began there. It meant a long drive to Monmouth Park in New Jersey each day. When he and Harlan Floyd got back to the club one night, Freddie Green was standing outside enjoying the evening air.

"How did it go?"

"Real well. A horse in the last race called *Fiddler's Green* paid seventeen to one."

Freddie smiled his biggest smile, remembering his predecessor in the band, Claude Williams. Claude, who played violin as well as guitar, had been nicknamed "Fiddler."

Although Basie always speaks warmly of Fats Waller, and the encouragement and organ tuition he had from him at the Lincoln Theater, the Harlem scene obviously didn't have the impact that Kansas City's did.

"For twenty-five blocks, there used to be joints, sometimes three or four doors apart, sometimes every other block," he recalled. "There were burlesque shows, too, and all this was established before I had a band, before I even started to work there. There was an awful lot of good music, and it was like everything happened there. It was the first place I really heard the blues played and sung as they should be, and I heard all the great old blues singers of the twenties. This was all in Kansas City, Missouri. There was a big difference across the bridge, because Kansas City, Kansas, was dry."

Jimmy Rushing, who was subsequently his singer for fifteen years, played an important part in his early career.

"I didn't audition Jimmy," Basie continued. "Jimmy auditioned me. I was in Tulsa, Oklahoma, with a little show—Gonzel White and The Big Jamboree. We used to ballyhoo out on the sidewalk before each show, move the piano out, play a few tunes, and say, 'Right inside, folks!' The Blue Devils were in town at that time and Jimmy happened to pass by. He invited me up to the hall that night, when I met Walter Page. They let me sit in, and that was how we got acquainted."

After his period with the Blue Devils and Bennie Moten came the Reno Club. "Basie told me he thought he'd try getting a band together," Jimmy Rushing remembered. "At first, he had a little combo, just rhythm and two or three horns. Then they started jam sessions and began to broadcast. Blue Monday got to be a big night—Sunday night, Monday morning—at the Reno, and they wanted to put a rope between white and colored, but Basie said, 'Oh, no, we don't go for that!' And there never was any trouble. Blue Monday started as a thing for entertainers. We'd send out invitations to the other clubs around, and everybody would come in and blow, or sing, or dance. The other clubs started the same thing on different nights. Basie was very success-ful at the Reno, and the band increased in size. He was always very conscientious about his music, and Walter Page was like a daddy teach-ing some of the boys to read."

"I had had a little organ thing going each afternoon," Basie supple-mented, "and then I was lucky and got a sustaining date with the band. That's when I got a professional nickname. Dick Smith, one of the announcers then, said, 'Listen, we've got the Earl of Hines, the Duke of Ellington, the Baron of Lee, and Paul Whiteman is the King of Jazz. So you be the Count with His Barons of Rhythm.' The first part stuck."

On his way from California to New York, Buck Clayton stopped off in Kansas City to see his mother. Lips Page had just quit Basie. Clayton joined the band at the Reno Club and was with it for two months there, until it left Kansas City on Halloween Night, October 31, 1936, right after playing in a battle of bands with Duke Ellington at the Paseo Ballroom.

"Our reputation before we came east," Buck Clayton has explained, "was built on nine pieces, and I don't think we ever had a bad night in

Kansas City; but when we added five or six men it made a lot of difference. The band had to be enlarged to go on the road, but it slowed everything down and made it sluggish. . . ."

The aid of John Hammond, Willard Alexander, and Fletcher Henderson helped the band through difficult days, and when men like Benny Morton, Dicky Wells, Harry Edison, and Earle Warren came in, it began, Clayton added, "to sound like a good big band."

A great period in jazz history ensued. The 1936 Roseland engagement in New York did not insure the band's acceptance, but after it played the Famous Door there was no doubt anywhere.

As Basie tells it, talent was acquired almost casually, but it is his good ear and careful listening that brought that talent together.

"Someone had recommended Prez," he recalled. "He was working up in Minneapolis, and we had sent for him to join us. It was the strangest thing I ever heard, and the greatest. We got Herschel [Evans] from California while we were at the Reno, too. In those years, he represented 'soul.' That's where *he* was—a beautiful saxophonist.

"Somebody from St. Louis mentioned a drummer with the Jeter-Pilars band by the name of Jo Jones. We sent him a telegram, and he came to us and played two nights. The third night, there was no Jo Jones. 'What happened?' I asked. 'The boys came for him,' they said, 'and took him back to St. Louis.' But he got away and was with us until he went in the army.

"Freddie Green joined when we were working at Roseland. John Hammond came by one Sunday afternoon and said he had a guitarist he wanted me to hear. It seemed strange to audition a guitarist, but we went down to the dressing room. He was on the bus the next day when we went to Pittsburgh, and he's been with us ever since. Freddie Green is Mr. Hold-togetherer!

"When we were at the Brass Rail on Randolph Street in Chicago, with Clark Terry and the small group, Joe Williams used to come around and sing one song in the last set. Then we came back with a big band to the Trianon Ballroom, and Jonesy [Reunald Jones] came in very excited one night. 'You ought to hear this cat singing down there,' he said. 'Okay, tell him to come up here!' So Joe came, and you know what happened. He broke it up. To me, he's the tops. He's not limited. He can sing anything. We weren't doing any good, but then that thing came out—*Every Day*—and put us back on our feet.

"Sonny Payne was recommended to us, and he was pinchhitting for Gus Johnson, but he knocked a home run. Now we have Harold Jones, a young guy out of Chicago. He swings, and that's very necessary. The drummer is the boss of the band, not the bandleader. If the drummer's not right, nothing's happening."

The episode with Clark Terry and the small group in 1950 separates the story of the Basie band into two different chapters, and more definitely than might be expected of such a brief hiatus. Before 1950, despite many personnel changes, the band retained much of the character of the original. It was looser, and the contributions of the individual soloists, as compared with that of the ensemble, were stressed more. From 1952, as the new personnel stabilized, there was more emphasis on ensemble precision, and a very high standard has consistently been maintained in this area ever since. A perceptible difference in the two groups' approach to tempos was perhaps accounted for by the different nature of the audience. "A big difference between now and the thirties and forties is ballrooms," Basie said. "Everybody has converted over to jazz concerts, and there's a different atmosphere altogether."

Significantly, Basie never seemed to have difficulty in finding talented musicians, not men already established as stars, but men who would gain international fame in his band. Thad Jones, Joe Newman, Benny Powell, Ernie Wilkins, Frank Wess, Frank Foster, and, later, Al Grey were among those who grew greatly in stature during the fifties.

The band of 1968 was a well-balanced unit, and hardly less endowed than the band of the fifties. Each horn section had a first-class leader—Marshall Royal, Gene Goe, and Grover Mitchell. Each section boasted attractive soloists—Al Aarons, Sonny Cohn, and Oliver Brashear on trumpet; Harlan Floyd, Richard Boone, and Bill Hughes on trombone; Marshall Royal and Bobby Plater on alto; and Lockjaw Davis and Eric Dixon on tenor. And on baritone, the vastly underrated Charlie Fowlkes was the anchor man. Despite drum changes, the ticking heart of the band—the rhythm section—with the worthy Norman Keenan on bass, still provided the healthiest pulse in jazz.

Keeping a band of this quality together is evidence enough of leadership. It was never easy, and the itineraries, even with occasional aerial assistance, are still tough. One month in 1968, for example, the Basie band went from Florida to North Carolina, to Kansas, to Oklahoma, to Texas, to California, to Arizona, back to Kansas, to Iowa, to Illinois, to New York, and to Connecticut. Jumps and journeys may not be good for morale, but the leader makes them, too.

Transportation is a part of the enormous financial problem facing all big bands. They have to move to work. Other aspects of the same problem explain albums on which the band accompanies singers or records material unworthy of it. The reality of the conditions within the record industry must be taken into account. But at night, when the audience is right, everything is changed, and a big book of jazz instrumentals is opened up. For example, in the sympathetic atmosphere of one of Gene Hull's Bridgeport presentations, a program included

Cherry Point; Cottontail; Lonely Street; Bye, Bye, Blackbird; Li'l Darlin'; Shiny Stockings; When Your Lover Has Gone; Moten Swing; Every Day; Boone's Blues; King Porter Stomp; Satin Doll; Jumpin' at the Woodside; All Heart; Blues in Hoss' Flat; Whirlybird; Squeeze Me; Nasty Magnus; The Midnight Sun Never Sets; The Sidewinder; and *Why Not?*

Such a program, with its arrangements by Neal Hefti, Frank Foster, Eric Dixon, Sam Nestico, Nat Pierce, Bobby Plater and Quincy Jones, suggested that, like any other institution, the Basie band is too often taken for granted. And it *is* an institution, an American institution, a jazz institution. Its policy has changed only superficially in more than three decades. It still stands for forthright, swinging music, and the responsibility for it belongs to the man who, in Duke Ellington's words, "is still the most imitated piano player around."

(1968)

Jimmy Rushing

(VOCALIST)

"Both my parents were musical. My mother played and sang in the church choir. So did I. My father played trumpet in a brass band. But I also had an uncle, Wesley Manning, who used to play and sing in the sporting houses—forbidden territory to me—and he'd come home at night with a hatful of money. *Tricks Ain't Walkin' No More*, which I recorded in 1956, was a song he used to sing in the houses. He was the one who taught me to play the blues.

"I used to go by the red-light district on my way to school, and I'd see the girls in the windows, looking very pretty. I was eager to get in there, and one day I knocked on a door and a girl let me in.

" 'What can I do for you?'

" 'Well, . . .' I began, looking around, but not knowing what I was looking for.

" 'Aren't you too young to be in here?'

" 'I guess I am, but when I'm passing I often hear the blues.'

" 'Can you play?'

" 'Yes.'

" 'Then sit down and play.'

"So I sat down at the piano and played, and everybody gathered around, and I guess I was satisfied; but if my daddy had passed by there, that would have been *it!*

"He had bought me a violin, and he had forbidden me to touch the piano. When he left the house, he'd lock the piano and give my mother the key. We'd watch him away, and then she'd give me the key. When he came back at night, he'd say, 'Get the violin out!' But I wouldn't know anything. It got to the stage where I just couldn't play it, and he told me, 'If I ever catch you on that piano again, or dancing, I'm gonna run you away from home!' I had really tried, but I was gone from there in about two weeks! He lived long enough to see my success with Basie, and he agreed to it, although he never said so. But he'd have a smile on his face and say, 'Well, I guess you're doing OK.'

"He didn't approve of blues like Bessie Smith's. That was honky-tonk music to him. I was official pianist at our high school 'drags,' as we called dances in Oklahoma City, where I was born on August 26, 1903. Then I went to Wilberforce University, where I met quite a few great pianists, but my biggest thrill was when I met Jelly Roll Morton.

"The first time I left home, I went to Chicago and heard a lot of bands and musicians. I liked roaming around by myself, and I went through states like Ohio and Texas, wherever I heard of bands and singers that were making an impression. Then in 1921 I left home again and went to California, where I sang professionally for the first time. That was in a little club with the Sunnyland Jazz Orchestra. Buster Wilson was the pianist. Papa Mutt Carey, Buddy Petit, Ed Garland, and a whole lot of New Orleans fellows were out there in the early twenties. When I went to the club where Jelly Roll Morton was playing, I thought he was the greatest thing I ever heard; so I made myself acquainted and we got to be real chummy. One night I was hired as intermission pianist and *he* played drums, although I could still only play in three keys. In those days, when a party came in a club, got himself seated and ordered a drink, the entertainers would ask if there was anything particular he wanted to hear. So on this occasion one of the girls wanted me to change keys—I guess she had a cold. I was swinging away in E-flat and she said, 'Change to B-flat,' but I just kept on playing in E-flat. She came back and called me everything under the sun. Jelly Roll spoke up then. 'Don't worry about it,' he said. 'I'll play for her.' He was a great fellow.

"There's a difference between the blues of the New Orleans guys and anyone else, and the difference is in a chord, but I can't figure the name of it. It's a different chord, and they *all* make it. I know people stamp

New Orleans as the home of the blues, but I don't because I found the blues everywhere in my travels. In the old days, a lot of people used not to like the blues. If you played blues, you were a nothing to the public—but they were always a kick to me. They always had a good feeling. Guys would walk around with guitars and mandolins, playing and singing the blues on the streets and on the corners. The blues tells a story in itself. It can make you happy or give you a feeling to swing. Here, lately, it's gotten to the place where they've given it a new name—'soul music.' It's always been a *soul* music.

"I heard a good blues singer we knew as Cut as long ago as 1918, in Tulsa, Oklahoma. He had a little band and they played blues in the sense we know it today. Their theme song was *When You Come to the End of a Perfect Day*. They played it at medium tempo, and people flocked to hear them. Cut had drums, sousaphone, trumpet, alto and tenor saxophones. They'd play dances during the week at Nails Park, and the place was always packed. There were after-hours spots they would go to, too. Mostly they played blues, twelve-bar blues, with a few pop songs of the day thrown in. They were not from New Orleans. Most of them were born right around Tulsa. Ernie Fields was around, too, and he had two bands at that time.

"Although I could only play in three keys, I made a living playing piano, but after a time everything began to sound alike to me, and it was then they told me to sing. I was working with Carrie Williams, a very good blues singer out of Chicago. During intermissions, she had to sing suggestive songs like *My Daddy Rocks Me*. She called on me one night and I nearly died. The first number I had to sing was *You Gotta See Mama Every Night or You Can't See Mama at All*.

"When I got homesick and came back from California, in 1926, I worked in my dad's hamburger stand and got to be a pretty good cook. It was a good business, but I used to listen to records and go see the touring shows, and music kept calling me. By 1927, the Blue Devils were getting very big in the state, and when they heard me sing one night I was gone again! We toured all over the Southwest and were recognized as one of the top bands.

"There were no microphones in those days, and unless you could overshadow the horns they wouldn't let you sing. You had to have a good pair of lungs—strong!—to reach out over the band and the people in those big dance halls. Later on, they brought in megaphones for singers like Rudy Vallee, but the crooners and sweet singers couldn't make it before that. As I remember, microphones came into use around 1933, and then you got a different type of singer like Orlando Robeson with Claude Hopkins, and Dan Grissom with Jimmie Lunceford. There was a very good Texas blues singer with Troy Floyd's band called Kellogg Jefferson. He was a kind of male Bessie Smith, but he could also sing high and almost in an opera style.

"Scat singing was just beginning to catch on with the public because of Louis Armstrong. George 'Fathead' Thomas, with McKinney's Cotton Pickers, was a good ballad singer *and* a scat man. A lot of singers tried to copy Louis, but not very successfully. George Thomas was one of the notable exceptions. He was the first I heard sing *I Want a Little Girl*. He did a marvelous job on *Baby, Won't You Please Come Home* and *If I Could Be with You*, too. When he was killed in an accident, I had a chance to take his place, but I couldn't because I had just joined Bennie Moten. I was well known in that part of the country by then, and Bennie's records were coming out on Victor.

"The first record I ever made was *Blue Devil Blues* by the Blue Devils when Walter Page was the leader. A guy had come to Kansas City from Chicago to make records for Vocalion. The number on the back, *Squabblin'*, was Basie's tune.

"Basie had come to the West with a show. He couldn't play the blues then. He was an 'actor' when I first saw him. They would ballyhoo in front of the show, take a band and play a number, and have fellows singing. They would be out on the street, and Basie would explain the show as a crowd gathered around. We'd stand through all the ballyhoo until Basie would play. 'That guy's crazy,' we'd say, because he played so good.

"The first time he heard the Blue Devils, we were ballyhooing on a big truck in Kansas City. There was a lot of that in those days. Wherever you were working, you had to go out and ballyhoo for the place. Coming back from downtown, we struck up with a good blues. Basie heard this and thought it was a record, but somebody told him, 'No, that's the Blue Devils!' He ran down and met all the fellows. Not long after, he quit the show and joined our band.

"The best band in Kansas City in those days was reckoned to be Bennie Moten's. We battled all the bands around, but he avoided us until we caught him one night and tore him up. Then he began to take guys from the Blue Devils when Walter Page had trouble with bookings. Basie went first, then Lips Page and I. Later, Walter Page broke up his group and joined Bennie, too. We also got Ben Webster, and Moten's band was soon more exciting than it had ever been before. But those were difficult times, in the thirties, and business was just beginning to get better for us when Moten died during an operation for tonsils. After Basie got a little band together at the Reno Club, we still had to scuffle for a while till things clicked for us.

"Bennie Moten had been very well established in Kansas City, although he had started out with just three pieces. I guess the kids would die today if they heard just a piano and drums in a place that would hold six or seven hundred people. The pianist would sing and the drummer would sing, and then they'd sing duets together. They'd play blues and foxtrots. There were fellows then that never did get to the limelight, you know. Did you ever hear of the human-voice whistle? They'd have those and it would sound like someone singing. George and Julia Lee were one of the best teams you could ever hear. Around '23 or '24, Alphonso Trent and Troy Floyd had bands of six or seven pieces in Dallas, more or less what they'd call Dixieland bands today. Different bands and different entertainers were popular in different parts of the country in those days. Work was plentiful in the Middle West. Grant Moore worked out of Omaha and played in Chicago, around Minneapolis, down in Iowa, in Idaho, and all like that. He had great musicians and would play picnics, dances, boat trips, and excursions, for colored and white. Besides all the bands already established there, Bennie Moten and the Blue Devils would play in Kansas, Oklahoma, Tennessee, and Texas. But because most of the recording was done in the East, they never got quite the same attention.

"I used to listen to Alphonso Trent's band whenever I could. Though they played for both races, the dances were always segregated. They were one of the top attractions and played at the Adolphus Hotel in Dallas for years, but they had to use the back door and go up on the freight elevator to the roof garden where they worked. They had a real routine, and for most of the years they could work at the best hotels in Texas. People knew them from their broadcasts. The rest of the time they would tour through states like Oklahoma and Colorado, or take a vacation. They were much better off than most of the guys who were gigging around. They powdered up and had beautiful clothes and automobiles. There weren't many personnel changes in that band.

"There was more harmony in the bands then. I was offered all kinds of money to go with Trent, but I stuck with the Blue Devils and Bennie Moten. We had a lot of good musicians who were offered good jobs in the bands that were making the big money, but they stayed because we had a better time together. Sometimes, when the Blue Devils finished playing a dance, after the cost of the hall, placards, and traveling expenses had been deducted, and the take was split 60–40, we had done so badly that the man gave us his part because he wanted us back. Maybe rain had stopped the crowd turning out, but he knew we had top musicians. Whether we each had a dollar and thirty-six cents coming, or seven dollars and ten cents, we knew we all had the same, and we were happy. It was averaged out and divided up in front of us. Maybe when we played a Fourth of July breakfast dance it would be as much as forty dollars apiece. They'd keep a bank to pay for gasoline and the notes on the cars. In a cooperative like that, if a guy was late we'd bawl him out just as quick as any manager would.

"Lunceford had something like that at one time, but you won't find it anymore, because now a man thinks he has to have more money once he's a soloist. It used to be thumbs down on that. A man took a solo because he *could*. If a guy started drinking or coming late, he'd get three warnings, and then he was replaced. There were no ifs or buts. But sometimes, when we had maybe run through our reserves, whoever was in charge of them would say, 'We haven't much in the kitty, fellows, and it doesn't look as though we are going to make anything tonight, so you had better grab your girls.' Then we'd beg those girls, and in those days, if they liked you, they'd feed you and give you a small piece of money.

"When it came to parties, we used to be like one big family. If one couldn't go, none of us would! People liked to entertain the band. That really began when Basie first started with us; but later, what with being around New York, mixing with other musicians, and with the guys who were taking the solos feeling they ought to have more money —well, it wasn't the kind of band I had originally come out of. New York is something else. Guys wouldn't think of rehearsing without putting in a charge. In Kansas City, when a man wasn't working and was asked to rehearse, it was always, 'Sure!' But here it's 'Forget it, man!' The music game used to carry a certain amount of brotherly love, but it isn't that way now.

"As I said, Basie couldn't play the blues when he first came to Kansas City (and he wasn't 'Count' then), but he soon caught on when he heard Pete Johnson and some of the other great blues players around. In fact, he soon became, with Pete, the best of the blues pianists. Of course, Jay McShann is one of the very best still around today. I tried to get Columbia to send for him when I was recording, but I haven't been able to persuade *anyone* to do that yet. I don't know what it is, but there are some players who come out of the West, the Midwest, who play just exactly what you want. Others, you can't tell them what you want. If I say, 'No, change that chord,' they don't feel it that way and it's something different. There's also the question of touch, and time!

"Now, Earl Hines is a good one. He may say he can't play the blues, but he will for me. He used to play for Chippie Hill at the Golden Lily and the Sunset in Chicago. Guys like that are not always comfortable playing their natural style. They feel they've been playing it so long they need to dress it up to make it sound different today. And that's not good. It's a serious thing that they are made to feel they have to be different. Regardless of everything, Earl Hines is Earl Hines, a great pianist.

"Nat Cole is another one for playing the blues. He was a great admirer of Earl Hines, and you have to remember that. I used to sit down at night and listen to Earl for hours in after-hours spots. He was a pacesetter in Chicago for years, and everybody tried to play like him.

"This business of switching styles can't be done honestly by one man. As soon as he can play his instrument well, he can express himself, and all his life he has only one self.

"Basie used to please people with his piano, but he got away from it when bop came along. He got shy. I used to say, 'Come on, Basie, play one!' He'd say, 'Oh, man, I can't play no more.' But Basie can play a whole lot of piano still. When people asked me about it, I would say, 'Well, Basie's gotten lazy, and he hides behind his band.' That was only partly true. We used to go to house parties where he wouldn't be criticized, and Basie would play. How he played! Oh, God! You hear him on Bennie Moten's *Lafayette* and *Prince of Wales.* That's true Basie. But he wouldn't play like that now any more than the man in the moon. What if it's old, if it's good? He could still do it, but I think he got a little self-conscious about his playing. I know when I was with the band he would lay out and let the band take it on down. The record companies used to fight with him. 'The people want to hear the piano,' they'd say. 'That's what they want.' And that's why those Kansas City Seven records sold like they did: because there was some Basie on them.

"You could take Basie, Duke, Earl, Nat Cole, and Erroll Garner, and out of all of them Garner would be the only one not self-conscious about his playing. The others couldn't even play in the way they were raised in, although if they did you would hear some of the finest of music. For instance, people kind of frown on stride piano, even though it's hard and they can't play it.

"I worked with Ralph Sutton in California. I hadn't worked that way in years, with just piano and drums, and I was so well pleased. Ralph carried such a heavy left hand, it sounded like a bass. We broke the show up for two weeks and I didn't feel tired once. I've seen the time when I've had five or six pieces in there, but they wouldn't carry the time the way he did playing stride piano.

"I've been trying to get Ralph and me together as a combo for the past year. He can play all the stuff like Willie The Lion. I wanted to have him with a small combo in Toronto, but the guy there couldn't see it. In a way, Ralph doesn't even need drums, but he can be more relaxed when he can hear that beat all the time and he doesn't have to play so hard. It's the same with me. I'm more relaxed when I can hear the beat clearly all the time I'm singing.

"To go back to the old days, to the twenties . . . I remember when we had a small combo of seven or eight pieces. The sousaphone was just beginning to go out, and they were bringing in the bass fiddle. We had a drummer who used to beat the side of a leather case and get a sound like a rimshot. Believe me, that kind of beat does something to you. When a guy took a solo—a 'Boston' in those days—everybody in the band used to hit that beat; and on a swing tune you were home free. You had no worries. Then they brought the after-beat in on the high-hat, and now drummers like Sam Woodyard are bringing it back with rimshots. I like it, especially on a going-out chorus. Sometimes, when the drummer is playing fast—not clear and definite—the average guy in the horns can't hear the beat and gets lost. Many times I've heard musicians like Earle Warren and Dicky Wells say, 'What's the matter with the drummer? Why doesn't he stay in there?' When you've got a big ensemble going, you've got to be able to *feel* those drums, not just hear them. I've noticed on a lot of records you hear all top but no bottom to the drums. You must feel that bottom, and they should put a microphone on the bass drum.

"Not that they used the bass drum the way they ought. I walked behind a drummer on stage one time, and he had his right foot wrapped around his stool.

" 'What's wrong, man?' I asked him.

" 'What?' he said.

" 'What do you use that foot for?'

" 'I don't use that no more.'

" 'I'm not going to tell you how to drum, man, but give me that four,' I said.

" 'Oh, yes, yes . . .'

"Even before I heard Chick Webb, the drummer with the Blue Devils, and all those in the other bands in the Midwest, used to play that four on the bass drum. They all played but one way. Where they got this thing about neglecting the bass drum and carrying all the time on top, I don't know. A lot of young people don't know what's missing. They've been brought up without it and they don't know how it should be.

"Alvin Burroughs, who was with the Blue Devils, and later with Earl Hines, was one of the great drummers. He came to us from Little Rock, Arkansas. Another drummer who was the Jo Jones and Gene Krupa of the day before yesterday was A. G. Godley. He was with

Alphonso Trent's band for a long time until he quit playing and went to work. They used to use those little sock cymbals with their hands. (You can hear them on *Squabblin'* by the Blue Devils.) They used to shove the spotlight on A. G. Godley and he would drum for half an hour, years before Buddy Rich. There was another fine drummer out of Chicago, in Grant Moore's band. We used to call him 'Jeans.'

"In the old days, too, you could name almost as many good women pianists as men. Besides Mary Lou Williams, there were Countess Johnson and Julia Lee in Kansas City, another girl in Oklahoma, and a girl out of Minneapolis. But apart from pianists, there were never too many girls who could play in bands.

"So today [January 23, 1963] I was surprised to find that Patti Bown could sit in with a big band. I knew she had worked with Quincy Jones, but she was so relaxed on my date. And you can't be relaxed unless you know what you're doing. I think this album* was sort of on the new side for me, compared to what I had been doing. We have a little touch of the 'progressive' in it. It's all right for pop tunes, and I think people will like it, but I wouldn't get away from the things that made me popular in days gone by.

"When we went out with Basie once in the forties, he had changed his style to a certain extent. He had a bunch of new arrangements, and some fellow yelled out, 'Come on, Count! What the heck! You trying to sound like Stan Kenton?'

"I always say that Basie had a style he never should have changed. He came back to some extent, and he keeps it pretty simple, but the public grows with you and likes to hear you the way you came up. Once you've established yourself, they don't want you to get too far away from there. When I talk to people in the audience, they so often tell me, 'I have all your old records, and I won't let anybody borrow them.' Or, 'When I want a big kick I play the old arrangements—you and Basie.' It's dangerous to get too far from what they identify you with.

"I understand how fly-by-night things like bossa nova are introduced and promoted, but when they've gone you've got to get back to the main source—the blues. I can sing anything I want, maybe two or three songs before the blues, but the minute I begin *Goin' to Chicago*, or something like that, I hear that scream start. So if I told a guy who requested *Goin' to Chicago* that I didn't sing it now, or said I couldn't remember it—that would be very funny.

"I play the Playboy clubs and a lot of other clubs across the country, but I never thought the time would come when I would go up on the

---

* *Five Feet of Soul* (Colpix 446).

bandstand, call this or that familiar number, and have some of the cats on the stand say, 'Don't know it!' And they don't. They're younger musicians and most of them don't know anything farther back than Charlie Parker.

"I've been asked several times, 'What's going to happen to American jazz?' It's a big question. 'Well, Jim,' people ask, 'what will happen when you and Duke and Basie have gone?' We are not the patterns anymore. Years ago, when you heard a pianist, you'd say, 'He sounds like Earl Hines.' Or it might be Fats Waller, or Pete Johnson, the boogie-woogie man. You don't get that anymore. Musicians are afraid to pattern themselves on the great artists for fear someone will tell them, 'You sound like so-and-so.' Everybody's trying to create I don't know what. Maybe I should say a style of their own; but they try so hard to be different that they lose the soul.

"I met a fellow out in Detroit some years ago, a pianist who could play his ass off. He was very good. He came to New York, went to Juilliard, finished there, and went out on his own. Now when he plays for you, he mixes in the progressive style and augments the blues chords. That causes trouble, because you can't add to the blues. But it's *different*, even if he does lose the blues! The blues are just the old church chords, two- or three-part harmony, and that's all. When he makes the big chord, it's something else, and he loses the feeling.

"When I get to singing, with someone like that behind me, I may be feeling pretty good, but he'll strike one chord and take everything away from me. Such a lot of beautiful songs and solos have been built around the blues chords that the big chord seems like a big mistake to me.

"There are not as many good blues pianists as there used to be, but Jimmy Smith—though he plays organ—is a real blues man. He builds his whole repertoire around the blues. Ray Bryant is a very good blues pianist today, and so is Sir Charles Thompson, if you can make him play it. The 'progressive' kick has changed many people. A lot of musicians feel they're obsolete if they play the way they really should, the way they were taught years ago. They think that makes them 'webby,' as though they'd got spider webs on them! Not Basie, though. It's amusing. Sometimes, when he takes a solo, and then the band comes in, it's like two entirely different things. *He* is true to his first love in music.

"When I go in front of an audience, I'll admit I sometimes have a certain amount of fear in me, because maybe the people are not going to accept what I'm doing today. That's bad for any artist, especially if what you're doing is not in line with what's happening today. If you don't get the right amount of applause, you feel you're not doing the right thing, and you get nervous. Automatically, you begin to wonder if you're too old or passé, and that will work on you if you're not careful. It's not a matter of ability or, if you like, artistry. I remember singing *I Want a Little Girl* one night—and that's normally one of my big ones, after *Goin' to Chicago*—and the crowd just looked at me, as much to say, 'What is *that?*' That drug me. Other times, people know it and request it. But the performer always has his problems before he goes on. He tries to figure what will hit the crowd, like going for the jackpot. If I sing *When You're Smiling*, and they scream, I do another like that; and meantime someone will probably yell for *Goin' to Chicago*. When I get a good reaction on that, I go right into *St. Louis Blues*. It's surprising, though, how difficult it is to pick right.

"When I come out with a new album, guys will say, 'It's a typical Jimmy Rushing record.' Well, who else would it be? If I'm going to do blues, it's going to be a typical Jimmy Rushing record because I don't think any other way. It's impossible for me to be like anybody else. If it doesn't sell, if a guy doesn't like it, that's something else.

"I'm funny about recording something someone else has done and made a hit out of. When I did *I'm Walking Through Heaven with You*, I took the tempo a little up as compared with Lunceford's. I'm not being egotistical, but after I made *Goin' to Chicago*, a lot of people said, 'Nobody can sing that but Jimmy.' In the same way, I don't think anybody could make *I'm Walking Through Heaven* other than Lunceford's Dan Grissom; so if I'm going to record the same number I want a different tempo or something. Like this number of Billie Holiday's they wanted me to do. 'Oh, no,' I said, 'I have always cherished Billie and I don't feel anyone else could do the things she did.' The artist who establishes a number, in other words, has the edge. Like some of those Louis Armstrong made. Nevertheless, I love that song of his, *Someday You'll Be Sorry*, and I'm going to try to do that in my next album."

(1963)

Jimmy Rushing died June 8, 1972.

Lester "Prez" Young

Lester "Prez" Young haunts the pages of this book in the memories of those who knew and admired him. François Postif's famous interview with him, shortly before his death in 1959, was finally printed unexpurgated twenty years later in the French magazine *Jazz Hot* (nos. 362 and 363). The 1958 interview with Chris Albertson, which follows, is very different in tone, but not less revealing of the gentle, considerate person Young basically was.

The second, somewhat impressionistic section was written for the British magazine *Melody Maker* in 1956. It is included here primarily because Young liked it, and had his manager, Charlie Carpenter, write to tell me so.

I

Chris Albertson. First, I want to, if you can, talk about the old days. . . . You played with King Oliver for a year, didn't you?
Lester Young. Yes, about a year.

A. That was after Louis Armstrong moved away from the band, wasn't it?

Y. Many moons after, you know, because that was an older tribe than me. I came like in the middle of that.

A. Then you played with . . . Let's see, from there where did you go?

Y. From King Oliver? Then I played with a band called the Bostonians. They were out of Salina, Kansas. It was a nice little group, about eight or ten pieces.

A. Anybody we might know in the band?

Y. Oh, I'm sure you wouldn't. The boss-man's name was Art Bronson, so I know you never heard of him. He played piano.

A. Did you make your first records with Basie?

Y. Yes. My first records—I made 'em in Chicago.

A. With the old Basie band?

Y. Right. We were playing at the Grand Terrace.

A. Did you always play the way you did? Coleman Hawkins was *the* tenor sax man in those days.

Y. Yeah. . . . Well, I had a lot of trouble along in those days, because the people couldn't understand the way I sounded and they wanted me to play like Coleman Hawkins. Well, to each his own. So . . . I played in a band and there were about three boys from the West. They fired the trombone player . . . a great big envelope. Then they fired the trumpet player. When he was gone, well, I'm the third party. I know they're going to fire me, too. You dig? We were all from Kansas City, you know, and we came to New York and we weren't in the New York clique. So that made a difference. So I went to him and asked could I get a recommendation so I could split and go back home. So he did, and I went back, and then I started playing with Andy Kirk.

A. But you replaced Hawkins, didn't you, in the Fletcher Henderson band?

Y. Yes, I did.

A. Wasn't it pretty tough for you to replace him, when everybody was so used to the Hawkins style?

Y. Oh, yeah. I got all kinds of trouble, because most of the people would come out to hear him, and see me up there and listen to the way I sounded. . . . They were looking for him. I think he was in Switzerland, or Sweden, or something like that.

A. When did you first meet Billie Holiday?

Y. When I came to New York, in 1934. I used to live at her house, with her mother, 'cause I didn't know my way around. She taught me a lot of things, and got me little record dates, playing behind her, and little solos, and things like that.

A. You're her favorite soloist.

Y. She is mine, too. So that's a draw.

A. I understand she gave you the name Prez, didn't she?

Y. Yes, she did, and I gave her the name of Lady Day. So that was even.

A. I think she has said that her style of singing is formed after your style on tenor sax.

Y. Well, I think you can hear that on some of the old records. Sometimes I sit down and listen to them myself and it sounds like two of the same breed if you don't be careful, or the same line, or something like that.

A. Tell me, did you ever make records with Hawkins?

Y. With Hawkins? No, I never did.

A. You probably will some day. Now, is there anything you can tell us about Billie Holiday? Or any funny incidents when you were on the road with the Basie band?

Y. Oh, no, I couldn't think of anything like that. I just know we were all happy, always waiting to go to work, and things like that.

A. I was talking to Basie the other day, on this same show, and he was telling me that he preferred recording in the old days, when you had just one microphone. Now, he said, he has the rhythm section around the corner . . . and it's so confusing. Do you feel that way?

Y. One microphone?

A. Yes, in the old days, when they had just one microphone. Now it's become so technical. There are microphones all over the studio, and you're so split up. You're not together, the big band . . .

Y. I don't think I'd go for that. If you've got one mike, you've got to run over to the mike and play and then come and sit down, with only one mike. Now they make it convenient, with a mike here and a mike there, and a mike everywhere.

A. Did you use one mike when you recorded with Basie?

Y. Yes, that's true.

A. Well, several musicians whom I have interviewed have said the same thing, that they felt the spirit was more there in the old days, when you were recording. There were clinkers, but there was more feeling in the music because it wasn't so technical. Nowadays everything is technical, with high fidelity and everything, and they feel they just can't get into the right feeling.

Y. I still don't buy that. To each his own. No, I don't think like that.

A. What other bands have you played with?

Y. Well, with Teddy Wilson, records and things like that. I never played with him regular.

A. Do you have any favorite records of your own?

Y. No, I really couldn't say. When I get by myself, I just play them and enjoy them all.

A. Did you ever hear Bessie Smith? I'm sure you did.

Y. Yeah. I thought *she* was a wild lady with her blues.

A. Do you think there's anybody nowadays who can sing like her?

Y. Yeah.

A. Of the vocalists today, whom do you like?

Y. Oh, you left Bessie Smith, huh? Well, sometimes you think upon Kay Starr and listen to her voice and play one of Bessie Smith's records, and see if you hear anything.

A. You feel there is a similarity there?

Y. Yes, very much.

A. We have played Kay Starr records on this show, and she definitely does have a good voice for jazz. How about some of these new singers that are coming out nowadays?

Y. No. I can tell you really my favorite singer is Kay Starr. No . . . that's the wrong name. Her husband has a band. . . .

A. Jo Stafford?

Y. There you are! I'll go there. Yeah. And Lady Day. And I'm through.

A. Jo Stafford doesn't sing jazz, does she?

Y. No, but I hear her voice and the sound and the way she puts her songs on.

A. That's amazing. How do you feel now when you hear your old records?

Y. I think it was nice during those days. I have a lot of trouble on the bandstand, people coming to ask me, "How come you don't play like you played when you played with Count Basie?" Well, that's not progressive. If I'm going to stay there and play that same stuff year after year . . . I'll be an old man! I don't think like that, so I have to try to think of little new tricks and little new sounds and things like that—that's the way I do.

A. Are there any tenor sax men nowadays, newcomers, that you like especially?

Y. Well, I imagine I'll say I like them all. They all sound the same to me, because almost all of them went to Juilliard and whoever that teacher was, he taught them all the same thing. This one will start playing it, this one will pick it up and start playing it, the same thing. In my mind, the individual is going to come out and play for himself. Like, if you have thirteen people and the teacher teach all thirteen of them, you mean to tell me out of the thirteen he can't get *one* individual? That's the way *I* think.

A. So you don't have any favorites?

Y. Oh, no; I like them all. I like modern . . .

A. But you think there should be more individual styles?

Y. Yes, that's all.

A. How do you feel about Coleman Hawkins' style?

Y. Well, the way I look at him . . . he's the first person who played the tenor saxophone who woke you up and let you know there *was* a tenor saxophone. So when I see all the kiddies who are copying his style . . . That's about all I could say on that.

A. You don't think very highly of his style? It's not your type of music?

Y. Well . . . that's incomplete . . . !

A. You've traveled a lot with Jazz at the Philharmonic. How do the Europeans react to you? Do you feel any difference in your audience in Europe?

Y. They're very nice over there. I've been over twice.

A. Dizzy Gillespie feels that they appreciate the music more than the American audiences. How do you feel about that?

Y. I don't think I'll buy that. If a person likes you, they like you, and if they don't, they don't like you, that's all.

A. Do you ever play the clarinet anymore?

Y. Yeah. I just made some records for Norman Granz, about four or five or six months ago, on my clarinet.

A. I heard some records that you made with . . . was it Walter Page and His Blue Devils?

Y. Yes, many moons ago.

A. . . . *Way Down Yonder in New Orleans?*

Y. Right.

A. Are the records you made with Norman Granz the latest ones you've made?

Y. Well, the way we make records, Norman and I, he'd make so many records and then he'd put them in a vault, and he'd stash them away. Then when he wants to go and get them, he'll bring them out. And you can never tell when you'll hear one, 'cause that's his business, you know. So that's the way it is.

A. How do you feel about the reissue of the old Basie records? Do you ever go back and listen to the old records?

Y. Um-hum. I have some in my room, and I listen to them and try to dig little mistakes, little things that you could have done a little better.

A. We did a show on Coleman Hawkins the other day, two weeks ago, and we explained the difference between your styles and played one of your records, *Lester Leaps In,* with Count Basie's Kansas City Seven. That was a long time ago. Do you still play **that** number?

Y. I must have made about three or four different records of that. That's just like a crib. I used to play it all night long.

A. Like Hawkins. They're always asking him to play *Body and Soul.* So what are you doing now, just touring the States and playing various spots?

Y. No, I've been off. I was a little sick and had to go to the hospital and all that. I haven't worked since the fifth of August—I mean July. This is my first week that I have. It takes a little time to build your chops up.

A. Before we close, I want to ask what you think of Mahalia Jackson?

Y. I think she's great.

A. She has been compared with Bessie Smith. Do you think she could sing like Bessie Smith if she sang the blues?

Y. That's a little deep for me. She's religious, right?

A. Yes. She won't sing anything but religious songs, but she has the tremendous voice, very powerful voice.

Y. Yeah. I heard her . . . *Hold My Hand*, or something like that?

A. She has so many, I'm not sure . . . *He's Got the Whole World in His Hand.* . . .

Y. Yes, something like that.

A. Thank you very much.

Y. It's a pleasure meeting you, Chris.

A. A pleasure meeting you.

(*1958*)

II

To some, Lester Young was the Trojan Horse of jazz, dragged into hot and happy Troy by Count Basie and his carefree men. To others, he was a voice crying in the wilderness, a herald of glad, cool times to come. To others again, he was the lonely signpost at the meeting of the ways, indicative of both, but committed to neither.

Whatever view you hold, the fact remains that in the jazz story Young is one of those key figures whose style, nurtured in one era, profoundly influenced the course of the next. We can look back now and see how the brilliance that was Armstrong's leapt out of King Oliver's orchestra like a Roman candle's fireball to presage the next decade's solo idiom. And we can see now how Young's revolutionary approach to sound, tone, and phrasing was full of implications of the shape of things to come.

Young had the background. Born in New Orleans in 1909, his expe-

rience went all the way back to King Oliver, with whom he worked a
year. After a phase in Kansas City, he took Coleman Hawkins's place
with Fletcher Henderson in 1934, to the inevitable dismay of Hawkins's
admirers. Returning to Kansas City, he joined Basie for the second
time in 1936, and an epic four-year partnership began.

By that time Kansas City had made up its mind which way it wanted
to go. It was swinging with uninhibited violence, with a direct, uncom-
plicated beat. When the Basie band came east, it had a rhythmically
elemental quality which made even the best New York bands sound a
little prissy. The heart of the band was the famous rhythm section, the
heart of the rhythm section was Basie, and what stimulated Basie
was Lester Young. No matter how much the band played, there was
always that *duo* feeling between these two.

The driving, extrovert, rhythmic kick was not entirely Young's way.
He needed the inimitable Basie rhythm behind him to insure the
initial lift and subsequent freedom to fly (and never afterward was he
afforded such security). Once away, however, soaring, his improvisa-
tions were to a considerable degree independent of the necessity to
emphasize the beat audibly, although his musical heritage insured that
it was always implied.

Hawkins had gone to Europe in 1934, but he had left behind the
memory and influence of the style he had perfected during his decade
with Fletcher Henderson. His was the big sound, with the rich, sensual
tone, warm vibrato, incomparable rhythmic power, and unlimited
imagination that assure him a place among the First Five of Jazz
Giantry with any unbiased assessor. His seemed the ideal way of playing tenor, and with the exception of Bud Freeman, the Chicagoan
whose tone approximated Lester's, all the leading tenor players drew
inspiration from him. One of his disciples was Herschel Evans, who
also played in Basie's band.

The rivalry between Evans and Young probably pushed both of
them further in their respective directions than they might otherwise
have gone. Evans has been overshadowed by Young, and as a result
of his early death it is not always realized how great an artist he was;
but the invention, the virtual creation of Young, was more readily
apparent when contrasted with the approved and recognizable style
that Evans played.

Compared with the big sound of the Hawkins tradition, Young's
sound was diminished and light. He used far less vibrato. Where
Hawkins was all power and confidence, Young was cool and detached.
Irrespective of tempo, his melodic invention was always strange and
haunting. On a jump number, he would impose a weird mood; a ballad

was transformed into a nostalgic song, searching and mysterious. His phrasing was astonishingly varied rhythmically, rarely pushing, often lagging in a fashion new to the times and unique to himself. All of these qualities in the music were reflections of Young's unusual personality.

Those who knew him well would tell you that Young was no grabber or boaster, but essentially a gentle soul, a lover of beauty, of beauty as he saw it in beings, values, and things. Quick-witted, hip to everything of moment around him, experience had shown him the wisdom of detachment. He lived in a world of his own, accepting the fact that his highest, most idealistic values were out of reach. His fellow musicians were quick to sense the maturity of this acceptance and of its expression in his music. The young strive—with heat, anxiety, and impatience—for the impossible, whereas Young, like a wistful lover, was content to sing about it. Consistency of outlook and single-mindedness of approach sprang from this acceptance and his desire to come to terms with life. We may be sure that he would not have accepted many aspects of life had he had the choice, but that intuitive insight into cause and effect allowed him to practice tolerance while observing critically.

A sensitive person like Lester Young undoubtedly suffered much initially from those who compared his sound unfavorably with Hawkins's. It is a tribute to his artistic integrity that by 1940 he had compromised not at all. In fact, in an era when the tenor saxophone became the paramount solo instrument, his style was more influential than Hawkins's, earning him the nickname of "President" and its affectionate abbreviation, "Prez," and even influencing a singer like Billie Holiday, who tried to improvise in the same way. Charlie Parker admitted admiration but denied being influenced. That may be. Yet when the artificial attitudes of bop, physical and musical, were introduced, many of those attitudes had already been given expression with casual innocence by Young. He had made it quite clear where he stood. "I play a *swing* tenor." So he did, and so did his disciples, like Allen Eager, Paul Quinichette, Gene Ammons, and the late Wardell Gray, whenever the rhythm sections permitted. That Young liked more than a "listening beat" from his accompanists is evident from the superiority of his work with rhythm sections containing such swinging musicians as Count Basie, King Cole, Johnny Guarneri, and Teddy Wilson.

His cat-footed walk, his eccentric but unstudied stance, his hat, his exciting contributions out of a personal dream on a roaring J.A.T.P. stage, and his water pistol duels at Birdland all go to form the legend of the giant and genius that was Lester Young the President. On an inspired liner, David Stone Martin once depicted Lester and that famous Tower of Pisa. Lester was leaning the opposite way to the tower.

No copy-cat he!

(1956)

Lester Young died March 15, 1959.

Buck Clayton

(TRUMPET AND ARRANGER)

"I first began to get interested in jazz when I was twelve. I was learning to play piano then in my hometown, Parsons, Kansas. It was a small railroad town of about eleven thousand people. The Missouri, Kansas & Texas Railway—the M.K.T.—had their headquarters in Parsons, and because it was a railway junction all the trains from Texas to Kansas City used to stop there.

"My father was a minister and a musician, and he taught me to play piano. He played tuba. Every Sunday, the church orchestra would rehearse at our house and the guys would leave their instruments there until the following week. So there were always plenty of horns to pick up and blow, and we had two pianos as well. A girl called Noreen Tate, who has been in New York, was in my father's band, too. She made some fine piano records with Sonny Greer playing brushes.

"Wild Bill Davis's father and mine were very good friends. They used to sing in the same quartet. He had a beautiful baritone voice and my father sang bass. Sir Charles Thompson's father was a church pastor, and they lived in Parsons, too.

"I suppose because I'd had the piano tuition, I was the one who organized a little six-piece band of kids aged from about twelve to sixteen. We had a drummer and the rest of us mostly played combs. We used to try to play tunes like *Hard to Get Gertie*, and we would maybe make a dollar apiece most weeks playing rent parties. We had a lot of records and the Bennie Moten and George E. Lee bands would play Parsons on their way through from Oklahoma to Kansas City. We also used to hear Coon Sanders on the radio, which we called the 'wireless' in those days.

"At one time, I liked George E. Lee's band best. He had a novelty band and they used to stand up and swing their trumpets around. Later, as a professional musician, I realized Moten had the better band. I'd take a girl to a dance at that time and not dance at all, but stand in front of the band and listen to the music all night long. She'd get mad at me, and the next day I didn't have a girl!

"I really got on the trumpet after one of George E. Lee's visits to Parsons. I met a fellow named Bob Russell who was with him. Although I had been very interested in trumpet, I had never really tried to play it. Bob had a very sharp personality, and he dressed well, and he had a mellophone and a slide trumpet—about five different horns. He talked to me and encouraged me very much, and at that time I had never heard Louis Armstrong, so Bob was really the very first trumpet in my life. I thought he was good then, but I haven't heard him since. I think he's out in Washington, around Seattle.

"Jazz was looked down upon in those days, but my father wouldn't be at the house parties! My mother told me she didn't want me to play jazz. There would be someone playing cornet down at a little dive, the Bucket of Blood, and somebody was always getting killed there. There was another place in Kansas City, the Yellow Front, and every Saturday night somebody would get killed in there, too. They tried to check the knives at the door as you went in, but people would be killed anyway. So my mother didn't want me to play in places like that, and I don't think she changed her mind about jazz until 1938 when I played at Carnegie Hall with Benny Goodman. There's no drinking at Carnegie Hall!

"I left home when I was nineteen, but I didn't leave strictly for music. A friend of mine had emigrated to California, and he wrote me so many pretty letters about how beautiful it was that I decided to go. So I ran away, and hoboed out there, and I stayed for four months, doing different jobs in a garage, a pool hall, a barber's shop, and washing dishes. I even took a chance on being a prizefighter. I had been a pretty good wrestler before I left home, but in those days wrestling wasn't like it is now. Then it was more in the style of the ancient

Greeks and a matter of different holds. I went to the gymnasium about twice, but I didn't like it. I preferred racking balls in a pool hall to prizefighting!

"When school time came around again, I went home, finished high school, got my diploma, returned to California, and really started my musical career there. I'll never forget the last job I had before I began playing professionally. I was working in a barber's shop in Los Angeles, and I was about nineteen. I had my trumpet and I knew how to run a few scales on it, but not well enough to play. When I got to California, there was a little band led by a guy called Duke Ellighew. (At that time everyone was trying to be like Duke Ellington.) He was a young cat, a trumpet player, about my age, and somebody told him about me. He asked me to come to a rehearsal at nine one Wednesday night. I was supposed to mop and sweep in the barber's shop after eight o'clock. I decided to sweep it real good and hope they wouldn't notice it hadn't been mopped. The fellow who owned the shop had a cousin who wanted my job. I swept real good, split out, and went to the band rehearsal. The next day I go to the job and I'm fired. 'You didn't mop,' the guy says, and he gives the job to his cousin.

"So I go back to the band. They're only playing parties, one or two nights a week, but I was single and I could make it. I was living in a basement, paying two dollars a week, and I remember once I was thirty-two dollars behind in rent! I stayed with that band about six months until I got my first *real* professional job at a taxi dance—the Red Mill dance hall. After that I never went back to anything else. The band was led by Lavern Floyd, a piano player, and he'd heard about this little young trumpet player from Kansas City. I think I had been making around sixteen dollars a week with Ellighew and he could offer thirty-five. That was like a thousand to me. These were my first real professional jobs apart from once in Kansas when a five-piece band came through and the trumpet got sick. They came and got me. I couldn't play anything but *Dinah*, and I played that all night for five dollars.

"There had been quite a shift of New Orleans players to California, musicians like Papa Mutt Carey and Kid Ory. There were about eight taxi dances in Los Angeles at that time and Papa Mutt was playing in one of them. I liked the way he played with a mute very much, but he never taught me. He was very nice to me, but my father had taught me how to play scales and I think that was the only thing anyone ever taught me on the trumpet. From then on I had to go on my own, and I never had a lesson on trumpet. Another player I liked very much and used to listen to was Claude Kennedy from Texas. He was a whiz, but he died and you never hear of him now.

"I left the taxi dance hall for a fourteen-piece band led by Charlie Echols that played all the great big ballrooms. That was my first big band. Then Earl Dancer, a big-time Broadway guy, came to California from New York. He had put Ethel Waters way up on top and he came with offers to make movies, so we all left Echols and went with him. We had to eliminate Earl when we found out later that he was gambling with our money. Because I had been arranging for the band, they elected me leader. I already knew the keyboard, because of that piano tuition, and a fellow named Parker Berry showed me, 'This is the trumpet, this is the trombone,' and so on, and I had picked up on arranging.

"One of the things I remember from about this time was the earthquake in 1933. I went to the union that day and from there I went to the barber's shop, and the guy was cutting my hair when there was this rumbling like thunder. They had the radio on with Bing Crosby singing, and the announcer says, 'The next number you're going to hear is *You May Never Come This Way Again*,' or something like that. There was some more rumbling and the ceiling started cracking, and a mirror fell off the wall. The guy says, 'Earthquake!'—and I'd never had one before—but I was out of that chair and in the street very soon. The street-car tracks were buckling and bricks were falling off the hotels, but nothing hit me. There was a place that sold chickens nearby and I remember women going home with chickens tucked up under their skirts. That night, they had big bonfires going in the streets and everybody stayed around them, praying.

"I was twenty-one and a bandleader when I took the band to China. Teddy Weatherford came back with orders to take an American band to Shanghai—no particular one, just a good one. At that time there were really only two in California—Les Hite's and mine. Teddy liked mine and I don't think he could have gotten Les Hite's, because Les was at the Cotton Club. We considered it quite an honor to accompany Teddy Weatherford to China, and we found it very nice, very European —not wild. We hadn't anything to lose, but we did think it rather a daring step. The sidemen were going to make a lot of money, and in 1934, right after the Crash, a hundred dollars a week was a lot. So we went to Shanghai and stayed two years. Bumps Myers, Eddie Beal, Teddy Buckner, Baby Lewis, and Caughey Roberts were in the band.

"Teddy lived in a big house in Shanghai and my wife and I always went by his to eat. The White Russians were numerous in Shanghai then and they seemed to like to pile everything up with thick, white cream in their restaurants, which was another reason for preferring the food at Teddy's. I didn't learn Chinese and I had no desire to, because there are so many different dialects. It's like learning English in New York and going to Newark, New Jersey, and finding they don't understand what you're talking about.

"We played at the Canidrome Ballroom in the International Settlement. It was run by English people and everything was fine until we ran into some racial prejudice from Atlanta, Georgia. A fellow came in one night and called me quite a few obnoxious names. The place was so beautiful I couldn't believe what I heard. Anyway, I gave the downbeat for the next number, the band began to play and a bunch of girls from Hollywood—the Hollywood Blondes—ran out all over the floor. I went over to the table where this fellow was sitting, and it turned out he was a boxer and an ex-marine. Before I even got to his table, he popped me one between the eyes, and while I'm still shaking my head I'm aware the band is all jumping off the stand to get to him. So there's a big free-for-all and when it's over this guy is all beat up. He sued the place and we all had to go to court. One of our main witnesses was Madame Chiang Kai-shek. She always wanted to learn tap dancing and she was taking lessons from one of my trombone players. We testified and this guy lost the case and had to pay court charges and everything, but after that there was such pressure and prejudice that we left the place to avoid bringing more trouble to it. We had played many dances for the marines and had a lot of friends among them. Six months after the trial was over, they caught this guy—they called him a rat—and beat him, and left him draped over the steering wheel of his car. That's how he was found the next day.

"It was a big thing, and I have article after article about it in my scrapbook, but it cost us our job, and for three weeks afterwards I had to have a bodyguard if I wanted to go to a nightclub. The other place we went to—the Casanova—could only take half the band, so the rest of the guys went home.

"At the Canidrome, we had played for dancing every night, and every Sunday we had an afternoon matinee when we used to play quite a bit of classical music and things like Ravel's *Bolero*, and *Rhapsody in Blue* with Teddy Weatherford playing the Gershwin piano parts. We wore tails—we had gray, white, and black—and altogether it was a wonderful foundation for me. I remember I had to learn every note of that *Rhapsody in Blue* so that I could conduct it. Jack Bratton, who's now a druggist, and I used to write the arrangements.

"Eventually, we returned to Los Angeles, opened at Frank Sebastian's Cotton Club, and played there and at the Club Araby for quite a few seasons. I had seen China, California, and part of Mexico and

Canada, and then I got the urge to go to New York. I was hearing about the Cotton Club there and what was going on, and I tried to get my band to come east, but western boys like their home state and barbecue pits the way New York boys like their apartments and after-hour spots, so in the end I gave Eddie Beal all my arrangements and split.

"On my way east to join Willie Bryant, I stopped to visit and talk with my mother for a couple of days. Lips Page had just quit Basie and when I went back into Kansas City he had told Basie I was available. So Basie called me, said he knew I was going to New York right away, but if I waited two or three months I could go with him. I was with him two months at the Reno Club. We left Kansas City October 31, 1936, Halloween Night, the same night we had played in a battle of bands with Duke Ellington at the Paseo Ballroom. In our minds, we thought we had won the battle, but when we got on the bus to leave there wasn't one single friend of ours on hand to assure us we had. So probably we didn't, and knowing Duke as I know him now, I'm almost sure we didn't.

"Our reputation, before we came east, was built on nine pieces, and I don't think we ever had a bad night in Kansas City, but when we added five or six men it made a lot of difference. The band had to be enlarged to go on the road, but it slowed everything down and made it sluggish, because those extra men were not exactly the best musicians. Then Benny Morton, Dicky Wells, Harry Edison, and Earle Warren came in and it began to sound like a good big band. At first it was a disappointment, especially as compared with the band in Kansas City. Anyone who heard it there heard the swingingest band in the world. It was really a pleasure to play in it. Of course, we weren't making any money to speak of, but things were cheap then and I think my rent was only about three dollars a week. We always had fun some kind of way.

"From there we went to Pittsburgh and Chicago, and we opened in New York at Roseland just in time for New Year's, which I'll never forget. It was a sight that first New Year's on Broadway, in 1937. There were so many people.

"The band first started clicking in the Famous Door. We had made good changes and the band sounded well together. The place was small and we sat close together, and the low ceilings made the band sound beautiful, and it was a rocking place, and that's where business started picking up. Café Society was another valuable stepping stone.

"The first song I ever wrote for Basie was called *Baby Girl*. We never recorded it, but we—the nine pieces—used to play it and swing it. I wrote it for my sister's little girl. Others I did for Basie were *Red*

Bank Boogie, Taps Mills, What's Your Number?, Avenue C, and *Love Jumped Out.* I have arranged for Benny Goodman and Tommy Dorsey, and I did a couple of things for Duke. I wrote *Hollywood Hangover* when I was in the army, when I had plenty of time to write, which I didn't have with Basie.

"He was a leader all right, but not a harsh one. When someone got too unruly, he would eventually get stirred up and let him know he was the boss. He was very nice to work for, but he always knew what he wanted from the band and the arrangers. At the beginning, it used to take us so long to get through the arrangements. We'd have to help guys who didn't do so much reading, but who were great as soloists and were accustomed to the 'heads.'

"Lester and Herschel never said an unkind word to one another. There was some kind of feeling between them, but a lot of respect and no real animosity. I remember one time Herschel stopped speaking to me for about a month. I finally found out that he thought in writing my arrangements I was giving Lester all the tenor solos. All I was doing was giving the solos as Basie told me, and Herschel blamed me for it. I think Basie felt Lester showed the band off best when it was flagging and waving and carrying on, but for the mellow things—slow blues and sentimental numbers—he preferred Herschel.

"The only reason I played all those things with a mute with Basie was because he asked me to, and as he was the leader his wishes were like commands. When I came out of the army I was my own judge and I played like I wanted to. The funny thing about Basie was that he'd ask me to record with a mute, but when we got out on one-nighters he'd have me play the same thing open. I don't mind playing with a mute, but not all the time. I got so I hated the cup mute then. There's even a record called *Cup Mute Clayton* that I made with Ike Quebec. But there are some songs, like *Goin' to Chicago* and *If I Could Be with You* which I like to play with a cup mute. I played plunger when we recorded Jimmy Mundy's *Fiesta in Blue* in 1941. I remember I was the last trumpet to play it, the fourth one to try it. It wasn't written for anyone in particular, but Mundy seemed to like the way I was playing it. I don't often use a plunger, but there are times when I like it. I can play with mute *and* plunger, but a mute will make you tired. A bucket is the easiest, because it lets the air out, and it's the only one you can play practically like an open horn. Nowadays, you don't see many people use a derby like Snooky Young did with Basie, and I saw him use a cup mute like a plunger down at Birdland one night. He had his fingers sticking in there and he played in and out—something you seldom see. Ed Lewis used to do that. The buzz mute is uncommon now, too. I think that was invented when fellows couldn't get to growl like Cootie and Duke's men. A lot of trumpet players, corny ones, couldn't growl, so the only thing that would give them a somewhat similar sound was the buzz mute. Roy gave me one and I used to like it. It's made on the principle of tissue paper and the comb, but with wire. It makes a mechanical buzz, but nothing on the order of Cootie's sound.

"I was with Basie seven years before I went into the army. I was luckier than Lester. He didn't make the band and when his time came they shipped him down to Alabama. It nearly happened to me, too. I went up to the reception center where everyone goes to be screened. After that they send you anywhere in the country for your basic training, and then they ship you. Dave Martin, the pianist, was stationed at that reception center and he had a five-piece band without a trumpet, so they were glad to see me. I started playing with them for officers' dances and everything, and they canceled every call that came up for me to be shipped to Georgia or somewhere for basic training. 'Not in camp—on leave,' they'd say, and they did that so many times. When finally a requisition came to go to Camp Shanks where Sy Oliver was, they said, 'Okay.' Otherwise I would have gone many times before as a soldier, not as a musician.

"The main job of the band I was with was to be at the port when the soldiers got on the boat, and to play them away and make them feel good. We had to meet them when they came back, too. Some days, when we played a boat away, it was so cold the valves of the horn would freeze. Then they'd send us in to the stoves to thaw them out. We'd come out and blow for fifteen minutes until they froze, and then go back in again. We might be playing from five o'clock in the morning until ten o'clock and then be through for the day, or they might call us out again the same evening. We used to play *Lay That Pistol Down, Flying Home*, and numbers like that.

"We started out with about thirty-five pieces and it got down to where I was the last trumpet player in the band. That was because I was the last to go in. Sy Oliver was in charge and a top sergeant. Others in the band were Mercer Ellington and Joe Turner. Sy had to arrange military music for ten trumpets, and so on. Another of his main jobs was to do the arrangements for an army broadcast we did every week. He used to play trumpet in the band, too. We were at Camp Shanks, only forty-five minutes from New York, and I stayed at the Hotel Theresa nearly the whole time I was in the army. I'd come home most nights and we'd call up the camp in the morning and ask, 'Anything for us to do?' They'd often say, 'No,' and sometimes we'd stay in town two or three days at a time. Then we'd go and play one boat and come right back!

"At first, I liked it, because it was a rest, and it was good for me after the years with Basie, but I didn't like wearing the uniform all the time. I was always wanting to change clothes. There were the M.P.'s, of course, and at one time there was a law which said soldiers had to get out of nightclubs and bars at midnight. We'd have to get up and leave our friends there, even if we had nothing to do next day.

"We had a certain amount of military training, but the main thing we had to do was to rehearse. And I don't regard it as a period of musical stagnation, because we tried hard to make ours a very good band. In fact, we could have washed away a lot of civilian bands that came out to entertain the soldiers.

"When I got out of the army in 1946, I joined Jazz at the Philharmonic. I'd known Norman Granz a long time. He had taken a group up the West Coast, but the very first real cross-country contingent he had was three horns, three rhythm, and Helen Humes. The horns were Lester, Coleman Hawkins, and myself; the rhythm, Kenny Kersey, Billy Hadnott, and Jackie Mills. Trummy Young, Rex Stewart, and Illinois Jacquet came later. We didn't have sax battles between Prez and Hawk. I'd solo between them and keep them apart.

"From 1948 on, I free-lanced around New York and toured abroad. I played in the Savoy Ballroom with Jimmy Rushing's band, which was practically the same as the one I took to Europe. It included Emmett Berry, Dicky Wells, Buddy Tate, and Buddy Johnson. After that I went to the Embers with Joe Bushkin. When we went into Lou Terrassi's on 57th, between Broadway and 8th, Tony Parenti taught me Dixieland. I didn't know anything about Dixieland until the fifties! Tony took me to his house and taught me solos and routines. He had a little band, with Sandy Williams on trombone, and he needed a trumpet. I didn't know the songs, but some afternoons he and his wife would cook a big dinner, and I'd go by his house and we'd take off our coats, and he'd teach me four or five songs that day. We did that quite a few times until I had learned about twenty songs.

"Now how long would you say it takes a trumpet player to mature from the time he first starts playing? When I joined Basie, I had been playing just four years and I felt I shouldn't take Lips Page's chair. I like some of those early records, though. The one I made with Teddy Wilson and Benny Goodman of *Why Was I Born?* was all right as an example of melody, but when it came to real hot, authentic jazz, I didn't think I was good enough to follow Lips. He'd been playing a long time. Louis Armstrong had been playing a long time when he made the *Hot Five* records, too. I think if Basie had known I'd only been playing four years he wouldn't have hired me. I believe it takes a trumpet player at least twelve years to mature, and after that he should try to improve himself. I don't believe you should stop improving. Some fellows believe they've got as far as they can go.

"I think the trumpet player I used to sound most like, fifteen years ago, was Bill Coleman. We played together when I was last in Europe and we're very far apart now. Of course, I haven't said much about Europe here, because it's really a story on its own. I've made seven trips and I like it over there. There are some rough trumpet players in Europe, too, but the best are in England. All of Ted Heath's are good, and then there are Kenny Baker and all the trumpet-playing leaders of little bands. It's not that way in France or Sweden. There are very good musicians in those countries, but England has more good trumpet players. I don't know how you account for things like that, but then it's also strange that there was so much variety in the trumpet players who came up through the big bands, while the youngsters who have come up in little bands sound so much alike."

(1962)

Jo Jones

(DRUMS)

Jo Jones has a quicksilver mind and the interviewer soon discovers that he is not there to ask questions but to be instructed. Questions, in fact, are sometimes brushed aside, but more often they merely deflect his stream of consciousness unprofitably. What follows was taped one afternoon in Jones's hotel room on 49th Street in New York City.

"The average person who works from nine to five could not possibly go through what the professional and his body go through in one year—not physically, mentally, morally, or spiritually. Nobody has ever explained what it takes to perform, the driving force that makes a person get up on that stage and perform night after night. I've been in this business fifty years and ever since I was a kid I've been hearing this cliché that they come up with—*the show must go on*. A nine-to-fiver gets a headache and doesn't come to work. Or it's snowing outside and he says, 'I can't get to the office today.' Or he has an important meeting in San Francisco but he comes down with a cold and says, 'Can you postpone it? I'll be there next Wednesday.' That's

47

all right in a set business that doesn't fluctuate much, but when we're booked to go somewhere we are billed, and don't nothing stop us. We're worse than the mailman. We're going to be there.

"Show business has to be more flexible, but I've always been interested in the fact that if you take a thirty-five-year-old or a forty-year-old professional to the businessman's doctor, he's going to be in better shape than the nine-to-fiver. I remember we tried a thing once with two or three people who followed the Basie band. They tried to do the same things they *thought* we were doing. They tried to drink as much as they thought we were doing, and they tried to carouse around with the girls like they thought we were doing. It was that old wives' tale about a musician having a quart of whiskey on one arm and a chick on the other. I'd just like to see a man go to bed with thirty different women in a given month!

"You can take the average musician, any guy that plays music, and he's better off than anybody in any other walk of life, I don't care who—doctor, lawyer, teacher, minister, businessman, or what have you. He doesn't need what they need. He'll come out of the hospital after an appendix or tonsil operation and get right up on the bandstand and play. The other guy has got to *recuperate*. You can check it with any reputable doctor who has musicians and performers—that goes for dancers and singers—as patients, and he'll tell you that in comparison the nine-to-fiver is in bad shape. You're right, irregularity may be good. They're forever trying to find out about our bodies. They give new medicines to the army, because the foot soldier has to go through circumstances and conditions different from those of the ordinary layman. If it's tried and proved on him, then the patent is approved."

"When I was starting out I tried to do everything. I tried to sing, to dance, to do dramatics, to play the trumpet, to play the sax, to play the piano. When a distant cousin of mine took me to hear Mr. Louis Armstrong in Chicago, I said, 'Well, that's the end of my trumpet playing!' When I went to the sax, I got smarter than the music teacher, but here comes Coleman Hawkins, so that was the end of that! Right afterwards I met Lester Young. So now I'm going to the piano, and I know I'm very great, but then I met Mr. Art Tatum, and that ended my piano career!

"When we started out as youngsters, a lot of us—like Johnny Hodges—were fortunate enough to be around our elders and we weren't allowed the luxury of playing around like teenagers, because we were around older people with experience. They didn't lecture us, but they showed us the way. The boy who stayed home with Mama and Papa had a good routine, but the people I'm talking of were passing on the benefit of their professional experience to us. When we got so smart that we knew everything, they'd let us go and jump off a cliff. But they'd have a net there to break our fall, and then they'd let us know we weren't so all-fired smart.

"I was just always a gypsy, and I had an unusual urge to be in carnivals or circuses. I wouldn't have gained the knowledge I have by reading. It took a whole lot of experience and a whole lot of *helping* to make me what I am, because I realize that personally, myself, I'm fifty people. We were very fortunate, and ofttimes those of us with certain backgrounds could sit down and talk about them, but as of today I don't know nobody I can talk to but Roy Eldridge, because there's nobody playing in the music business that has had the kind of experience he and I had. I used to talk a lot with my very good friends Sidney Catlett and Chick Webb, but they hadn't met the people, hadn't had the experience, hadn't been in the states, the villages, and the hamlets that I had. In my formative years I didn't rightly know where I was, because I didn't major in geography. All I knew, I was just traveling. And I was fortunate enough to have a whole lot of mothers and fathers, sisters and brothers, and aunts and uncles, out there in the shows. In the carnivals and circuses you had mostly European performers, and they'd tell you about different things to come, and they'd give you addresses. They'd find out where you were going, from one town to another, and you'd look up retired and semi-retired people and ask questions—that is, if you were going to be in the business. It was a sort of protective thing, especially when your time was taken up with your music, your instrument, and getting the precision you had to have. Our hearts bleed now for the kids coming up who don't have the dance floors and the theaters we had. They took them away. A boy asked me the other night to explain to his wife, who was twenty-five, what a chorus girl was! She didn't know."

"A friend of mine, who knows more about me than anybody, is Wilson Driver. When I first saw him in Atlanta, he had a xylophone, a cornet, a set of drums. Another multi-musician I remember was Jimmy King. They both impressed me, but I wasn't thinking that I'd play drums as a livelihood because I had other things on my mind. I saw many drummers, many banjo players, many guitar players, many tuba players, many violin players, many piano players, and to make me what I am I collected many mannerisms and moral things from them. 'Come on, kid,' they'd say, 'sit down and watch this.'

"I'd hang around theaters and spend all my time running errands

for different people. I ran errands for Butterbeans and Susie. I'd mown
lawns and I'd washed windows, but I was always asking, 'Show me
how to do this.' They could only show me through their eyes, because
my imagination wasn't keen enough to grasp the experience. I ran
errands for chorus girls and soubrettes, too. Most clubs had three or
four women who sang different kinds of songs for different kinds of
people. You'd call to 'em and this one would come up and sing risqué
songs, this one would sing the blues, and another would sing pretty
songs."

"When we first came to New York, I told 'em I didn't want to know
anything about a drum or a woman until I was ninety! I have yet to
see a man who knows anything about a drum. And I haven't read or
seen anybody who knows anything about a woman. All you can do
is leave her happy. You can't satisfy her! Years ago Mr. Ellington
wrote *A Drum Is a Woman*. And it *is* like a woman. Because there is
a type of woman you can talk to, there's one you have to shake, there's
one you slap, and there's another you have to break a chair over her
head. Yet she still loves you—as much as she can.

"You never know what that drum is going to do, and it has fasci-
nated me all my life. I remember my aunt taking me to a circus when
I was a kid, and I can still feel that bass drum. Later, she bought me
a snare drum, but I didn't ever think I would really play drums. When
I really switched over to them was when I found the drummer was
the highest priced in the orchestra, because it was required of him to
know as much music as the conductor, the first violinist, the first
trumpet player . . . So I began.

"Samuel 'Baby' Brothers told me what to do. He was going to Australia with Sonny Clay. I was fortunate to be in Omaha then, because
there were a lot of musicians around to help me. I went to Hospe's
Music Store and got vibes, chimes, and tymps, and I went to a couple
of teachers who showed me how to do things.

"The one I learned more *music* from than anyone was Henri Woode.
I roomed with him when I was with Lloyd Hunter's band. He played
piano and accordion, and sometimes I wanted to get my pistol on him
because he would have music paper spread all over and he'd be using
the bed as a piano, writing and singing. 'This guy's going crazy,' I
thought. I didn't want to go out and sit in the park! When we were
on one-nighters in Iowa, I used to watch him. He'd come back in
with another idea and start writing—with no piano. I picked up so
many things with that ten-piece band, and he really gave me an
insight into ear training.

"He was the band's musical director. In most cases you are either an arranger or a performer. Few people can ever be both. Even as of today, if Henri Woode brings in an arrangement to an orchestra, and he sits down in front, and you're looking at the music, there will not be one mistake. And when he stomps it off you will play it from start to finish, and you'll feel relaxed. All his arrangements are relaxed.

"I was sheltered by two or three people who told me to study music, to go down to catch classical music, to do this, to do that. These guys were pool-hall characters. You must remember the social conditions in the country at the time. One of them owned a pool hall and he caught me using profanity. 'You use that kind of language in my pool hall again, I'm going to hit you in the mouth!' So then I pawned the pistol, broke off my knife in a tree, and he took me to his home and gave me a key. The guy could speak five languages, and he said, 'I'm going to lock you in here with these books, and you will *learn*. No sneaking out, because I'm going to ask you about what everything is!' Then I asked, 'Why do you talk like this in your home, Ralph, and a different way in the pool hall?' He explained that the people he was dealing with—laborers and guys from the packing house—would not understand. But here was a guy who could speak Greek and Latin, and in the pool hall he was talking about 'dis, dat, and da other.' So the people I've met have been very responsible for and to me.

"The guy that played the bass drum in Mr. Sousa's band was a Mr. Helmich. Later, he played with the Goldman band in Central Park, and I had the pleasure of taking several drummers out there with some popcorn to get some music. 'Now they're going to do this,' I said, 'and I want you to hear this bass drum.' I used to love to go back after the concerts to see him, and I always tried to get him a nice stein of beer. The last time I saw him he was about eighty-three years old but still very immaculate and dap. He could take that bass drum just by itself and get eight notes out of it. He was the only one of his kind.

"Experiences around the people I met make me create, and I must play *music*. I try to keep my drums in tune, although I have a very hard bass drum. The reason Mr. Chick Webb took an interest in me was that he found out I played with a tympany head. In old pictures, when I used two tom-toms, you can see where I have tympany rods on. It's very difficult to tell an individual how to tune up his drums. Most of the guys in my formative years would play with one band for ten to twelve years, but after World War II a guy's over here for three months, over there for two weeks, and he never gets to play with one group of people over a period of years. You see some young musicians get together and they've a good group for about six months, then something happens and they break up. Somebody has told one of the guys he should get a group of his own. They should have pooled their resources to make it one solid thing."

"You have to remember social conditions as they were in Chicago in the twenties and thirties. It's no secret that the people who controlled things would demand and tell you what you were going to do. If you were going to survive, that's what you did. If they wanted your services, you played where they told you to play. You did exactly what they told you to do or you were dead. That's what happened to me one time. I have crushed fingers, you see? You've met Mr. Earl Hines. So far as I know, the man had to play with a knife at his throat and a gun at his back the whole time he was in Chicago. You tell those people you were taking your horn to get it fixed, and they'd say, 'Leave it here. We'll get it fixed.' They knew you might have been thinking of going to Kansas City or someplace else.

"Chicago never was like Kansas City. Which was worse? Not worse—it was good, clean, wholesome fun. You did what they told you, and that was it. You had no worries, remember, when you were working for *them*. You see, there was a dearth in the United States from 1926 to 1936. We lost more music then than the world will ever know, because we hadn't got tape-recorders and all that modern boom-boom-boom. There was so much music and so many musicians, but if you didn't belong to certain cliques, didn't do this, didn't work for this guy or that guy—then you were just out of it. So guys said, 'Oh, what the heck!' Some got day jobs. Some began to drink and became winos. Some got jobs in department stores or running an elevator, or in the packing house, in order to survive. Some just gave up, because they weren't allowed to play the way they wanted to play."

"When it comes to wealth, musical wealth, I'm the richest drummer that's lived in fifty years, because nobody ever had what I have. Nobody ever had the pleasure of sitting up with a band night after night that had a Herschel Evans, a Lester Young, a Harry Edison, a Buck Clayton, a Dicky Wells, a Benny Morton, a Freddie Green, and a Walter Page. No band ever had that. Well there was one, but Mr. Ellington was always for presentation. I'm speaking in the pure sense of jazz—they never had all that ability. Everybody in that Basie band was capable of standing up and playing with just the rhythm section.

"Jack Washington was the brightest thing in the reed section, but everyone was talking about Herschel Evans and Lester Young. Jack just stayed in the background but ofttimes when guys acted up Basie

would let Jack play two or three choruses. If he let him play four or
five choruses, there wouldn't be any other saxophone players up there.
That's right. Ask Mr. Benny Carter when you see him!

"Mr. Benny Carter lived across the hall at 580 St. Nicholas Avenue,
where I was across the hall from Willie 'The Lion' Smith. Herschel
Evans and Jack Washington roomed together in the next building.
Mr. Benny Carter had just returned from Europe and sometimes he'd
be there listening when they were working out. When Jack picked
up the tenor, Benny would be listening to *him,* and Herschel would be
shaking his head. And at other times, when the guys couldn't play
an arrangement, he'd be sitting there, looking straight ahead, waiting
till they got through, and then he'd play it. I remember once, too,
when somebody was fooling around, Mr. Walter Page left his bass,
went down quiet as a cat, got the baritone, played the sax parts, and
went back to his place. So what else is new?

"You must remember there were about four drummers in Basie's
band. Besides Basie, there was Freddie Green, and later on there was
Joe Newman. I didn't need to worry about Gene Krupa or Buddy
Rich. I was catching hell sitting up there, trying to play in Basie's
band.

"There will never be an institution like the Basie band that came to
New York in 1936. Until we came, musicians didn't fraternize with
one another. It was a very cold, clique scene. Because they didn't
know any better, and they still don't. I can remember everything that
came through Kansas City. I used to run up and say, 'You guys gonna
sit in?' And they'd say, 'No, it's against our contract.' I'd laugh, because they better *not* sit in and play with nobody there.

"At that time in Kansas City a local band had to play opposite
visiting bands, and when some met up with Basie's raggedy band they
got egg on their faces. They'd rather have paid us and had us not play.
You ask Earl Hines about the night his band and ours played together.
Or ask Duke Ellington what happened the night Basie's band left
Kansas City. Fletcher Henderson? McKinney's Cotton Pickers? They
never had a rhythm section. Chick Webb? Great, but never had a
rhythm section. Everybody went north, east, south, and west.

"We worked at it, to build a rhythm section, every day, every night.
We worked alone, not with the band all the time. I didn't care what
happened—*one* of us would be up to par. If three were down, one
would carry the three. Never four were out.

"What other rhythm section? None. None. The greatest band I've
heard was Mr. Walter Page's Blue Devils. I heard all the bands in
'26, '27, '28, '29, '30. . . . I used to go to Detroit. I saw Edward's Collegians, Fletcher Henderson, McKinney's Cotton Pickers. I'd see them

in Battles of the Bands, when they had five-band tours. I saw Blanche
Calloway, Belton's Syncopators out of Florida. But I never heard a
band like Walter Page's.

"Naturally, you know about Hot Lips Page, but Mr. Louis Armstrong and I used always to talk about one guy, Harry Smith, who
took Hot Lips Page's place with Walter Page. When I saw him, I
quit dancing. And I used to love to dance. But I just took a look at
this man and did a very foolish thing. I didn't know he wasn't supposed to drink, and I just bought him all the whiskey my little money
would buy. Later on they left and went to Kansas City. He was in a
hotel. He drank and died. Harry Smith—he never recorded.

"When I first joined Basie, I played with him one night and I quit.
'I'm going back to school,' I said. There I was, sitting up there with
all those fantastic guys. I went back to get my drums, and they im-
plored me to go to Little Rock with them, and I did. See, Basie had
two bands that never came to New York, but he never had a band
after that, not a band like that one. I can't explain that band, because
there's no record of it.

"It is very wonderful that the young musicians today have a
chance to make records, good, bad, or indifferent. At least they get a
chance to hear themselves, and they can improve. There were so
many people back then that you never heard about. The East Coast
guys didn't travel around much, didn't go in all the different places in
the Midwest. It takes all types of people to make a world, but there
are so many that come to mind that nobody ever speaks about. As
Dizzy Gillespie was saying, I'd like people to know about me being an
innovator. It's not quite the same as wanting credit. Please let me
know I was the innovator of this, or that I started that."

"At one time I had about seventy-five records of Duke Ellington and
I used to carry my record-player around. I think Freddie Green and
I must have put words to about twenty of Mr. Duke Ellington's tunes,
before anybody else thought about putting words to them. We'd just get
in a room and play the records and find words to go with the tunes.
He wrote a four-part thing called *Reminiscing in Tempo*, and every-
thing is in it that you could ever get—the whole embodiment. And
I'm supposed to be a connoisseur of Mr. Ellington, you know.

"'What do you think of Duke Ellington?' somebody asked me once.
'Well,' I said, 'you know how this slavery started, and who started it—
the Africans, the Arabs, etc. But Mr. Ellington is the only slaver I
know. When the so-called white people act up, he'll write a tune and
spank them. And when the black people act up, he'll write a tune and

spank them, too. He just keeps *everybody* in line. He's a slave-driver
if ever there was one! Every time some little moral or civil upheaval
comes along, he sits down and writes something, scratches it off, and
bang!' They used to say at the theaters, 'Well, Duke is all right, but
he can't write nothing popular.' I'd go by and tell them everything he
wrote was 'popular.' I'd have some of the things Freddie Green and I
had written down, and I'd say, 'Look, here's some words.' But they
forget, how easy they forget!

"In 1930, I had Duke's record of *Three Little Words* and I took it
'round to the Ritz Café to play on the juke box.

" 'That can't be a colored man,' they said.

" 'He's very colored,' I told them.

" 'Here's a band you should book,' I told Jimmy Jewell. 'They're
making a movie, *Check and Double Check,* with Amos and Andy.'

"So when Duke did come to Omaha, he had to play uptown and
downtown. Not that it made any difference because at that time it
was still a checkerboard. But he played in the small places, and then
the people just had to have him in the big places. He came back and
played the *other* theater, and I'm looking at them playing *Mood
Indigo*, and for two or three years Barney Bigard made the clarinet
famous. This is where it gets ridiculous. I *know* what I've got in my
scrapbooks, because this was before Benny Goodman. Well, he was
playing in the studios or with Ted Lewis, and nobody wrote the truth
about Bigard. I used to follow what they were doing. I went from
Cleveland to Boston—650 miles—to catch two shows of Duke Ellington, and then I got on a plane and went back to Basie's band."

"There will never be an institution like the Basie band was when it
started out. All these other people, they started out *with* something.
But we were really behind the Iron Curtain. There was no chance
for us. So there was nothing for us to do but play for ourselves. You
see, in Kansas City you had ten or eleven bands, and the only band
that came in there and made any impact was McKinney's Cotton
Pickers. They had a thing going and it was a different thing. Of
course, the brass was electrifying. But Don Redman left them shortly
after that.

"Now Bennie Moten's band played one and three, but Walter Page's
played two and four. Walter joined Bennie in 1932, as Jimmy Rushing
and Basie had already done, and then other guys from the Blue Devils
got into the Moten band. East and West—it became a wedding. Instead of one and three and two and four, it became one, two, three,
four, and then it was like a lilt. That's how you got rhythm.

"The first night I played with the Basie band was in Topeka. Tommy Douglas, at the Cherry Blossom, had said, 'How would you like to join a band?' 'That would be nice,' I answered, 'but I don't think I'm ready yet.' But I left, and I had two quarts of whiskey coming to me, which I didn't drink. I took it home and put it in my suitcase. Then I went to Topeka and played with Basie's band. I was doing all right until they played *After You've Gone*. When Lester Young jumped up and took the second chorus, I was ready to go home. I went downstairs and sat in a cab, looking for them to give me my money. They came and begged me. 'No, no,' I said, 'I'm going home.' Then Walter Page, Joe Keyes, and Ben Webster got me in the gents' room in the hotel. 'You can't leave us,' they said, because they knew Mack Washington was going back to Bennie Moten. Then I took out a great big quart of whiskey and said, 'Here, y'all! I'm going to Omaha, Nebraska, to go back to school.' But I went with them to Little Rock anyhow!

"What had upset me? Well, when they played my heart leaped in my mouth. I just jumped out of my seat. I didn't know what they were doing. 'My God,' I said, 'what am I doing here?' There, in the Metropolitan Hall, Topeka, that band just floated me and threw me off!

" 'Mr. Basie,' I'd said, 'you got a nice band. I wish you a lot of luck.'

"But then they conned me in that outhouse, until I said I'd go for two weeks, which became fourteen years! I really didn't think I had the experience to play with them, because there was no music. They'd just call a tune and play it.

"The man who taught me how to think was Joe Keyes, the greatest first trumpet player. He was a very remarkable man. He knew everything, all the arrangements. He was from Texas, I think, and there was never anybody able to outthink Mr. Joe Keyes. He taught me how to read shows and he taught me how to change tempos. He sat next to me and said, 'Watch it!' He'd come to work and not speak to anybody. He'd get off work, drink two quarts of whiskey, and come back to work next night. He sat over there on that bandstand and if anyone got hung up, he knew the whole arrangement. He went straight ahead. In his later years, when he was going down slow, there was a band room down in the Braddock. Little trumpet players would catch him and buy him a drink. Then he'd take 'em downstairs and show 'em things. Those he helped could tell you how wonderful he was.

"Mr. Cab Calloway came and got him, bought him a uniform and bought him a brand-new horn. He played one show, pulled the uniform off, gave him his horn, and went back to the Braddock bar. 'It's no use, Cab,' he said. 'Your music is not interesting.' "

"Dancing? It helps to give me my sense of timing. If you notice, anything I play I have to play dancing and singing to it. Because I was never allowed the luxury of playing a tune unless I could sing the lyrics. My sense of timing and dancing helped when I had bad luck with my legs and had to switch to drums. The actual experience, to be around the thing in person, is what counts. Like in Kansas City, you had your farm teams. You played down here and then you graduated. It was like going from grade school, to high school, to college. You didn't just jump into a particular thing until you were ready. Here in New York, there were guys with horns who had no business on the bandstand. 'I played with Lester Young last night,' they'd be saying, 'I played with Roy Eldridge . . . I played with Charlie Parker . . . I played with Dizzy Gillespie. . . .' It wasn't like that in Kansas City. You had to wait until they asked for you to sit in. They had enough respect to say, 'We don't belong here. We're not ready to play in this league.'

"The other bands didn't have the flexibility we had. Everything Basie had was flexible. In those days we were thinking about nothing but music, not about going in and making a hit record, nothing like that. We exchanged ideas and there was a continuity that only got broken after World War II, or during it. We used to go around and show kids how to formulate, how to play fours, how to get more leverage out of what they were doing, and it was very wonderful.

"I went to a drum clinic once with Charles Mingus, for three days. I'd ask each of the kids, 'Why do you play like that?' One would say he'd seen Max Roach, another Philly Joe, another Art Blakey.

" 'How long you been playing, son?'

" 'Oh, four years.'

" 'Wait a minute! Have you played with the people Max (or Philly Joe or Art) play with? It's *who* you play with should shape the way you play.'

"When they heard Lester Young play, they said, 'Oh, Prez, he don't sound like he used to.' So I said, 'Well, who's he playing with?' Then when they heard the album he made in 1956 with Roy Eldridge, Vic Dickenson, Teddy Wilson, Gene Ramey, and me, they said, 'Wow, that's a difference!' Now that kind of thing is hard to explain, but people can understand when they hear it. And that's the reason I always want to tell promoters that, when they put something together, be sure to put compatible things together, like bacon and eggs. You don't just throw different people together and expect to get a performance, unless you know something about the experience *they* have had. They may set up a program in which one guy's not speaking to this other guy anymore. It is not a matter of hate, but of self-respect. If they're playing off a sheet, then it doesn't make any difference. All they've got to do is say hello. But when you haven't got a part, and you've got to play from here [heart], you'd rather not play with this other guy because you'll get in his way of thought. Always remember that we are playing our experiences, have got to project our experiences, of what we've had in common. We set that to music, according to the tune. When you say you want me to record with Earl Hines, it's okay. You bring in Al Hall on bass, and he and I are together, but I can't really bring Paul Gonsalves in on this record of our experiences because when *we* start going somewhere we haven't got time to explain our references."

"Basically, people are not bad. Some people do good because they know better. Others do bad because they *don't* know any better. They're ignorant of the facts, and two college degrees are not the answer. Intelligence doesn't mean the individual is wise. Let me point out a mistake that was made with Dick Wilson, the tenor player who'd been with Andy Kirk. He was in the hospital and he was not supposed to have salt, so all he'd ask everybody to do was to bring him a box of salt. So one of his visitors brought him a box and he put it in the drawer. After everybody had gone, he was eating salt in his food. The person who brought it thought he was doing good, you follow?

"People think they're being nice when they press drinks and hospitality on you, but some musicians don't know how to say 'No.' Now I may be the most disliked musician that has ever been in New York, because I don't visit, I don't go to parties, and I've never been in but three after-hour spots in the whole city. I'm a loner, a street boy, fifty years without a home.

"Then you have to watch for the eager beavers, the guys that really want to do you in. They go for the Academy Award every night. They *mean* to put a stumbling block in front of you. There's one statement I'm going to have printed, and I'd like the guys to stick it right on their door, where they'll see it as they go out: *There's nothing wrong with the music business that we ourselves can't cure.*

"Everybody who goes to a bar don't get drunk. But that *bar* is a detrimental thing. Everybody knows that. Then people began to make money off other things—the narcotics agents, the police, the shakedown artists. They said nobody but musicians used pot, until a few years ago, when they found out that in order to get some pot you had to go back to school, to grade school, that is. Marijuana has never been habit-forming and it has never hurt anybody in the world. In fact, they should hurry up and give me the concession, so that people won't be going around with catarrh, sinusitis, and all that. See that bag there? I had it full of marijuana once and I set it right down by Lester Young.

"'What do you want?' I asked.

"'Coca-Cola,' he said."

(1971)

Eddie Durham

(TROMBONE, GUITAR, AND ARRANGER)

"My daddy was a musician, a fiddler, and he played numbers like *Turkey in the Straw* at square dances. They'd have just him, nobody else, just a fiddle. He died when he was quite young and it was Joe, my oldest brother, who taught me and my other brothers. He subscribed to lessons from what was called the U.S. School of Music, and we were all able to learn pretty good from them. The system they had of teaching was a start, to train you, but it didn't go very far. Nobody knew more than two- and three-part harmony. A sixth was unknown.

"Roosevelt, my youngest brother, and I were about ten months apart. I was born in San Marcos, Texas, in 1906. I had another brother, who died in childbirth, and a sister four years older than me. My oldest brother went in the army during World War I, and it was when he got back that he was teaching us youngsters. He was with us a long time and we formed a family band, the Durham Brothers Band. Earl, who played saxophone and clarinet, eventually went to Connecticut and stayed there. Roosevelt remained with the minstrel shows for a time, playing piano, but I sent for him later and we were together quite a while. Our cousins, Allen and Clyde Durham, were also in the band. Herschel Evans was another cousin, and he joined us in Dallas. He was playing alto then, but he couldn't read and we tried to teach him. We put him on tenor and he was better on that than on alto, but he never did read very much. We used four saxophones in four-part harmony, and just about the first time down he didn't hit on anybody else's note. So if he didn't play the note *you* played, he'd found his own!

"After my oldest brother married, he organized Blanche Calloway's last band for her. She made him a trustee and he went to Kansas City and brought Ben Webster back. Joe was a technician and as fast on cello as Oscar Pettiford was on bass. He was with Nat Cole for a little while, and he was playing *some* bass! He was way ahead. When Nat got on top, he tried to get him to go in his trio, but he just hung around his wife and wouldn't leave. Then he was working in a shipyard and playing gigs, and he never really made the most of what he had.

"I played banjo first, then four-string guitar. Later on, I added trombone and six-string guitar, and played both in the band. I think I could have been a kind of genius on that six-string guitar, but after I started getting up in the world I divided my time between arranging, composing, trombone, and guitar, not sticking to any one. Mostly our band worked traveling shows. At one time we were with Doug Moyne's Dramatic Show, a white show. They had a terrific piano player named Neil Heller to accompany the singers, and they used us to back up other things.

"After our band split up, I went with the 101 Ranch Circus on trombone. Edgar Battle was there, too, and that's where I really taught myself to write, to express my own voicing, because we had a lot of horns to play around with.* The circus band was a big brass band, a parade band. We had four trombones, two or three French horns, and peck horns, but we didn't use all of them when we played for the minstrel show. They had very good men in those days, and

---

* Edgar Battle claimed that the 101 Ranch Rodeo Show was comparable to the Ringling Brothers or Barnum and Bailey circuses. It originated at the second largest ranch in the country, the King Ranch in Texas being bigger. The performers and animals moved from city to city on a train, Battle said, of about thirty cars. Over a thousand people were involved—"cowboys, Indians, Negroes, white folks and Russian cossack riders." The musicians would sometimes play from a big red wagon pulled by ten black horses.

they could read rings around me. They had trumpet players who could triple-tongue and double-tongue when they were playing high-powered marches.

"They could play a little jazz, but they stayed very close to the melody. I was trying to solo a bit, and it wasn't hard for me to learn the value of notes, but a guy who could swing a break was something new to them. So when we played for dances at night, I asked them if I could swing in the jazz breaks. They were all trained musicians playing solid trombone—no faking—so jazz breaks on trombone were different.

"The show used to be out at nine and we didn't leave town right away, so that gave us the idea of putting on a dance. The leader of the band said, 'How can we have a dance when we ain't got no piano?' We said we'd fix up something, so they got me some manuscript paper. I was just beginning to write and I wrote harmony for some of the horns so it sounded like a piano. We had saxophones in the minstrel show, and I'd use them, too. It worked out all right. We'd find some little hole in town and charge a quarter at the door. Each of us would make two or three dollars a night, so we were on our way!

"The minstrel show was like a sideshow and not in the big tent where the circus was. It didn't start till the big show was over. In the parade, the big band from the circus would come first, and further down the band from the minstrel show, and that would be playing the jazz."

After leaving the 101 Ranch band in 1926, Durham worked with many bands in the Southwest, including Edgar Battle's Dixie Ramblers in the 711 Show with singer Mamie Smith, and the Blue Devils.

"When I went with Bennie Moten in 1929," Durham resumed, "he had only three saxophones and two trumpets. Although I didn't care for the instrument, I was playing valve trombone in order to help the trumpets. I worked very hard, playing awful high with the trumpets to give a three-trumpet effect, then switching back to make a two-trombone sound. There was a lot of pressure on the brass, but those guys wouldn't play a sixth or a ninth chord. They were playing the fifth, tonic, and third, and they couldn't hear the sixth. So then Moten brought Lips Page into the band. 'What's he gonna play?' the guys wanted to know. 'He's all right, but we don't need another horn.' Then I stepped the band up to ninth chords, and they could hear a ninth better than they could a sixth. Lips was pretty true on his horn [trumpet] and he could hear the sixth, so I gave him that and played the ninth myself. That's how we started getting five-part harmony in the brass, and they came to see why we had needed another horn.

There was nobody playing *their* note, where before they'd been saying 'You playin' my note? Get off my note!'

"I remember when the band started swinging, but I can't remember the year. Walter Page had played sousaphone, but he played good baritone saxophone, too, and he started doubling on baritone and bass with the Blue Devils. I went down and heard what he was doing. I stayed just long enough to steal him, and then he came with us. He was playing baritone, but then I got an idea about the rhythm. 'Who wants a bass fiddle in a band?' everybody wanted to know. They preferred sousaphone in a dancehall, because you could hear it better. Without amplification, a lot of guys weren't strong enough on bass fiddle. But Walter Page you could hear! He was like a house with a note. He didn't have the best ear, but he worked hard, and the string bass was in demand. How was his sound produced? I think it's in the coordination of the stroke in the head. The bass is one of the greatest things in the world for rhythm, but instead of writing a two-beat bass on the fifth and tonic, I kept it moving on chromatics to the chord. It sounded good, but when they saw it on paper, musicians said, 'This has gotta be out of tune!' Walter Page is the guy that created that walkin', walkin' . . . I wrote it long, but I couldn't control and master that swinging motion till I'd been in the band a long time. Of course, Willie McWashington, Moten's drummer, was a two-four man. He played that Charleston beat and cut wood all the time.

"I used to get through with Moten around two or three in the morning. When Jo Jones came to Kansas City, I used to take my guitar and trombone and jam with him from four in the morning till eight or nine. He was playing that modern stuff and it sounded good. He was was sharp on it and he was really creating a style. I don't know where he got it from. He hadn't been east—he hadn't been any place. But he was something else! It was *natural* with him, and maybe he doesn't get enough credit for it now. As a solo man, Chick Webb was the best up to that time, but he was too weak physically to play a whole lot of rhythm. He should have had a deputy. If I were Basie right now, I'd get me a good piano player and just come out to make an appearance with two or three numbers. But I think if he didn't sit at the piano, the band would lose something. I doubt if anyone else can do what he does. He's got a style. You've got to give him credit. Everybody was playing *all* the piano they could play to get famous, and here comes Basie saying, 'I play as *little* as I can.'

"While I was with Bennie Moten, I played a straight guitar with a resonator. It was about the size of a ten-inch record, made of tin, and it went right under the bridge. When you hit it, especially near the mike, you got an electric effect, and it carried like a banjo. Later,

I made a record of *Honey, Keep Your Mind on Me* with Jimmie Lunceford, and it sounds like electric, but it wasn't.

"When I met Charlie Christian in Oklahoma, I had a straight guitar and would just go to the mike with it. He was playing piano, but he had a cheap old piece of guitar. I was there three or four weeks and he told me how much he liked guitar, but he didn't know a lot about it. 'You've got an awful stroke and conception for guitar,' I told him, 'but I can give you a lot of pointers. One thing, when you press the guitar, use a downstroke. You can get that punch like a saxophone. When you come up, it may sound legato, but it's staccato.' So he started that downstroke stuff, and not much more than a year later he was with Benny Goodman.

"Same way with Floyd Smith in Nebraska. He wanted to play guitar, and he could play a little, but he hadn't an instrument of his own. 'If you go talk to my mother,' he said, 'she might get me one.' So I was around a few days and when I went to see her she gave me the money. I went down to the store with Floyd and bought a guitar. About three years later *he* was so good that he claimed he was teaching guitar.

"Of all the arrangements I did for Bennie Moten, *Moten Swing* was the biggest. We were at the Pearl Theatre in Philadelphia when the owner, Sam Steiffel, complained about us doing the same things over and over again. 'You've got to get something else,' he said, but we didn't have anything else! When Bennie said we'd got to have a new number, I asked him to let me lay off one show to get it together for him.

"I went downstairs and Basie came with me. He was often my co-writer. He'd put a little melody in there, so he'd have an answer when Bennie asked me, 'What did he write?' This time he gave me the channel. Horace Henderson was there and saw me write it, in pencil. We took it upstairs and the band went over it once, and then played it on the next show. It stopped the show every time. When we went to the Lafayette in New York the following week, we played it as the last number, and it took seven encores. The manager said, 'If you play it one more time, I'm going to throw the doors open.' And that's what he did, threw them open to the street, and people crowded around the doors to hear us.

"One reason it was a big hit was the tempo. That was one of the main things I concentrated on, and so did Basie, but Jo Jones was the key man for tempos. I'd say to him, 'Jo, this number I wrote here—don't let the leader, don't let the band, don't let anybody ever change this tempo!' That was the secret of Basie's band—not to let the tempo get too fast or too slow. But one number they spoiled was

One O'Clock Jump. It was not a real swing-out number. It was meant to be played at a good medium tempo. One of the things that went wrong with the band business was that the bands got too wild in their tempos.

"Another trouble with the later musicians is that they don't want to bend a note. They want to hit the note straight. But Basie's guys bend the notes around the corner. That's why the band sounds so good. He lost all the powerhouse men he had, but the guys he's got right now make the band sound so far ahead of others. He may not have the soloists, but he's got showmanship in the voicing and flexibility in the way the arrangements are played. He has still got some of the style there in the rhythm section, but modern amplification makes problems. The mikes pick up the sax and brass sections so well that you have to watch out and step up the volume of the rhythm. I like the kid Basie's got on drums now [Harold Jones]. He plays quite a bit of rhythm, and he can swing. The band swings *him* quite a little bit, too. I think Basie likes that, when you've got the band swinging the drummer. What could the drummer do but swing on an arrangement like *Moten Swing*? The band is based on hot licks, and the arrangements he played the other night at Roseland were all hot licks. The drummer can play all those licks along with the arrangement.

"To go back a bit, after I left Bennie Moten in 1933, I went to New York to join Willie Bryant's band. Teddy Wilson, Benny Carter, and Cozy Cole were in it, and I wrote arrangements like *Chimes in the Chapel*. Teddy Wilson was always late to rehearsals, and when he came in he'd find me at the piano, stretching those big chords. 'Stay right there!' he'd say. 'Don't get up!' He was always kidding me about that.

"After about a year, I got in the union and went with Jimmie Lunceford. Although I had never met him, he had been trying to get me for some time. There were two trumpet players in his band from Kansas City—Paul Webster and Eddie Tompkins—and we'd worked together and were buddies. Paul was always telling Lunceford, 'I gotta go get that guy,' and when we met I'd just tell him, 'Oh, I'll see you in New York.'

"I first caught the Lunceford band at the Apollo Theatre. There was nobody could play like that band! They would come out and play a dance routine. The Shim Sham Shimmy was popular then and six of the guys would come down and dance to it—like a tap dance, crossing their feet and sliding. Then Willie Smith would put his bonnet on and sing a sort of nursery rhyme. Eddie Tompkins hit the high notes and did a Louis Armstrong deal. Then they had a Guy

Lombardo bit and a Paul Whiteman bit. See, they imitated bands. The lights would go down next and they'd all lay down their horns and come out to sing as a glee club. They had solo singers like Henry Wells, too. The next number, they'd be throwing their horns and hats up to the ceiling. That was all novelty, and I liked it. So I joined them, as a trombone player and an arranger.

"I always liked the trombone sound in the circus band. And I liked the instrument because a guy could make it sound like he was crying. I just liked trombone players from the start—Big Green, Jimmy Harrison, J. C. Higginbotham, Joe Nanton with Duke, and later on, because he was sweeter, Lawrence Brown. Then I got crazy about Tommy Dorsey. He had a wonderful tone and it didn't sound gooey. I was crazy about Trummy Young, too, and I think he has been underrated. And then, yeah, there was Dicky Wells, who took my place in Basie's band. I liked all these guys, but I didn't copy any of them. The instrument itself moved me for inspiration. I didn't play many solos with Lunceford, because the section needed support in that band, so people didn't know too much about me. That was like Jack Washington with Basie. He was a good team man and he was fast on his baritone, but if you don't get up and take solos people don't know what you contribute.

"Sy Oliver and Eddie Wilcox were writing for Lunceford, but they'd had only three trumpets, two trombones, and four saxes before. They hadn't had much experience with wider arrangements, and few of the bands had more instruments than that. When Dan Grissom, the singer, played sax, he used to double, but now I fixed him a part of his own. I wrote a few things for them like that, stepping it up to five saxes. I showed Wilcox how to voice that way, and coached him with the sax section. I was also teaching Willie Smith how to voice for the instrumentation we had, and he was even willing to pay me. He wrote one or two things like *Running Wild*. Now we could have six brass, too, and I could handle that without any trouble. Where they had arrangements already set up, I wrote a part for myself, sometimes in the bass and sometimes above, but either way to get that extra note. I had a good range and could play it, but it was hard to set some of their earlier arrangements in six-part harmony. When Trummy Young eventually took my place in the band, they had to give him three weeks to go over the repertoire so he could get with my parts.

"I didn't get too much recognition for the numbers I wrote, and some weren't well recorded. I could write flagwavers like *Harlem Shout*, and they always opened and closed the show with a number of mine. When we were at the Larchmont Casino, there was a moving stand that used to excite people. The opener was always crescendo and loud. The band would be sitting on this stand, about a foot higher than the regular stage, and as they hit, the stand started moving forward, right up to the edge of the stage. It used to scare some people. They'd jump up and want to get out.

"I was with Lunceford about three years, and then Basie came to New York to play in Roseland at the end of 1936. They came to me and said he needed new numbers in my style. Although Lunceford was getting top money at the Larchmont, he was only paying about seventy dollars a week at that time. He wasn't a crook, but he always thought the leader should make all the money. A few weeks before he died, he told a reporter that that was where he made a mistake, that he had found out the men should make money, too.

"To cut a long story short, Willard Alexander offered me seventy-five dollars a week to play with Basie, and another seventy-five to write for the band, so it was a hundred-and-fifty a week. News got to the papers that I was on notice, so they booked a battle of music between Basie and Lunceford in Hartford, Connecticut, the night my notice expired. The radio stations were talking about this man who had been with Basie, then with Lunceford, and was now going back with Basie. 'He's going to let us know who's going to knock who down,' they said. I don't remember how the 'battle' came out. Basie could swing and he had Jo Jones, but though Lunceford's was a show band, it could swing, too. Nobody could wash Lunceford away at that time. Nobody! I had some swinging numbers in his book, and then they'd go back and put novelty on top of them.

"That night, when we packed up, the valet switched my stuff to Basie's band. We went to the Ritz-Carlton in Boston. That's where I started writing, and where we made *Blue and Sentimental* with Herschel Evans. Of course, Basie's was strictly a rhythm band, not an entertaining band like Lunceford's, and it wasn't as big, but they started adding guys.

"I had written things when I was in Kansas City with Bennie Moten that were in Basie's book. For instance, there was *One O'Clock Jump*, but we originally called it *Blue Ball*. Back then, it meant you've got the blues and ain't having a ball! Buster Smith in the reed section worked on that, and it was really a three-way deal. I was always looking to do something else with the trombones, always looking for a counter-melody. They used to call me 'Circus Guy' in those days. 'Here comes ol' Circus with all his slurring,' they'd say, but later they started liking it, and all the horns started doing it. Four weeks after I left to

come east, Moten had a tonsil operation, and he died. There wasn't
anything wrong between him and me. We were close, but I just wanted
a little eastern air.

"During the year I was with Basie, I got a lot of ideas off him. He
has a lot of hidden talent, but he'd only go about four measures, and
that's all. Just enough to know the song. He was contributing enough
to be acquainted with the arrangement when you wrote it. If I could
have got him to go along—his ideas along with mine—he'd have
twice the stuff he has now. He wanted the arrangements simple, to
swing, not what they'd call 'far out' today. When I was with Lunceford, I could stretch out with my own ideas and put anything down,
like on *Running a Temperature* and *Bird of Paradise*. You can be
ahead of the public all the time, so they never catch up with you.
Stan Kenton stayed ahead for a while.

"I had agreed to go with Basie for a year, and I guess I could have
stayed longer, but I had really been with Lunceford too long. He was
a college man, a different kind of leader. Nearly all the band were
college men, and I never heard a word of profane language with them.
But Basie's was a regular type of band like all the others, and it got
to the point where I couldn't stand much of the radical stuff. The fellows were nice in Basie's band, but his attitude was different to
Lunceford's. The only guy I knew to come near Lunceford was
Glenn Miller. Tommy Dorsey was rough, rougher than Basie. I'd made
tours opposite him with Lunceford. 'What's the matter back there?'
Tommy would shout, and then he'd throw a trumpet player out of the
bus and leave him on the highway. Things like that. Basie didn't
bother after his men, but he wanted to have a good time all the time,
and he wanted me to have it with him. 'You've been working so long,'
he'd say. 'Now's your chance. Let's have some fun!'

"When I left Basie, I fooled around, arranging for Jan Savitt, Artie
Shaw, and Ina Ray Hutton. I remember Ina asking me one day,
'Eddie, why do the two tenor saxophones have to be separated like
that?' It was a good question, because all the bands used to put the
two tenors and the two altos together, but all of a sudden they began
putting one tenor on each end of the saxes. It began with Lester
Young who couldn't sit beside Herschel, because he didn't like that
vibrato in Herschel's tone. That's what started everybody doing it,
even though they didn't know why they were doing it.

"I got a band of my own in 1940 and had guys like Joe Keyes,
Buster Smith, Ben Smith, Eddie Williams, Doles Dickens, and Arthur
Herbert in it. The president of Local 802 told me it was too smooth
for a colored band, and that I'd be more successful if I went with
Glenn Miller. I actually had two styles. I could swing or play sweet

as any white band. I had a white boy playing first alto, and that was the trick. White boys have thin lips and get a very pretty sound on saxophone, and this boy could make the whole section sound like him. That band was so good that when we played Pleasure Beach all Connecticut state was trying to get in the park, and we were hurting the business of the big names they'd hired. But in the end I let them talk me out of it. I was having trouble, so I let the band go and carried my book to Glenn Miller.*

"Then I got the girls' band together. That was the only way I could stay out of the army. I met an old West Indian guy, a politician, who got me with the Treasury Department's bond drives. So long as I kept the girls' band, I'd be deferred from the army every six months for the duration. And so long as I gave some service to the USO, the Treasury Department cooperated with whatever agency I was with. I did one day a week for them and six days for myself. I played all the camps and did over four thousand miles in Canada for the Canadian government. For four years during the war I was the only leader who had a sleeper bus and used gas from the government. That's how I got involved with the International Sweethearts of Rhythm!

"After that, I got a six-piece band of my own together and went on the road for nine years with Wynonie Harris and Larry Darnell, a couple of blues singers. I had to treat them both like babies, but I could always handle people. Wynonie was wild, really radical, and he drank a lot, but I had a big old athlete on the show as bodyguard and bouncer. He'd run all the women out, drag Wynonie out of bed, throw him over his shoulder, and put him in the car. Wynonie liked that! He knew this guy would break the door down to get him. He'd do Larry, too, the same way.

"My resistance was very low when I came in from traveling with those guys; and I just retired from music for about ten years. I had a few dollars saved up and I played a few jobs out on Long Island, but I wouldn't go anywhere. I looked all right, and I wasn't too disgusted with the business, but I had had pneumonia and it took me a

---

* For a 1940 *Down Beat* story by Dave Dexter, Durham variously cited as his best or favorite arrangements the following: for Lunceford, *Harlem Shout, Honey, Keep Your Mind on Me,* and *Lunceford Special;* for Basie, *Topsy, John's Idea, Jumpin' at the Woodside, Out the Window, Sent for You Yesterday,* and *Swinging the Blues;* for Shaw, *My Blue Heaven, Sunny Side of the Street,* and *I've Got the World on a String;* for Savitt, *Tuxedo Junction, Wham, Dear Old Southland, Turkey in the Straw, Blues in the Groove,* and *It's Time to Jump and Shout;* and for Miller, *Sliphorn Jive, Wham, Glen Island Special, Tiger Rag, Baby Me,* and *I Want to Be Happy.*

long time to get over it. I gradually regained my strength and I've played a few concerts in the last four or five years. Right now, I think I'm going to start playing again. I've made two or three arrangements for the big band Edgar Battle has been organizing. The only fault with Edgar is that he has still got flexible musicians, who can play anything, on his mind. You've got to kind of forget that. I don't think you can pick up fellows of that kind today. You've got to condense your arrangements and simplify them a little, so these guys can play 'em. He's going to be a long time finding guys who can play like they used to play."

(1971)

Earle Warren

(ALTO SAXOPHONE)

Earle Warren was born in Springfield, Ohio, on July 1, 1914, the second son in a musical family. His father played mandolin and piano, his mother piano and guitar, an older brother drums, one sister piano, and another violin. When he was ten he began three years of piano tuition, but his father also bought him a banjo-ukulele, which he played on the family band's weekend engagements.

Warren, Sr., was a truck driver and an enterprising man. He had a small gym in which he trained fighters, and he taught both sons to box. Later, he presented and danced in minstrel-type shows at local affairs. One Christmas he bought Earle his first saxophone, a C-melody, on which he played in the school band before switching to tenor in an Elks band. Out of the latter, a nine-piece group was formed, which became known as Duke Warren and his Eight Counts of Syncopation. Earle played alto saxophone in this band. His father booked and promoted it energetically, and the band soon became well known in the territory around. Eventually it merged with another Springfield group and grew to fourteen pieces. Its size necessitated working farther afield, and during the ensuing period Earle Warren worked with Fats Waller and the Mills Brothers, encountered many musicians later to become famous, such as Roy Eldridge, Chu Berry, and Joe Thomas, and led his own group called the Varsity Seven.

After graduating from high school, he left home to work around Columbus before joining a band led by Marion Sears (the older brother of Al Sears) at the Furnace Club in Cleveland. It was an after-hours spot run by gangsters, and the working hours were tough, from 10 P.M. to 6 A.M. each night, but the money was good. So was the experience, playing for a show with dancing girls, a comedian, and other acts.

"Art Tatum was working at another club around the corner," Warren recalled. "It was a place called Jimmy Jones's, down the street from the old Majestic Hotel, right off of Central Avenue. I had heard of him before, in 1931, when I went to Detroit to play at a food show in an auditorium—one of those things where people showed what they grew. Musicians told me about this young, blind man in Toledo who played such remarkable piano. I made up my mind to search him out, especially since Milton Senior, a fine saxophonist from my home-town, was in Toledo. Milton's dad played tuba and they both had been in our Elks band. Milton had gone on to play with McKinney's Cotton Pickers.

"The whole reed section from the Sears band—two altos and Andy Anderson on tenor—used to go down to Jimmy Jones's after we got through. Art Tatum was the featured attraction, and that's where the jam sessions started, in the early wee hours of the morning. The Jeter-Pillars band was also in Cleveland then, playing the Creole Club, and Harry Edison was with them.

"After an election and a few shakedowns, Jimmy Jones's club began to lose business. I didn't understand the politics involved with that, but Art went to play in a little house off of Cedar Avenue, around 89th Street. It was among some little shacks, and the man had a bar, a few tables around, sawdust on the floor, and an upright piano with a little dim light over it. That became the new after-hours spot. It was one of those old-time upright pianos. It was kept in great condition and it made a beautiful sound. Of course, Art would make *any* piano sound good. We visited there all the time, and I used to sing *Body and Soul, Once in a While,* and other songs of the day with him. We would split any tips we made right down the middle, because he could use the money the same as I could!

"All the big bands that came through—Glen Gray, Jimmie Lunce-ford, Jimmy Dorsey, and Paul Whiteman—had heard of Art Tatum, and sometimes you couldn't get in the place, because it was really only a house. The people with money would sit at the tables, and the price for drinks was quite a bit for those days, like a dollar or a dollar-fifty. Art would have beer lined up on top of the piano, and he would play there six or eight months of the year. Those were lean days for black artists on radio programs, but I think it was Jimmy Dorsey who got him featured in a kind of jazz spectacular. Jack Teagarden used to come there and play, because he loved Art. So did Don Byas, and they played together in New York.

"Jam sessions there used to go on until seven or eight in the morning. Art was a good feeder and didn't get in the way. When it was his time to play, he'd really play, but then he'd come up to the service end of the bar and start arguing about football. Art loved to discuss the football and basketball players that to his mind were the greatest. He used to go to games, too, and when people hollered he'd know someone was running. One eye was better than the other then, and he could hold an envelope up to the light and tell what was written on it. And he could tell the difference between a one, a five, or a ten when he was given money. He hit a couple of guys that got cute. He was no baby. He was a man, and a fine one. If you hit a guy good, whether you can see or not, he doesn't want to come back for more.

"If a cat could play, Art loved to hear him. I never saw him show any particular partiality, although I know he loved to play with Don Byas. Of course, he didn't want to play with some lane,* because that would have been a waste of everybody's time, but otherwise he was wide open. He was just a lovely man to know and be around. Even as early as when he was at Jimmy Jones's, he used to get a lot of respect. He'd come in and hobble over to the piano with that funny walk of his, sit down and take himself a drink of beer, run a couple of quick arpeggios, and start off with something smooth, like *Deep Purple*. He had a God-given talent, like Erroll Garner, but Art always sounded schooled. I don't know how much of Fats Waller and Earl Hines there was in Art's style, but I used to see and play shows with Fats Waller when I was at a club in Dayton, Ohio. He came out of Cincinnati, where he was on WLW, a radio station. I didn't hear too much Fats in what Art did, except when he wanted to 'walk' on the piano.

"His knowledge of chord changes, and the way he'd go 'in and out,' as we say in jazz, were what impressed me. On a lot of his records you can hear how he carried progressions outside and then brought 'em back. 'Where's he going?' you'd say, and then he'd come back in so beautifully. One fellow that got very close to him was Lanny Scott.

---

* An inadequate performer, a square.

Whenever Art went to New York or somewhere else, Lanny would take his place. And often Lanny would sit beside the piano, and when Art got up Lanny would take his seat. He used to kill me, but he lost quite a bit of it when he came to New York. Communication is a wonderful thing. It keeps thoughts alive that haven't particularly originated in your own mind. When you're in communication with someone like Art Tatum, he stimulates many different thoughts. Away from real stimulation, you lose a lot of real things, real sounds. Art would come up with chords and changes an ordinary mind wouldn't think of.

"I think Don Byas was one of the few instrumentalists that really grasped what was happening. He learned those changes and his knowledge of his instrument was affected. After they had worked together on 52nd Street and Don left, it was hard for anybody else to work with Art. I think that background and Art's influence helped Don blossom out and become a stellar saxophone player. Only God can bring forth a forerunner, a man of a special type like Tatum. It was the same thing with Prez, Lester Young. No sound or approach to the tenor prepared us for him, because Hawk was *it* before he arrived."

"I first heard of Prez when I was in Cleveland, years before I ever dreamed I'd hear him. Leroy 'Snake' White had told me, 'Boy, if you ever get a chance to hear Lester Young . . . !' He'd known him as an alto player but knew he'd tried out for Fletcher Henderson on tenor. Fletcher, having had guys like Coleman Hawkins with a heavy sound, found Prez a little light. I was working in Sandusky, Ohio, when I first heard him over the air with Basie from the Reno Club. 'Boy, this guy is playing!' I said. And then there was Herschel Evans, too, with his big Hawkins sound.

"Leroy 'Snake' White always bragged on Lester Young. Leroy was a great trumpet player out of Des Moines via Minneapolis, with a background in bands like Zack Whyte's and Walter Page's Blue Devils. He knew what he was talking about. When I eventually joined Basie, I swear to God I had cold chills, because I never heard anything so fabulous in all my life. Prez had an approach to his horn that has been carried on down, but there are so many guys who would have given a right toe or something to embellish on their horn and come up with original ideas the way he did. He knew changes like nobody's business, and he was, of course, a great advocate of Art Tatum.

"About his tone, I should say I knew he had previously been an alto player, but I'd also heard Bud Freeman and Eddie Miller, who had tones just a little different but formed almost the same way. The inimitable sound coming from this man was a matter of the echo chamber and the lipping of the mouthpiece. By that I mean the nasal quality, up in your jaws, and the way you feed the reed. Buddy Tate had a different sound. Herschel Evans was *his* love and he tried to get a sound like his, but he wound up with a sound you can always tell is Buddy Tate's. But he got the job with Basie because he played more like Herschel than anybody we'd ever had. I studied singing and I know that the chamber within you is what determines an inimitable sound. It's from you personally, in the way you deliver it, in the way you feel, in your expression, and in the way you let the sound resolve and go through the chambers of your head.

"Lester was from the Deep South and he'd played in little jazz groups, including his father's family band. Probably his first horn was the cheapest or quickest thing he could get his hands on, and that way he may just have happened on the alto. I never heard him play it, but as an alto player myself I could always hear how fabulous he could have been on that, too. In fact, I'm sure that if he had gone back to alto he would have been world renowned in the same way. I don't know why he switched to tenor, but situations call for certain instruments. I've played tenor and baritone at different times, and with Basie I played alto and baritone—Jack Washington and I together. A guy wants to keep a job!

"The first time I heard Prez in person was in the early spring of '37. He came through Cincinnati with Basie and, to be honest, he didn't impress me at all. Herschel impressed me much more, because I was able to *hear* more. Prez turned his horn up in the air like he was smoking a pipe! Some idiotic idea he'd got, but it amused me greatly. It was a different story when I joined Basie. Jack Washington was sitting between me and Prez, and Herschel was next to me, and I could hear everything. 'Ee, shuckins!' I said. 'He's blowing, baby!' And Prez blew right on into world fame, you believe it!

"Herschel had been an alto player, too, but when he heard Coleman Hawkins he didn't want any more alto. He got him a tenor and worked on it. Hawk showed what the instrument *could* produce, but when I first heard him with Fletcher Henderson he used to play real high on that horn. In later years, he never played what you call those altissimo notes.

"I got the chance to meet Hawk when the Henderson band was in Cleveland in 1933. I remember Jeff [Hilton Jefferson], Procope, Dicky Wells, Pop Smith, Bobby Stark, and John Kirby were in it. Smaller sax sections could maybe move more, but when we went from three to four it opened up more of a basic harmony spread, which gave the reed section more substance. Then Duke came along with Harry Carney as *the* baritone player, but back in the twenties the baritone was thought of as a parade-band instrument and there just weren't real baritone players around. If you wanted a good subtle sound, you would get the alto players to double. That's what we did in Basie's band. A lot of people don't remember when I played baritone. Jack and I would be playing two baritones alongside two tenors to get a dark, deep sound on ballads. Then I'd go back to alto and he'd stay on baritone. The baritone is sort of harmonically based with the trombone, and at that time we had only three trumpets and two trombones so it gave a little more depth. One band that really used to make the baritone travel was Ozzie Nelson's. He had a sensational baritone years ago named Charlie Bubeck. Whoever wrote the arrangements put the alto and the baritone on the same melody. Duke did that quite a bit, and when he wrote that way Harry Carney could be the lead. It was an effect, but not everybody could get that sound because nobody else had a Harry Carney. For a while, some bands had baritone and bass saxophone, but that went out because the sound lacked finesse, was too guttural. A baritone is not an easy saxophone to play, in any case. Some people say, 'You play one saxophone, you play 'em all.' But that's not true.

"Alto saxophone players are usually either playing lead or third to a lead. There are good lead altos and good third altos, but a third alto very seldom makes a good lead alto. He's underneath, a follower; he lays right there with you, and his concept of his position is reverent. He accepts it and he does all he can to be right under the first man. Some guys get to be beautiful at that. But there are some third altos who want to be first altos, who play *over* because they're afraid they're not being heard. They say to themselves, 'Well, I don't like the way he [the lead] played that passage, so I'm going to see if I can't kind of influence him.'

"Years ago it used to be one-three-five harmony—first alto, third alto, and the fifth part for the tenor. Then arrangers began to find different ways of handling chords, whereby they could voice a reed section into four-part or five-part harmony at times, not that they didn't double on other horns in the band, but it gave body when it came to five saxophones. Saxophone choruses were very interesting in the thirties and forties. But all at once there was a change, more emphasis on trombones and not too much on the melodic sound of saxophones, except in solos. The battle of the tenors began to be the thing, and you could almost forget alto players. Some who had established themselves earlier, like Johnny Hodges, survived. What happened to me in the Basie band was that I got all the bridges, eight bars in the middle of everything. The only number I remember opening up on was *Out the Window,* and I got a lot of compliments for that."

"I was relieving Al Sears in his band at the Cotton Club in Cincinnati when Basie came. Al at that time played alto and clarinet, and well. He had to go to Detroit for the weekend and I had a seventeen-piece band down the street at the Sunset. I'd get my band started and go up and play the show at the Cotton Club. Basie and his band would play between the shows, and while they were on I'd go back to the Sunset. On the Sunday there was a matinée, and I played all the afternoon, and they heard me. I was reading the buttons off the music, and all our stuff was real bouncy but with a lot of sixteenth notes.

"After we closed, Herschel Evans came over to talk to me. Caughey Roberts had put in his notice, because he was getting lonesome and wanted to go back to California. I decided I would go with Basie and I joined him in Pittsburgh in April. Caughey played on a couple of days but then he was gone and I never saw him again until he came back for a hot minute as third alto. Buster Smith was also in the band for a month or so in 1938, the year his arrangement of *Blues I Like to Hear* was recorded. He was like Ben Webster. He would always go home to visit his mother. If he knew she was all right, he was all right, and then he'd come back to New York.

"I was twenty-three, younger than most of the guys in the band. I'd met Jack Washington, Ben Webster, and Eddie Barefield years before, when they were with Bennie Moten. They used to come to my home when they were stranded in Cincinnati during the hard times of 1932. One time they'd be there and they'd be real sharp. The next time they'd be kind of shopworn and their horns would be in pawn. Different things happen. Dates are canceled and hotel bills are due, but everybody's got to eat! Some took out on the lam, and others pawned clothes as well as horns.

"Cincinnati used to be called 'The Gateway of the South,' and all the bands used to stop off there. There was a Greystone Ballroom in Cincinnati just as there was in Detroit, and everybody wanted to play there. The big fabulous place was Castle Farms, but they didn't play many colored bands at that time. Colored bands used to play dances in the South, but you would be harassed, insulted, and not respected. You could play wonderfully, but they'd still make very derogatory remarks about you. It was a most grievous time.

"The Basie band was very insecure when I joined. Willard Alexander had something to do with the booking, but there was no money.

Three of the boys in my band had left to go with Walter Barnes when he offered them eighteen dollars a night, but they and Walter all got burned up in a fire in Natchez. I had gone to the secretary of the Cincinnati local and found that about sixty dollars was scale for a musician on the road, but when I first went with Basie I was making $6.25 a night. After Social Security came into effect, I made seven dollars a night—the nights we worked. I hadn't been making much with my big band, and after the Cincinnati flood the city was in terrible condition. Further, I had married in 1934, so I had my responsibilities!

"There weren't many black hotels around in those days, so we had to walk up and down the street in the black neighborhoods trying to find a room. If they knew you were a musician, a lot of people weren't going to give you a room even when they had one. But because of so many bands traveling through so many territories, there came to be more rooming houses and that's where we would have to stay, but they'd charge three-and-a-half or four dollars, and that was quite a bit of money then.

"When we finally got to New York, I moved into the Woodside Hotel, on 142nd Street, with Ed Lewis, the first trumpet player. He was a great big cat and I was real small then. We roomed together and I think we paid about six dollars a week. I'd go across the street where they'd have bologna or liverwurst. You could get that, an egg or two, some toast and a cup of coffee for a quarter then. Whenever I broke a dollar, I'd save three dimes in my little piggy bank in order to be able to eat later. Sometimes I didn't have a nickel to ride the subway, although I was with Count Basie's band!

"When they told me we were staying at the Woodside Hotel, I pictured a big, palatial place with a circular driveway in front. So when we pulled up in front of that hotel I almost died. A great big cat was sitting in the middle of the lobby. There were a lot of ballplayers and a guy who had worked with Basie for a long time, by the name of Jack Castor. He was like the bellhop, the impresario *and* the greeter. The band had stayed there before, when they played the Apollo, so all the guys knew what it was like. June Clark, the trumpet player, and the Mills Brothers' sister were there, along with a lot of show people. There were cooking facilities in some rooms, and a big kitchen where people could cook and take food up to their rooms. Jack Washington's wife, Jimmy Rushing's, and Ed Lewis's all lived there. It wasn't by any means luxurious, but it was like a music house, and we rehearsed in the basement. When we really started cooking in 1938, after the records of *Every Tub, One O'Clock Jump,* and *Jumpin' at the Woodside* came out, things improved and I brought my wife to New

York. We moved to where we could have our own little place, and everything became quite nice.

"I wasn't what the cats call a 'straw boss' at the beginning. I don't like that word, anyway. Up until the time he went into the army, Buck Clayton was the assistant conductor. He had had bands of his own, just as I had, and any time we did shows and stuff he conducted. The Holy Main [Basie] didn't want to be bothered with that anyhow. He wasn't much interested in conducting for an act because his name was becoming quite well known and he wanted to have his time for himself."

"Herschel was a most likeable guy, and he and Prez really weren't bitter enemies. Herschel was outspoken. He was a man. Little things that happened between him and Prez were of no great consequence. So far as sitting on the bandstand and not talking to one another— that's a lot of hogwash. Like guys would say to me, 'Man, that Prez. . . . I dug the way he walked. Is he kind of on the lady side?' So many times, I've had to tell them, 'No, definitely not.' There's no way in the world I can accept that. At one time, he, Walter Page, and I were all three living in one room, and I was so tired of looking at chicks running in and out of there I was sick. So I tell guys not to talk to me about Prez in that way. He nearly got arrested once on a train going out to Long Island, when a guy started hitting on him. Prez almost cut his suit off him, his army suit. He didn't bother anybody ordinarily. He wouldn't even say hello if he didn't know you.

"I remember when Lady Day was in the band, and how it would be some hard nights when Prez was blowing his brains out. We'd be soaking wet when we finished and got on the bus. If he had been able to cop a bottle, he would have his little gin. The first thing he'd do was come walking up the aisle with the dice in his hand, shaking them in everybody's ear. 'Sweet music,' he'd say, 'sweet music!' He had his special seat on the bus like everybody else, but now they'd be shooting dice, rolling 'em all up under the seats and everywhere. Usually he'd be the first one broke, and when that happened he'd go on back to his seat and sit down. He was just a beautiful cat.

"We had a softball team and Prez was the pitcher. He threw a backspinning ball which made the guy hit the ball on the ground. I played shortstop, Herschel was first base, Jack Washington was second, and I forget who was on third. We used to practice on the roadside in the spring when we were down south, and all through Texas.

"We were down in Columbia, South Carolina, one year, and we had a bus from America Orchestra Service over in Jersey. Little Jimmy

LeMarr was our driver, and if we didn't have him we weren't happy. We were crazy about him. He had a lot of gall and he was our mainstay. If something happened to the bus, we'd be out beside the highway with our gloves for batting practice while Jimmy fixed it. This time we were running up and down, and the ball went over two or three times into a field where a guy had some wheat planted. Meanwhile, Prez, Freddie Green, Lady Day, and Shad Collins had made a little trip, you know, in seclusion. All at once we see this guy coming up the road on a motorcycle, a big South Carolinian. When he got through getting himself off that cycle, he must have been six foot six and about 240 pounds. Maceo Birch was our manager then, and when he saw this cop coming he ran in the bus, pulled his hat down over his head, and made like he went to sleep. Jimmy was up under the bus when this guy asked, 'Who's in charge of you so-and-sos?' We pointed to Jimmy and he kicked him on the foot. 'What's the matter with you?' Jimmy said, coming out from under.

" 'I want you to get these so-and-sos out of here. This ain't no place to play! You better get that thing fixed right quick.'

"There was nothing to do but grab the bats, the ball, and the gloves and go on about our business. Prez and the others showed up just as we were getting back on the bus, and the cop told them to get moving, too. I don't like to embellish on things like that, but at the time it was quite scary because we knew what Columbia, South Carolina, meant in those days. We went over to a place called College Inn in Allen, hoping they'd have rooms where we might stay, and then we played the big Columbia auditorium, where the white people sat on one side and the Negroes on the other. Some people would want to dance, and others would throw money to 'em and act like a bunch of nuts. It was embarrassing. The band was beginning to gain fame and we needed scenes like that like a hole in the head.

"When we were in Memphis, playing a theater, Freddie Green left the window open. Somebody broke in and stole a brand-new coat he'd just bought, and the long black coat Prez always wore with his porkpie hat. Freddie had a little black spring coat and a trenchcoat as well, so whenever Hawk was really asking for them,* Prez would be trying to wear Freddie's trenchcoat and Freddie would be in his spring coat. We used to make fun of them and call them the Dootsie Twins.

"When Buddy Tate came to the band, he had an overcoat that came down around the ankles. He'd come out of Omaha from Nat Towles' band, and he'd just had a case of pneumonia. He was wearing long

---

* Whenever the weather turned really cold.

drawers, too. We'd see him outside crossing the street to the hotel, and the wind would be whipping that coat every which way. 'Whew,' he'd say when he got inside, 'that wind tore me up out there!' It seemed as though everybody had a joke to tell on somebody else in those days.

"Noble Sissle had been looking for a saxophone player before I joined Basie, but I didn't care for his style or the way he dominated his men. He was quite forceful in his language, and I guess it was just a lingo out of New York, but I was from Ohio, the Midwest, and if a person can't talk to me like I'm a man I don't have any respect for him. After I'd heard Basie, I figured that was *it*, anyhow, but even in that band I met the kind of talk that ran racial—bad words, and calling each other names. 'Well, wait a minute,' I said, 'I don't dig this. We never used that kind of language around where I lived.' So I cut that off. But I had the same problem Willie Smith had with Jimmie Lunceford, until people had seen him a few times and the word was brought out.

"People who didn't know me, even Negroes, assumed I was white. Years before, I'd played with an Italian guy who was darker than me and called himself Richard Sherman. There were his cousin, a couple of Jewish boys, a Pole, and an Irish kid in the band, but we were all real close and it didn't matter what race or denomination the other was. Only the leader and his cousin knew what *I* was. When we played the Pick Hotel in Owensboro, Kentucky, I did all the negotiating with the peckerwoods there. 'Mussolini's in town,' they said when we arrived in dark blue suits and yellow ties! Later I went back to Owensboro with Basie and I was scared to death. But musicians came by and said, 'Warren, we remember how you played here, and we know doggone well the best thing you ever did was get in a band with a bunch of niggers. You've got that kind of sound, and when we saw your picture in *Life* magazine we knew you were going to be the happiest man alive.' It made me laugh more than anything else, but when some of those hillbilly characters came to New York they wouldn't even speak to me anymore! Somebody must have told 'em, 'Man, are you kidding? He's colored, like everybody else in the band.'

"I got a lot of harassment from my own people. I objected when they started calling me 'white folks,' 'redneck,' 'albino,' 'peckerwood,' and other nicknames. I know Willie Smith would sometimes get quite venomous when they pulled that on him.

"In 1937 and '38, when I wasn't making any money and was trying to squeeze out a living, I stayed in the little old crummy places I had to stay in. Some of them were terrible. I got eaten up by bedbugs, and you had to keep one eye open all the time to keep from having your stuff stolen. I roomed with other guys in the band, and altogether I paid my dues, but when I got my raise I stayed in nice hotels.

"We came into Lincoln, Nebraska, one time, and it was so hot. There was a little white-run hotel near the station that accepted bands. Of course, it *had* to be down by the tracks! The band jumped out and went to this place, but we couldn't get rooms. I walked straight up the street with my clothes, bag, and horn to the Lincoln Hotel and checked in for $4.50—a nice room with ice water running out of the spigot, and big fans in the window. That night I told Basie, 'Come by and see me. I've got two beds, beautiful fans, and everything. Ain't no use sleeping some place where you're going to smother to death! Come by like you're talking business with me, and you can have four or five hours' sleep before we leave.' But he wouldn't do it."

"I first met Harry Edison in Columbus, on Long Street, and we struck up a friendship. He was just a young fellow out of high school, playing with some little band around there. Then he disappeared and I didn't know where he had gone, but when I got to Cleveland in the fall of '33 he was playing at the Creole Club in the Jeter-Pillars band. After an election, a new regime came in, the racketeers were washed away, and the club scene kind of dissolved. Next time I saw Harry, he was with Lucky Millinder's band in New York. Dicky Wells, Herschel, Harry, and I all lived in the same place, 2195 Seventh Avenue. It was strictly a show business building, run by Mrs. Cotton and her husband, two lovely people. Jimmy Jones, the bass player who used to be with Noble Sissle, Emmett Berry, and a lot of dancers lived there. My wife and I had kitchen privileges downstairs, and we used to eat with Mrs. Cotton, who was a very kind lady.

"Anyway, with us all in the same place, we managed to get Harry Edison over to the Basie band. He really added zest, fire, and punch to the trumpet section. I still maintain he's one of the world's greatest. He was a good reader and no novice. He already had a style of his own, and he was good fanning a derby to make hanh-hanh sounds. He and I were about the same age, and we used to wrestle and roll over the yard. He played short-center on the softball team. Sometimes we'd get mad at one another, but there were no fights. We were just like brothers. Just like Buck Clayton. I see Buck every Wednesday when I go to the union and I put the whistle on him. He'll cock an ear, because everybody from the old Basie band will recognize that whistle, even if they're in Istanbul. Where did it come from? From Prez. It says, 'I want you to get way back, babe!'

"It was Prez who named Harry 'Sweets.' I don't know why. You couldn't ask Prez why he did anything. He called me 'Smiles,' because when I play saxophone I smile, from the embouchure. 'Man,' he said, 'you're about the smilin'est son-of-a-gun I ever saw. I'm gonna call you Smiles.' Then he changed it to 'Smiley,' and later to 'Smile.' "

"I think Basie's more projective now. He's got more confidence in his position than in the olden days. Then he was more like one of the guys, an ordinary cat, but everybody loved Basie. Everybody knew he could play. Man, he was no dummy setting at that piano! And when he spoke up, expressed an opinion, everybody listened. You must understand that nobody in that band was a novice, and nobody was just a guy who came in gangbusting. That never worked anyhow. Basie started the band, although I heard years before that it was actually supposed to be a thing between him and Walter Page. That's beside the point, because it takes a leader. I don't think Basie got himself into a position to be a leader until about two or three years after the band was really going. He never was a forceful arbitrator, nor a disciplinarian. He'd wait till something just blew up, and then he'd tell the manager, 'Here, give him his notice! Tell him to take a walk.' He's always been a gentleman, but he can blow up like anybody else.

"I'm the godfather to his daughter, Diane Catherine, and my wife, Clara, was the godmother. Adam Clayton Powell was the pastor that baptized Diane. That was back in 1944. We stayed close together until I felt it was time for me to get out and try to help myself. It was like a sorry day, and I got a lot of venomous and nasty remarks from people I never expected them from.

"I had some money saved up and a whole, good band waiting for me in Cincinnati. My trombone player, Bob Kennerley, put it together. A guy named Murray Deutsch, who used to manage Woody Herman, became my manager, and Paul Ash of the Roxy Theater was taking out a $100,000 insurance policy on me and putting $50,000 behind the band. He liked my playing and singing, and he thought I had potential as a new bandleader.

"Mr. Ash and I went to Moe Gale's office when Ralph Cooper was there. Moe came on with the real funny Italian talk. So I said, 'Now, wait a minute. I don't need your money. I've had bands since I was sixteen years old. I want to know if you will take me as a prospective money-maker for your organization.' He had the Savoy in New York and the El Grotto in Chicago. But he turned me down, although Jimmy McCarthy, the publicist, had already got my picture in the papers all across the country. It seems that Moe and Paul Ash had had some words over Connie Stevens sometimes. Paul went to other agencies, and Willard Alexander naturally closed the door on me.

"I went to Cincinnati, but before I got there Moe Gale had sent somebody to take most of the men for Billy Eckstine's band. I got together twelve pieces and worked for the mother of Ezzard Charles, the prizefighter. She had what they called a coliseum on Ninth Street. Erskine Hawkins came through a couple of months later and said, 'Boy, where'd you get this band?' But we weren't making any money and I ended up with six pieces in New York, at the Concord—Charlie Lewis on trumpet, Bob Kennerley on trombone, a new piano player, Kenny Johnson on bass, and Khalil Mhadi on drums. From there we went to the Paradise in New Jersey, then to Kelly's Stables in New York for six weeks, after which we went up to the Savoy in Boston. We rehearsed all the time and emphasized jazz. I had a trio singing and wrote little original things myself. Charlie Lewis and I would sit down and arrange the format for certain tunes. I kept that group for two-and-a-half years, and did very well with it, but then in 1946 my wife became *very* ill with cancer. It just washed her away, and she passed in '51.

"I hadn't been in the service during the war, because I had terrible ulcers, starting in 1939. It may have been a nervous situation, but I can't recall being worried. In 1947, I got a telephone call and went back to Basie. Preston Love, who admired everything I played and tried to play just like me, was there. He fitted very well, but I took his place in Omaha. C. Q. Price was third alto and he wrote good. He never was promoted on alto, and I don't think he was justly paid for what he did do in the band, but he was so withdrawn—a rather timid, yet nice man. Another saxophone player nobody knew or recognized was a boy named Marvin Johnson, who was in the Basie band at the same time as Don Byas. He and his brother had a little combo in Los Angeles, and he was a marvelous player. He was in the post office, and he was only with us a few months, but he was on that record date when I sang *Time on My Hands.*

"Tab Smith and I got along beautifully. He would play first on the arrangements he wrote, and play all the alto solos on them. Nothing wrong with that. He and Buddy Tate were real close friends. He was a formidable musician, a nice guy to know, with an even personality and no animosity toward anyone. You never heard him talk about anything he disliked. He just took life as it came, and he was happy with Basie, but that was his last big band. He left to go out with a small group. His mother and sister were in St. Louis, where he had property.

"Playing in those days wasn't particularly healthy, especially in those old tobacco barns down south where there was so much dust and everything. I got sick in 1948 and the doctor told me not to blow anymore. 'If you lost a finger, you'd still be a doctor, wouldn't you?' I asked him. 'Well, that's the way I am. I'd rather die blowing than sit around moping away.' So I came back, and I've been blowing ever since.

"Of course, the war years brought so many changes. Jo Jones, Jack Washington, and Buck Clayton went in the army. We had a whole lot of different tenor players, including 'Sam' Byas (that's what we always called Don), Paul Gonsalves, Dexter Gordon for a little while, and Weasel Parker. Weasel is from Akron, and we got him from George Hudson's band. But everything was getting too difficult, so in 1950 Basie dissolved the band. Since then I've done all kinds of things, mostly with small groups."

(1969)

Dicky Wells

(TROMBONE AND ARRANGER)

"Basie sent for me in 1938 and told me to come by his house, because Herschel [Evans], Lester [Young] and some of the fellows in the band liked my blowing with Teddy Hill.

" 'Okay,' I said, 'but how about you?'

" 'Well,' Basie said, 'so long as they like you, you must be okay.'

"We went to play in a country club in Plainfield, New Jersey. It was a small room.

" 'Come on,' Basie said, 'take your axe out, and sit down and blow with the cats. See if you like it.'

" 'Where's my music?' I asked.

" 'Sit in and see what happens,' he said.

"I took Ed Durham's place and they had only the two trombone parts for Dan Minor and Benny Morton.

" 'Grab a derby and start fannin'!' Basie called.

"I was so busy getting my kicks, because Billie Holiday was there, and Jimmy Rushing, and Herschel Evans, as well as Prez. Herschel and Prez had their battle going, and it was the swingingest band I had been in since Fletcher's. Basie would start out and vamp a little, set a tempo, and call out, 'That's it!' He'd set a rhythm for the saxes first, and Earle Warren would pick that up and lead the saxes. Then he'd set one for the bones and we'd pick that up. Now it's our rhythm against theirs. The third rhythm would be for the trumpets, and they'd start fanning with their derbies. (Derbies were very effective with brass sections then, and it's too bad they're so little used now. Derby men like Lips Page, Sidney De Paris, and Harry Edison could always make your insides dance.) The solos would fall in between the ensembles, but that's how the piece would begin, and that's how Basie put his tunes together. He had a big band, but he handled it as though it were six pieces.

"When we got through, Basie asked me how I liked the band. I told him I was crazy about it.

" 'Am I hired?' I asked him.

" 'I didn't fire you, did I?' was his answer.

"It took me quite a while to pick up on some of the psychology he used. He was the first leader I ran into who used jokes as hints, along with nicety, to whip you back into line—maybe damned near too late! I found out afterwards that his motto was: 'I'm not going to fire you— you're going to fire yourself.' Just about the only way I had seen cats whipped back in line in Louisville was when others whipped out their shooting irons or blades. The leader I first worked with, the one who was pocketing the other half of my weekly pay, carried the longest rod in the world. It should have had wheels on it. He said he had it for pink-toes, but he must have been color blind because I've seen him pull it on some pretty dark pink-toes. Anyway, give me Basie's style as a leader and I can make it.

"It was a happy band. Even when Herschel and Lester weren't speaking, they were the best of friends! There was so much humor in that band. It was like being part of a family. And all kinds of people liked Basie. Sometimes there were so many millionaires on the bus there wasn't room for the guys to sit down. Walter Page was very popular, too. Carloads of people used to come long distances just to hang out with him. I'll tell you another thing. We were a clean band. When we played hotels, we didn't leave the stand littered up with cigarette butts and chewing gum. They used to be so surprised they'd say, 'Hey, didn't you guys work here last night?'

"Soon after I joined, we went into the Famous Door. It seemed that everything they had then turned out to be a hit, like *Jumpin' at the Woodside*, and *One O'Clock Jump*, and *Doggin' Around*. And Jimmy Rushing had his hit songs, too, like *Good Morning Blues*, *Sent for You Yesterday*, and *Don't You Miss Your Baby?* Billie didn't stay long, but she had her songs going as well. This was about the time she began to make a name for herself on records.

"We were supposed to be in the Famous Door six weeks, but we stayed three months. Basie and I had a little spat there one night, and he told me to go home until he sent for me. I thought he would never send for me, but he did. So I went back after a couple of days and was there until the job ended, when I was supposed to quit. He asked me if I wanted to stay a bit longer and go on the road. The band was swinging, so I said, 'Yes.'

"The bus left from outside the Woodside Hotel. Herschel was sitting in the front and he started cursing me out right away:

"'You knew you weren't going to leave in the first place, and here you come dragging back! Get the hell in the back of the bus and set your red ass down.'

"He made me kind of angry, but the other guys said not to pay him any mind, and soon we were all smiles. He turned out to be one of my best friends, and they used to call him, Buck [Clayton], and myself brothers, because we were about the same height and color. I soon seemed to settle in in that band, although the only guy I'd known before was Benny Morton. I remember him coming to Louisville with Fletcher, and everybody marveling about how well he played.

"So we went out, and that was the beginning of my eleven years with Basie—what was supposed to have been six weeks. We went touring, mostly in the South, because Basie didn't cover the wide area he does now. In fact, he almost never goes south now.

"The band gradually took on a lot of arrangements as well as the heads. Don Kirkpatrick, the pianist, used to bring in arrangements while we were at the Famous Door. He was a wonderful writer. Now, Herschel was a slow kind of reader and didn't care about reading at all. So after we had spent about three hours rehearsing, Basie would call out that night:

"'Get out that number Kirkpatrick made!'

"'I can't find my part,' Herschel would say.

"We'd all be down, looking under the stands, and Basie would be looking through the piano music. Herschel would be real busy helping Basie look for it, but after the gig he'd tell me:

"'Man, I tore that damn thing up and sent it down the drain—all them sharps and things. I didn't feel like fooling with that.'

"That happened three or four times, until Basie got wise. He said,

"'I believe that rascal's tearing up our music.'

"But I don't think he ever actually *knew*. Herschel would wait until after rehearsal and tear it up, six or seven sheets for saxophone. Well, he read slow, but that was one of the reasons why he swung so much.

I asked Fletcher Henderson once why he wrote so much in those keys like B-natural and C-sharp, and he said he'd been doing it so long because it meant less notes and the band would swing more. Sandy Williams verified that later on. He said when he left Fletcher he couldn't read fast in flat or natural keys.

"Basie really began to get a book together when Ed Durham was in the band. Basie and Ed would lock up in a room with a little jug, and Basie would play the ideas and Ed would voice them. Durham could write real well then, as he did later for the Glenn Miller band. After Durham left, Basie began to buy different arrangements from outside. Even so, Basie always played a big part, because he would cut out what he didn't like, what wasn't Western style, just as he does today, until he got it swinging. He always said you could swing a piece no matter how fast or slow it was. He always believed in making people's feet pat, which is one reason he still has a swinging band. And he had that feeling for tempo. He'd start the band off, maybe fool around with the rhythm section for thirty-two bars, until he got it right, and then it would stay that way right through.

"I don't think the Basie band had anything *new* except the idea of the two tenors. After all, Fletcher had swung just about everything that could be swung. Maybe Fletcher's things were a bit more polished, but Basie had those tempos like Bennie Moten had. Bennie's brother used to play accordion and I believe it helped to groove the band. If you were standing in a corner, you'd hear it coming through with the rhythm. Ed Durham contributed a lot, too. He didn't write too complicated and he voiced so open, like Jimmy Mundy, and I think it caught the dancers better. Now Don Redman and Benny Carter wrote tough parts for trumpets, but their style couldn't be better for trombones. Benny's writing for saxes was something else, and there was no limit to what Don would write if he could pick his men.

"Basie's two battling tenors were two of the best, and the crowd went for them. I heard them going like that at the Cherry Blossom when I was in Kansas City with Fletcher Henderson. Plenty of bands had two trumpet soloists or two trombones, but not two tenors. I noticed their effect for the first time when we played the Paradise Theater in Detroit, a place like the Apollo. As soon as Herschel stood up, before ever he went down front, the people would start yelling. The same when Lester stood up. I think that started the tenor sax duet within a band. Before that it had been drums and trumpets. The flute's popular now, but I think it's more of a novelty. It has more of a symphonic sound, but that's the way it's gone lately, as though everyone wants to see how technical he can get. So they've tried to squeeze the older sounds under the rug. The older people you used to see, you may see now in a ballroom, dancing to a band like Buddy Tate's. That they can understand. The more Buddy swings, the sooner he fills the floor. And the blues still fills it up. I always remember Buchanan at the Savoy saying, 'The best band is the one that keeps the floor filled.'

"Herschel had a kind of first tenor sound that made a real contrast with Lester's, and Herschel was playing that way before he ever heard Hawk in person. When Buddy Tate, Lucky Thompson, Don Byas, and Paul Gonsalves were in the band, though they were tops, there was never the same contrast. It's pretty hard to duplicate the original, especially when the original is perfect—and that it was. Wow, what a team! I think, though, that if any of the fine fellows with real tenor tone, like Don, Paul, Lucky, Jacquet, or Buddy, had been on the scene *at first*, it would have been pretty much the same. Don, Lucky, and Paul were supreme technicians. Illinois Jacquet was an all-round man with something of Herschel's style. Buddy was tops for gut-bucket, and he had a lot of Herschel in his playing, too. Those three, Herschel, Buddy, and Illinois, all came from Texas, and they have that big Texas sound.

"Buddy came in when Herschel left, and Basie liked him because he had a quality like Herschel's. So had Illinois, but there was never again quite the same effect, although Basie always had a contrast going. He wouldn't put Don Byas and Lucky Thompson together, or Don and Paul Gonsalves. He aimed for two different sounds and styles. He had fine tenor players, but it was as though he was really lucky the first time. He could never get that flavor after Lester left, but at least the first two gave him a pattern. He came closest to it when he had Paul Quinichette.

"Basie is always listening, and he's the one who gives the band its character. Like if I had a band, and he and I bought the same arrangement, and rehearsed it with different bands, when we came to play it most people wouldn't know it was the same arrangement. He'd have whittled it down, maybe only kept the introduction, though he'd have paid good money for it. So it was Basie music! As great as Don Redman was, he'd rearrange his arrangements, too. Basie told me once about one of mine:

" 'That's good, but you've got enough there for fifty arrangements.'

"When he'd finished tearing it up, I didn't know it, but it was swinging.

"Andy Gibson wrote things for the band like *Tickle Toe* and *Beau Brummel.* He knew about Basie's way with arrangements, so one night he brought one in written on a bit of paper about the size of a postcard.

" 'Turn it over when you get to Letter B,' he said.

"Basie had gone to the phone. When he came back he heard us playing this number, said it was swinging, and wanted to know what it was. When he saw the size of it, he said, 'This one must be on the house, man!'

"So I think the real difference between the Basie band and most others was in the way they broke down arrangements the way they wanted them. Sometimes, Benny Carter's bands sounded almost too perfect. That's the funny thing about jazz. You may rehearse until you're hitting everything on the head, and here comes a band like the Savoy Sultans, raggedy, fuzzy-sounding, and they upset everything. 'What am I doing here?' you wonder. But that's the way it is. That's jazz. If you get too clean, too precise, you don't swing sometimes, and the fun goes out of the music. Like Fletcher's arrangements—they'd make you feel bright inside. You were having fun just riding along. You could almost compare it to a lot of kids playing in the mud, having a big time. When the mother calls one to wash his hands, he gets clean, but he has to stand and just look while the others are having a ball. *He's too clean and he can't go back.* Same way when you clean up on that horn and the arrangements are too clean: you get on another level. You're looking down on those guys, but they're all having a good, free-going time.

"Basie's book was probably more varied in the old days than it is today. Buck Clayton used to know just what to write for the guys, and Basie would often suggest the number he wanted. Besides Andy Gibson's things, Don Redman wrote some good ones like *Old Manuscript* and *Down, Down, Down.* I wrote *Stay Cool* and *After Theater Jump.* He used to play my *Kansas City Stride* every night, too, the one we recorded on V-Disc. One of the last the band recorded was *Just a Minute. Dickie's Dream* was Lester's tune. He made it up in the studio. We hadn't got a title for it, so John Hammond said, 'Let's call it *Dickie's Dream.*' I sometimes get a request for it, but until recently I had forgotten how it went.

"When the band first came to New York, it was pretty rough, but the time at the Famous Door ironed out quite a bit of that. Each section used to iron out its own problems. And then we used to have different guys for different chairs, sometimes maybe two first men. Like in Smack's band: Joe Smith wouldn't play first, nor would Louis. Today, everybody wants to be so great on their horns technically that they can say, 'I play first.' I once heard Sy Oliver say, 'If a man can't play first, I don't want him.' That's all right, but if everybody can play first you end up with a similarity of sound in solos. When you had definite first, second, and third chairs, I believe you got more of an individual flavor in the different solos. I go along with each playing *some* first, but there should be a key man. If everyone plays first, what about cats like Louis Armstrong, Buck Clayton, Emmett Berry, Bill Coleman, Bobby Stark, Bix Beiderbecke, Red Allen, Jonah Jones, Bobby Hackett, Miles Davis, Dizzy Gillespie, and Harry Edison, all of whom I consider great? There are many more, not to mention saxes and bones, who have a beautiful color (musically), who are also great and don't play first or care to do so.

"Now, Arthur Pryor, who had a band like Sousa's and started lip vibrato for trombone, was one of the greatest trombone soloists, but he always kept one or two of the best first bone men in his band. He used to demonstrate trombones for Conn, and he gave me lessons about 1936, when I was with Teddy Hill. Keg Johnson and Claude Jones went to him, too. He was one of the best artists, but when he was teaching you just had to watch and listen. He was so very fast, you had to tell him to slow down. There was nothing stiff about his playing; he was very flexible.

"Basie was one of the best to work for. He takes quite a bit, and then he may get mad and explode. Could be that you're on the way out and don't know why. Well, it's a poor guy who doesn't know he has done wrong and keeps doing it. Basie's pretty easygoing, but he still lets you know who's boss. He doesn't want you to drink too much on the job. That is, he wants you to be careful. I think Prez was about the only man he let have a taste on the stand, and he always hid it and wouldn't make it obvious.

"I don't think Basie plays enough piano solos today. One guy in the band used to kid him and say, 'Man, I hear you reaching way back!'

"He acted as though he were kidding, but he meant it, and that was no good, because Basie is kind of shy, and sincere about his work.

"Whether it's old-fashioned or not—and I don't think it is—the real question is, is it good? A lot of new-fashioned things are no good. That's what I like about European audiences. They don't just want the newest, they want the best. The Basie rhythm section could still be featured by itself like it used to be, because it's still a good rhythm section.

"When we were at the Lincoln Hotel in New York, the owner, Mrs. Kramer, was fond of swing, and she'd pull up a table near the stand. She especially liked the rhythm section, and sometimes they'd play alone for maybe an hour, and Basie would tell us we could leave for a while, and we'd be in the bars around, drinking.

"One of the things that keeps tension down in a band is a drummer who plays for the band, and for the soloists, rather than for himself. Basie's rhythm section used to be so light, and so strong, that it was a real inspiration. My idea of a rhythm section is one you feel or sense, one that doesn't disturb you. In the forties, some of the drummers got so technical they spoiled everything. Before he died, Shadow Wilson told me that before he went with Basie he had one way of playing in mind—the latest thing, that was it! Then he got hungry and found out, and began playing with a beat to satisfy the band. He was very versatile and a good drummer, and he played for the musicians on the order of Big Sid. At its best, the Basie rhythm section was nothing less than a Cadillac with the force of a Mack truck. They more or less gave you a *push*, or a *ride*, and they played no favorites, whether you were an E-flat or B-flat soloist.

"It was at the Lincoln that Prez got his little bell. If somebody missed a note, or you were a new guy and goofed, you'd hear this bell going— '*ding-dong!* ' If Prez was blowing and goofed, somebody would reach over and ring his bell on him.

" 'Why, you . . .' he'd say when he'd finished.

"Jo Jones had another way of saying the same thing. *Bing-bing-bing* he'd go on his cymbal rod. When you first joined, you would take it kind of rough, but later you'd be in stitches with the rest, and take it as a joke. They'd ring a bell on Basie, too. And if Prez saw someone getting angry, he'd blow the first bar of *Runnin' Wild*.

"Harry Edison named himself 'Sweets' because he was so rough, always kidding, hiding your hat, and things like that. Sweets, because it was the opposite of what he knew he was. He and Prez just about named everybody, and when Prez named anybody the name stuck.

"Basie was 'The Holy Main.' That meant 'tops' in the way you'd apply it to someone you greatly admired. Buck Clayton was 'Cat Eye' and Snooky Young was 'Rabbit.' Ed Lewis was 'Big D.' George Matthews was 'Truce,' and Benny Morton was 'Mr. Bones.' After Benny left, I became 'Mr. Bones,' but before that I had been 'Gas Belly' on account of my troublesome stomach. Freddie Green was 'Pep.' Walter Page was 'Big 'Un,' or 'Horse.' Jo Jones was 'Sampson.' Buddy Tate was 'Moon,' and Herschel was 'Tex.' Rush was 'Honey Bunny Boo' or 'Little Jim.' Earle Warren was 'Smiley,' and Jack Washington was 'Weasel.' Emmett Berry was 'Rev.,' and Eli Robinson was 'Mr. Eli.' Jimmy Powell was 'Neat,' and Helen Humes 'Homey.' It was Prez who named Snodgrass, the manager, 'Lady Snar.' Everybody had one of those names.

"Herschel worked up to the day before he died. I think it was dropsy. He swelled up so he couldn't get his hat on. It could have been cured if he had gone to the doctor earlier. Everybody loved him.

"Helen Humes did well as Billie's successor, and her blues style fitted the band. Even her pop songs had a blues flavor. She and

Jimmy Rushing used to get along well, telling tall tales and keeping the bus in an uproar all the time.

"Jimmy used to come aboard the bus with a bag of food, chicken or something. We'd be leaving around two o'clock and he would wait until everybody was asleep, snoring, and then open his chicken bag. I was sitting behind him one time, hungry, and saw his jaws working, so I touched him on the shoulder.

" 'Ah, man, I thought you were asleep! Here, fool, eat this and go to sleep.'

"He passed me a very small bit of chicken. I'd wait a couple of nights and then touch him up again.

"Rush is a big man, but he's real light on his feet and can move fast. The only time that I saw Rush depressed was when his wife or mother was sick. He's something like Earl Hines. Earl may have troubles, but he doesn't let you know it. Earl told one of his guys once, 'You may have holes in your shoes, but don't let the people out front know it. Shine the tops.' And Rush never forgets anything. He can tell you exactly what happened twenty, thirty years ago.

"Basie kept going all through the difficult period when most other big bands broke up. Somehow, he always managed to get good transport and accommodation during the war. But then conditions caught up with him, too. It began to get rough some time before he cut down to six pieces. The band wasn't drawing, things were rough all over, and guys were coming in and out of the band fast. He asked me if I wanted to stay, and I appreciated it, but by that time I had had enough of the road, so I told him I thought I ought to stay home for a while.

"Before that I had been out of the band for some time. I had my tonsils removed, because they kept swelling, and I also had stomach disorders. That was because I was drinking quite a bit, trying to stay together. I guess anyone but Basie would have fired me long before. He didn't want to have you on the bandstand if you felt bad, and I'd lay off a week or two, and he'd tell Lady Snodgrass to bring me my money! After I'd had my tonsils out, Lester's burst on him. That was in Chicago. They got the house doctor in the hotel, and Prez said afterwards, 'Where the hell did you get that cat from? He must have been a horse doctor, cutting away at all the wrong places in my throat!'

"He got better, but he took it pretty hard when he had to go in the army."

(1970)

Harry "Sweets" Edison

(TRUMPET)

"My mother and father separated when I was six months old. My father was a Hopi Indian, a very handsome man, and I only saw him once or twice when I was about seven, but I still have a vivid picture in my mind of how he looked. My mother worked very, very hard, at two jobs, so my grandmother was my babysitter until I was five, when she died.

"I was born in Columbus, Ohio, on October 10, 1915, but after my grandmother died my mother sent me to my uncle, Robert Woodard, in a little place called Beaver, in Kentucky, ninety miles from Louisville. Do you remember a tune I wrote for Basie called *Beaver Junction?*

"My uncle was married to my mother's sister, and her folks were called Schultz, a German name that doesn't seem befitting to blacks, but they were all mixed up and there were so many Schultzes in one little Kentucky city that it was called Schultztown. My uncle was a coal miner and a farmer. Everything we ate and accumulated, so far as the house was concerned, we grew. There was so much work to do! I had to hoe the garden, I had to plow, and I had to feed the chickens.

95

We grew sweet potatoes, tomatoes, corn, sugar cane—just about every-thing. I had a paper route, on a horse. My uncle had to get to the mine early, so I had to get up first and light the fire to warm the room. When I got home from school, around four in the afternoon, I'd have to work in the garden, and study. I could always tell when my uncle was on his way home, because I could hear his horse hitting the bridge to the farm. Then I would have to get water and feed the horse. My life was no different from that of any child whose parents were farmers. If I had to do it over again, I wouldn't want to change a thing. It taught me something. But my uncle was lord and master of his house. Whatever he said, he meant.

"He had a pump organ and he would have me play something for him every day. He'd sent away for books from a mail-order store, and he'd just picked up some knowledge of music. He taught me the scales, and he was always trying to form a band among the youngsters in Beaver. When he succeeded, we went to little country towns like Bowling Green, Owensboro, and Hartford. We even went across the Kentucky border to Indianapolis, which is not far. There were usually ten or twelve in the band. I had gotten to where I finally played organ good enough to play in Sunday school! But my uncle had an old York cornet lying around, an old beat-up thing, and it intrigued me. After he got the valves working, he sent away to Louisville to get a mouth-piece. He taught me the scales on it, but after a while I laid it down and started playing trombone. Then I went back to trumpet. I still hadn't learned to read well, but the scales were a foundation, and you never get away from basics.

"Our little band would get on a wagon and play for church fairs, what they called chautauquas, an Indian word for a gathering. Every woman would make something—a pie, a cake, potato salad—and bring it to a kind of church bazaar. We'd play marches, like *Washington Post March*, but no jazz. I was about eight or nine. There was some Dixieland music around there. I used to stand outside a place we called a dancehall—a shack, really—and listen. They had a couple of banjos, a washboard, and a tub with a post and string on it like a bass. They had something going, and they had everybody dancing. It was jazz, and it sounded good to me.

"Then I used to listen to all the records of the old blues singers like Bessie Smith and Blind Lemon Jefferson. And I happened to hear Louis Armstrong backing up Bessie Smith. That was for me! That was where it all started, the direction I wanted to go. Louis Armstrong has been my idol ever since.

"When I was about eleven, I got typhoid fever. There was no swimming pool there, but on the way home from school we'd pull off our clothes and jump in those old ponds, so the water probably had something to do with it. I was deathly ill, burning up with fever, and the doctors gave up and said there was nothing they could do. My mother came from Columbus, and my great-grandmother, who lived to be 108 years old, said she'd use her last resort in medication. She got some fresh cow manure, made a tea out of it, and they gave me that tea all day long. I was delirious and didn't know what it was, but that night my fever came down. The doctor was absolutely amazed, but I had no strength left and almost had to learn to walk all over again. Old people like my great-grandmother had a lot of remedies. They'd dig up roots and make a tea that did more good than medicine. She was always giving me herbs, and there must have been something in the grass the cows ate that was good for my fever, just like the way they got penicillin from mold. They'd use tobacco as an antidote for wounds, and once when I was hit on my forehead by a baseball bat, my great-grandmother took soot out of the stove and filled the cut with that. I think the trumpet was a body-builder for me after that typhoid, too, because when you blow you exercise your lungs and your heart.

"My aunt played the organ in the church, and she could read. She played all the hymns and she helped me, but she was so busy most of the time. A woman's work was really never done in those days. She worked all day, every day. My uncle would be tired, too, when he got in, but Saturday and Sunday were his days to do what he wanted, mostly on the farm. But if the boys in that little country town wanted to know something about music, or wanted to rehearse, he would leave everything. He loved music.

"One of my most glorious moments came after I joined Count Basie in 1938. We played a dance in Owensboro, about thirty miles from where I was raised. My aunt and uncle came in a horse and buggy to see me. My uncle was so proud! He came up to the bandstand and told everybody, 'I taught him! What he's doing today, I taught him!'

"When I was twelve, my mother took me back to Columbus, Ohio. There was a fantastic trumpet player there, a friend of Sy Oliver's, named Pete France, and he and I became friends. But I still wasn't really enthused about trumpet, not even when my mother bought me a new horn, an Olds. I think it took her about five years to pay for it, at fifty cents a month. I loved *sports*, and got a letter in school for baseball, but after a couple of tackles in football I went back to trumpet. Pete France had joined the band at Central High School, and I began to play in it, too, because we could get in the football games free.

"At that time *all* the big bands came through Columbus. It was a big dance town and they had a fantastic dance hall called Valley Dale.

Blacks couldn't go in there, but we could stand outside the fence and hear the bands playing. I heard Louis Armstrong, and when Bennie Moten played there I met Ben Webster and Hot Lips Page for the first time. I was living next door to a beautiful girl, and when I was coming from school one afternoon I saw Lips sitting on the porch talking to her. Musicians were getting all the girls at that time, and here was one accomplishing overnight what I'd been trying to accomplish for years. Of course, the girl was much older than me, but that's when I decided to be a trumpet player! Then, too, I loved the way musicians dressed. They had style about them. They wouldn't come out on the street unless they looked the part. Ben Webster had big shoulders, but he had Little Caesar coats with padded shoulders, and when he put them on he looked like a football player. His shoes were always shined, too, and altogether musicians had an entrée to conversation with a lady the average layman would never get.

"When Pops [Louis Armstrong] came to town in his early days, he was so sharp! The compass of a trumpet was reckoned to be from low C to a high C, and to play over that was considered impossible, but here was a man doing the impossible, hitting three or four tones above the impossible. When he came the first time, my mother asked the manager of the Palace Theater if I could be allowed backstage to hear him. This was downtown and blacks were not allowed in the place. We had a theater of our own. Columbus was segregated, but the schools were mixed. We all played together, but after school the white kids went to the white part of town and the blacks to the black part. I had two or three white friends, and when I go back they are still my friends today. One of them used to stay at my house some weekends, and some weekends I'd stay at his. So I grew up not having that complex about being black or white, although I was very concerned about not being able to hear Louis Armstrong!

"Some of the symphony musicians thought he played a freak horn to get those high notes. Some trumpet players used to make the hole smaller with chewing gum to play higher, but then they couldn't play low. Pops was getting all *over* his horn, playing high *and* low. Anyway, the symphony musicians went to the first show at the Palace Theater, and he showed them his horn and mouthpiece, and even let them blow the horn. It was not the horn, but the man behind it.

"As I was standing in the wings, Louis announced that he was going to play *Tiger Rag*. Since some of the audience still thought he played a trick horn, he had a local trumpet player come up and play it first. Then the band started out, and I never heard a man blow like that in my life! He hit two hundred high Cs, and they counted them as he went around the stage, and he ended on a high F. It looked like the lights shattered when he hit that note. He had phenomenal chops and they never went down, not even when he traveled by himself, just barnstorming. 'Who can play?' he'd ask. 'We're playing a dance tonight.' They had some pretty good musicians around Columbus, and he'd get four or five of 'em. There was a trombone player called Archie White who'd been with Jim Europe years before. There was John Hooks, a fantastic trumpet player. Sy Oliver was around, and a good saxophone player named Paul Tyler. He played in Earl Hood's band, and Johnny Hodges knew him well. The neighboring cities were good dance towns, too, and bands used to station themselves in Columbus. Cincinnati was ninety miles. So were Akron and Dayton. Cleveland was a hundred-and-fifty and Steubenville only sixty. Columbus is the capital of Ohio—Ohio State University, the state penitentiary, and the capitol are all there. Besides Valley Dale, there was a Greystone Ballroom, another called Lane Askins, one on Long Street in the black neighborhood, and both the Pythian Temple and the Masonic Hall were used for dances. So every night there was a different band to hear, and there were always a lot of good musicians around in Ohio.

"Paul Tyler lived next door to my mother's home and he heard me playing all the time, so one day he asked me to a rehearsal of Earl Hood's band. Hood liked me and I joined his band, playing around Columbus and Chillicothe, mostly Saturday nights. He'd tell me, 'You're playing for experience,' and wouldn't pay me. I'd be so sleepy on Monday, I wouldn't have my homework done. My mother, who had bought me a trumpet and a tuxedo, thought Hood was mistreating me, and when she eventually went to see him he started paying me thirty-five cents a night! We were playing dance music and everybody was taking solos. One night I just started playing one myself on *Limehouse Blues.* Everybody turned around asking, 'Who is this kid?' That was my debut as a soloist.

"I continued going to school until a band called Morrison's Grenadiers was organized. Some rich family of that name loved music and backed it, and they got the best musicians, like Sy Oliver, Jimmy Crawford, and Joe Thomas. They were going to Cleveland for an engagement at the Cotton Club, and they asked my mother if I could go. She agreed, so long as I came back and went to school. We were eight pieces, and later we added Jimmy Miller on guitar. There were all kinds of clubs in Cleveland, and that was where I first met Art Tatum. He was playing at Val's in the Alley. There were other very good piano players there, too, like Lanny Scott and a man named Pickett who married Rose Murphy, the Chi-Chi Girl. I was nearly sixteen and music had gotten in my blood, but my mother came and made me go back to Columbus to school.

"The Alphonso Trent band from Texas had been doing one-nighters until Trent got sick in Bangor, Maine. He went back to Fort Smith, Arkansas, and the band broke up in Columbus. It was a very good band, and two of the saxophone players, James Jeter [alto] and Hayes Pillars [tenor] decided to get a band together again. My mother agreed for me to go back to Cleveland with them, and we started playing in the Creole Club. That's where I met Basie's wife, Catherine. She was a dancer in the club. We were all youngsters then, but we became friends and she would take me out to her mother's house, Mrs. Morgan's, and feed me quite a bit.

"Then we got another job at the Heat Wave Bar in the Majestic Hotel. Besides Jeter and Pillars, Snub Mosely was playing trombone, A. G. Godley was on drums, and Slim Waters was on tuba. Slim was from Jersey, and he could play tuba like other guys played trumpet. In fact, when we got off at four in the morning we would go places, and he would jam with the trumpet players. Wherever there's an underworld, there's plenty of money, and there were a lot of speakeasies there where you could buy whiskey. The town was flourishing, and that attracted musicians. Caesar Dameron, Tadd's brother, was a good saxophone player at that time, and Poison Gardner, a piano player and entertainer, was also at the Heat Wave. But there was no one like Art Tatum. He was a genius from the time I first knew him.

"The Ohio State School for the Blind was on Parsons and Main, right across the street from me in Columbus, and he graduated from there. They taught him to read braille first, and then to read music in braille. He certainly got some of his training there, but I think he was born with a gift and went to that school to improve it. In later years, he did have more finesse, but he always knew how to keep people involved. The more he played, the more you listened—and drank. There was no hour to quit in those days, but you had an hour to start, usually nine o'clock, and you left when everybody left the club. Art would play till ten, eleven, or twelve o'clock in the daytime. I know we were making only twelve dollars a week in Cleveland, but they had a kitty and we'd get five or six dollars a night in tips. Naturally, Art did better than that.

"I was getting pretty confident by this time, but we mostly played heads. The reading you had to do was not complicated, but more like what beginners play today, at least as compared with what you're expected to do now in the studios. I never forget when McKinney's Cotton Pickers came to Cleveland. They had Roy Eldridge, Billy Bowen, Teddy Wilson's brother Gus, Clyde Hart, and Cuba Austin. Roy came in after us one night and carried us from place to place. He almost made me want to quit. What chops he had, and how he could play! He and Pops were the only two people I ever heard who could play continuously like that. The longer they played, the stronger they got. Pops could play for hours and hours, never miss a note, and never crack or anything. He had good tooth formation and a perfect lip for playing. And he was just so far ahead of his time. It was absolutely amazing how a man could pave the way fifty years ago, and here we are, still playing his things. For any trumpet player to play a decent solo, he's got to play something Pops played. Dizzy still plays things Pops played. They can call it be-bop if they want to, but he was playing it in the thirties.

"The Jeter-Pillars band stayed in Cleveland about a year and then went to St. Louis for two or three years. We added George Hudson on trumpet there, and Carl Smith, a trombone player we called 'Trombone Smitty.' When he left, Gus Wilson took his place. He was a better musician than Teddy then. Besides trombone, he could play good piano and write beautifully. After A. G. Godley left, we got Sidney Catlett on drums, and when our bass player decided to stay in Cleveland we got Jimmy Blanton. Then Sidney Catlett got a call to join Fletcher Henderson in Chicago, so that was when Jo Jones and Walter Page joined us. Chester Lane, who now works with Teddy Buckner at Disneyland, was on piano, and Jimmy Miller was on guitar. Gene Porter, a tenor player who had been with Earl Hines, was also added.

"Some stories have put me in Alphonso Trent's band, although I never met him. I have also been connected with Eddie Johnson and His Crackerjacks, but I never did play with them. They used to come through Columbus and I got to know Hal Baker quite well. The first time I heard Tab Smith play was in that band, and later he recommended me to Lucky Millinder.

"Where we were playing in St. Louis was the Plantation, a big club with fantastic chorus girls. The girl I'd been going with left before I did, to dance in the New York Cotton Club. I guess I would have stayed if she hadn't left, but then Lucky Millinder sent a telegram and tickets to a friend of mine, Harold Arnold, who was playing tenor with the Crackerjacks. Lucky had wanted some other St. Louis trumpet player, but Harold suggested I go with him. So I got on the train and went to New York, where Tab Smith told Lucky I was a good trumpet player.

"I think I stayed with Lucky about six months before I joined Basie. Lucky had a good band. He had Charlie Shavers, Carl Warwick, Billy Kyle, Tab Smith, Don Byas, and Andy Gibson. O'Neil Spencer was on drums, but when he got sick Walter Johnson took his place. We played opposite Basie in Baltimore, and we played an arrangement I'd written called *Every Tub*. It upset the crowd before Basie could get on the bandstand. 'Where in the hell did these guys come from?' he asked.

"Lucky fired me for Dizzy Gillespie. Charlie Shavers and 'Bama Warwick had played with him and they were good buddies. I was from St. Louis, you know! But Dizzy and I got to playing *Body and Soul* in some place in Philadelphia one night, and I made a little noise, so Lucky hired me back and Dizzy went to Teddy Hill.

"Then Bobby Moore, who was with Basie, took sick. He was a good trumpet player, but he had trouble with his teeth, and they had a bit of a problem replacing him. I was staying at the same boarding house as Jo Jones and Herschel Evans, and they recommended me to Basie. So I joined his band at the end of 1937.

"Lucky had a guy named Chappie Willet who used to write such hard arrangements, but when I got with Basie everything seemed to be head arrangements. I bet they didn't have ten manuscripts. I still wanted to learn more about music, so I recommended Andy Gibson, who made *Louisiana, Tickle Toe, The World Is Mad*, and all those arrangements.*

"Basie's was not an ensemble band. Everybody in it was a soloist. I think Basie had become the leader because he was very popular in Kansas City. It was logical, too, in an era of piano-playing leaders like Duke Ellington, Earl Hines, Fletcher Henderson, and Claude Hopkins. They could direct from the piano, but if the bandleader played tenor or trumpet he had to hire another to play while he was directing.

"By this time I guess I had developed a style. I didn't have the chops to play like Louis Armstrong or Roy Eldridge. To play high as they did is partly a gift, but you also have to be dedicated to practicing to play high. Red Allen was one of my idols because he played in the register of the horn I love to play in. I think he thought the same way I did, too. Jeter and Pillars were both very good musicians, and they stressed quality in their band. You had to have tonal quality and you really had to express yourself on the lower part of your horn. They had more of a sweet band—not like Guy Lombardo—and after the show at the Plantation we'd play for dancing, mostly stocks of show tunes and numbers like *The Continental*. It was a white club, and blacks weren't allowed in there. They had a special door for us. It was the same old thing, the same old South, just like the song! But there wasn't much room for playing solos in that band, and it wasn't at all like Bennie Moten's or McKinney's Cotton Pickers. I didn't forget about Pops and Roy, but I was only a kid and this was a job where I tried to play with the tone and quality they wanted.

* For more details on Gibson's career, see *The World of Swing*.

"When I got with Basie, I was still playing that way, and in the lower register, which is why Prez started calling me 'Sweets.' At first I tried to play pretty all the time, and I took a lot of solos Buck Clayton got the credit for.* He already had a name, but people hadn't heard of me. It didn't matter then who got the credit, just so you got to play. If you didn't swing, Basie would take the solo away from you and give it to someone else. Prez had a bell he would ring, and that was the cue that the solo was not for you.

"What a thrill it was to play with that band! It was the greatest thrill of my life. We couldn't wait to get on the bandstand at night. It was just like a horse prancing to get out on the racetrack. We were nervous if we weren't on the bandstand. I don't think there is a better bandleader on earth than Basie. He's a very humorous guy; he's easy to get along with; and he knows how to handle men. He knew how important the soloists were at that time, and he didn't try to make an ensemble band out of it. He loved to hear Prez play, and he loved to hear Herschel play. He liked to hear Buck play, liked to hear me, and he liked to hear Jo Jones. He was and is the greatest for stomping off the tempo. He noodles around on the piano until he gets it just right. Just like you were mixing mash and yeast to make whiskey, and you keep tasting and tasting it. Or you're making a cake and tasting the mix to make sure you've got the ingredients and everything to the point where you know it's going to be all right. Freddie Green and Jo Jones would follow him until he hit the right tempo, and when he started it they *kept* it. They knew where he was going at all times, but if the tempo was too fast he would bring it down gradually, not abruptly, so nobody would ever know. And if it was too slow, he would bring it up until it was *just* right.

"Of course, Walter Page contributed a lot, too. He was a good musician and a teacher from the University of Kansas. Besides playing bass, he was also a fantastic baritone player. He started that 'strolling' or 'walking' bass, going way up and then coming right on down. He

---

* On Basie's early records, Harry Edison has solos on *Sent for You Yesterday; Every Tub; Now Will You Be Good?; Swinging the Blues* (second trumpet solo); *Texas Shuffle; Shorty George; Panassie Stomp; Jive at Five; Rock-a-bye Basie; Jump for Me; Twelfth Street Rag; Miss Thing; Pound Cake; Riff Interlude; Hollywood Jump; Let's Make Hay; Louisiana; Easy Does It* (second trumpet solo); *Blow Top; Super Chief; Moten Swing; What's Your Number?; Five O'Clock Whistle; Broadway; Stampede in G Minor; Rocking the Blues; Wiggle Woogie; Beau Brummel; Jump the Blues Away; Tuesday at Ten; 9:20 Special; H & J; Tom Thumb; Something New; Platterbrains; Feather Merchant; It's Sand, Man; Ain't It the Truth?; Taps Miller; Avenue C; Queer Street; High Tide; Lazy Lady Blues* (obbligato); *Bambo; Stay Cool; Open the Door, Richard* (vocal); *One O'Clock Boogie; Guest in the Nest; Money Is Honey;* and *Just a Minute.*

did it on four strings, but other bass players couldn't get that high so they started making a five-string bass. That rhythm section would send chills up me every night. The whole band would be shouting, and then all of a sudden everybody would drop out for the bridge and there would be just the rhythm with Page's bass going up and down. Oh, my goodness! That was the greatest band that's ever been on earth! I've never heard any other swing like it did.

"We were all very close in the band. You couldn't just say, 'This is my best buddy.' Buck was a very good friend. Freddie Green is about the closest friend I have. Basie is a good buddy to me, and I always looked upon him as a father. When I joined the band, he just took a liking to me. I used to listen to him, because I had no fatherly advice when I left home. He took me everyplace in New York and introduced me to Duke, Don Redman, Clark Monroe, Benny Carter, and Chick Webb—to the whole scene. It was a thrill to meet James P. Johnson and all the people I had read about and admired without thinking I'd ever be shaking hands with them. I met them through Basie, and he introduced me to the older dancers in New York at that time. I'm really grateful to him for my whole career. I was with him from '38 to '50, but I still go back to him. There's a chair in that band I consider mine. I'm sure anybody still active that has been in the band can always go back. He'll make room for you.

"Early on, I put in my notice. There was so little written music that I wasn't accomplishing what I wanted to accomplish. I wanted to read well and be a really good musician. I told him that nobody could play those head arrangements like Ed Lewis and the guys who had been in Bennie Moten's band. Every night I was trying to pick me a note to play.

" 'Well, you sound good,' Basie said.

" 'But I don't know what note to hit,' I said.

" 'Well, if you find a note tonight that sounds good, play the same damn note every night!'

"That was the beginning of a beautiful friendship.

"Basie gave Coleman Hawkins all the respect in the world, and he respected Chu Berry and Joe Thomas, too, but it was Lester Young's playing that he *loved*. Everything Prez did was a classic. Like the names he had for different people. He nicknamed Basie 'Holy,' the Holy Man, the Holy Main, the Main Man—Holy, because he was the bandleader and did the paying! He named Billie Holiday 'Lady Day,' Earle Warren 'Smiley,' and Herschel Evans, because he came from Texas, 'Tex.' He had a name for everybody, and a knack for doing comical things. He'd be the first to start a crap game on our old bus, and the first to go to sleep. We were so short of space, we'd take turns sitting on the outside seat so we could stretch our legs in the aisle. Sometimes, when we were all asleep, he'd wake up, take the dice, and shake 'em in everybody's ear all down the bus, saying, 'Sweet music, sweet music!' He'd get another crap game started, but he would be the first one broke. Originally, he didn't drink or smoke at all. When he first left Kansas City, he had an old cob pipe he used to hold in his mouth, but he never had any tobacco for it. New York is so fast you have to have a lot of willpower to stay within the bounds of your teaching. In later years, after he started drinking, he never ate anything. He might order a good meal, take a bit of this and try that, but then leave it. He never had what you'd call a good appetite, and alcohol will take your appetite away. His body was just saturated with alcohol, and Coleman Hawkins was the same way towards the end.

"We got an engagement at the Strand on Broadway, and it was our big chance. Basie wanted a production number and Jimmy Mundy did an arrangement on *I Struck a Match in the Dark*, which Earle Warren was to sing. When the lights went out and Earle started, we were all supposed to strike a match and light up the stage. Well, when Earle made his introduction, Prez struck a match, held his part up, and set fire to it! That was the end of that. He didn't like Earle Warren's singing, and he always imitated singers and made a comedy out of it. He liked Helen Humes and Jimmy Rushing, but after Billie Holiday left we didn't really want a singer anyway. The singer was just an ornament on the bandstand in those days, more of an accompaniment to the band. Sing a chorus and sit down! Now it's the singers' era and the band is an accompaniment. Most of those making the money, to me, are not good singers. If you put Ella Fitzgerald and Sarah Vaughan aside, I'd say Streisand is one newcomer who can sing. Frank Sinatra, Billy Eckstine, Carmen McRae, Peggy Lee—the ones that sang with the old bands—were better singers than today's crop and had something of quality in what they did. The record companies take all the equipment and put it behind somebody who doesn't have quality, but they won't take that equipment to make someone who already sounds good sound better. The electronics are the worst thing that ever happened. If you've got quality, you don't need them to make you sound good, but take them away from some of today's musicians and they'd be absolutely horrible to listen to. I once made an album of thirty-six tunes in three hours with Ella Fitzgerald. Art Tatum would make several albums in a day. But I read where they've given Stevie Wonder a year to make one album! They're really trying to wash out black music. They'll promote any kind of mush, but not jazz. Rock 'n' roll is strictly white music. Country music came way after the blues, because cowboys came way after slavery! Norman Granz is the only man I know who really promotes jazz.

"I just wish they would give the originator credit while he's living. To me, Coleman Hawkins is just as great as Thomas Edison. He originated something on tenor saxophone that had never been heard before. Louis Armstrong broke all the rules of trumpet, and Duke Ellington broke all the rules of those who said you cannot play dissonant chords because they're displeasing to the ear. There's only one Dizzy Gillespie, but the beginning of most of the white soloists' prominence was bebop. Dizzy started playing the trumpet like a virtuoso, with a lot of notes, and there were many white players who had been taught to get over their horns fast. What they couldn't do was hit one note, or two notes, and make it sound effective by putting a lot of feeling in it. That was the beginning of a lot of white musicians, who didn't have to have quality to play. Charlie Parker could swing, but his swing was getting over his horn—speed. But when it came to melody, nobody in the world could play like Johnny Hodges. He could play a melody note for note and make it absolutely expressive. And nobody could play a melody as *pretty* as Ben Webster. There was no quality in Charlie Parker's tone, not like there was in Johnny Hodges', Benny Carter's, or Hilton Jefferson's. Jeff was magnificent and a schooled musician, but he never got the recognition. I can't allow for an imitator. There's no substitute for originality.

"I think there's nobody more influential on tenor players today than Lester Young. More than Coleman Hawkins now. Prez would try anything on the bandstand, anything he thought of. He maintained that if he didn't try it there, where was he going to try it? If it didn't work in the first instance, you kept playing it until it did. It was like an experiment, and the bandstand was his proving ground.

"We used to do like three hundred one-nighters a year, because we had no place to sit down and play. Jimmie Lunceford had the Cotton Club, and when he came out of there he would go on forty weeks of theaters, where we had fifty weeks of one-nighters. But one time we were supposed to battle Lunceford in Hartford, Connecticut. He came out from New York in a big, air-conditioned Greyhound bus. We came from Pittsburgh, Pennsylvania, to Hartford—a long ride, and we were so tired. Basie said, 'Well, I'm tired like everybody else.' Willie Smith was one of the warmest guys you could ever meet, and Joe Thomas was very friendly, but most of the guys in Lunceford's band didn't even speak to us. We were only Count Basie's band, and we got out of a ragged bus, but when we got on that bandstand we started jumping and showering down. Prez played like he'd never played before. Before you knew it, Lunceford and all his guys were coming up to the bandstand. We put a hurting on them that night and washed Lunceford out of the dance hall.

"Our head arrangements sounded good, because we had them so well together, but as musicians were added to the band we had to have written music. We had to rehearse and learn it. Because you're looking at the music when you're playing, you don't have the freedom you had when everything was head. Therefore you lose a little of your feeling. Yet when you've got your own notes and *know* what you're playing, you are more at ease. As more instruments were added, the band became more musical and more of an ensemble. Today, the band is strictly an ensemble band, and one thing I think Basie misses, too, is soloists, because he was always used to having solos.

"After Prez went in the army, and didn't come back, Basie got musicians who could read and blend in with the sections better. In the late forties, Jimmy Mundy and Don Redman were writing for the band. Buck Clayton was doing a lot of writing, and Benny Goodman gave Basie some of Fletcher Henderson's arrangements. All that required more rehearsals than we were used to. Quite a few of the tunes we recorded were mine, like *Every Tub, Sent for You Yesterday*, and *Jive at Five*.

"While I was in the Jeter-Pillars band, Gus Wilson and I had become very good friends. He was a beautiful arranger and I used to ask him questions. How do you voice the altos? How do you put the trumpets here? The E-flat scale is different from the B-flat scale, and he'd tell me where to put the note to experiment. 'After you hear it one time,' he'd say, 'change it and put it in a different perspective, a different place.' So I started doing that, and sometimes it sounded pretty good, but after hearing what guys like Benny Carter wrote, I kind of got discouraged. I love to play, and the only man I know who writes as well as he plays is Benny Carter. He can make a living doing either one.

"After I went to New York, I went from place to place, listening to solos by Charlie Shavers, Roy Eldridge, and Erskine Hawkins. Erskine had a style and fantastic chops. He was promoted as the Twentieth Century Gabriel, and in those days playing high and reaching the stratosphere on your horn was popular, even if it wasn't tasteful. The musician I really liked in his band was Dud Bascomb, a remarkable trumpet player.

"All the big bands were collapsing. Only Duke's ASCAP rating kept his going, and he was paying good salaries even when other bands were in trouble. Johnny Hodges was making five or six hundred dollars a week when we were getting fifteen dollars a night.

"I left Basie when the band broke up. Little groups had begun to take over, dance halls diminished, and people didn't dance anymore. When we played we became more like a concert band, and in the clubs people would just sit and drink. It was nightclubs instead of dance halls. So in 1950, Basie formed a small group with Clark Terry and Serge Chaloff. Clark had been in the trumpet section a year or two, and it had been a very good section with Snooky Young, Emmett Berry, Clark, and myself. Snooky was a more flexible trumpet player than Ed Lewis, and the new arrangements we were getting required flexibility. Right now, I think Snooky's the best first trumpet there is. He's a good soloist, too, and good soloists make better first trumpet players than just strictly first trumpet players because, although they may be the most reliable guys in the world, when it comes to bending a note, and being flexible, and phrasing as only a soloist can, the first trumpet who is also a soloist has an edge. Snooky once had a band of his own in Dayton and *had* to be a soloist. Then he took it to the Three Sixes in Detroit, and he had to solo there, too. When Basie had only three trumpets—Ed Lewis, Buck, and me—Buck wouldn't play first, and I wouldn't because Buck wouldn't, so Ed had to play it all. But after I got a band of my own and came out to California, I had to play a lot of first parts.

"The first thing I had to do when I left Basie was join Local 802, because we'd been a traveling band all those years and the only members of 802 were guys like Dicky Wells and Benny Morton who lived in New York. A lot of people wondered why Basie didn't take Dicky Wells, myself, and older guys out of the band, because he had enough soloists to keep the thing going. Somebody must have sold him a bill of goods for him to take Serge Chaloff and Buddy De-Franco! We didn't even know he had a small band till Freddie Green, Ted Donnelly, and I met one afternoon. 'Man, how come you-all aren't going to Chicago?' somebody asked. 'Basie and them just caught a plane to open up some bar in Chicago.' I said, 'You got to be kidding!' and Freddie said, 'Aw, that can't be true.' But we found out it was.

"That's when I became almost hysterical. It's very easy to be a sideman. The bandleader has to get all the work. All you have to do as a sideman is lie around until you get up to play, or until you get a telephone call saying, 'We're leaving at four o'clock tomorrow and we'll be out for three months. Get your things packed.' All those years with Basie, I didn't have to worry about work. I'd been irresponsible and I'd depended on him just like I would on a father. I was twenty-one when I joined him just before Christmas in 1937, and now it was 1950 and I was a married man. I was afraid and really depressed. I didn't know where I was going to get any money from.

Nobody knew what Basie was thinking. He hadn't said, 'This is it. You go your way and I'll go mine, because it's come to the point where I just can't afford the big band any longer.' Yet it happened for the best, because it made me realize I'd got to look out for myself.

"I played around New York with all kinds of people and I recorded quite a bit. I went out with Jazz at the Philharmonic. With Coleman Hawkins, I went to Toronto and Cleveland. We were good friends and I played with him a lot of times. It was an experimental period in music, I think, because everything was happening. I couldn't understand what some of the guys were playing, but I never said anything. Who's to say who's right and who's wrong? But if it was not understandable to a musician, how could the average person understand it? The right hand was coming into prominence with the piano players in the small groups. The left hand was like the drummer's right foot. It went from bass drum to no bass drum, from left hand to no left hand, just that quick. It went from holding one note to making a whole lot of notes on your horn. It went from making a simple chord to putting in a flatted fifth, or a thirteenth, or a suspended note, or whatever.

"I always play the melody before I start improvising. One of the hardest things to do is to play straight melody without deviating from a note. You can originate a lot of little things around the melody without changing it till people don't know what you're doing. I'd rather be a mediocre originator than a perfect imitator any time."

Harry Edison's career from 1950 onward was one he could scarcely have anticipated. In 1952 he became Josephine Baker's musical director and toured with her for a long time, spending six months at El Patio in Mexico City. Deciding to settle in California, he became acquainted with Nelson Riddle. Although at first reluctant, he gradually became involved in studio work and persevered until he was completely accepted. He credited much of his success to Riddle's patience and the help of established studio trumpet players like Mannie Klein. He began recording with Frank Sinatra in 1952 and was in the band that accompanied him on the *Wee Hours* album, which Edison considers the singer's best. At Sinatra's request, he continued to record with him for six straight years, often with headphones at a mike separate from the trumpet section. He was thus free to make his own muted trumpet commentary on the singing. Soon in demand as an accompanist for other singers, he also recorded with Nat Cole, Margaret Whiting, Bing Crosby, Jerry Lewis, Billy Daniels, and Ella Fitzgerald, not to mention with jazz musicians like Shorty Rogers, Ben Webster, Arnold Ross, and Conrad Gozzo. He was featured in the film *Jammin' the Blues* and also played on the sound track of such movies as *Step Down to Terror, Houseboat, The Girl Most Likely,* and *Lady Sings the Blues.*

As a result of the popularity Sinatra's records brought him, he went to New York in 1958 and formed his own group consisting of Jimmy Forrest (tenor saxophone), Jimmy Jones (piano), Joe Benjamin (bass), and Charlie Persip (drums). After signing with Roulette Records, Edison opened at Birdland, where he often played opposite Count Basie's band. When Joe Williams left him, Basie thought it would be a good idea to put the Edison quintet and Williams together. It was a successful combination until the singer decided to operate on his own with just a trio in support.

The sixties were a busy time for Edison. He toured Europe several times, with Norman Granz's Jazz at the Philharmonic, George Wein's Newport package, and as a guest alumnus with the Basie band. Returning to Los Angeles, he again became involved in studio work. He did *The Hollywood Palace Show* with Mitchell Ayres for three years, playing all kinds of music in what was essentially a variety show. Other television shows followed, with Della Reese, Frank Sinatra, Rosemary Clooney, Bill Cosby, Don Rickles, Leslie Uggams, and Glen Campbell. He was also on many record dates during this period, and, having got his own group together again (with Jimmy Forrest), he played extensive engagements in Las Vegas and Los Angeles.

In 1977 he teamed up with Lockjaw Davis, an old associate and Basie alumnus. Usually picking up local rhythm sections in the cities they played, they began to tour the world with great success. This gave Edison opportunities to indulge his taste for history and art; much of his spare time abroad was spent in art galleries, museums, and historic buildings. (His discriminating taste is, incidentally, indicated by the excellent prints of Constable, Goya, Rembrandt, and Van Gogh paintings that adorn the walls of his apartment.) One of the most exciting experiences of his life was a tour of the Middle East made for the U.S. State Department in the Bicentennial year. As a member of a quintet led by Benny Carter, he appreciated the VIP treatment they received, but most of all he enjoyed seeing the Blue Mosque and St. Sophia's in Istanbul, the beauty of Isfahan, the Nile, the pyramid at Karnak, the Sphinx, the treasures of Tutankhamen, and a little town where Jesus walked. Perhaps this breadth of interest helps account for the fact that Harry Edison is today one of the most renowned and best preserved of all the Swing Era's famous trumpet players.

(1979)

1. *Bennie Moten's Orchestra, 1931. Left to right: (front) Vernon Page, Count Basie, Lips Page, Ed Lewis, Thamon Hayes, Eddie Durham, Woodie Walder, Buster Berry, Harlan Leonard, Booker Washington, Willie McWashington, Jack Washington; (rear) Bennie Moten, Buster Moten, Jimmy Rushing.* (Courtesy Jimmy Rushing)

2. *The Blue Devils, Oklahoma City, August 10, 1928. Left to right: Lips Page, Buster Smith, unknown, Walter Page, unknown, Willie Lewis (piano), unknown, Ernie Williams, unknown.* (Courtesy The Last of the Blue Devils Film Co.)

3. *Count Basie*. (Stanley Dance collection)

4. *Lester Young.*
(Courtesy Dicky Wells)

5. *Buck Clayton.*
(Courtesy Dicky Wells)

6. *Earle Warren.*
(Courtesy Earle Warren)

7. *Walter Page.* (Courtesy Dicky Wells)

8. *Dicky Wells in Harlem.* (Courtesy Dicky Wells)

9. *Edgar Battle, Valentine Billington, and Eddie Durham with the Seven Eleven and Mamie Smith Show, 1927.* (Courtesy Eddie Durham)

10. Count Basie and Freddie Green. (Courtesy Freddie Green)

11. *Count Basie and Billie Holiday.*
    (Courtesy Dicky Wells)

12. Left to right: *Jo Jones, Walter Page, Buddy Tate, Count Basie, Freddie Green, Buck Clayton, Dicky Wells.* (Courtesy Freddie Green)

13. *Count Basie and His Orchestra, 1941.* Left to right: *(front) Ed Cuffee, Dicky Wells, Dan Minor, Helen Humes (vocal), Count Basie, Buddy Tate, Tab Smith, Earle Warren, Jack Washington, Don Byas; (rear) Harry Edison, Al Killian, Ed Lewis, Buck Clayton, Jo Jones, Freddie Green, Walter Page.* (Stanley Dance collection)

14. *"America's Number One Band,"* 1941. (Courtesy Dicky Wells)

15. Left to right: *(front) Count Basie, Buddy Tate, Earle Warren, Jack Washington, Lester Young; (rear) Walter Page, Freddie Green, Benny Morton.* (Courtesy Freddie Green)

16. *Count Basie and Duke Ellington.* (Courtesy Columbia Records)

Buddy Tate

(TENOR SAXOPHONE AND CLARINET)

"Pilot Grove in Texas is where my parents and grandparents came from. It's between Dallas and Sherman, which are about fifty miles apart. There's a place called McKinney and a little town called Van Alstyne. Pilot Grove is out from Van Alstyne, one of those in-between stops in north Texas near the Oklahoma line. My grandfather was a very good businessman and he taught all four boys the importance of owning property. There's a whole country of Tates down there. At one time my father owned three farms. He gave one to his brother and sold another to my mother's brother. My father was pretty well-adjusted and he left my mother straight with all the farm paid for. He was forty-six when he died, and I was three.

"I had two brothers, one ten years older than me, and the other eight years older. I also had a sister who was six years older. I was the baby, and I think I was kind of spoiled, although at the time I thought they were the meanest people in the world! We had plenty of cattle on the farm, near Sherman, when I was born in 1915. We had everything and hardly had to go to town to buy anything. My mother canned, and we had a big smokehouse with hams and sausages hanging in it. When we killed hogs, we'd still have hams from the previous year. We had good water from a spring that never failed. My daddy and granddaddy had fixed it with cement all around.

"My two brothers weren't really old enough to run the farm when my father died so my mother had to have help. When I was about twelve, she told me we were moving into town, three miles away. It broke my heart. We were leaving a brand-new house, and I loved that farm and the outdoor life. We had horses to ride and I could go hunting whenever I liked. I even liked walking through the woods on the way to school with fifty or sixty other kids. Mother had a hard time keeping me in the city at first, but she rented the farm to a friend, a school teacher who farmed and taught. We had five hundred acres and we grew cotton, wheat, corn, and grain. After my brothers died my sister sold some of it, but I think we still have nearly four hundred acres. Now the government has taken over and they only let you cultivate so much of your land. Farmers are always independent and they don't like that because they can't always cultivate enough to live comfortably.

"One of my brothers played piano, and the other played C-melody saxophone. I used to listen to them and I wanted to play, too, but not saxophone. I liked the sound of trombone better, and I got an old curtain rod with the rings on and I used to slide the rings up and down, imitating a trombone. I'd stand around and watch my brother change reeds on his saxophone, but he'd never let me touch it.

"When I started listening to the radio, I used to hear Guy Lombardo, and then Alphonso Trent over WFFA from Dallas. They used to broadcast every night from the Adolphus Hotel, a fine, exclusive place. That was a band, man! We had a Victrola, too, and I used to listen to all of Bessie Smith's records. Mother loved music and she liked those records, but she had so many that after a while when my sister and I got tired of some of them we'd take them and sail them through the air, throwing them at each other.

"We used to have what people called picnics, or chittlin' suppers. We could stay up all night and make as much noise as we wanted, when we were out in the country. My brothers would play and I wanted to join in so badly. Sometimes, when my brothers were away, I'd sneak in and try to put a reed in the saxophone and play it. I broke up so many reeds he'd box me upside the head. Finally, he went to school in Dallas and was working on the side. When he came back one time he had bought me a brass alto saxophone.

"'Okay, now,' he said as he gave it to me. 'You want to play so bad, you've got to get a teacher and learn *how* to play it!'

"There weren't many teachers around in those days, but there was a boy called Emmett Malone, a brilliant musician who played trumpet. Where he got his knowledge from, I don't know, and he never really made it, but he knew chords and changes inside out. And all kinds of times. He used to try to tell me about times like twelve-eight, but it sounded like Japanese to me. He taught me how to read. He gave me books and wrote out scales for me to practice. I had a good ear and my mother would pay him, but we could never keep him at home long. Three months, six months, and then he'd be gone. When a minstrel show or a circus came around, he'd run off with them.

"Eventually we had a little family band. Malone was the only one in it not related to us, but he was engaged to my cousin. He always wanted his own band, and later we played with him a little while when he was in Sherman. But by then ours was better and more popular.

"We used to rehearse by listening to records. I remember how we listened to Pops [Louis Armstrong] playing *West End Blues*. Then we got records by the Coon-Sanders Kansas City Nighthawks. They could swing! In those days you could get stock arrangements with the solos all written out just like on the record. That was a help, but I can remember how we scuffled with Coon-Saunders' *Brainstorm* and Fletcher Henderson's *Deep Henderson*. What we couldn't read, we'd clap our ear to on the record. And we would slow the record down so that we could get it. We rehearsed every night and we were tight. We must have had a hundred numbers, and the band got to be pretty popular, playing dances.

"We got us a manager, a white fellow named Red Jackson, a college kid, and after about a year we added another saxophone. His name was James Johnson, and he played good violin as well as C-melody. My cousin, Roy McCloud, played trumpet; another cousin, Hazel Jones, played piano; Ralph Arterberry, a third cousin, was on drums; and Bernice Douglas, a boy despite the name, played banjo. Leroy Porter was the original banjoist, and he had had a lot to do with getting us together and getting us jobs because he worked uptown and people asked him about music. Leroy was another cousin, but when we started playing from stocks we got Bernice instead because he had a good piano foundation and played beautiful chords.

"I must have been thirteen or fourteen when we started playing dances for all the high schools. Bernice and the drummer were about my age, and nobody more than three years older. As soon as we began to make some money we started buying uniforms. At one time we each had seven of them. Then we bought tuxes, and we used to wear spats with them. I'll never forget that—tuxedos and spats! When we'd go to a town and fall out of the car, people would just stare at us. Man, we were so sharp! We spent all our money on ourselves, and we were making good money. Families were making it then on ten dollars a week, because you could get a loaf of bread for a nickel, but here were we making twelve dollars a night!

"Those were the days of territory bands, before the booking agencies monopolized everything. You could rent a hall for twenty-five dollars, and after all the expenses for placards and everything had been paid we'd split the swag down equally. Sometimes we'd give the leader five or ten dollars extra for the work he'd put in. That's the way it used to be.

"As our band became popular, they started asking for us farther afield. We went to Oklahoma City all the time, and all over Texas. We traveled in cars with wide running boards and on one side we'd have a rack with all the instruments lined up on it. You couldn't get out that side. We'd have something to cover the instruments so they wouldn't get splashed. We had a Model T Ford and no one but me and the manager could drive it. I remember lots of nights when the manager didn't go with us and I had to drive home, and all those cats in the car would fall asleep.

"There were two towns we could always expect to make fifteen dollars apiece—Ardmore, Oklahoma, and Paris, Texas. Bonham, between Paris and Sherman, was a good town, too. It was Charlie Christian and Nipsey Russell's hometown, and I guess the population was around 25,000. We'd just play dances in a hall. Put up our placards, go in and start playing, and people would start dancing. A lot of white people would come, but they just listened and didn't dance, although eventually we were playing more white dances than black.

"There were four or five colleges in Sherman, where I was raised, and they always paid a good, flat guarantee. Red Jackson was booking us into all of them, because he had connections.

"There were five or six white theaters there, too, and each had a band, but they were all white musicians, playing for the pictures. There was a saxophone player named Frank O'Banner who played one of those theaters, and he had a beautiful sound. He used to come to our dances.

" 'You play so pretty,' I told him one time.

" 'But I can't play jazz,' he said. 'Man, if you snatch this sheet of music away, I'll have to fold up.'

" 'Well, I can't handle that sheet . . .'

" 'That's nothing,' he answered. 'I'll see to that. Why don't you come to see me?'

"This was after Malone had left, so I used to go around midday and stay sometimes till he had to leave for the theater at 2:30. The first thing he taught me to do was transpose, playing from the piano sheet music, playing a tone-and-a-half down. Sometimes, if I'd goofed my money off, I'd miss a week and tell him I had had to go out of town, but he'd know when I was lying and he'd want the truth. When I told him I didn't have the money, he said, 'Don't you ever let that stop you from coming. Money isn't why I have you here. I want you to continue. Someday you may remember what I've done.' I don't know what help I was to him, but I'd have him taking solos and getting off. He's in another business and doesn't play anymore, but his father lived on in Sherman and I used to go by and see him when I was home.

"So Malone and O'Banner were my two teachers. They got me where I could go for myself after that. They really put me ahead, because so many of the guys weren't reading then.

"Sherman was swinging in the twenties. It was a good dance town. It seems as though one of the name bands would come up from Dallas every week. It was a rare treat to hear Alphonso Trent. I remember seeing Rudolph Valentino at the Adolphus Hotel one day when I happened to be in Dallas. He was touring the country in patent leather boots! I heard Paul Whiteman's band the same day at the same hotel, and my brother got me backstage to see Bix Beiderbecke and Frankie Trumbauer. Whiteman's band had come in for the automobile show, and I think he had thirty-six pieces. Frankie Trumbauer had a style, and a lot to offer. He and I became real friends in later years when I used to go to Kansas City with Basie. He was in aeronautics there and he would come backstage and stay all day. The first time I ever spoke to him—in 1927 or 1928—he said, 'Practice. You don't get this overnight.' He was a beautiful person. In 1942 he said, 'I remember you, the kid your brother brought backstage. I see you practiced!' I have a box of reeds he gave me in 1943. He bought them in 1924 and I keep them—in a sealed box—for sentimental reasons. I didn't use them because they were for C-melody, but they still *look* good!

"He used to tell me some of his experiences with Paul Whiteman. He had his own plane and used to fly to his gig. One night they were opening at some big hotel in San Francisco. On the way his plane developed engine trouble and it ended up falling on the hotel they were to play. He *swore* this was the truth, that the plane just sat right on top of the hotel. 'See this?' he said, pointing to a scar on his nose. 'This came from that.'

"I used to visit my aunty in Dallas and stay with her. She had a big house and some of Alphonso Trent's boys roomed with her, including

Gene Crook, the banjo player who lives across the street [in Harlem].
It was a terrific band and they had a terrific drummer in A. G. Godley.
He was the first real *solo* drummer I ever heard. That band was always
some mess! Later on, Trent had Snub Mosley, Peanuts Holland, Sy
Oliver, and Stuff Smith.

"Our little band, which we called McCloud's Night Owls, lasted
four or five years. It seemed longer to me then. After we hired the
saxophone player who doubled on violin, we decided we had to have
a trombone player. One of our friends who used to go to the Holiness
churches said, 'I have just the fellow for you guys! You ought to hear
him play. He's a good salesman, too. He can get on his belly and play!'
So we figured we should go and listen to him. We could hear this cat
a block away, he had such a big sound. He could swing, and he could
read. 'He really does sound good,' we said, but when we asked would
he want to join us he said, 'I can't play good enough for your band.'
But we talked him into it. I can't remember his right name, but we
called him 'Booley.'

"Next we added another alto player, Leo Wright's father, whose
name was Mel Nash Wright. By this time, I was playing tenor as well
as alto. When we found we couldn't keep Booley, we got Booker
Ervin, Sr., in his place. Augusta Arterberry, another cousin, came in
on sousaphone, and Rudolph Collins on trumpet. Rudolph was good,
but not an Emmett Malone. We couldn't keep Emmett, he was so
brilliant. So here we were, up to ten pieces, a big band and very popular. We were buying stocks, listening to Fletcher Henderson's records,
to Alphonso Trent's broadcasts, and making up heads of our own.

"My main influence on tenor then was Prince Robinson. I loved that
cat! He was doing some things that were complicated. I always remember him on McKinney's Cotton Pickers' records—*I Found a New
Baby, Zonky, There's a Rainbow 'Round My Shoulder*. He was a pio-
neer, but he didn't keep up. In those years, though, he was out there
with Hawk, and his modulation on *Zonky* used to knock me out.

"On alto, my two idols were Harris Erwing and Booker Pittman.
Booker was the grandson of Booker T. Washington and he played in
a band led by Fred Cooper. Booker was a daring, pretty boy, who
could outplay everyone. The chicks were crazy about him. Then he
was in The Blue Moon Chasers with Budd Johnson. They had eight
or ten pieces when we had only six. We heard them when they came
to Sherman, or when we went to Dallas. The Erwing brothers had a
family band in Kansas City, but their parents were from Sherman.
When I heard Harris in the twenties, he was just the best alto I had
heard in my life, but he never did learn to read. Buck Clayton played

with them, and they went out to Los Angeles. Marshall Royal heard Harris and dug him, too. He said I was right in my opinion of him.

"Marshall's daddy was a bandmaster who played everything. I always knew about Marshall because his mother was from Denison and he was born in Sapulpa, Oklahoma, but I didn't get to meet him till I went to Los Angeles with Basie in 1939. He had a band of local musicians playing *One O'Clock Jump* to greet us on arrival, although the Palomar had burned down the night before we were supposed to open. Charlie Barnet's band lost all its instruments.

"Back with our ten-piece band . . . I was still going to high school, but I was getting that fever. I wanted to play with people like Budd and Booker. Then T. Holder and His Clouds of Joy came to Denison and Sherman. When I heard them I said to myself, 'Man, I have to get with one of those bands!' You get to the stage where you figure you're not learning anymore. Holder was a fine trumpet player who had left Alphonso Trent and organized his own band. He had Theodore Ross and Fats Wall on altos, Slim Freeman on tenor, Big Jim Lawson on trumpet, and Andy Kirk on sousaphone. They were working in Tulsa just before Christmas, and T. took off with all the payroll to see his wife in Dallas. He came back after three or four days, and he hadn't spent any of the money, but the guys called a meeting and made Andy Kirk the new leader. So T. went back to Dallas and formed a second band with Budd Johnson, Booker Pittman, and a boy named Fred Murphy, who looked like Cab Calloway and played alto almost as well as Booker except that he wouldn't play lead. T. had Eddie Tompkins, Eddie Durham, and Jesse Stone, too, and it was a terrific band. Later on, when I was with Andy Kirk, Andy told me T. came through Oklahoma City and looked him up. Andy's band was scuffling and T. said, 'Well, I want to wish you a lot of luck. I've got two or three jobs you can have.' Andy said, 'After me taking his band, for the guy to come by and offer us work like that . . . well, you just can't say anything bad about him.' When T. got to Kansas City, Jesse Stone took the band over. That's that territory thing again. Jesse had had a band there and was better known.

"In the meantime, I left home and went to Wichita Falls with the Night Owls. There was an oil boom and a lot of sporting people there who were spending money like water. It was winter, and *cold*. We went to play a week, but Roy McCloud and I decided to stay and make some money. The other guys quit, because they wanted to go to school, and home. We were making over sixty dollars a week, and it cost only about four dollars a week for a room and three meals a day. I felt I couldn't turn that down! I had one year more to do at school, but I kept thinking that I had time to make that up, and I had my heart set on being a musician anyway. Ross and I joined a band called the St. Louis Merrymakers and one of the musicians in it was Herschel Evans. I had met him a couple of years before when we were playing a job in Van Alstyne. He was in a band coming from New Orleans called TNT, or Trent Number Two! Trent was so popular that they named themselves after him, hoping some of his luck would rub off on them. Where we were playing was a ballroom near the highway, with a swimming pool and everything. There were hundreds of people around, so they decided to stop and join in the fun. Then they asked if they could sit in, and we wanted to hear them, of course. They had so many instruments, those cats would scare you to death! Even if they couldn't play them all too well, they had saxophones standing around like a show. They had lights in the drums, too, and the bass drum head looked like a reflection of water in the ocean. It all made the bandstand look so pretty!

"Herschel had heard about me from my brother in Dallas. He was playing alto then and had about a thousand rubber bands around his instrument, but while all the other guys looked beat he was immaculate, sharp as a tack. He always looked good. He'd been riding all day, but his clothes were pressed and he was a picture of health. . . . He was a good alto player, and he sure did play that night! He was still playing alto in Wichita Falls, where I was playing tenor.

"Then Troy Floyd came out there. He was from Dallas and he'd been working the Gunter Hotel in San Anton', another big white hotel. He had got a job at Shadowland, a ballroom about eighteen miles out of San Anton'. That was when they had roadhouses where people could get drunk. You'd drive five miles up some country road off the highway to a place that turned out to be a beautiful nightclub. The police never came by.

"Troy heard Herschel play on Fletcher Henderson's *Stampede*, and Herschel killed that thing! Troy took him, although he didn't read too well. When they needed an alto later, Herschel told me to come to San Anton' and take the job. 'We'll alternate,' he said, and we both played tenor and alto with Troy.

"While we were out there, the Alphonso Trent band came to San Anton', to play a dance. Herschel asked Troy to lay him off that night.

" 'No,' Troy said. 'If you take off it will cost you five dollars.'

" 'Here's my five dollars right now,' Herschel said.

"Everybody in the band wanted to take off, but the manager of the club told Troy, 'If they do, I'll hire the band you're going to hear.' But all the local bands in San Anton' did take off that night. This was when A. G. Godley had gone to the Blue Devils and Alvin Burroughs had taken his place. Stuff Smith was in the band, and Sy Oliver was director.

"After four or five months, I went back to Dallas, and that was when T. Holder came back from Kansas City to put together his third band. I joined him, playing tenor. Sam Price was on piano, and we had a wonderful drummer named John R. Davis. Red Calhoun, who was Money Johnson's cousin, played brilliant alto. He taught himself everything and he could write anything he heard, so that it sounded just like Duke. He played the blues better than anybody I ever heard in my life. He never left Dallas, wouldn't go any place else, but he could really have made a name for himself had he come to New York. He died of cancer a few years ago, about the same time as Willie Smith. Besides T. playing trumpet, we had Norris Wilson on trombone. When we went to Bonham, Texas, to play the fair, we ran into a college band out of Austin. It was led by Wesley Smith, a fiddle player. Lloyd Glenn was on piano, and there were three Corley brothers—one played tenor, another trumpet, and the third trombone and sousaphone. Wesley had about twelve pieces, but he knew T. had this big, beautiful reputation, so he asked him if he would take over the whole band. When T. became leader, I went along with him, for five years. In 1930, I hired Earl Bostic for him! He had sat in and cut everybody one night. He could do anything on alto, and he could write like crazy.

"When T. Holder's band broke up in 1933, Wesley Smith organized a band for Victoria Spivey. She and Nina Mae McKinney had just made the picture *Hallelujah,* about the first black movie ever produced. Victoria opened a show in Dallas called *Tan Town Revue,* and then we played the circuit of vaudeville houses all through Oklahoma, Texas, Arkansas, and Missouri. Half the band came out of T. Holder's, the other half from Troy Floyd's. We had Joe McLewis on trombone, Nat Towles on bass, a pianist named Jeffrey Perry, and John Humphrey on drums. John was a great drummer, not a soloist but a rhythm man who never varied an inch. Al Johnson was on trumpet and Slow Wilson, C. Q. Price's uncle, played alto. Wesley played fiddle, of course, and he was also a very nice arranger.

"After that, Nat Towles, Al Johnson, and I went to Little Rock to work with Ethel May's band. In those days they used to put an attractive girl in front of a band to sing and direct, and that was what Ethel did. About the time her band broke up, Basie brought a band to Little Rock and I joined it. As I understand it, Bennie Moten hadn't any bookings and agreed for Basie to take most of his band for an engagement in Little Rock. When Moten picked up some bookings, the fellows began slipping off one by one. Lips Page went first. Then

I met Jimmy Rushing one morning about three o'clock. He said he was
going downtown to the drugstore, but I knew there was none open at
that hour in Little Rock. He was sneaking off to the bus station, you
know, to catch a bus! That's the way guys would leave a band in those
days. I stayed because I knew I could go home any time I got ready.
I called Nat Towles in Dallas and told him the band was breaking up.
'Doesn't anybody need any money?' he asked. 'This cat I'm working for
over here has got so much, you can have anything you want.' When
Buster Smith and Joe Keyes found they could get as much as a hundred
dollars, we three went back to Dallas. Towles sounded like Santy
Claus to them. The others all went back to Kansas City.

"Nat Towles was working for a gangster who was really pulling the
strings. He owned twenty-six nightclubs in the city. One of them was
called The Big House, and it had bars inside so it looked like a prison.
We all wore striped prison uniforms, and it was there I met Bonnie
and Clyde and Pretty Boy Floyd. That gangster loved me, said I had
potential, but I didn't want to be obligated to him. T-Bone Walker was
with Towles then, and he was the one who used to go out on the floor
and make all of the money for us.

"Now, after Fletcher Henderson got rid of Lester Young, they sent
to Kansas City for Ben Webster, who was with Andy Kirk. When
Basie heard Andy needed a tenor player, he said, 'Man, we just left one
down in Texas. Send and get him.' So Andy sent me a ticket, and I told
Towles I was going to leave. No contracts in those days! Do you know,
I walked around with the ticket in my pocket for about a month, trying to make up my mind! Dallas was jumping, and we were really
swinging every night. The money was no better with Kirk, but in the
end I went, just to see what was going on in Kansas City. The Kirk
band had a good reputation by then [1934]. Mary Lou Williams, John
Williams, and Pha Terrell were in it. We went east and through New
York State with Mamie Smith, playing theaters, and we were booked
into the Vendome, a very popular place in Buffalo. Then we played
dances as McKinney's Cotton Pickers. McKinney had a lot of dates but
he had nobody to play them because he had lost his band. He would
just make a brief appearance on drums, but he was a good businessman, just like Troy Floyd. When Don Redman fronted the band, I don't
think McKinney did anything!

"The Kirk band broke up in Cincinnati, and I decided to go back to
school, to Wiley College. They'd give you a scholarship if you had an
interview and agreed to play in their band—one of those deals! Joe
'Trombone Buddy' McLewis, who was later with Earl Hines for years,
went with me. He was way ahead, a hell of a trombone player. He
was Henry Coker's idol. Some of the others there were Tom Pratt, a

bass player who could have been another Jimmy Blanton; Duke Groner, who was to be singer and director with Nat Towles; Walter Duncan, a fine trumpet player who's now a doctor; and Earl Bostic.

"Most of us were in there to be in the band, and just jiving. We toured a lot for the school, and for the football games. I see my mistake now. I could have got a lot of theory, and I'm sorry I didn't study to be a teacher. Bostic tried his best to get me to do that. He became a teacher there, and although he was only a year or so older, he later taught Joe Newman. Joe seemed so much smaller and younger then, but when you saw them together in later years they looked to be the same age.

"When we came out from Wiley, about everybody who'd been in the band went with Nat Towles—except Joe McLewis, who went with Clarence Love and Eddie Heywood. Nat was from Louisiana and had originally worked out of Monroe and New Orleans. Now he got some bookings in Omaha. I think Duke Groner had something to do with it. He was a house-stopper, a singer with a high voice like Orlando Robeson, only I liked him better. He used to sing *Trees* and *I'm in the Mood for Love*, and women would just fall out.

"We made Omaha our headquarters and were there three years. We just took that territory over. We played all through the Dakotas, all through Minnesota, and we'd go as far as Chicago. It was very good dance country and mostly one-nighters. We'd go sometimes to a place that looked like a barn in the middle of a field. They were cultivating all around, but inside it would be a fine ballroom.

"We had a sleeper bus, like a Pullman car. There was a cab up front and then seats you could let down like a bunk. There was plenty of room and next to the cab a huge closet with shelves where we put all our uniforms and instruments. There was a john on it, too, and altogether it cost Towles a lot of money. A fellow in Sioux City, Iowa, made it, and not long afterwards all the big bands started getting them.

"There were about four big black bands in Omaha besides ours— Lloyd Hunter's Serenaders, Red Perkins', Ted Adams', and Warren Webb's. When we came there, we just cut them down to nothing! Lawrence Welk was working for the same agency as us, and he was already very popular with his polkas.

"Sir Charles Thompson, Henry Coker, Fred Beckett, and Money Johnson weren't part of the Wiley Collegians, but they joined us there. In those days we all called Money Johnson 'Satch.' 'Money' is a New York nickname. (Later on I got him in Basie's band, in Chicago.) Bob Dorsey, from Lincoln, Nebraska, was formerly a piano player, but he, Lee Pope, and the boy who played with me, Lem Talley, were good saxophonists. Then there was a trombone player named Archie Brown.

He played just like Tricky Sam, but nobody ever got to know anything about him. Debo Mills was the drummer the band always needed.

"Towles had a big book and I learned to read a lot in that band. It was harder music than Basie's, because it was an entertaining band and we did everything, all with a lot of class. We did ballads, and we had good singing groups like Lunceford. Then, too, we had so many guys who could write well. Sir Charles was writing every day. C. Q. Price was terrific, and so was Weldon Sneed, the trumpet player. He was Erskine Hawkins's first cousin. They look alike, and he had real strong chops like Hawk. We used to have two or three arrangements on one tune. For example, *Dinah, Dinah No. 2*, or *Dinah No. 3*; or 35A, 35A–2, 35A–3. This was unusual, and if we played *Dinah* three times in one night the tempos and treatment would vary very much. It was a very interesting band and ready for the big time. We used to beg Nat to go into New York, but he wouldn't and then the boys kind of lost interest. Sir Charles left. Then Coker went to Honolulu. I had a choice to join Basie or go with him to Honolulu. Francis Whitby, a very good tenor player, went in my place, and they made barrels of money over there.

"After I had left Towles, Horace Henderson, Emmett Berry, and Israel Crosby went out to Omaha and took Nat's band, took everybody.

"Basie had sent for me. I didn't know that Herschel Evans had died, didn't even know he had been ill, but I *dreamed* he had died and that Basie was going to call me. That's the truth, so help me God. I had married in Omaha in 1936 and I told Vi, 'Honey, I dreamed Herschel died and that I was going to New York to join Basie.' It happened within a week or two. I still have the telegram Basie sent me.

"When I joined the band in Kansas City, Prez said, 'Come on, Lady Tate, let's go have dinner!' We went to a little place where we always ate in Kansas City, and you know what he ordered? 'I'd like a bowl of red beans and rice,' he said, 'and give him the same.' He didn't give me a chance to order!

" 'Have you been keeping up on your horn?' he asked.

" 'Well, I've been trying,' I answered.

" 'If you're playing anything like you did the last time I heard you, it'll be your gig.'

"This was 1939 and he hadn't heard me play in five or six years. He had kind of settled down and was faster than when I'd heard him before. That time I'd come into Tulsa with the *Tan Town Revue* and he was in the same hotel. He was with King Oliver and he'd checked in that morning and had just gotten to bed. Downstairs in the Small Hotel (the biggest colored hotel in the country), they had a room where you could jam, so I went and woke him up. 'I'm going to make this cat play some this morning,' I told our piano player, Jeffrey Perry. He came down, and I wish I could hear again what came out of that horn! I listened, and then he had me play. He dug what I did and he told me so, which is what he meant when he spoke of the last time he heard me.

"There were plenty of tenor players who wanted the gig with Basie. 'Lots of ladies have eyes,' Prez said, and mentioned the names of several guys who could have had it in terms of reputation. But Basie had remembered me, and had sent for me!

"We played a colored dance the first night, and I'll never forget how those cats sounded and how they swung. They had Skippy Williams traveling along with them, and he wanted the gig, too. We'd each play a while, and he'd say, 'I hope you make it.' He was a beautiful cat, and sincere, and I felt badly when they hired me because he had wanted the job so much.

"The next night we played Kansas City University—a white dance— and the kids kept asking for *Blue and Sentimental*, which had been Herschel's showcase. Basie looked down at the piano and asked, 'Hey, do you know that?'

" 'I can try,' I said.

" 'E-flat,' Basie said, and made the introduction.

"I walked out to the mike and it seemed like a mile. I knew *Blue and Sentimental*, because I'd listened to the record often enough, but I'd never played it. Everybody danced as I played and it broke the house up. All the guys in the band stood up and shook my hand when I finished. 'You're in,' they said. Everybody, that is, but Prez. He just looked up and winked.

"We had kind of a long tour, and then we came into New York and made records like *Rock-a-Bye Basie* and *Taxi War Dance*. I'd never been to New York, and the band had been out so long doing one-nighters that all the guys were glad to get in. I'd never seen a station as big as Pennsylvania Station before, and the guys were all going this way and that way, running and grabbing cabs. I was standing there with a pocket full of money, not knowing where to go, when I saw Prez standing in a corner. So then he looked out after me, carried me along in his cab, got me a kitchenette right next to him and Mary at the Woodside Hotel.

" 'I knew you didn't know where to go,' he said. 'The ladies are excited. They haven't seen their Madam Queens for a long time. You understand?'

"He was a beautiful cat and he had a lot of class. When he was on

the road, he'd have a ball, but when he was in New York he'd stick
with his old lady, just as though he were a one-woman man.

"What set him on the road to ruin? I've often tried to figure that out.
We were in the band together from '39 to '41, when they let him
go because he wouldn't make a record date on Friday the thirteenth.
He had his superstitions. He came back in the band in '43, when they
fired Don Byas. The reason for that? Well, Ben Webster came down
one night when we were at the Hotel Lincoln, and he sat in Don's
chair and played. I never heard anyone sound like that in my life, and
all the cats flipped over Ben. Poor Don went across the street and got
stoned!

"Prez worked until they got him in the army. The way he was drinking whiskey, I didn't think they'd ever take him, but he was healthy
then and he passed *every*thing. He had a big, healthy chest and, although he smoked, he didn't inhale. But the army did him in. He was
actually a jolly, happy cat, but he got sad after that. They put him in
the brig and kept him there a long time. He had made that movie,
Jammin' the Blues, for Norman Granz, before he went in, and Norman
used to send him money all the time he was in there. If you ever did
Prez a favor, he never forgot it in his heart.

"Prez had beaten induction for quite a while. Like a lot of guys
would say, 'Well, I wasn't at that address when . . . I'm traveling with
this band all the time.' When we opened in Los Angeles that year, there
was a sharp young cat there who kept looking at Prez and Jo Jones.
That wasn't unusual, because they were stars. He sat there drinking
whiskey all night, but when we got through he came over and said,
'You, Lester Young, and you, Jo Jones, I have to serve you with these
papers. Be down at the Induction Center tomorrow morning!'

"They thought Prez was crazy down there, because he was talking
his special kind of talk, like, 'Well, boot, then.' . . . 'I see you got
hangman's eyes.' Or: 'I'm with you, ladies.' They thought he might be
putting on an act, so they passed him.

"When they went in the army, Buddy Rich took Jo's place and Artie
Shaw played Prez's part until Lucky Thompson came in the band.
Artie had just given up his navy band, but Buddy was working with
Tommy Dorsey in Hollywood. Tommy started early in the evening and
got through about ten, when Buddy would come over to the Plantation,
a big ballroom in Watts, where we were playing. It was packed every
night and Buddy was our drummer till we got Shadow Wilson. Artie
Shaw was playing tenor parts on clarinet, but Basie wouldn't let *us*
play clarinets. I think the only clarinet player he really liked was
Benny Goodman, although he used to let Rudy Rutherford play, and
Rudy was playing his ass off in those war days.

"When Lucky Thompson arrived, he continued the Byas approach. Lester had naturally been featured more than me, and Lucky was in his chair. Lucky quit when he decided he wanted to stay on the Coast, and then Illinois Jacquet came in. I'd heard him—and Arnett Cobb—when I went to Houston with Nat Towles. They were with Milt Larkins. Norman Granz offered Illinois all that money to play in Jazz at the Philharmonic, so he left and later Basie got Paul Gonsalves.

"We didn't have cliques in the Basie band. Everybody seemed to dig each other. If a cat really got out of line, he'd be over in left field by himself. Then he would come on back in. When we had a disagreement, everybody would help straighten it out on the bus right then and there. Basie was like one of the guys and he'd have a ball with us, but we always knew when he was serious, when he meant business.

"The band broke up in 1948, right after our engagement with Billie Holiday at the Strand on Broadway and 47th. The bop era was coming in and people were confused. Rhythm and blues and rock 'n' roll were getting big, too. Packagewise, bop hadn't really gotten big, but the booking agencies started sending out packages of five or six attractions, each one able to hold its own. It got harder and harder for a band operating by itself when people could see a bunch of acts for maybe just a quarter more.

"I'd been with Basie for ten years, but by the time Murray Bloom, the road manager, called and said the band was getting back together and they were going to rehearse I'd make up my mind I wanted to try something else and stay around New York. After I'd put my transfer in with the union, I soon had all kinds of gigs coming in. There were single dates and a lot of recording.

"I worked with Lucky Millinder at the Savoy for three months. I don't know where he got it from, but money didn't mean anything to him. If he wanted you, he'd pay what you asked. Tab Smith was making four or five hundred dollars with him when most people were asking no more than two hundred and fifty. Lucky hated it when I wouldn't go out on the road with him, but I quit and went to work with Lips Page. He had a good, eight-piece band and we were playing theaters. That's where I met Skip Hall, the piano player. Lips had Vinnie Bair-Bey, a good alto player, Flat Top Wilson on bass, and Herbie Lovelle on drums. When jobs ran out for Lips, Billy Shaw—God bless him—got me some dates, and I asked Lips if I could use some of his guys. He said he didn't mind, and I got Irvin Stokes on trumpet. While we were in Philly, Lips got some work and was peeved with me because he couldn't get his guys back.

"Next, I took Sam 'The Man' Taylor's place in a band led by Ted Fields at the Celebrity Club in Freeport, Long Island. Ted was a drummer who had been to Europe with Sam Wooding. I was living in New York then and I used to hate going way out there. It was too damn far!

"Then Jimmy Rushing got a good nine-piece group together and took it into the Savoy. He had guys like Buck Clayton and Jimmy Mundy writing for him, and the band was very popular for a while.

"After that I was in Lucille Dixon's band at the Savannah Club in the Village for about a year. The front line was pretty—Taft Jordan, Tyree Glenn, and me. Jimmie Evans played piano, Lucille bass, and Billy Smith drums. It was a big club with a floor show, and packed every night. There was a line of girls, about fourteen of the prettiest chicks you ever saw in your life, three acts, three shows a night.

"Irving Cohen, the owner of the Celebrity Club in Freeport, had another club with the same name on 125th Street in Harlem, and he called me one day. He'd noticed that I didn't drink, and he wanted me to take a band in there. He said 'booze was getting the best of all the guys' in the group he had. I couldn't leave Lucille Dixon right away, but after a couple of weeks I opened with Pat Jenkins [trumpet], Shorty Haughton [trombone], Ben Richardson [reeds], Skip Hall [piano], Flat Top Wilson [bass], and Fats Donaldson [drums]. That was in 1950 and I've been there nearly twenty years. That's been my main thing. Eli Robinson took Shorty's place in '53, and we've had several changes in the rhythm section—Sir Charles Thompson, Sadik Hakim, Johnny Acea, and Kenny Drew on piano. Everett Barksdale played fine bass guitar for a time, and he used to break it up with *One O'Clock Jump*. He is a well-schooled musician, and when we had to play a waltz he'd add things, build rich chords. The old piano was always out of tune, so I ended up with George Baker playing electric guitar instead.

"I have to play what the dancers want at the Celebrity. If they're mostly kids, I have to play more boogaloo or James Bond–type things. It's getting so I can play less jazz as time goes by, but I play as much as I can—to their beat. So long as the rhythm is there, they dance to that, and it doesn't matter what the horns play. Sometimes we get people who say we don't play loud enough. What they really want is three guitars amplified to the point where you can't hear yourself talk! But when European fans come over, the Celebrity is one of the first places they go to, and they want to hear jazz. On the other hand, I've never seen any of the well-known New York critics there. The band nevertheless got quite a reputation, so that we'd be hired for social dances at downtown hotels and ballrooms. Depending on the size of the room, I might have to augment to meet the minimum number of men the union required. They usually send a delegate around and if I were not employing the full number I'd be in violation. So that's when I'd have a gig for some of my old friends in the Basie band.

"The last time I saw Prez was at Newport. I'd gone up to play with Benny Goodman in a big band. That was the time the guys got high, played badly, and really let him down. The trumpet players threw their derbies down on the stand while he was trying to make an announcement! John Hammond asked me to stay over to play for Billie Holiday the next night, with Buck Clayton, Jack Teagarden, Georgie Auld, and Pee Wee Russell. We played for Joe Turner and Chuck Berry, too. And Prez came up from Birdland. A friend brought him in a big Cadillac. He was already so weak, he just dragged his case along. We were rehearsing when he came in, wearing that big hat. He'd had a lot of trouble finding the tent, and we were just about ready to quit.

" 'Voo,' he said, standing in the entrance.

"Everybody burst out laughing, he was so funny.

" 'I don't want to hear any of you bitches laughing,' he said. 'I had a helluva hard time finding this molly trolly. I'm tired, and you're all laughing.'

"I didn't know what he meant by 'molly trolly,' but that's what he called the rehearsal. When we finished, he sat at the back of the tent for several hours and drank a little.

" 'Lady Tate,' he said, 'I really don't dig you laughing at me! But I want you to be like my manager and get my money for me. Take out a hundred and send it to my wife. Don't say a fucking thing except, "Hundred dollars, Lester." They're going to dock me at Birdland tonight. They didn't want me to come, but I needed the money.'

"It was three hundred and fifty dollars.

"I went on first that night and later we played together. After it was all over, I went back to New York with him in the Cadillac. We got lost and it took us eight hours from Newport. He talked all the way. I remember parts of our conversation.

" 'You know,' he said, 'I never really made it on my horn.'

" 'Don't feel like that,' I said.

" 'I never really made it on my horn,' he repeated.

" 'What are you talking about? You and Coleman Hawkins have more imitators than any tenor players in the world. They play like you *or* him. So you know you made it.'

" 'But the *other* ladies, my imitators, are making the money!'

" 'You shouldn't say that. I'm not a booker, but I could sell you, because they know you everywhere in the world. The only thing is, you haven't taken care of business like you should have.'

"He was my friend, and I didn't pull any punches when I told him that.

" 'Yeah, I guess you're right,' he said.

"Just a few months later he was dead."

(1969)

Helen Humes

(VOCALIST)

"I was in Bessie Allen's Sunday School band in Louisville, along with Dicky Wells, Jonah Jones, and Bill Beason. I had had piano lessons from a German teacher, but I tried to play trumpet in the band. I didn't really care for it; so when we went out on trips to some of the small towns around I'd play piano in the little jazz group we called The Dandies.

"A lot of us kids in Louisville started singing as soon as we could talk. I used to sing all the time, but I guess I really began seriously at the Baptist church down the street. My father and mother both sang there, and they'd sing duets together right here in this house. My mother had been a schoolteacher, and she was half Cherokee. Her name was Emma Johnson. They used to call my father 'Judge,' because he was in and out of the courthouse all day. He was among the first black attorneys in the city, and he did well in real estate. Besides this house, he owned a farm and other property at one time. He was John Henry Humes, and he had a reputation for being kind to people. I was an only child, and we were a *very* happy family. My parents were always so good to me.

"Our little band would sometimes play at the Palace Theater, and when they had amateur contests I'd slip off and go down there. I remember that the first song I ever sang in public was *When You're a Long, Long Way from Home*; and the first song I sang with a band—in 1926—was *I'm in Love with You, That's Why*.

"It was at the Palace Theater that a guitar player by the name of Sylvester Weaver heard me. He had made records for Okeh and knew Tommy Rockwell, who was producing for that company. He told him I sounded like Ethel Waters; but I was only fourteen, and nobody had influenced me at that time.* We had a piano at home, but no record player or records, and I didn't know anything about Ethel Waters. When I got to hear her later, I preferred her to others, and I've always liked pretty songs, torch songs. Bessie Smith and Ma Rainey were too bluesy for me, but people have always tried to make me a blues singer, right from my first record date.

"Mr. Rockwell had my mother and me go to St. Louis, where I recorded *Black Cat Blues*, *A Worried Woman's Blues*, and a couple of sides that were not issued. I don't know whether the record sold anywhere else, but I know people around home bought it. When Mr. Rockwell wrote us and wanted me to go on the road in some show, Mother told him no—I had to go to school. But she and I went to New York and I made a second lot of records. Then we came right on back.† Of course, I didn't know then what the words of the songs really meant.

"After I got through high school, I took a business course and worked in my father's office. Then I got a job at the first black bank in Louisville, typing and doing shorthand. I had no idea of making a career in music, but I *knew* I didn't want to keep typing! So then for a time I was a waitress in a place called the Canary Cottage, a lovely place right down in the heart of town.

" 'Have you ever worked before?' the man asked me when I went in first.

" 'Yes, but only in nightclubs,' I told him.

" 'Well, go into the kitchen and get me a demitasse cup,' he said.

"I didn't know nothing about a demitasse cup, but I asked somebody

---

* On the early records, Helen Humes sounded more like Mildred Bailey, whom she had never heard and who made no records until a couple of years later.

† The titles were *If Papa Has Outside Lovin'*; *Do What You Did Last Night*; *Everybody Does It Now*; *Cross-Eyed Blues*; *Garlic Blues*; *Alligator Blues*; *Nappy Headed Blues*; and *Race Horse Blues*. Discographies credit J. C. Johnson as the pianist, but John Hammond recalled a conversation with James P. Johnson, who remembered the session and spoke enthusiastically of the singer.

and they showed me. When I went back with the cup, he hired me right away.

" 'You work with the captain today,' he said.

"So I worked with the captain, and the next day he gave me a station of my own. I was so *happy*! I loved that work, and I was there until I left home to go to Buffalo. I went there to visit Margaret Stewart and her husband, Luke, who was a terrific banjo player. He's retired now; but I heard from him last week, and I asked him why he didn't get his guitar out and do something. He goes to visit Jonah Jones all the time. They were in the same school, and they're real buddy-buddies.

"We went to a club in Buffalo called the Spider Web, where Al Sears had the band. 'Make her go up there and sing,' Luke said to Margaret. I was scared, because this was a large place and I hadn't been out in front of an audience like that before. But I got up and sang, and they liked me so well the man asked me would I come and work.

" 'Well,' I said, still scared, 'I'll come back tomorrow and let you know.'

"I went back and stayed for I don't know how long. Then I left and went over to the Vendome Hotel, where Jonah Jones, Luke Stewart, Stuff Smith, Joe Thomas, and all of 'em worked. I was in Buffalo a couple of years, and then I came home. I never was a person to stay away from home too long. Later on, I would always make it my business to come home once or twice a year.

"The following year, I went back to Buffalo, just visiting, not working; and from there I went to Albany. Virginia Scott and her husband, George, were there, and I got to know them when they were in Buffalo. He was a saxophone player, and she was a singer and a dancer. She would do splits, high kicks, and all that kind of stuff. I worked in a club there, but I can't remember the name. While I was back in Louisville again, some man called from Cincinnati. He wanted me at the Cotton Club, and when I got there I found Al Sears had the band —a lovely band, eight or ten pieces. Basie came through in 1937 and heard me sing. He said Billie Holiday was going to leave, and he asked if I'd go with the band.

" 'Well,' I said, 'what does it pay?'

" 'Thirty-five dollars.'

" 'Oh, shucks, I make that here and don't have to go no place!'

"A bit later Al Sears took the band to New York, and I went with 'em. Al got a job with Vernon Andrade's band at the Renaissance, and I would go up there and sing. I guess Basie had told John Hammond about me, because I think John heard me at the Renaissance for the first time. He asked Al and Vernon to see if they could get me to join Basie.

"In the meantime, they had had an amateur contest at the Apollo, and I had come in second. The girl who won sounded *just like* Ella Fitzgerald. She had listened to all Ella's records; and Ella was the biggest thing in show business then, along with Billie. I was happy to be second, but it was like an audition for Basie, because after they had tried that girl he came after *me*. I was glad he did, although the pay was still thirty-five dollars a week, which is what all the guys in the band were getting. Our salaries went up to ten dollars a day when we were on the road, and a little more when we worked theaters. We went into the Famous Door on 52nd Street, and that was where the band really took over. I was with Basie four years, and when I left I was getting more than thirty-five dollars!

"One thing I always remember about Basie was what happened when we were traveling in the South. They have a lot of wooden bridges down there, and when we came to one he would have the bus stop. Then he'd get out and walk across.

" 'What about the boys and me?' I asked him one time.

" 'You can get off if you want,' he said.

"Jimmy Rushing sang all the blues and originals with the band, and I got mostly ballads and pop songs, some good, some not so good. I did *If I Could Be with You; Someday, Sweetheart; Don't Worry 'Bout Me; All or Nothing at All; Between the Devil and the Deep Blue Sea; Sub-Deb Blues;* and a number by Leonard Feather called *My Wandering Man.* My very first record with the band was *Dark Rapture,* but before that I had recorded with Harry James. He used about half of Basie's band on those sessions—Buck Clayton, Herschel Evans, Earle Warren, Eddie Durham, Jack Washington, Walter Page, and Jo Jones. I sang on *I Can Dream, Can't I?; Jubilee; Song of the Wanderer;* and *It's the Dreamer in Me.* That was before Harry had a band of his own.

"Jimmy Rushing and I were close friends in the band, and we always kept in contact. I had a Christmas card from him a while back, and then it seemed right after that they sent an announcement that said he had passed. 'Well, for pity's sake,' I said. I thought of all the laughs and good times we'd had. We made some records together for Columbia out in California, but I don't think they ever were issued. Irving Townsend was in charge of the session, and I remember we did *Outskirts of Town.*

"I used to pretend I was asleep on the Basie bus, so the boys wouldn't think I was hearing their rough talk. I'd sew buttons on, and cook for them, too. I used to carry pots and a little hot plate around, and I'd fix up some food backstage or in places where it was difficult to get anything to eat when we were down South. Playing cards was the best way of passing time on those long trips, but sometimes when I won money from them I found I had to lend it back! I wasn't interested in drinking and keeping late hours, so that part didn't hurt me. But my kidneys couldn't stand the punishment of those long rides. I was too timid to ask the driver to stop when I should have. Then, too, I got tired of singing the same songs year after year.

"So I went home to Louisville, but I hadn't been there long when John Hammond called me to go into Café Society in New York. I had Mr. Teddy Wilson to accompany me, and you know that wasn't bad at all! Then I had Art Tatum for a while. My goodness, that was such a ball! Sometimes he'd play too much, but then I'd tell him: 'Wait a minute now! Give me a chance. Just play something pretty.' He understood, and we were really good friends. It was nice working down there, and I was at Café Society several times. But I remember one time they had a picture of me in the paper right next to some movie star, and in the picture I looked so *fair*.

" 'Miss Humes,' the headwaiter said when I went in that night, 'there's a gentleman waiting to see you.'

" 'Okay,' I said. 'I'll be out in a few minutes when I've got my things on.'

"When I came out, the headwaiter took me over to the man.

" 'Oh, you're colored!' he said, and he looked so shocked.

" 'I certainly am,' I said, and just walked away from him.

"He continued to sit at the bar, but we didn't speak again. I don't know who he thought I was, from looking at the paper, but I'm telling you, you meet some weirdos in this business.

"I was driving through Arkansas one time with my cousin, his wife, and their little girl. The baby wanted to go to the rest room, so I drove up to this gas station and asked, 'Do you have a toilet we could go to?' The man said, 'Yes, back there.' So I said, 'Well, fill the car up with gas.' When I found there was no bathroom, I came back and asked where it was.

" 'Didn't you see it?' he said.

" 'No, I didn't.'

" 'Well, they must have it locked.'

"Then my cousin remembered he knew a doctor three blocks down; and when we came back there was this old gas attendant and the police.

" 'That's the woman, that's the woman!' the attendant shouted. 'She was talking back to me.'

" 'Don't talk to me like you're talking to some of these kids around here,' I said, 'because I came to you like a lady, and you're gonna come to me like a gentleman.'

" 'Well, you know, you're down South now,' the police said.

" 'I was born in the South and I know exactly where I am.'

" 'Well, let's go on and try to forget it,' the police said.

"There are diehards down there, of course, but then you meet others who are just so wonderful.

"Besides Café Society, I also worked on 52nd Street and at the Village Vanguard. It was while I was at the Vanguard one year that I got to thinking that I wanted to be back in Louisville for the Derby. I didn't want to leave Max Gordon without anybody, so I ran around trying to find a singer for him. Somebody suggested Pearl Bailey, and I went all over Harlem looking for her and finally found her. She went from the Vanguard to the Blue Angel, and I don't think she has ever looked back since. She's a wonderful entertainer, and I was so happy for her.

"After I left New York, I went on another tour through the South to New Orleans in a package show. Then I went out to California in 1944 with Connie Smith, the piano player. She was from Atlanta, Georgia, and she had a left hand like a man. The way she hit those keys—oh, she could play! We worked as a team at the Streets of Paris and just upset everything. The people loved us. Lately, she's been playing cocktail piano in hotels.

"I also worked with Nina Russell out there. She played piano and organ.

"I stayed out in Los Angeles and did four or five seasons with Jazz at the Philharmonic. I made a few records and had hits with *E-Baba-Le-Ba* and *Million Dollar Secret*. I never got a nickel of royalty out of *Million Dollar Secret*, but I did get between three and four thousand dollars out of *E-Baba-Le-Ba*. When I asked the Modern people about *Million Dollar Secret*, they said they didn't know it was selling, that somebody must have been selling it 'under the table.' Knowing those fellows, I knew better, but what could you do?

"While I was on the Coast, I played a part in Langston Hughes's *Simply Heavenly*. It didn't last long, but I always remember a review that said, '*Simply Heavenly* is simply Helen Humes.' My voice was used in three movies, *Panic in the Street*, *My Blue Heaven*, and *The Steel Trap*—as well as in the television version of *Come Home, Bill Bailey*.

"In 1952, I was working at a club in San Francisco when I got a phone call from Dorothy Johnson, a very dear friend of mine. We sometimes say we're sisters.

" 'Well, now,' she said, 'you might as well get yourself together, because you're going to Australia!'

" 'No, I ain't going to Australia,' I said.

" 'Yes, you are, because I told the man you were going.'

" 'You better call him and tell him something different.'

" 'You're going with Red Norvo. I know you'll enjoy it.'

"I had met Red casually when he and Mildred Bailey were together. (And I just loved the way *she* sang.) So I met Red again up at the office and we got everything all signed up. 'Oh, Helen,' he said, 'there's nothing to it. You'll like it.'

"But I was scared to death about going that far. I thought the little plane we were in would never make it. At that time you didn't have great big planes like today. 'If I ever get there,' I kept saying to my-self, I think I'm going to stay, 'cause I don't want to come back like this.' They have good musicians in Australia, and after Red had put a quartet together we went over big and had a wonderful time. The promoter wanted me to stay and work by myself, but I told him no, that I had to go back home—because I didn't want to make the trip alone! And Red Norvo had some more work lined up for us here. By the time I went back, in 1962, they had jets and everything, and I didn't mind going by myself. I had a very good Australian group to accompany me, and we played clubs and major hotels for thirteen weeks. The third time I went, in 1964, I stayed ten months, and they tried hard to get me to become a citizen.

"In 1962, I toured Europe with the first blues festival package. T-Bone Walker and Memphis Slim were big names over there, and we did very well. Then I was out in L.A. again, working in Redd Foxx's club, when Mama took sick in '67. I went back to Louisville, and she died soon afterwards. My father was sick, too, and I knew I had to stay. I knew it was what I was supposed to do. I haven't sung since. I got a job in an ammunition plant and, you know, I enjoyed it, enjoyed being with the people there. When we got laid off, I still had my father to care for, and in the afternoons I'd drive with some other women to bingo games. I don't know what Louisville people, particularly the older people, would do without bingo.

"I caught Eubie Blake on the tube the other night, and, gee, he was good—just full of life! This is a funny business. People get out of the picture, and then first thing you know they're big again. I don't know what Newport will do for me. I hope you're right; but it's been so long since I've even tried to sing. I might get a piano back here and rehearse by myself. That would be a way of trying to remember some of those songs."

(1973)

The preceding interview took place in Louisville in 1973, when the writer succeeded, on George Wein's behalf, in persuading Helen Humes to participate in a tribute to Count Basie at the Newport

Jazz Festival. Her appearance was a great success, and it was followed by records, lengthy engagements at The Cookery in New York City, at prestigious clubs and hotels all around the country, and frequent European tours. Her cherished father, who had encouraged her to resume singing, died in 1975, at the age of ninety-six.

In preparation for a European tour, Helen sent a list of her preferred songs for arranger Buck Clayton's consideration, as follows:

Between the Devil and the Deep Blue Sea
'Deed I Do
You're Driving Me Crazy
Don't Worry 'Bout Me
Honeysuckle Rose
Mean to Me (use verse)
Someone to Watch Over Me
I Wish You Love (use verse)
Today I Sing the Blues
I've Grown Accustomed to His Face
A Hundred Years from Today
If I Could Be with You One Hour Tonight (use verse)
Million Dollar Secret
Woe Is Me (a cute calypso)
Kansas City

A charmingly modest note added: "I love the old songs, but the keys I had them in may be too high now. Anyhow, tell Buck my low note is G under middle C, and C above. That will leave me room to play around, because after I sing a while I get clear and higher. Please see if Buck can pick me up a copy of *You've Changed, I Could Have Told You So,* and *You've Got Your Troubles, I've Got Mine.* I like those songs, and one of these days I'm going to sing *I'm Satisfied,* Duke's song that Ivie Anderson used to sing so good. I loved it from the time I first heard it, but nobody ever does it now."

Like the late Louis Armstrong, Helen Humes takes pleasure in what is now almost a lost art: she writes lively and informative letters.

Snooky Young

(TRUMPET)

Count Basie was relaxing in his dressing room before a concert at Carnegie Hall. The conversation touched on tempos, his own preferences and those of different audiences; on the sight-reading ability of today's bands as compared with those of yesterday; and, inevitably, on personalities within his present group.

"Snooky Young? He's very likeable, and wonderful, and dependable," he said warmly.

"Snooky's a gentleman and very pleasant to work with," Buck Clayton had said a few days earlier. "He has a good lip and he's very consistent. In fact, I'd say he's one of the most dependable trumpet players in the business."

"Snooky'll just stand up in the section to take his solo," Emmett Berry remarked on another occasion, "and not come down front. He doesn't have to. He's the kind of trumpet player who can wash everybody away."

Public recognition of the talents engaged in jazz is a haphazard matter, but the musicians themselves judge more surely and have

137

longer memories. Records, fortunately, can often prove the validity of their opinions.

For instance, the two choruses on Basie versions of *Who, Me?* may be compared with the two on Lunceford's *Uptown Blues*, which marked Young's recording debut. Not a few years lie between, but the polished young musician with Lunceford and the seasoned professional with Basie are clearly the same man. There is the same artistic integrity in the solos, the same poise, the same disciplined imagination, the same precise articulation, and the same brilliancy and beauty of tone.

Young was born and raised in Dayton, Ohio. The first instrument he remembers playing was an unlikely one, a zither, but he came of a truly musical family, one that actually operated a "family band." Young's father played saxophone and taught the children music. His mother played banjo, and later, as it became more popular, guitar. His sister, Mary Louise, played piano, and he and his brother, Granville, trumpet.

"Granville and I had a teacher named Ed Sanders, who played in the old Don Redman band and used to come to Dayton," Young recalled. "He took a liking to us and really taught us how to play trumpet. Granville is older than me and there's always been a lot of controversy among our friends. Some of them claim right today that he was a better trumpet player than me. He played with Floyd Ray's band in later years, but he gradually gave up music. He shouldn't have done it, because I think he had a wonderful future ahead of him.

"When I first went out from home professionally, in the family band, it was with a road show called *The Black and White Revue*. They added a drummer, another saxophone, and one or two pieces to our band, and we accompanied the show, but we were an act in ourselves. A drummer called John Godley played with us around home but didn't go on the road. He always said he was a cousin, but he really wasn't any relation at all.

"We went south and got stranded. My father had to take all the blame for that! But I met a couple of people there who were a help to me in terms of experience. I played with Eddie Heywood's father (Eddie Heywood, Sr.). He was a fine pianist and arranger and at that time he was writing for shows and everything. I also played with Graham Jackson, who had a band in Atlanta, Georgia, and because I was so young he featured me out front.

"It took us six months, but we came back from there to Dayton together, the whole family, and we weren't in any hurry to leave again. While we were on the road, we'd had a tutor, but now I went back to school again. I did a lot of playing at night, in clubs and so on, while

I was still in school. I was generally considered fairly advanced for my age and I played with the Wilberforce Collegians before I graduated from high school.

"Louis Armstrong used to come to the Palace Ballroom in my hometown, but I wasn't old enough to be allowed inside. I used to stand in the street—and even the street would be crowded!—and Louis would be playing the most beautiful trumpet I ever heard. This was before air conditioning became so general, and in the summer all the windows would be wide open, and you could hear all right. So when I first began to play, Louis was my influence. I liked the way he played melodic things as well as the 'hot' solos. I thought a lot of Roy Eldridge, too, and though I liked what Dizzy played I never tried to play like him. There are guys like Charlie Shavers and Clark Terry whose work I'm crazy about, and you can't beat those men, but my main influence was Louis.

"After the Collegians, the next band of any size I worked with was Chick Carter's. If it could have stayed together, I think it would have become famous. Most of the musicians in it—like Gerald Wilson, Booty Wood, Ray Perry (who played alto and fiddle), and Eddie Byrd, the drummer—went on to make their names in other bands.

"My next move was to get married, and in that same year [1939] I joined Jimmie Lunceford. Gerald Wilson had gone into that band about six months before and had told Lunceford about me. My wife's cousin had gone to school with Lunceford, and I think his friendship helped me. Gerald always admired my playing, thought I should go places, and used to tell Jimmie, 'If you ever need a trumpet player, I have a young kid around here who can play.'

"It was a great break for me, because Lunceford's was one of the top bands then. I was only twenty and, although I hadn't had so much training, I had had a lot of experience. I replaced Eddie Tompkins, the first trumpet, and I had to play lead. I really wanted to be a soloist, a 'hot' man, and I did get plenty of solos, but since that time I've played lead in most of the bands I've been in. I think I must have been cut out to play first, and now I really like it.

"But it was different in those days. They usually had a lead, a growl, and a get-off man, but today the lead is thrown about more. In fact, I don't think one man could play lead on *every* number in today's books. So much of what we play is upstairs that it would wear one man down. They used to have a high-note man (Lunceford had Tommy Stevenson and then Paul Webster), but now the lead is expected to take care of the high notes. They'll write an F or a G or an A right on the lead sheet, but before, when they wrote an A or a high B-flat, they'd write it for third or fourth chair, the high-note man.

"There was a time when it was a thrill to hear a high note, but now you hear high notes all night long. I think sometimes the arrangers make a mistake in taking such advantage of the musicians' ability to play more. You don't get so much contrast from the brass if you don't have them playing soft and pretty as well. And if the listener gets tired of high notes, you can bet the trumpet player does, too! It's a kick to play them, but if you have to keep pounding them all night, it gets kind of rough."

Young was with Lunceford for nearly three years, and besides the famous *Uptown Blues* he was heard as a soloist on records like *Dinah, Twenty-Four Robbers, Wham, Blues in the Groove, Red Wagon, It Had to Be You, Swingin' on C,* and *Monotony in Four Flats.* "It was a good band," he said, "one of the greatest I was ever in, but what with the war, and the older guys leaving, there was a lot of confusion. When I left and went back home, I asked for the navy, because all my friends were stationed up at Great Lakes, and I was accepted and passed physically fit, but they never called me.

"Count Basie came through Dayton at a time when Buck Clayton was sick with tonsils, and he asked if I would play in the band for about a month until Buck was well. I think that was how I made my way with Basie, because he liked my playing, but the next time I joined him it was to take Al Killian's chair, not Buck's, and at a time when the lead was split between Al and Ed Lewis.

"I went back to Dayton and gigged around for a while. Then I was on the road with Lionel Hampton for about a year. Next, I went out to the Coast to join Lee and Lester Young. They had a trumpet player by the name of Paul Campbell. I stayed at the house with Paul and got to like him, so I wouldn't take the job, because he liked it. I gave Lee back the money he had sent for me to come out and joined Les Hite. Gerald Wilson was with Hite, and I consider Gerald my closest friend, so we were back together again. Eventually, when things began to slow down, we moved the whole trumpet section over and joined Benny Carter—Gerald, Walter Williams, Jack Trainer, and myself.

"While I was out on the Coast, I played in most of the musical sequences in the pictures Lena Horne was making, and I was the off-screen trumpet in *Blues in the Night.* I like the Coast, but things haven't broken yet. I really don't think they've improved *that* much.

"I stayed with Benny until Basie came out and Al Killian was leaving. So I took Al's place, and that was when I was first really one of Basie's men. Later, Gerald Wilson came up with an idea for forming a big band, so I went out to the Coast again and joined him. We came east and played New York, but things got rough for the band in Chicago and St. Louis, and Basie took me back again.

"In 1947, I quit the road, went home, and organized a seven-piece band. I had four rhythm and three horns—trombone, tenor, and my trumpet. Slam Stewart was on bass and Eddie Byrd, who was with Louis Jordan a long time, was on drums. My sister played piano and later on my younger brother, Don Leroy, came in on drums. Booty Wood played trombone for a while, until he formed his own group with three trombones, and he had a good thing there. I gave Frank Foster his first job after he came out of Wilberforce University. Charlie White did the arrangements, and we always tried to keep a big-band feeling in the writing. We traveled all around the territory, in Michigan, Ohio, Indiana, and Kentucky, played all the best places, and I think it was the best band in that area. We opened the Flame Show Bar in Detroit, where we also accompanied Billie Holiday, and we played the Club Valley there. In Dayton, we worked the Classic, a club which ran shows and big names.

"Every time Basie came through Dayton he would ask me to come on back, and I always told him I wasn't coming back anymore. Finally, he called me one day in the fall of '57 when, I guess, I was pretty low in mind, because I said 'yes,' although all the other times I'd been saying 'no.' When I quit the road in 1947, it was to be home and to bring up my three children. They grew up during that ten years. It was a gap in my career, but I thought it was the right thing to do, and I wasn't forgotten completely—not by Basie, anyway.

"I've written a few tunes but I've never done any arranging. One Basie recorded, a little swing thing, called *Let's Have a Taste*. Another I did with Freddie Green a few years ago was called *Free Eats*.

"I feel very happy about being back on the scene. I got attached to the big-band sound and I like playing in a big band better than in a small group. There was a period when I wanted to blow all the time, but now I like to listen to the other guys and I don't care about solos the way I once did. What I really like is to hold the section together, to get that section feeling."

"It's probably only because he's so valuable in the section," Benny Carter said at the end of a Basie record session, "that Snooky hasn't received his due recognition as a soloist. He's equipped to solo well in so many ways. He can play with wonderful expression, as he did on *Pensive Miss*, or he can play real, swinging jazz—just whatever's required. He's an outstanding musician and a powerhouse in any trumpet section."

(1962)

Joe Newman

(TRUMPET)

"My daddy was a musician in New Orleans, where I originally came from. He played in the first Negro band to have a sustaining radio show in New Orleans, on WWL. The band was known as the Creole Serenaders and was approximately six pieces. The three Bocage brothers played in it—Peter, Charlie, and Henry. Peter played trumpet and doubled on violin. Henry played tuba. Charlie used to sing. I didn't like his voice, and there were many other people who didn't, but they still went along. My dad played piano, Louis Warnick played alto and clarinet, and a guy we called Mr. Martin was on drums. During the Depression, they played at the famous old Absinthe House. Before that, I remember, they'd played in a jitney dance hall, where they had girls and the band segued from one number right into another. Men would come in and buy tickets to dance with these girls. They also played in Gretna, just across the river, and my sister and I would go over when they played dances.

"There were six of us children, four girls and two boys. My father and mother both married twice, and they each had two children in

142

their first marriages. My sister Georgia and I were the children of their second marriage. We all lived together and I never could find the slightest bit of difference between us except in terms of complexion. My mother was a Creole, very fair, and with very straight hair. My father was much darker, more Negro. The children of his first marriage were dark, my mother's very fair. My sister and I have the same complexion.

"We had two pianos in the house, one a big, regular upright that would play rolls, the other a big concert grand. The grand was kept locked, but we found how to open it with a pair of scissors. My father discovered we were doing this because the little brass ring that fitted in the keyhole got loose and would fall out. So he forbade us to touch it after that.

"I began by studying drums for about two weeks, but I never cared too much for them. This was around home. I originally wanted to play tenor saxophone. The guy who impressed me most on tenor was Dick Wilson, with Andy Kirk. With the exception of Herschel Evans, I don't think anybody captured that particular style. It really got to me, but I think the style is lost now.

"I always wanted to play music. I can remember times I used to sit up, or *try* to sit up, to hear Louis Armstrong. He used to come to a club called the Club Forest, out near the Jefferson Racetrack. On a few occasions, too, I heard Earl Hines broadcasting from the Grand Terrace. These bands were my beginning, and later the Benny Goodman and Count Basie bands. They all fed my desire to play tenor saxophone. One day I found some zinc pipes that had elbows on them. They curved like the neck of the tenor saxophone, and the bottom curved up like a bell. In the center there was an extension that came out, another pipe, and I used to put my fingers over this, I used to blow it as you would blow a trumpet, and I'd get tones out of it, all with my lip.

"Soon we formed a little band that played birthday parties in the neighborhood, getting maybe five dollars for the whole band. My brother imitated a trumpet with a kazoo, which he had inserted in a can and fitted with a regular funnel, like a trumpet bell. We had one real instrument, a banjo, which belonged to Ernest Penn, whose father was a minister. Ernest could really get over his instrument, and his solos at that time, to me, were amazing. Then my father bought my brother a Conn cornet, one of those horns with a key on it so you could change to A-flat and back to B-flat. He also bought a clarinet for my sister.

"They began giving free music lessons in the high school, but my brother got so he didn't really want to play the instrument. He fooled with it for some time, but then he would take it away from home, hide it under the bridge, and pick it up on his way back from school. Then it got so he didn't take it at all, and it just laid around the house until I picked it up and learned to play tunes on it.

"Sometimes the Creole Serenaders would rehearse at our house, because my father was more or less the leader. One night I went in the back yard, sat on the steps, and started playing along with them. The musicians heard me and came out to see what I was doing. They suggested to my father that I ought to have lessons. The teacher who started me off was David Jones. He had played saxophone and mellophone on the riverboats with Fate Marable, and he gave me very good backgrounds. He had a band of students, most of them older than me, some very much older. We used to rehearse on Sundays. It was a dance band, but it never worked much. Guys in it used to come and get me for gigs. They were like fathers to me and never let me do anything wrong.

"After the Jones band, I remember working in an uptown section of New Orleans with a drummer called Big Warren, who was always smoking cigars. The piano player was Percy Washington, and we used to rehearse at his house most of the time. We played for dances, picnics, or whatever the occasion was. Many weekends, too, I used to play in small groups at beer taverns—like trumpet, saxophone, banjo, bass, and drums. All this was experience.

"I guess I was seven when I began playing cornet. I've been playing all my life, really! There's a special day in New Orleans called McDonald's Day, in memory of a guy who had donated a lot of money to the public schools. All the schools would go to his monument and lay flowers, and all the school bands would play. Earl Bostic had become bandmaster at my school and had started the first band there. I was a tiny little guy, about eight, and he stood me on a chair to solo on a tune called *Washington and Lee Swing*. It was a march, and I always remember that because it was the first solo I took in public. We gave concerts in several different sections of the city. I guess I was pretty versatile at that age, because I also used to do tap dancing and a little singing at concerts and school affairs. We had a quartet for dancing, and other schools like Hoffman Junior High would send for me and my buddies. We'd walk there, nearly ten miles from our school, but our instructors would let us out maybe an hour early. I've really walked all over New Orleans.

"Our closest neighborhood theater was the Tivoli, in Zion City, but my parents would never let me go by myself. The father of one of my friends owned a truck, and on Friday nights he'd pick all of us children up and take us to the show. There was a Buffalo Bill serial then, and I'd have a fit if I missed a week and didn't know what had happened. The point of this is that the theater started having amateur contests. It was part of a chain in New Orleans, and each week there would be a contest in one of the theaters. So I started at the Tivoli, did nothing but play my trumpet, and won second prize. After that I went to a lot more contests, won five or six first places, several seconds, and some thirds. The older brother of one of my friends used to go with me as guardian and manager. It was a nice little hustle for me, because I was able to give this guy a small fee. By this time I was thirteen or fourteen and going to high school.

"I left New Orleans for the first time when I was fifteen. I had met Allegretto Alexander, a marvelous piano player who had worked with Fate Marable on the *St. Louis* riverboat. He was in charge of the music department at St. Francis Xavier University. I was christened Catholic, and that's where all my background comes from. I think it's a very good background and both my kids are Catholic. I'd like for them to come up in Catholic schools. Although I was still in high school, Allegretto had heard of me and the amateur contests. He also happened to be a very good trumpet player, and he took me out on a tour through Mississippi, Alabama, and Texas with the Xavier University Swing Band. My mother came to see me off that particular morning. We traveled in cars, and if we hadn't had to play a return engagement in Mississippi I would have seen her alive again. She died of heart attack the morning we got back. My sister saw me from across the street and burst out crying. I was very close to my mother, and when my sister told me what had happened I came as close to passing out as I ever did. I remember I went down on my knees, and then I came back up.

"Now after my first year in high school, I had a problem with the Sisters, the school instructors. They didn't think a high school student should play with a college organization. I was also playing jobs at weekends, and sometimes during the week at the Rhythm Club with Henry Horton's band. Then I got a wire from Alabama State Teachers College in Montgomery. A young man from New Orleans who was attending school there had told them about me. It was a state-supported school and they used to give scholarships to musicians and athletes. I finally convinced my father to let me go. He didn't want me to go at first, but I was pretty disgusted after my mother died.

"I was at Alabama State a little more than three years. I was in the band the first summer when it toured all through Ohio and then made the big jump to Chicago, where we played in the Beacon Ballroom. The following year I decided to go home for vacation and stay a while. I went by bus, and while I telephoned my father to pick me up I left my bag outside the booth. Somebody stole it and I was really upset, because he took my horn as well. They finally caught the guy, but it soured me and I went back to school after a week, to play with the band, although they didn't tour that year.

"The band got to be so good before I left that we could go to a town like Dayton, Ohio, when Lunceford and all those bands were there, and *still* have a packed house! We used to copy arrangements from Lunceford's and Basie's records, and we'd have others that some of the guys wrote. I remember one in particular on *Avalon* that Dick Hailie wrote. He later became music instructor at Florida A & M. There was another guy named Handy, a funny looking guy whose parents were at Tuskegee Institute. He came down to Alabama State because it was known to have the best band. As a matter of fact, in Erskine Hawkins's time, before I went there, they had three bands, the Collegians, the Revelers, and the Cavaliers. Just before I left, we had two very good bands, and everybody thought a great deal of my playing ability.

"We used to hitchhike to different towns to hear touring bands, and some of the guys went to Birmingham—about a hundred miles away—to hear Lionel Hampton's band. I had a bad cold and couldn't go, but Leroy Williams (we called him 'Monty Googoo,' and he was Cootie Williams's brother) and Isaac Livingston, who played trombone with the Revelers—they found out Hamp needed a trumpet player and they spoke highly of me to him. Hamp asked me to come up to Atlanta, Georgia, the next night. I didn't have any money, nor did my two friends, but they pawned some of their clothes to get me the fare and some money to go up and let Lionel Hampton hear me. So I took the train up, and Hamp said I was to join the band, but he would let me know when. For months I didn't hear from him. I got my father to get me a card from the New Orleans local, because he was on the board of directors. So I was ready.

"The purpose of college bands like ours was to create funds to help keep the school running properly, because state support didn't represent enough money. The music was just a means to our tuition. I had a place to stay, I had my meals, I had doctor care, and I had my books—I didn't pay anything. My parents gave me spending money and some to buy clothes. But by this time it was in my blood to leave.

"Some of us decided we would form a band from the better musicians in both bands. The music belonged to the guys anyway, because the school only gave us the paper to put it on. We took the arrangements and left. The fact that Erskine Hawkins had done it earlier gave us a little inspiration. We made a contract with Dillworth Attractions, an agency in Atlanta, and they sent a bus for us. I hadn't quite made up my mind to leave then, but the guys packed my bags and carried me bodily on the bus. They also said that if I went I could be leader of the band. So I went, although it was supposed to be Joe Morris' band. Joe was a trumpet player, too, but I fronted the band and was really the leader.

"We got to Miami and played our first date in a club owned by Bill Rivers, a pretty wealthy Negro. When this guy Dillworth messed up some kind of way, Rivers decided to furnish our keep. We worked in his place weekends and he took over the band, buying stands and uniforms for us and putting us in hotels and private homes. He was a wonderful guy. We were there two or three months, and then Lionel Hampton got in touch with me again. So now I didn't know whether I wanted to leave or not. I spoke to Bill Rivers about it, and he said it was my decision to make but he offered to buy me a wardrobe, a diamond ring, and any kind of horn I wanted if I stayed. In the end I decided to go, and I joined Lionel Hampton in Chicago early in 1941. I was eighteen then.

"Lionel had formed his band on the West Coast the previous year, and we had heard it on the air. He had a lot of good men like Ernie Royal on trumpet, Dexter Gordon on tenor, Jack McVea on baritone, Marshall Royal on alto, Ray Perry on violin and alto, Vernon Alley on bass, Sir Charles Thompson on piano, Irving Ashby on guitar, and Shadow Wilson on drums. They had something different, and they were really swinging. But what chiefly influenced me in going with them was Illinois Jacquet. Most of the guys who were from Texas in our band knew him, and they all spoke very well of him and his ability.

"I stayed with Hamp till December 1943, when I went with Basie at the Lincoln Hotel. What encouraged me to go with him specifically was Lester Young and Jo Jones. Hamp's band was at the Famous Door, over the House of Chan, back of Birdland and on Seventh Avenue. The night we closed, Jo Jones came by and said Buck Clayton had to go in the army, and would I come and sit in with the band? Basie decided to keep me, and I worked with his band a year or so until I decided to stay in New York and get my union card. I was with Cootie Williams about a month, and we did theaters in a package deal with Ella Fitzgerald and the Ink Spots.

"During the time I was getting my 802 card, Basie was in California. By this time he had Illinois Jacquet and Shadow Wilson, so when he called me I went out, rejoined the band, and came back with them to New York. I stayed with Basie until Jacquet decided to leave and form his own group, and I went with him. At first there were just the two of us. We'd go to different towns and hire a rhythm section. One night we played a dance for Norman Granz in Washington, D.C., and that was where Leo Parker joined us. He was one of the best modern baritone saxophonists. He used to make it pretty hot for Jacquet, without knowing it. He loved Harry Carney, and Harry would tell him things. Leo really *manhandled* that baritone, but he got messed up, which was a shame. Later he contracted TB and one of his lungs collapsed. He had a tune called *Mad Lad,* and I made several record dates with him.

"After a time, Jacquet wasn't getting enough work, so I went with J. C. Heard's band at downtown Café Society for almost a year. I took George Treadwell's place. It was the last job he worked as a musician before he went with Sarah Vaughan and took over her affairs. J.C. had a very good band: Big Nick Nicholas on tenor, Dicky Harris on trombone, Jimmy Jones on piano, Al McKibbon on bass. We started off well, but a little incident came up when we took off and played a benefit at the Apollo. Barney Josephson, at Café Society, was pretty torn up about it when we got back to the club. J.C. had a six-month contract and when it was up Barney wouldn't renew it. I went back to Jacquet for about a year, and then rejoined Basie in January of '52. I'm still with him, and I've had many happy, lovely days with the band.

"I haven't said much about my own musical influences. The first and biggest, of course, was Louis Armstrong. I went to hear him when I was still in grade school. He was playing at the fairgrounds, and I got on my old man so there wasn't anything for him to do but give me the money to go. Somebody must have told Pops about me, because he gave me a mouthpiece. I also became interested in Fats Waller. They used to play his records on the radio, and my sisters were crazy about him. He was so jolly in his way of putting tunes over. But Louis Armstrong was my first idol, and the biggest influence of my whole career. I liked everything about him—his singing, his playing, and what he played, all seemed very colorful to me.

"After Louis, I guess it was Roy Eldridge, because I had a picture of him on the door at home where I could look at him. I used to hear him on the radio, and they were hopping, one of the hottest groups you could ever hear. When bop, Dizzy Gillespie, and Charlie Parker came along, I realized that what I was hearing was something very advanced, but I didn't quite get with it at first. A lot of it I didn't understand, and some of it I didn't like. But now I think the world of Dizzy and admire him. He's one of the greatest, personally as well as a musician. I like the way he treats me and other people around him. If there's anybody to follow Louis in the public's mind and eye, it will be Dizzy Gillespie, in spite of his clowning.

"I don't like some of the things Louis says and does, but to be his age and still able to do what he's doing today—well, I don't think there's a person living as great as he is. Most of the trumpet players who've come behind him have failed to realize that Louis made it all possible. I'm not trying to get on a soapbox about it, but this is the way I feel. There are guys younger than me who don't feel this way about him, because they don't know what he accomplished and can't see what I've seen through *experience*. There are so few musicians today who could really play in bands like Basie's. They don't have the background, and they haven't had the opportunity to hear the old stuff. There are guys in the band right now who never heard Lunceford's band, and that, to me, seems fairly recent compared to a lot of other things. We have a younger influence in the Basie band now, but the old flavor's still there. The changes mostly reflect the work of the arrangers.

"People throughout Europe are more serious-minded about jazz and not, in general, as prejudiced about it as the American public. A lot of our critics, and the younger fans, frown on older guys like Louis Armstrong. The only reason I see why Basie's band is as well received as it is is because there aren't many other big bands. We've had the opportunity to reawaken the older people's interest, and by surviving we have attracted a lot of youngsters too. We've been criticized in many ways. Some writers have said the band plays good ensemble but doesn't have any soloists. That's usually because they're prejudiced in favor of a more modern type of soloist. But as I was saying about Louis, it took the other styles to make the new styles possible. They couldn't have been if the guys hadn't listened to what went before. From Louis came Roy, and from Roy came Dizzy. Dizzy was imitating Roy at one time. It takes a while for a musician to realize what he really wants to play, what he wants to do on his instrument, and where he wants to go.

"Dizzy is more mature now and knows where he's going. A lot of guys *don't* know where they're going. They're not sure. . . . Some of them don't know the first thing about music to begin with, and then there's the matter of jumping on the bandwagon. A lot of people like Basie because the majority likes Basie. Apart from Duke Ellington's, there are so few other bands really surviving.

"We always play music that can be *felt*. At many places we've played, the people could not dance, but they *wished* they could. It's the beat that really gets under people. Of course, a lot of people want to be critics, but there aren't many critics who have the nerve to say, 'Well, I don't think much of Basie now.' There was one who compared us very unfavorably to the old band and said that we were *nothing,* but he lied, because he'd come in, sit down at ringside, and pat his foot all night! His feeling, when he wrote his article, was just a sentimental feeling.

"Musically, anything that isn't melodic doesn't really impress me. No matter how much you vary music, you've got to have a melodic line somewhere. You don't get over to the ordinary listener if he can't remember some part of what you've played. By the same token, how many of the people who claim an abstract painting is the greatest can tell you what it is?

"There's a type of person who wants to be right all the time, wants to be *with* whatever's happening. So many different types of people follow music. Some do, not because they love it, but because it provides an outlet for them. Like when we play Birdland, a lot of guys and girls come down there of the sportin'-life type. They come because at different times the band has had a following of a lot of chicks that came around not because they like the guys but because they like what we play. I think women are more true in their convictions about music than men are. They're more apt to say what they really feel than men. Then, too, a lot of men who come to Birdland don't give a damn about us, but come to make contacts with those girls.

"People also follow music because they think it's glamorous. I did, too, at one time in my life. But recognizing it for what it is, I love music for what I feel in my heart, not because somebody else likes it. There are some musicians I don't care for, just as there are probably some who don't care for me, but if I can't say anything good, I won't say anything."

(1960)

Preston Love

(ALTO SAXOPHONE)

"I joined Count Basie's band as Earle Warren's temporary replacement on September 6, 1943. Except for the fact that Rodney Richardson had recently taken Walter Page's place, and that Lester Young was absent, most of my early heroes of the band were still there. All of the early Basie aura and atmosphere were intact, and the band was still at an absolute peak. Everything about playing with a 'name' band was new to me, and the six weeks I spent in it were utopian.

"The band was still playing nearly all the great hits from the early years when Basie 'exploded' on the music scene. I owned all his records and had listened to them ecstatically thousands of times. I had also heard them on network broadcasts and in person. It was like being in heaven to play the first alto part on *Swingin' the Blues, Goin' to Chicago, Harvard Blues, It's Sand Man, More Than You Know, One O'Clock Jump*, etc. The first time I played *Moten Swing* with the band, I could hardly restrain my emotion and excitement when Dicky Wells began to blow those incredible and uniquely colorful obbligatos behind me. The other trombone men became a bit annoyed

151

at my youthful enthusiasm as I fidgeted around and exhorted 'Mr. Bones' to 'pour it on!'

"*Moten Swing* had a special meaning for me, because when I was with Lloyd Hunter's band in 1941, Lloyd and some of the older members of the band sharply criticized Basie's recording of the number. They said Buddy Tate's tenor part stood out as loud as the lead alto's in the organ harmony behind Sweets Edison's trumpet solo. They also found it unforgivable for the lead trumpet and lead alto sax to play the same melody notes, doubling together as they did in the last chorus. With all my youthful zeal, I would remind Lloyd and the older guys that it was stupid to become analytical where great art and jazz were concerned. The final product is all that counts, regardless of how the artist arrives at it. And they had to concede that in spite of breaking rules, Basie's *Moten Swing* was beautiful, soulful and that it 'sure did swing.'

"I was barely twenty-two in 1943 and it was understood that I was only 'spelling' Earle Warren. My ability to imitate him closely, my youth, and enthusiasm for the band made me quite a novelty, so that I became a kind of pet with the older Basie band members. I enjoyed that immensely! The more experienced men by this time took for granted such things as the high-class mode of travel, the fancy ballrooms, nightclubs, and theaters, but they were all novel to me. I felt my life and musical experience were absolutely complete when we played a one-nighter at Castle Farms in Cincinnati and I made my first coast-to-coast broadcast. I could hardly believe that Omaha's 'Love Boy' was in Earle Warren's chair, broadcasting over WLW with Count Basie.

"During this 1943 period we played a one-week stand at four theaters and two weeks of one-nighters. My last week was at the Apollo Theatre in Harlem, where Earle Warren played some of the shows and I did the others. At that time it was the ambition of all black musicians to play the Apollo, so naturally I was very excited to be there. An even bigger thrill was in store for me, because Lester Young rejoined the band, taking Don Byas's place. This was my first and only opportunity to work in the same reed section with my favorite tenor sax player, one of the geniuses of jazz history. I could hardly play my part, because I kept glancing to my left to observe Lester and his unique playing pose. We opened with an up-tempo version of *Swingin' the Blues*, and at the first notes of his famous recorded solo the whole house went wild!

"Playing for stage acts as at the Apollo was another first in my musical experience. Backing comedians, dancers, acrobats, magicians, and other kinds of performers was so new and different from playing in ballrooms or for listening audiences. I loved the variety of music and changes of tempos theater acts required. Basie's band put the same feeling and personality into the show music as they did into their own repertoire. To me, in 1943, playing shows seemed to represent the real big time of the band business.

"My six weeks ended all too quickly and abruptly for me. I had just begun to feel comfortable with the repertoire and to relax a bit. In that era, the Basie mystique was probably matched only by that of Duke Ellington's. There was a personal style about everything these two bands did, including their dress, their slang, their humor, and the relationships within the personnel. Earle Warren, or 'Smiley' as he was called, was part of all this, so I couldn't help feeling like an observer. I never really felt like an insider, but my enormous admiration for Earle and the band did give me a special status in the Basie 'family.'

"As an alto man, I also admired other lead men. I rated very highly Willie Smith with Lunceford, Otto Hardwick with Ellington, Hilton Jefferson, Milt Yaner, and a young man I heard with Fletcher Henderson called George Fauntleroy. So long as Willie Smith played in the context of the Lunceford style, I admired him as much as Earle Warren, but when I heard him later with Charlie Spivak, Duke Ellington, and Harry James, he sounded less impressive. In fact, I think Willie played far below his own personal standard in every setting I heard him in outside that of the Lunceford band.

"Apart from who was the best or greatest alto sax man, Earle Warren's sound and conception were for my taste always ideal, but I question whether his style would have fitted the Lunceford band, where the reeds used straight tone without vibrato and put more emphasis on the 'moaning' quality.

"After Earle returned to Basie in late October 1943, I went back to Omaha and worked with Lloyd Hunter a couple of months. Trevor Bacon, Lucky Millinder's singer, had heard me at the Regal Theatre in Chicago with Basie, and he urged Lucky to send for me. On January 4, 1944, I received a train ticket from Millinder, and I joined his band two days later at the Fay's theater in North Philadelphia.

"Millinder's band was not the equal of Basie's, but it was a fine one, and now I had the opportunity to work with Tab Smith, whom I had seen playing third alto next to Earle Warren when Basie played Omaha in 1940 and 1941. I worked with Millinder intermittently until April 1945, and I made my first recording in May 1944 with his band. We made five sides for Decca, including Wynonie 'Mr. Blues' Harris's first records, *Hurry, Hurry* and *Who Threw the Whiskey in the Well?* The other titles, on which Judy Carol sang, were *Darlin'*, *Lover Man*, and *I Just Can't See for Lookin'*. Judy was born Winelda Carter and, like Wynonie, she was from Omaha, so that made three of us.

"When the Millinder band was in New York, I would hang out with Basie's musicians if they were in town, too. I would go down to the Lincoln Hotel or backstage at the theater, wherever they were playing, and I was more awed by the band and Earle Warren than ever. My dream of playing in Earle's chair seemed remote, until one day in the spring of 1945 he told me he was going to leave and form his own band, and that his chair would then automatically be mine. I quit Lucky Millinder in a state of jubilation and went home to Omaha. Basie called me on May 25 and I set out for New York again the next afternoon. My ecstatic family and incredulous friends were at the railroad station to see me go, and it would have been a really triumphant moment if my brothers had been there, but I was the only male member of the Love family in Omaha during these wartime years.

"When I arrived in New York, I took a cab to the Braddock Hotel at 126th Street and 8th Avenue, where I had stayed before. Then I took the subway downtown to the Roxy Theatre, where Basie was playing. The band was on stage and I eased into a place between the curtains only a few feet from the reed section. (The wings of a theater are by far the best vantage point from which to hear an orchestra.) Buddy Tate was nearest me, and when he caught sight of me he nudged the other sax players—Earle, Jimmy Powell, Lucky Thompson, and Rudy Rutherford (on baritone sax). Jimmy had been alto in the 1943 band, and I had worked with Lucky briefly in the Millinder band in 1944.

"There were several new faces in key positions in this wartime Basie band, but it was still fantastic, and still *Basie*. Shadow Wilson had replaced Jo Jones when Jo went in the army, but Basie, Freddie Green, and Rodney Richardson were there as in 1943. Karl George on trumpet and J. J. Johnson and Ted Donnelly on trombones were the only members of the brass new to me. Jimmy Rushing acted as my 'guardian' at this point, and Earle Warren encouraged me about my future in the band, counseling me on negotiations with Basie management. When the Roxy engagement ended, we left for a one-nighter in Johnstown, Pennsylvania. Earle came down to see us off in the charter bus in front of the Theresa Hotel on 125th Street. I detected a little melancholy in his manner, but he couldn't know how happy he had made my life.

"This 1945 band was a formidable group of musicians, but without Jo Jones, Jack Washington, Walter Page, Buck Clayton, and Earle Warren there had to be a difference. I constantly measured my performance against Earle's, and came up very short in my own estimation. I actually resented it when fans and columnists compared me favorably with that great man. One reviewer caught us at a Cleve-

land theater and wrote: 'At least Basie's reed section has gotten together, thanks to the presence of a fine young lead sax man who replaced the erratic Earle Warren.' I called him the next day and told
him that he knew nothing about lead sax, that Earle was the greatest
lead man in history, and that to compare me with him, especially in
Basie's band, was stupid. After many years and much more experience, I am even more amazed at lead men like Earle and Willie
Smith. They are as incredible in their way (of leading a section) as
were geniuses like Art Tatum, Lester Young, Charlie Parker, and
Clifford Brown in their solos.

"On October 15, 1945, I had the great personal thrill of making my
first records with the band at CBS in Hollywood—*Queer Street*,
Jivin' Joe Jackson, *High Tide*, and *Blue Skies*. That night, our road
manager handed out a new itinerary for our trip back east. My heart
almost stopped when at the top of the list I saw 'Orpheum Theatre,
Omaha, October 22–28'! Ever since I was ten years old I had been
going to the Orpheum to see all the famous bands and their stage
shows—Duke Ellington, Cab Calloway, Erskine Hawkins, Jan Garber,
Lucky Millinder, Charlie Spivak, and for the first time, Count Basie. To
go from the poverty of the Love Mansion and Omaha's ghetto to the
Orpheum stage seemed too far-fetched to a black kid of my generation. Nearly every kid I knew, musician or not, had dreams of per-
forming on that glittering stage some day. The Orpheum simply represented the 'big time' of Omaha.

"I began counting the seconds when the Union Pacific *Challenger*
pulled out of Los Angeles and headed east for Omaha. Union Station
seemed to be crowded with members of the Love family and friends.
They were there to greet me and Buddy Tate, whom they thought of
as an ex-Omahan. If Jo Jones hadn't been in the army, there would
have been a contingent of his friends there, too. After directing some
of the band members to the best rooming houses in the ghetto, I was
whisked off to one of the nightclubs on the main street of the black
community.

"North 24th Street was buzzing like a bee that night, with Count
Basie's band in town and with a night off before the Orpheum opening. I almost got tired of taking bows at the clubs on the 'Avenue,' the
term we used for the area of 24th and Lake streets, the main intersec-
tion in our part of town.

"My wife and I still maintained our Omaha apartment. She and our
three-year-old son had been with me in California for three months,
but they had left a few days ahead of the band's departure. I awoke
earlier than usual, because I had invited Bill Doggett to breakfast.
Being an early riser, he arrived promptly on time at ten A.M. He was

traveling with the band as staff arranger, and occasionally Basie would let him sit in on piano. We had our bacon and eggs and set off in good time for the theater. I stopped on the way to pick up some accessories at the Hospe's Music Store, sauntered south on 15th Street, and turned into the alley leading to the Orpheum stage door.

"The movie was on and I could see that the band valet had been there earlier that morning to set up the bandstand before it began. The five chairs for the reed section were on the side nearest me. A lot of friends and well-wishers were standing around, but I finally found one of the better dressing rooms upstairs that Buddy Tate had staked out for himself and me. In a few minutes they called the 'half-hour' before the show so I changed clothes and warmed up my horn. It seemed like no time at all before someone yelled 'All on!' Down the steps and into my seat I went. Then I remember Basie's piano intro to *One O'Clock Jump* and his signaling 'Line Ten,' which meant for the reed section to begin its opening riff on the number.

"All the lights were bright on the stage and the curtain began to open as the moveable stage rolled forward. So here I was before a hometown audience at the Omaha Orpheum Theatre. Blacks were still 'requested' to sit in the balcony of downtown theaters then, but there in the front row were a gang of my life-long buddies, among them 'Brother' Joe Allen, Maxine 'The Red Fox' Parker, Basie Givens, Bernice Donaldson, and Bernard Butler. They cheered and pointed to me, and I could also hear a murmur of excitement from the balcony, where other ghetto friends were seated.

"After a short version of *One O'Clock Jump*, the band launched into an up-tempo number called *B-Flat*. For the next hour, Basie and his stage show had the audience wild with delight. He never gave any special recognition to band members when the band was playing their hometowns. That was the band policy, so I had only a short solo on each of the five daily shows—the eight-bar bridge Earle Warren had played on *Jumpin' at the Woodside* or the one on *Rock-a-Bye Basie*.

"Pop, the backstage doorman, soon learned I was a hometown boy by the visitors who came to see me. He had instructions from the management to curtail the number of people backstage, but he realized this was my moment of glory, so there would always be a crowd of my friends and relatives backstage, in the wings or in our dressing room.

"My mother had purchased a fine home in 1944 with money sent by my brothers, Norm and Dodda, from their army pay, and during the week my sisters gave several huge parties there for the entire Basie band and show cast. At each of these affairs, Jimmy Rushing and

Sweets Edison were the life of the party. What with playing piano and telling jokes, they kept everybody lively. I think of them as two of the cleverest individuals ever in show business.

"The night we closed at the Orpheum, we had to hurry to Union Station to catch a late train to Minneapolis, where we were to open at another Orpheum. I was very excited again at the thought of seeing my brother Dude there, when he would get to hear his kid brother play first sax with Count Basie for the first time. (When the band returned to Omaha the following year, it was an added pleasure for me because my two other brothers were home from the war in Europe.)

"Nineteen forty-six was really the most significant year of my stay with the band, because Jo Jones and Walter Page returned to reunite the famous Basie rhythm section. Jack Washington was back from the army on baritone saxophone, and in some ways this little giant was the greatest saxophonist ever to play in the band. If Buck Clayton and Earle Warren had only been there, it would have been one of Basie's best bands. In the summer of 1946, too, we 'discovered' a young tenor sax man named Paul Gonsalves, who replaced Illinois Jacquet, who had taken Lucky Thompson's place in October 1945. I never felt Paul's style fitted Basie's band ideally, but he was a true virtuoso and we became very good friends. Of course, he went on to distinguish himself in the great Duke Ellington band.

"Perhaps the most overlooked member of the original Basie band was Ed Lewis, the lead trumpet player. Ed played nearly all the lead on the 'classic' recordings when Basie had only three trumpets, Buck Clayton and Sweets Edison being the other two. In person, Buck or Sweets would occasionally relieve Ed by playing the lead on a riff or a prolonged number, but even after Basie added a fourth trumpet, Ed still played a predominant part of the lead.

"Much of the Basie sound was Ed Lewis. He 'grew up' with the original Basie style from Kansas City and captured the essence of the Basie feeling and the Kansas City charm. Ed had a sweet, delicate sound, but he played definitively. Basie's was the greatest swing band with the most relaxed feeling in jazz history, and Ed always swung like no other lead trumpet probably ever did. We always referred to his lead as 'funky,' far before the word came into common usage in connection with rhythm and blues.

'I rate Snooky Young as the greatest of all jazz lead trumpets. For power, finesse, and the ability to interpret a part, he is without equal. But in Basie's band, Ed's lead had a very special quality that fitted the Basie style. I heard Ed and Snooky together nightly for nearly three years, and although Ed was nearing the lower curve of his greatness as a lead man, he still gave a beautiful account of himself on the more characteristic Basie arrangements. He would still 'spit out' the lead on numbers like *It's Sand, Man*, just as he had years before. Then, towards the climax of the arrangement, the younger man, Snooky Young, would take over with high notes on 'shouting' out choruses.

"Ed Lewis gave his all to the Basie band during its rise to the top. He may even have burned his lip out by playing *all* the lead in the young powerhouse band of 1937, 1938, and early 1939. Unfortunately, his kind of dedication was never properly rewarded.

"Nineteen forty-six was really the last 'glory' year for the Basie band of the thirties and forties. Bookings were still good, crowds were still large, and the band still regularly played the most prestigious nightclubs, theaters, and ballrooms. However, storm clouds were brewing. Bebop was becoming the popular craze in jazz, and Basie hadn't had a hit record or anything dramatic happen in quite some time. When the war ended, the country's economy changed drastically. Early in 1947, as if at some prearranged signal, things declined sharply for the Basie band.

"After a tour of the West Coast, we played a one-nighter at a ballroom in Philadelphia on our way back to New York. It was late January of 1947 and the crowd and enthusiasm were much less than when we played there before. Before intermission I noticed a group of young fellows standing attentively in front of the reed section. Occasionally they would whisper to each other. From their manner I judged them to be young musicians from the same orchestra or local clique.

"At intermission, they beckoned me to join them in front of the bandstand. A spokesman for the group said, 'Man, we want to talk to you because you're a young cat. How can you stand playing those old-fashioned arrangements, man? Diz was here with his big band, and that's what's happening! Basie better get hip and get some new stuff. We know if you tell him what's happening, he will listen to a hip young cat!' Then one of them pointed to Buddy Tate. 'They don't play like that anymore,' he said. 'That other tenor man [Paul Gonsalves] can kinda get by, but that old cat has got to go!' The whole group laughed in agreement.

"I was twenty-five years old, the youngest member of Basie's band, but I felt nothing in common with these beboppers. But I did realize that the mania for change and newness in both show business and the music business had finally caught up with even my beloved Count Basie band.

"Looking back to that night in 1947, I wonder how those young musical 'revolutionaries' feel about youth, age, and changes in music now that they must all be in their early fifties. Buddy Tate has survived as a highly esteemed figure in jazz, but I wonder if any of that clique ever made a name for posterity to remember. Buddy always played tastefully in the purest jazz idiom, compensating for a lack of virtuosity with expression, a big sound, a driving beat, and by always telling a meaningful and unpretentious story in his solos.

"Bookings fell off sharply as 1947 progressed, as did the caliber of the places where we were forced to work and the size of the crowds. Some of the better bookings were retained, but there were more one-nighters, unpaid vacations, and 'short weeks' in which we worked less than five days for reduced salaries.

"In early June, Basie called a meeting and announced that summer bookings were few, but that his manager had the opportunity to book the entire summer season at the Club Paradise in Atlantic City if the payroll were reduced to meet the club's top offer. It meant a sharp reduction for all of us, but we agreed to it rather than go through the summer unemployed.

"Although the cost of living in Atlantic City was staggering, by careful budgeting all of us were able to have our families with us to enjoy the resort atmosphere. The hours at the Paradise were brutally long, but we had a fine show complete with Ziggy Johnson's revue and a line of attractive chorus girls. Like a well-conditioned athlete, any band shows the effect of a long location by becoming tighter, and on its better nights, the Count Basie band almost 'burned down' that little Club Paradise.

"Our competition in Atlantic City came from the other main black club, the Club Harlem, which presented the Coleridge Davis big band, Larry Steele's *Smart Affairs* revue, with twelve beautiful chorus girls, Moms Mabley, Billy Daniels, Top and Wilda, Derby Wilson, and others. The musicians and performers from both clubs soon had a wonderful rapport.

"Basie's band had a fine softball team organized by Paul Gonsalves, Jack Washington, Ted Donnelly, Sweets Edison, and me. We played several mornings each week after we got off at five A.M. We played teams from the Harry James, Charlie Spivak, and Louis Prima bands when they were working in Atlantic City. We also played teams made up of bartenders and waiters from the black clubs, as well as teams formed by the black policemen and firemen of the city. I played third base and Paul Gonsalves played shortstop. If you could have combined my ability to catch sizzling grounders with Paul's riflelike throwing arm, we would have had the finest shortstop–third-base combination in jazz. But Paul was prone to miss a few catches, and I always had the worst throwing arm in the world. We won only occasionally, but the games were great fun. The stands would be full of celebrities, because nearly every star of black show business visited Atlantic City during the season. Some of them would play with us for laughs, and after each game there would be a big party.

"Freddie Green, Ted Donnelly, my son, and I went crabbing once a week. We had bought ropes and crabbing baskets, and we would walk several miles to an inlet where we stood on a little bridge and caught hundreds of ocean crabs. Freddie was from Charleston, South Carolina, so he was right at home on the seacoast with crabbing basket in hand! He was also a master swimmer. Emmett Berry, singer Bob Bailey, and I once made the mistake of trying to swim with him in the ocean. The three of us had a frightening time when we found ourselves far out beyond our safe limits.

"Snooky Young, his wife, and three children, C. Q. Price (the third alto man) and his wife Mildred, together with my wife, son, and me, shared a three-bedroom apartment, which reduced our costs to a minimum. The three families worked out the cooking arrangements very harmoniously, considering that there were ten of us in a rather small space.

"The season at Atlantic City traditionally ends with Labor Day, but Basie's management got a booking at the Strand Theatre on Broadway in New York, so we closed at the Paradise on August 22. It had been a surprisingly enjoyable eight weeks.

"Hot Lips Page opened at the Paradise the day after we closed with a hastily put together band. We stayed one day to catch his opening with the same show we had played. Hot Lips had a much smaller group and most of his men were good jazz players, but not adept at reading show music. It was a disaster, though Sweets Edison got up on the stand with his trumpet to help them. Sweets even conducted some of the more difficult show numbers. When he played for dancing after the show ended, Hot Lips rewarded us with some of the richest, purest Kansas City blues I ever heard.

"We opened at the Strand August 25 with the picture *Deep Valley*, featuring Ida Lupino and Dave Clark. We had an excellent stage show with the Edwards Sisters [tap dancers], Lewis and White [Slappy White] comedians, and Pearl Bailey as the headline. This was Pearl's first Broadway appearance and she was sensational. But a weak movie on Broadway meant a short run, so the Strand gig lasted only two-and-a-half weeks. After a two-week 'vacation' without pay, we set out on a string of one-nighters. The Orpheum in Omaha passed this year, but we played a one-nighter at Dreamland Ballroom, where I first saw Basie in 1938 and where I auditioned to replace Earle Warren in 1943.

"This 1947 gig was enjoyable because all my family and hometown friends could stand right in front and chat with me between numbers. Jo Jones and Buddy Tate were still sensations in Omaha, so coming there was a pleasure for them, too. The visit was marred for me by the fact that I had the only argument with Count Basie that I ever had. He called all the members of the band to the office during intermission to discuss salaries for the rest of the tour, and somehow the road manager maneuvered the conversation to make it appear I was being mercenary. I told him and Basie that, if they couldn't pay my full salary, they could leave me in Omaha right then and there. I was contrite afterwards, because Basie seemed surprised and disappointed by my outburst.

"From Omaha we went to Denver for a one-nighter and then to the Rainbow Rendezvous Ballroom in Salt Lake City for a week. The ballroom afforded Basie valuable air time on a coast-to-coast network. I never quite got over the miracle of broadcasting on the networks, which enabled my family and friends to listen to us at the very moment of our performance thousands of miles away. By this time I had made hundreds of broadcasts with Basie, but it remained a novelty to me till the end.

"We went to Los Angeles from Salt Lake City in our private railroad pullman car. Our arrival at Union Station had previously always been triumphant, with crowds of friends, relatives, and fans to greet us. But this November morning in 1947 there was only a handful, although Les Hite, Basie's faithful friend and admirer, was on hand. Les was formerly leader of the top big band on the Coast in the thirties and early forties.

"I realized then that the Basie magic was waning, but there was worse to come. We opened for a week at the Million Dollar Theatre, which had once been an ornate and prestigious venue, but it was on lower Broadway and it had declined. The Orpheum, where we had previously played, was on upper Broadway and was considered a higher-class place. Furthermore, attendance at the Million Dollar was far below what we had enjoyed at the Orpheum.

"Next, we went off for some weeks of one-nighters in northern California, Oregon, Washington, and Vancouver. We played a week at the Golden Gate Theatre in San Francisco. In nearly all these places we had played to enormous crowds in 1945 and 1946. I had also played some of them in 1944 when I was with Lucky Millinder and we played from Seattle down to San Diego. Now we were playing to far smaller audiences than Lucky had drawn. I was alarmed and I felt personally affronted by any serious threat to the sacred Basie 'thing.'

"We returned to Los Angeles for a four-week stand at the Meadowbrook Club in Culver City, which had been the Casa Mañana when we triumphed there in 1945. (Previously, during Les Hite's great days, it had been Sebastian's Cotton Club.) After the first week, the owners told Milt Ebbins, Basie's personal manager, that they couldn't honor the remaining three weeks of the contract because of the miserably poor attendance. Ebbins reached a compromise whereby the band would work only three nights over the weekends. Everybody in the band had to accept a large reduction in salary, and, with Christmas approaching, spirits were very low. The lack of enthusiasm on the part of the fans was also damaging to morale, but this didn't touch me deeply, because I was still with Basie and felt sure something would turn up to improve the band's fortunes.

"On the first night of the last three-day arrangement, I arrived at the club with Jimmy Rushing in the jitney we shared each night. Milt Ebbins was in my dressing room and he motioned for me to closet with him.

" 'Prez,' Milt began, 'Earle is coming back to the band.'

" 'I had heard rumors about that,' I said. 'I even heard the tape Basie made telling Earle that he missed him.'

"Milt became all flustered and protested nervously, 'No, Prez, Basie loves your playing and wants you to stay on and play with Earle. Isn't that what you've always wanted, to play in the same section as your man?'

"I knew the gesture of offering me the third alto chair was halfhearted, because C. Q. Price had become an important member of Basie's arranging staff. I had personally gotten C.Q. into Lucky Millinder's band in 1944, and was instrumental with Buddy Tate in getting Basie to hire him, so I wouldn't have done anything to cause his dismissal, even if I had felt the third-chair gesture was sincere.

" 'Listen, Milt,' I told Ebbins, 'this band is Earle Warren's home. As long as Basie has a band it should include Earle as first alto if he needs a job. Furthermore, I wouldn't play third alto under anyone, including Earle, and I think you and Basie both know this.'

"We could hear Basie signaling the band from the piano, so I asked Milt to excuse me and started to put my alto and its stand together before heading for the stand. As I came around the back of the band shell, I could see Earle Warren hurrying across the dance floor with his sax case in hand, heading for *his* chair in the middle of Count

Basie's reed section. He had arrived in Los Angeles earlier that day without my knowledge. I rushed to greet him in front of the bandstand. We exchanged a few warm words, and within seconds I was listening to the greatest first alto sax man in the world, in the band that was now made complete again by his presence."

(1978)

Marshall Royal

(ALTO SAXOPHONE AND CLARINET)

"Without Marshall Royal," said Sir Charles Thompson in 1961, recalling his days with Lionel Hampton, "it wouldn't have been the band it was. I looked to him as to a father musically, although sometimes his criticism made me so mad I could have cried. Later on, I saw its value. Several of the younger musicians disliked him for it, but they had such poor tones it was pitiful. He told them there was more to it than just blowing their horns, and he taught them about breathing together. He is one of the greatest musicians in the world. He can read any kind of music, play any kind of music, and he is—something few people know today—a genius on clarinet."

Some weeks later, Count Basie and his orchestra were playing at Birdland, a spot recognized as their New York home. While there, they were in the habit of rehearsing once a week. At two o'clock in the afternoon, the club presented a very different picture to that at two in the morning.

Thad Jones was at the piano. One or two musicians were on the stand, the others scattered in little groups at the tables. Benny Powell and Henry Coker were getting their kicks playing music out of a book for tuba by Don Butterfield. Marshall Royal did not appreciate their efforts and called the band together.

"You sound as though you were auditioning for the Salvation Army," he told them.

The band began to run through a new number and soon had the measure of it. Marshall turned around in his chair and gave some instructions: "At the end there, you guys make sure you push that right in tempo, so they don't think you're pulling out on them."

Other members of the band became impatient to give the number a real performance and began to call the leader:

"Base!"

"Basie!"

"Count!"

In answer to the last, shouted through Frank Foster's cupped hands, Count Basie emerged from the washroom in vest and trousers, carrying his electric razor. He bowed courteously to the band and took his seat at the piano.

The rehearsal rolled. Afterwards, at his hotel, Marshall Royal had this to say about his life and times.

"My father was a bandleader and music teacher. He played all the reeds, all the strings, and some of the valve instruments. He was a good musician. My mother was a pianist, and there were instruments around me all my life. I slept behind the piano on the overcoats from the time I was a month old. We had a kind of family orchestra, and my uncle played in it. Outsiders were recruited for the larger engagements, but the nucleus was always the family band. Everybody around my house was a musician, so I had to be one, and I *wanted* to be one. I knew nothing but music. That was it from the go, and I've never regretted it, never a day. I don't know that I could live without music.

"My father started me on violin, and I was very fortunate in being able to get any kind of tutoring I wanted right at home. That is, except in the case of my advanced styling, and then I studied with a graduate of the Paris Conservatory. I loved to play baseball and football when I was a kid, but the utmost in my mind was to be a good musician, and it was part of the deal at home that I always practiced before athletics. I used to practice hard, even when I was only seven or eight years old, sometimes at night after my parents had gone to bed, from nine to one or even two in the morning. The violin isn't loud, anyway, and I would put a mute on it. I'd be there playing what I wanted to play, and I liked it. I guess if I picked the violin up now and practiced for a couple of years I could be a good violinist. It goes, you know, if you don't keep up. It's the hardest instrument of all.

"I gave up the violin when I got into high school and started playing clarinet, and then saxophone. (I played a little guitar on the way, too.) I made the change for strictly economic reasons. Violins weren't popular. I used to play pretty things, and waltzes, on the violin in the orchestras when I first started out. In those days, most saxophone players were violinists who had changed over. Hardly any Negro orchestras were using violins in any capacity. Of course, orchestras like Paul Whiteman's still did, but they were larger, and they were founded on concert principles and on a more legitimate type of playing. The violins could do very well with the type of music that was written at that time. There was no getting hot, loud, and blary. Bands like that would have a full section of four fiddles. People danced then, and there were more waltzes.

"Saxophones hadn't been delved into very far. They weren't very good. They weren't made well. They were using C-melody saxes, rather as a substitute than as an instrument on its own. The real good sound of the tenor saxophone didn't come until Coleman Hawkins produced it. He had a different approach to the sound of the horn. Before him, they'd used a whole lot of wavery vibrato, and slap-tonguing.

"There were a few guys who started playing well on the alto, like Frankie Trumbauer. I was very conscious of him, long before I heard of Benny Carter. There weren't too many Negro orchestras being recorded then. In the early twenties, you could just about count on your fingers all the Negro dance bands that had ever recorded. There was Fletcher Henderson, of course. I can remember getting records of his like *Fidgety Feet* and *Sensation* in 1927. That was a turnover period in jazz then—arranged jazz, rather than everyone taking off for themselves.

"I think Benny Carter has always tried to play correctly, as I have. That may be why you hear a similarity in our lines and formations. I had never even heard a record of Benny's until 1940 or 1941, and I didn't meet him until World War II, when he had a band out on the West Coast. I was brought up there, although I was born in Oklahoma.

"While I was in high school, the music teacher came up one day and said someone called up and wanted a small group to work at the opening of a school market. They told him what *they* wanted, a drum, a saxophone, a trombone, and so on, six or seven pieces.

" 'You play saxophone?' he asked.

" 'Yeah,' I said, although I'd never played one in my life till then. But I'd been playing legitimate clarinet and there were always saxophones at my house. My uncle had a couple of them, and my father had two or three lying around. So I went home and got my dad's alto, and asked him how to play the scale on it. He told me, showed me how to use the octave key, showed me that it was built in octaves, so that once I'd learned one scale, all I had to do was press the octave key and play an octave higher. I practiced for one evening and started playing the next day. They had a platform out front, and music and bright lights to attract people to the opening. We had no arrangements. We just played the popular tunes of the day. One I remember was *Varsity Drag* from *Good News.*

"After that, I went into taxi dance halls, and I worked at night all during the time I was in high school, with different small bands, six, seven, or eight pieces. We'd get off at one or two o'clock in the morning and I'd have to make that class at eight o'clock. Not enough sleep maybe, but you can get a pretty fine education from seeing and meeting people when you're an entertainer. And you can systemize anything. When I got home from school in the afternoon, I would go to bed. I wouldn't run around. If there was a track meet or a hard baseball game, I'd stay out for that, but I'd still try to get home to sleep a couple of hours. I did that all through high school, and I learnt how to get two hours here and three hours there, and I've always done that. That life didn't harm me physically at all. I was always athletically inclined and I tried to keep my body in pretty good condition.

"There are two things that I think are overdone in this world—eating and sleeping. You really don't need as much sleep or as much food as most people get. So far as food is concerned, this is the land of plenty. Quite poor people here often have some of the fullest tables you've ever seen.

"After the taxi dance halls, I started working nightclubs. I'd be sixteen or seventeen. I went pretty fast, because I had a good background, and when I started working with professional musicians, I was competent to do so. I worked with Curtis Mosby, and then I had eight or nine years with Les Hite. With Les Hite, I was a sort of straw boss for the first time. As a straw boss, I rehearse the band. I try to make it sound good, and that's what I enjoy doing. If I succeed, that's another feather in my cap, and I'm very happy.

"I had complete charge of the rehearsing and putting together of Lionel Hampton's big band. I joined him in October 1940 and stayed until September 1942, when I enlisted in the navy and became straw boss of a very, very good band. During the war years, there was a shortage of good men around, and if I hadn't gone into the navy, I wouldn't have remained with Hamp. I would have become rich by being a bandleader myself! By now, I might have retired with my

laurels! There were more people getting by with little talent during
World War II than at any time in the history of music. There were
people who were garbage collectors or street sweepers who went back
to music because most of the good musicians were of draft age and in
the service. The bands that were on the road during the war weren't
too good, and that goes for colored and white bands. The bandleaders
on the road were struggling, but you could work day and night if you
wanted to.

"When I came out of the navy, I went with Eddie Heywood. The
big-band scene had become pretty bad. Why? Well, the band business
here has always depended on new dance crazes, but there hasn't been
a good dance invented in the last twenty-five years where you didn't
need to be a gymnast to do it. On top of that, during the war they took
up all the floors with tables to serve drinks, so there was no place for
the people to dance. That created a listening audience, which is good
in a lot of ways, but if you have no dance, dance bands can't exist.
They turned some halls into cocktail lounges and bars, and most of
the big ones just went under. Then there was the influx of Latin
American bands with their dances.

"Today's young people haven't discovered the big band yet. How're
you going to get them to discover it? I wish I knew. You take the kids
who came out and heard us at Freedomland. The only thing they ever
hear is those six- or seven-piece bands playing rock 'n' roll. So when
they hear a big band, it's new to them, but they like it. I think there
has to be more in-person and TV exposure of big bands. They should
take them for some of those summer TV replacements. That's where
Freedomland was very good for music. 'Gee, I like this!' young people
were saying. 'Why haven't I heard about this before?'

"I left Eddie Heywood at the Three Deuces in New York and went
back to California. I set down at home and only worked recording
and studio jobs. I did that for about five years without ever leaving
Los Angeles, and I made a very logical-type living. Now young fellows
like to go around and jam, and that's fun during a certain period of
your life, but after a number of years you look back, you get to be a
family man, and you see this guy who went to school with you is now
a doctor, and that one is now a lawyer. Each can provide well for his
family, and his wife doesn't want for many things, so if you're going
to be a real family man, around your mother and your wife, you'd
better get down to business and make a real business of this thing. That
was how I felt. Although it may become a matter of hard, cold business,
you try to get your enjoyment along with your business. Uppermost in
your mind is how to have a better type of existence for your family.
I try to go about it with a real business attitude, but I'm still doing

something I like. I'm doing exactly what I want to do and making my livelihood at the same time.

"I never did much writing. It didn't appeal to me, and then there was the eye strain in writing all those little old notes. I like to play, and to conduct, and to mold an orchestra. That's a different thing. I know enough about arranging and the fundamentals to correct a score, to read a score, and to know what's happening at all times, which is all I'm interested in knowing. So far as doing the writing—that's for the birds!

"I'd like to be sitting in one of those good studio bands in Hollywood, really making it well, because I like to play a whole lot of different things. I don't like just to swing hard all night. I like to play pretty things, too, and I like to play in big bands—thirty or forty pieces— where I have big sounds all around me and different things going on. That's my taste in music. I like contrast. I played in some of those studio bands and enjoyed it very much, but during the time I was trying to invade the field, there were no Negroes in those studio groups. I was one of the first, in the thirties and into the forties. It's a little better now, but it isn't that good.

"When I first came out with Basie, I did it more as a lark. I thought I would come out six months or so and then go back. I took Buddy De Franco's place, playing clarinet with Basie. It was a seven-piece group for about four months after I joined. Then the old Basie standards were revived. The big band was formed and it snowballed. I started to enjoy my work and stayed.

"I consider Basie is a friend of mine and I've always tried to keep my working conditions with him on a level of friendship and respect. In the early stages of the big band, it was just a matter of helping him. I will do anything with anyone I work with that will help to make the job better, easier, and more successful. Basie and I work together on a handshake proposition. I'm not contracted to him. I'm just the same as any other man in that band. Every band has to have a kind of deputy leader and my job may go a little further than that at times. I direct the shows in the theaters, rehearse the acts, put 'em together, and try to keep things going. I've done that kind of stuff all my life and know how it should be done. I just try to do a good job. So many people, who have resented at the time what I've told them to do, have come back in later years and thanked me, and that in itself is some- times enough reward. I remember working with kids like Illinois Jacquet and Dexter Gordon for the first time. I was eight years older than them, and that was a lot when they were only eighteen or nine- teen. I was only in my twenties, but I was a 'veteran'!

"When I joined Basie, I didn't have the least idea I'd be out here on the road, going into my eleventh year, not by any manner of means. In fact, I would have made a wager against that happening.

"My wife lives in L.A. and is very wonderful in her outlook on me. She wants me to be happy and she knows I'm happy when I'm playing my horn. Periodically she visits me, and periodically I go home, but she has been so great about the whole thing. A lot of guys I worked with in the early years, who were very good musicians, were told by their wives: 'I want you at home. If you're going to be a married man, you've got to be at home with me.' Well, the only reason the girl was attracted to the musician in the first place was probably because he was sitting up there on the bandstand playing music. After they get married, she forgets that and wants him home. She says she's lonesome, tells him she wants something secure, and takes him out of the band business 'You get yourself a job in the post office,' she says. 'You work twenty years and you can set down with a pension.' I look at a lot of those fellows and see the unhappiness deep inside them because they couldn't further their musical career. They were supposed to be musicians in the first place. Many of them have advanced well in terms of money, but money isn't everything. You've got to have peace of mind.

"I'm not minimizing the bad side of this. I'd like to be home right now for a couple of weeks, to be around things that are mine, to sleep in my own bed, and not wake up in some hotel room wondering, 'Where am I? What city am I in?' That happens quite often. Just to sit at home and look at my own TV, to ride in my own automobile, and to eat off my own table—that would mean a lot. The band may play on the Coast about once a year, for two weeks, a month. We used to play Vegas, but we haven't done so now for a couple of years.

"This band Basie has had the last eight or nine years has been an exceptionally happy one. They're wonderful guys, some of the nicest I've ever worked with, and there's been very little turnover, so that it's more like a family. We have our little ups and downs from time to time, but it all smooths out. And it's a very mature band. There are no teenagers in it. At this time, there's only one fellow even in his twenties —Al Aarons. He's a very nice boy and a good musician. This isn't a young band and that is one of the reasons for its success. There's enough age in it to give it stability, which is very important if you're going to keep a big band. Nowadays, the average young musician of the new era, who has been on the road three or four years, thinks it's time he became a bandleader himself. And if he's fortunate enough to get one album out, then he's really going out on his own. It's pretty hard to keep a youngster down if he gets a hit going, and I'm not censuring him, because if he can make a quick buck, then more power to him; but you need a bunch of settled people in a big band.

"In a big band, you play what's given you. I sat up in this one three or four years before I was given a solo to play. You don't worry about it. The main thing is to be able to play it when they give it to you. You're not trying to prove anything. It's mostly kids who are always trying to prove things, and that's because they feel insecure. Doesn't that apply in any phase of life?

"All four guys in a trumpet section should be able to play lead. That keeps the weight, the physical strain, off any one guy. The same thing should apply to trombones. There isn't the physical element with the reeds as with the brass, so the reed section may be led nearly all the time by one man. There's just a little more exertion to playing lead. You have to think a little harder and be more precise.

"There aren't many lead altos out now. Mostly the studios grab them. Willie Smith has always been considered an excellent lead alto. George Dorsey is wonderful. He was out on the road with Basie when Lucky Thompson was in the band. Benny Carter and Hilton Jefferson are two of the best. There are a lot of wonderful guys who can play lead alto, but they mostly have white-collar jobs and are not out on the road.

"In this day and age, the bands are at the discretion of the arrangers, and you get so much that is driving, driving. . . . The reason you like *Segue in C* is because some forethought went into it, both as regards the shape of the arrangement and the tempo. Even though the Basie band is expected to drive and shout, you can call one particular number on any dance floor anywhere, in any club or at any concert, and you will get instant applause at the start of the number. Overall, it's as popular as any Basie has in his book. We've been playing it for years —*Lil Darlin'*.

"You find out from requests what people want. A lot of people who come to Birdland would have us blast on every number. Sometimes, when we play a soft, easygoing number, we are almost forcing it on them. They seem to want a feeling of tension. And you could have a great big, roomy place, four times as big as Birdland, and people would stay away in droves. People like to feel all cluttered up. You don't believe it, you get a little restaurant and fine food, just a few stools and only five or six tables, and people will come and stand in line to get in there. When the manager renovates the place, enlarges it so they can have all the room they want, then they'll stay away—in droves. Same thing with music. You give them what they want in a place where they're all close together, and they feel they're a part of it, and they get mass hysteria. A person may come there not intending to enjoy it, but merely to say he's been there. Soon, he's patting like the rest. He's caught something from the people at the next table. But you'd be surprised the requests we get. If we played only requests, we'd play loud, blaring numbers all night long.

"It's strange, but when bands like Lunceford's were playing dances and one-nighters, there was more variety in the music than now, when we have a 'listening' audience. They had to play four or five tempos, and there was a dance for each of those tempos. You would think there would be more variety with a listening audience, but the people are sitting there waiting for something to happen, and it seems that to keep them going you've got to keep driving. Each set gets to be like a performance on its own. Some people only come into Birdland for the last set. They know exactly when to come in. (3:15 to 4:00 is the last set.) We get a lot of musicians at the bar then, but there are also a lot of music lovers who come in at 2:15 to catch the last two sets. Sometimes they're better than the first two, and sometimes they're not. Sometimes the guys are all fired up then, and sometimes they're tired.

"Music, like anything else, has its fads. One year, one instrument is top in the public's estimation; the next year, it's another one. For instance, there was the Louis Armstrong era, when everybody was mad about trumpet. Then you get along to the mid-thirties and it's clarinet —Benny Goodman, Artie Shaw, and a few others. The clarinet won public acceptance and people learned to know and appreciate the instrument's sound. It's almost the same with dogs. A year or so back the fad was for cocker spaniels. Now it's for poodles. Further back, it was for wirehaired fox terrriers, and airedales, and police dogs.

"If the clarinet seems a bit out of fashion now, you have to remember that it is a hard instrument to play. That is, to play freely. Most things originally set up for clarinet were stereotyped and supposed to be played from one certain angle, but when you go to play in jazz, you have to take off in all directions. Then the clarinetist who is not thoroughly prepared on his instrument is always afraid of the squeak. It's a fine type of precision instrument and that squeak is always waiting.

"The reason you hear more squeaks on tenor is because the players are involved in experimentation. They're trying to do something different. To get into something else, they may go beyond the realm of the tenor saxophone.

"I always play Boehm system on clarinet. The difference between the sound of the New Orleans musicians, who played the Albert system, and those who later played Boehm, didn't have much to do with the system. They sounded different because the style of playing and conception of sound were different, but that had nothing to do with the system itself. If they took enough time to learn the Boehm system, they would sound just the same way. The Boehm system is a reconstruction of the old Albert system and it has so many advantages.

"In this era, one instrument that has been really prostituted is the flute. There are guys playing flute parts on recordings who should never be on the instrument, because flute is a beautiful instrument which takes time and a lot of courage to play correctly. Just because a guy owns one and studies for a year doesn't mean he can go out and do a good, acceptable job on it. It doesn't make sense to me. It has become a gimmick in jazz, although there are only a handful of players in the world who can play jazz flute. We're fortunate to have a good one in our band—Frank Wess. There are so many so-called flautists!

"I've always tried to keep an open mind with my music. If you get to liking one soloist too much, you almost invariably tend to dislike someone else. I've tried to sort of space my feelings with regard to soloists by taking the good parts of each and ignoring what I didn't like. I don't necessarily look to reed soloists as my favorites just because I'm a reed player. I like to listen to excellent trombonists, and I like good bassists, and guitarists. I like to go all over the field. I've always tried not to be influenced much by others. There's always a certain amount of anyone that will rub off on you. For that reason, I've never had a record collection. I believe if you listen to one person long enough you'll unconsciously start playing like him. I listen to different people for short periods, so that I won't be taking their soul. That's a bit of a roundabout approach, but most people take it exactly the other way. I don't like copyists. I think each person is supposed to be his own individual self. I enjoyed listening to Charlie Parker very much, but I don't think I would have enjoyed playing what he did, because his line of thinking was different to mine. That's not saying anything he did was wrong. I just didn't want to play the way he did. Through the years, I've enjoyed Johnny Hodges and Benny Carter very much, and some of the things Jimmy Dorsey did. Besides Frankie Trumbauer, I used to enjoy Bix Beiderbecke and Eddie Lang. They had something going and they could play their instruments. I always appreciated Bix's *In a Mist*. He showed a little of his inner self. He had an inner beauty that was all right, and he played good piano.

"I worked with Lawrence Brown on the Coast and I thought he was one of the greatest trombonists that ever lived. He developed an entirely new outlook towards trombone. I never forget a thing he did with Paul Howard in 1929 called *Charlie's Idea*. I was still a teenager then, but I used to follow those bands. There's another trombonist out there I've always admired, a beautiful musician—Murray McEachern. Then I always admired the way Don Byas played tenor saxophone. We used to play and jam around together when he first came out from Oklahoma in the thirties. That's the kind of horn I like. Now Lester was a wonderful stylist, but if I played tenor I would like to play like Don. As for trumpets, there was no one to surpass Pops in his day. Then came Roy Eldridge, and he was wonderful. I like Dizzy and Miles. They all have something to offer.

"I'll eventually go home to California, the place I love the most. The studio position may improve, but a lot of young fellows will have come up. The only thing about those studios is that they want you to be a jack-of-all-trades—alto, tenor, alto flute, bass clarinet, baritone, and so on. I never thought that was quite correct. I thought a man should be hired for what he could do best, rather than for his ability to play a lot of instruments."

(1962)

Lockjaw Davis

(TENOR SAXOPHONE)

I

"You got him!" Count Basie exclaimed, as though relinquishing a not-unwelcome responsibility. "He was talking to me all the way from Idlewild to London."

Eddie "Lockjaw" Davis had just arrived in England for the first time. His tenor solos, sang-froid, and relaxed stage personality soon made him a great favorite with British audiences. During his free hours, he patiently interested himself in the ways of the natives. Maybe they had been doing things in this fashion for centuries, but why? "Theirs not to reason why" was no answer. Davis wanted factual explanations.

A diligent searcher after truth from way back, he admits to being the despair of some of his early teachers. "I didn't want to be told about Columbus discovering America, or America discovering Columbus. 'Where,' I'd ask them, 'did the Indian come from?' Same thing with the pyramids. They'd tell me who built them, when, and where, but they couldn't tell me *how* they were built."

An individualist with a naturally nonconforming mind, Davis is also a remarkable conversationalist with a formidable vocabulary. Had writing been his métier, he would have made a great essayist. All one has to do is to suggest a subject, or raise a question, put a suitable jug in a suitable position, and sit back to catch the news in a stimulating form. Some excerpts from a recent dissertation follow.

"Starting an evening, before all the gallant faces that expect a great performance," he explained, "you know you can sway them with a serious look. The public tends to go along with the characteristics you display. If we get on the stand and there's a lot of laughter and discussion amongst ourselves—'What did you do last night?'—the audience tends to feel we are a lackadaisical group, that we're just clowning. Later in the evening, we can get away with it, because everyone has had a few drinks and is feeling more gay. Working in all kinds of groups and with all kinds of fellows, I've found that that first set is the hardest. It's especially hard to get in the mood before a stony-looking audience, one that's considering the kind of tie you're wearing, or whether your shoes are shined. I've known it to unnerve quite a lot of musicians, but as the evening wears on, they become more at ease, more acclimated to the room. What I find very odd is that this may happen after they've been working there every night for weeks before. Sometimes a funny comment or a funny gesture is required to make the fellows relax, because, after all, this is just one out of five sets. What are you going to do for the other four?

"The next amusing thing after that first set is that the people become a little more talkative, and in the intermission they are surprised to discover that you are able to discuss subjects other than music. This astounds them, and brings me to a pet peeve.

"Apart from the fact that he plays an instrument, the audience really knows nothing about a musician. If you take an athlete, a footballer or a baseball player, the fan usually has some idea what the man does in his off-season. He may sell cars or insurance, or he may work for a tobacco firm or a brewery. The fan learns about his hobbies, too. He likes deep-sea fishing, he's interested in electronics, or he teaches in school. All this brings the fan or admirer closer to the performer, and that's what is missing in music.

"Among musicians, for instance, we have intellectual and sportsman-like types. We have some fine golfers like Freddie Green and Sir Charles Thompson. We have many jazz artists who could endorse golf balls, golf bags, and such products, if the manufacturers knew about them. In the same way, we have many musicians who are interested in the technical side of radio. I know one or two who are deeply interested in electronics, and others who have taken the IBM course. Facts like that are never brought out. You are always asked, 'How did you start in music? Did you sell newspapers to buy your first horn? Or did you sell apples, or shine shoes?' That's all people get to know about the musician, nothing about his personal life, nothing about the grown adult except when he violates the law, or something like that. JAZZ MUSICIAN COMMITS . . . the headline says, but when it's a baker, a butcher, or a plumber, the occupation isn't mentioned.

"If a musician saves a dog from the ASPCA, we don't read about that. If he saves a kid from being run over by a car, we won't read about that either. It's just the natural act of a citizen. When his services are required for a benefit, how often is the fact that they're given free mentioned? The distance he had to travel to make it, the sacrifice of a money-paying gig—these are taken for granted.

"The jazz musician in the eyes of the public is a villain!

"He's good copy in that role for the journalist, but if the public were told a bit more about the problems, a bit more about backstage, then I think there would be a higher appreciation of him. Various manufacturers would take a different view, too, and consider musicians for endorsing products.

"Now why doesn't the jazz musician endorse certain products?

"Tobacco, alcohol, and gasoline, for instance, are very much a part of his life, and he has had enough experience to know about differences in quality. Sure there's a difference in gasoline! If I'm using regular, I can get more out of W than out of X, more out of Y than out of Z. The same thing goes for automobiles. When I had that _____, the service was the worst. The musician who's traveling needs immediate service. He doesn't want to wait for parts to come from Detroit. When you deal with _____, they have parts in every section of the country, so this is advantageous to the traveling musician.

"I've certainly been in the business long enough to endorse liquors and beverages! The ones which won't give you hangovers. I have experience *nightly*, and right now I would like to endorse Cutty Sark! I have also had so much exposure to different brands of cigarettes that I really *know* which taste like a cigarette should. I remember how great they used to taste and I know what brings out the flavor. Like they say, 'Come up for a _____.' Don't stay down in this dungeon with the smoke! Who works more dungeons than the jazz musician? He's always in some trouble in smoke-filled rooms. Yes, he knows when to come up! (He knows when to throw up, too, with some of those funny-style beverages!) I mean, don't ask an athlete about cigarettes. He's in the locker room having a shower. How would he know? Ask the musician in the dungeon!

"For the musician who knows he's going to be drinking during intermissions, there are two rules. One, he must drink something he can control or handle. Two, he must select something that will be kind to his stomach, because there's always the next day to consider. I have a program where I drink beer in the early part of the evening. After drinking several bottles, I find I become irritated and agitated, and this agitation is projected through my instrument. I always have an excuse, you see, because if my music sounds offensive I can put it down to the beer, and there is one brand that does make my stomach feel particularly wretched. Later in the evening, I switch to Scotch and milk, but if I started off on this I'd become lazy, too relaxed. I have proof of this. I took my tape recorder and recorded a number of my performances when I varied my drinking program. Yes, really—a scientific project! But haven't you noticed that a group which began very sharp sometimes sounds all dragged out in its later sets? That's because they haven't programmed their drinking. Some, of course, do sound better as the evening progresses and the crowd grows larger, but others just seem to wane.

"One of our trials is the patron who asks, 'When are you going to play my request?' just after you get through playing it. He feels he's entitled to hear a version note for not as on the record, and this difficulty particularly applies to the artist who records with musicians other than those he works with. I think it's very important that a musician who works regularly with a group should at least make some recordings with that group, because then he's equipped to talk to the patron and explain that he does a variety of things, and that the number requested was made with a studio group. It's like people who record with strings. They may get a wonderful effect, but when they go out to work without them, there's a hell of a vacuum. It's amazing how many patrons can't tell a big-band sound from that of a little band. They listen to a soloist on a record and pay little attention to the support, but when they hear him in person, without that support, they decide the soloist himself is lacking something. You hear all these arguments about the critics and the musicians, but the patrons are most ill-informed. They are the ones who pay the bills, so you can't be too harsh with them, but they really know so little.

"You so often hear announcements like, 'Our next number, ladies and gentlemen, answers a request,' and you know it is self-manufactured. Nobody has asked for it. But take Paul Gonsalves playing *Diminuendo and Crescendo* every night, twenty choruses or so. The fact that you have something the people really want to hear—there's nothing awful about that! And it isn't that long. It runs about fifteen minutes, and that isn't so laborious, either. For Paul, it's an outlet, something everyone welcomes in a big band, something you can stretch out on, where the soloist is not restricted to one or two choruses. Even if it's monotonous to the listener, it isn't to the artist, because he doesn't know when he's going to get to solo again. This he welcomes, really.

"I deliberately handle the horn the way I do, to show I'm its master! I've always noticed how delicately so many tenor players handle it, as though it were fragile, as though it commanded *them*. I try to show that I have command of the horn at all times, whether I'm playing or just holding it. You take charge, it's yours, and I want the audience to feel I'm in complete command. Otherwise you can give the impression the horn is too big for you, whether you play it well or not. The visual impression is quite important. Similarly, the guy who acts as though the keys don't work properly, or as though he has a bad reed, gives the public a poor impression. The musician who comes in and must tune up before he plays is only too likely to give a sad performance. The seasoned musician plays and then tunes after his horn has warmed up. Then he gets a true sound. You can tune your horn with your lip, anyway. If I put my horn too far in, I may play sharp, but if I don't take too much of a bite, all will depend on the pitch of the piano. When they start asking for that 'A' before they've even played, you can bet they're relying on nothing but technicalities.

"Working in the quintet with Johnny Griffin, we had two styles. You might have a situation where a guy tried to capture the audience by having a substandard colleague along, but we tried to present two guys who were considered good musicians and could get over their horns. Then it was up to the public to decide which style they pre-ferred, and it gave them a chance to realize the range and capabilities of the instrument, which is why we played all kinds of material. It has been said that the tenor is a sluggish instrument. In fact, Charlie Parker used to say as much when he played with Earl Hines. It was too sluggish for him, but Don Byas proved you can fly with the tenor and still possess full quality. Its potentialities are enormous, and I think the patron got pleasure from making comparisons between two tenors where he wouldn't be able to compare the musicianship of, say, a trumpet and a tenor."

Dutifully skipping the newspaper-apples-shoeshine bit, it can be re-vealed that Davis began playing for $1.50 a night a few months after he bought his first horn. He joined Cootie Williams in 1942, played with Lucky Millinder, Andy Kirk, and Louis Armstrong, led his own group at Minton's for several years, was with Basie in 1952–1953 and again in 1957.

Largely self-taught, he credited Ben Webster with being his chief influence. Indeed, at one time, when they were playing together, Webster liked to refer to him as "Little Ben." The influence is most apparent on ballads, but at up-tempo Davis is very much his own man, and what Humphrey Lyttelton has termed his "slurred, insolent phrases" give to his interpretations an intensely personal character.

He realized the possibilities of pairing the tenor with organ when he first heard Wild Bill Davis, then playing as a single. He approached him about making records, but he was under contract, so Davis then engaged pianist Bill Doggett to play organ with him on his first tenor-organ session for Teddy Reig's Roost label. The date turned out so well that Doggett, who was accompanist for Ella Fitzgerald at the time, went right out and bought himself an organ. Billy Taylor and Jackie Davis also played organ for Lockjaw, but it was during the three-year period Doc Bagby from Philadelphia was with him that tenor, organ, and drums became a nationally popular combination.

"Nearly all the people who play organ in jazz have been converted from piano," Davis said, "and many of them knew so little they really cheated and exploited the instrument. Basically, it's the same keyboard, and there are only two things you must learn: the stops, which give you variations of sound, and the foot pedal, which is a substitute for bass.

"I got to the stage where I'd had enough organ. It was always controversial, because a lot of people thought it belonged to r. and b., and there's a faction that still refuses to accept the organ as a definite contribution to jazz. I made up my mind to go back to the conventional rhythm section, but rather than use brass I decided to revive the two tenors, because there had never been too much of that on records. There were Gene Ammons and Sonny Stitt, Wardell Gray and Dexter Gordon, but I don't believe any two-tenor unit stayed together so long and traveled the country as much as Johnny Griffin and I did."

(1961)

II

"You must be kidding," Count Basie said as he tore up the new business card he had just been handed.

This was not untypical of the reaction Eddie "Lockjaw" Davis met when he went to work as a booking agent for Shaw Artists Corp. in June 1963. Some of his closest colleagues among the musicians would not take the move seriously and laid bets that the job would not last six months. It would prove too boring, too tiring, or too monotonous.

"Another kind of reaction," Davis recalled, "was that I had a God-given talent and that I showed little regard for it by just stopping playing so abruptly. I had never considered it from a religious aspect. Then some people wanted to know if I was suffering from anything. Did I have some kind of bronchial disorder? Record fans kept dropping me cards. They were so disappointed, they said, and some suggested I was a defeatist. Did the popularity of other tenor players have anything to do with it? Some of the older musicians thought I had made a good decision, but they felt I should not have discontinued playing. They held that I should have tried to arrange my affairs so that I could still play saxophone as well as conduct business. But generally the comedy bit prevailed and Ben Webster even composed a poem for me called *Jaws the Booker*, which went like this:

> *Jaws is booking now,*
> *Jaws is booking now,*
> *Don't offer him a gig*
> *Or he'll blow his wig,*
> *'Cause Jaws is booking now."*

Later, as people grew accustomed to the idea, the repercussions were fewer and quieter. Just occasionally would someone ask Davis, "Are you still there?" or "Have you touched the horn recently?" Still, to many minds Davis's career was mystifying. Why should such a popular musician have ceased playing?

"There were several reasons why I decided to withdraw," Davis said. "And I prefer the term 'withdraw' rather than 'quit' or 'retire.' When you say 'quit' you mean you give up entirely, and when you say 'retire' it usually means you have reached a comfortable financial plateau. Neither applied in my case.

"I withdrew because I found myself becoming stagnant so far as musical progress was concerned. I was repeating a lot. It had to do with the fact that I was playing the same circuit and the same rooms, and that *had* become monotonous. Then I found I had a double job. I had to try to mold the youthful musicians into the type I'd been accustomed to working with. Oversaturation of records with insufficient variety didn't help either.

"Anyway, I began to lack enthusiasm and one club owner openly said I had become lazy. So I decided I wasn't enhancing the industry by my performances and I started thinking about getting into a different area, the booking agencies or the a. and r. field—working with musicians, but not necessarily playing."

The period of transition proved difficult for one who for two decades had worked by night and rested by day. "Acclimating to the other tribe—the nine-to-fivers—was a big problem for some weeks," Davis admitted; but he had an initial advantage in his familiarity with most of the rooms he was booking into and in his knowledge of the general background to the business. The hardest part, for him, was learning office procedure, the way a firm functions, and understanding the minds of those with whom he was now associated.

"It's a different way of thinking," he declared. "When you're working as a musician, you're in contact with people who are big spenders, busy drinking, gay, and out for recreation. In the office, the budget mentality rules with its problems of lunch money and carfare. The people are more settled and determined, and not as gay. You have to adjust to this and it's quite difficult if you've been accustomed to bartenders giving away drinks and all that sort of thing. Here, it was something if anyone gave you a coffee, but they could tell you all about fringe benefits and paid holidays, things I'd never given any thought to before. So now I became a member of the Budgeters Club, and when I went out at night I'd become so inhibited about spending that I was afraid of being called cheap. Yes, I was taking my daytime mentality out at night!"

Shaw Artists Corp. in New York was one of the biggest agencies and it handled such jazz artists as Miles Davis, Horace Silver, Art Blakey, John Coltrane, Sonny Rollins, Sonny Stitt, Roland Kirk, Oscar Peterson, Wynton Kelly, Hank Crawford, Shirley Scott, Milt Buckner, Wild Bill Davis, Bill Doggett, and Jimmy McGriff. Though well acquainted with them and their music, Davis found he also had to familiarize himself with a big roster of rock 'n' roll performers. The Coasters, the Drifters, the Contours, the Vibrations, the Sensations, the Shirelles, and the Miracles were only names to him, but now he had to know what they did, not to mention all the singles like Chuck Jackson, Jerry Butler, Marvin Gaye, Percy Mayfield, Major Lance, B. B. King, Fats Domino, Mary Wells, Gladys Knight, Maxine Brown, Betty Harris, Baby Washington, and Doris Troy. He had to check the record charts to see what hits they had last year and what they had going currently. He had to find out how many were in each group, whether they had any musical accompaniment of their own, and whether they were male or female. He listened to them on records and in theaters.

"Rock 'n' roll people," he claimed, "are active more in theaters and on one-nighters than in clubs. Some attractions appeal primarily to a colored clientele, others to a white clientele. We had one or two clubs with a basically white audience. We could send an r. and r.

group that had a big colored following and they would lay an egg there. And vice versa. We had expensive colored attractions that didn't draw a colored audience. It's a matter of taste and desire, but you cannot afford to make mistakes in that area, because it's costly for the club owner and it places the account in jeopardy. If you send the client a lemon, he assumes it was done deliberately just to raise the commission. When I had my own group, I used to say, 'You can afford a mistake on the bandstand, but you cannot afford one on the highway.' Now I found you could make a mistake in the office, but not one with the client.

"It was difficult, too, to sell an artist without a record. It didn't have to be a hit as long as he had made something. It's never a question of how good you are with a club owner, but of can you draw? A recording artist has a distinct advantage in that respect, but unfortunately there are a lot of good groups that haven't had the opportunity to record, and that makes it difficult to sell them. People used to call me as though I were a miracle worker, because I was aware of talent. When I found an artist with potential, the best I could do was to advise him on one or two record companies to approach."

The agency itself was divided into two sections: the Location Department, which served clubs on a weekly basis, and the One-Night Department, which handled dances and all jobs of fewer than three days. Each section had four agents, among whom the work was divided geographically. Davis was in charge of the East, as far north as Buffalo and as far west as Ohio, in the Location Department. An agent's major objective is always to route attractions in such a way that layoffs and big jumps are avoided. To this end, a booking slip was passed out every night to each agent and posted the next day in the route book. The agents could then see at a glance where each act was playing and know where and when to pick it up. In addition to the route book, there was a master book that showed specifics—the venue and the terms. "My three basic instruments as an agent," Davis explained, "were the route book, the master book, and the telephone."

Because he has a bigger and more detailed picture before him than anyone else, the agent obviously knows best about the general health of the business.

"According to the older hands," Davis said, "they've never seen it this bad, jazz or rock 'n' roll. Jazzwize, there's a combination of reasons. A lot of the club owners have found very few winners. The conduct of many jazz artists hasn't helped—the same old problems like showing up late, but also more profound ones. Jazz at one time was a happy thing, but now it has become so serious, even depressing in some instances. And there are too many experiments going on now.

The experiments should be in the studio, because you cannot expect an audience of musicians every night. Club owners claim there's a lack of entertainment on and off the bandstand. The relationship with the patrons is so distant. The artists stay in the bandroom during intermission or leave the premises, and the patrons feel this. The effect of a small group in a nightclub was to bring the artist and the patron close in a way big bands on a big stage never could. The patrons enjoyed this and it was a success. Today, a lot of them say they're almost afraid to go and ask the name of the artist's latest record.

"This need for entertainment can mean that the music will go in one of two directions. Maybe the older musicians and their values will be accepted again, or maybe the younger musicians will be groomed to realize the need for entertainment. Either way, it doesn't mean you have to become a clown."

Before Davis returned to music and Count Basie, he had begun to grow restless. As an agent, he could not perform before a live audience, but he was able to record and he thought a great deal about this as the backlog of his previously recorded material diminished. Shortly before he took Frank Foster's chair with Basie in 1964, he sized up the situation like this:

"I realize I had just as much security as a musician. My wife went along with my change of occupation because she felt it was important for me to have knowledge of another trade, in case I met with some accident or got so I didn't want to travel, but she prefers me to play. She says my personal habits have changed tremendously, that I have become more serious, more meticulous, and more grumpy. She has had to go through a transition herself, because when I was an active musician a lot of my time was spent on the road. Now she has had to acclimate herself to my grouchy appearance on a daily basis, and after twenty years this has been quite a job. I have really upset the household and all this can be eliminated if I go back to playing! It will only take a few days to pick up on the horn, and there's nothing, really, to compare with the musician's life for fulfillment and activity."

(1964)

Frank Wess

(FLUTE, SAXOPHONES, AND ARRANGER)

"You can play jazz on any instrument," Frank Wess said, "but you've got to have the feeling and conception for it. Where jazz and the flute are concerned, there's a whole lot more to be done on the instrument. The greatest flute players I've heard don't play jazz, but if we ever arrive at a really good academic flutist with an outstanding jazz conception, then the flute will really be appreciated in jazz."

Since he left Count Basie for the pit of *Golden Boy*, a Broadway musical, Wess had been studying again, and he reluctantly confessed that he had "made some progress." He was equally reluctant to discuss his own role in establishing the flute in jazz, yet there can be no doubt that the instrument's acceptance and popularity were very much due to his presentation as a flute soloist in the Basie band.

"Basie didn't know I played flute when I joined," he said, "but I used to practice during intermission all the time, and he couldn't help hearing me. So he told me to go ahead if I wanted to play any of my tenor spots on flute. The first number I was featured on—and that

185

we recorded—was *Perdido*. Of course, in a band like that you don't have time to warm up. You've just got to pick the instrument up and blow."

Born in Kansas City, Missouri, Frank Wess began playing alto saxophone in 1932. His parents were both schoolteachers, and his father headed a family band. "They were not professionals," Wess said in explanation of his musical beginnings, "but there were always a couple of cornets around." When the family moved to Washington, D.C., he continued playing alto in Bill Baldwin's dance band at the Colonnades. After that, he went into the house band at the Howard Theatre under Coleridge Davis's leadership.

"It knocked me out to see in that issue of *Down Beat* [March 11, 1965] that somebody had heard and remembered Biddy Fleet," he said. "I heard him in Washington and he was a helluva guitar player. He came to New York and played with Bird, and all around, but now everybody seems to have forgotten him. I guess if he'd had more recognition he would still be playing, but he was something else. I heard both Paul Gonsalves and Irving Ashby playing guitar in a New Bedford club a few years later. The guitar went out, but it's back now!"

It was in Washington, too, that pianist John Malachi heard Wess playing alto and suggested he should be playing tenor.

"When I started on tenor, I found I liked it better," he explained. "I went back to alto later only because Basie asked me. I liked Chu Berry and Ben Webster, and I'd known Don Byas from the time I was ten years old in Oklahoma. He went to Langston University, in Oklahoma, and I went out there during the summer, studying saxophone. He had a band there—Don Carlos's—and he always played the same way. But Lester Young impressed me more then. He was my inspiration.

"I jammed with him in Washington, and he showed me a lot of things about the horn, and how to make some of the sounds he got that other people were not making. For a long time I played more like him and sounded more like him than anybody, and I played nearly everything he recorded. Then one day a friend of mine, just a guy who liked music, came around where I was playing matinees in Baltimore.

" 'You know what?' he said. 'You sound just like Prez. You'll never get any credit for that. Everything you play just makes him bigger.'

"That made sense to me, and I gradually changed."

Blanche Calloway's was the first widely known band in which Wess worked. At that time, it included Ray Perry, the violinist and alto saxophonist, and George Jenkins, the drummer. In the army from 1940 to 1945, Wess was with Billy Eckstine during 1946–1947. Gillespie and Parker had left by then, but Gene Ammons, Fats Navarro, Doug Mettome, Shorts McConnell, and, for a while, Miles Davis were in it while he was. There followed a few months with Eddie Heywood, playing alto, tenor, and clarinet. ("I had played solo clarinet in the army, but I didn't care for the instrument.") Next, he played with Lucky Millinder, and then for a year with Bull Moose Jackson. In 1949, under the G.I. Bill of Rights, he began to study flute in Washington, D.C., with Wallace Mann, the flute soloist of the National Symphony, and eventually he got his degree on that instrument.

"I had heard Wayman Carver when those records by Chick Webb and His Little Chicks first came out," he said, "and I was always interested in flute, but then I didn't have a teacher. Carver did quite a bit of flute playing with Chick, but I don't think too much of it was recorded. Cats have really been playing flute forever, you know!"

Wess went on to speak with respect of Albert Socarras ("a beautiful flute player, a legitimate flute player"); of Esy Morales and his flutter-tongued *Jungle Fantasy* ("That was beautiful"); and of contemporary players he likes, such as Sam Most, Jerome Richardson, and James Moody. He was always at pains to make clear a distinction between what is acceptable as jazz flute and what is good flute playing from the academic viewpoint. He liked the alto flute, with which he recorded on the Impulse *Kansas City Seven* album: "It's a little different to play, and it has a nice, warm sound in the lower register, but it doesn't carry as well as the C flute."

When he joined Basie in 1953, Wess was already quite well known to musicians, but his was a new name to the public. "I think Basie first heard me when I was with Bull Moose at Ciro's in San Francisco," he recalled. "We had a pretty nice band then."

He and Frank Foster together perpetuated the image of two contrasting tenor soloists that was an established feature of Basie's presentation, but soon something new was added in the sound and shape of the flute. Basie used the flute increasingly and effectively, but the greatest impression on the public was probably made in *The Midgets* by Joe Newman, where it was complemented by Newman's fast, muted trumpet. Scores by Frank Wess also came to occupy an important part in the band's book.

"I started writing arrangements in the forties," he said. "I went to the Howard University Music School, where they had a fourteen-piece band called The Swingmasters. Some of the musicians in it were Benny Golson on tenor sax, Bill Hughes and Morris Ellis on trombone, Rick Henderson and Emery Pearce on alto sax, Pee Wee Thomas on baritone sax, John Watkins on trumpet, Carl Drinkard on piano,

Eddie Jones on bass, and Bertell Knox on drums. I enjoyed playing with them. Bill Hughes, Eddie Jones, and I went on to Basie, Rick Henderson to Duke Ellington, Benny Golson to Dizzy Gillespie, and Carl Drinkard to become Billie Holiday's musical director. Besides studying at Howard, I had private lessons on the side at the same time, so I knew what I was doing when I began arranging.

"*Perdido* was the first I did for Basie, and I think *Segue in C* was one of the more successful. I did another on *Dancing in the Dark* that I thought was pretty nice, and among the last before I left were a bossa nova and a couple of blues things that haven't been recorded. The more you do, the better you can do it. It makes a difference when you're in a band, because you have that orchestral sound in your mind, and you know what each guy can do. A band personality takes time, but if you grow in it, that helps, too. I'll get back to arranging eventually, but there are a few other things I want to get straightened out first—my instruments, my doubles, clarinet, and bass clarinet. I want to be proficient on them rather than a soloist."

When he left Basie, he knew he was going into the pit band of *Golden Boy*. It was, like, a new life to him, and he liked it. The band, which included Aaron Bell, Eddie Bert, Jimmy Crawford, and Benny Powell, was good. He could live at home, and he had three children, the youngest of whom was to go to high school the following year.

"The chief difference is not so much in the regularity," he observed, "but in the absence of all that traveling. I'd been on the road since 1939, most of the time, and if there were an opportunity for me to go into a studio band, I'd like that. It's mostly section work in the pit, although I have a few little fills on flute here and there. But no jazz. Clarinet is required as well as flute and tenor, and I hadn't played clarinet for almost twenty years. The only reason I can think of why that instrument has gone out of favor is that it is rather difficult to play. Many of the guys who are really proficient on it are not on the road. Marshall Royal can play it, but I don't know that he wants to. I heard that record of *Kansas City Wrinkles* recently, and his clarinet sure sounded good on it.

"Most of the recording I've done since leaving Basie has been transcriptions. I have ideas I want to record. I'd like to do an album of swinging things on flute with muted brass, and tenor with strings, but I've been thinking instrumentally rather than in terms of writing lately."

Conscientious, thorough, versatile, and well schooled, Frank Wess is one of those undemonstrative musicians who are the backbone of the profession and of any band they happen to be in. At one Basie recording session, when Marshall Royal was away, he played all the lead alto parts on a series of new arrangements by Benny Carter. He was quite unruffled, despite the fact that Carter was playing third alto beside him.

(1965)

Frank Foster

(TENOR SAXOPHONE AND ARRANGER)

"I was very assertive when I came into Basie's band in 1953, until I found out I wasn't as effective as I would liked to have been. I was relatively inexperienced and the band as a unit was very mature, getting on for twenty years old, and I soon realized that I had to alter if I was to fit. I had to learn to bend notes a certain way in order to blend with the section, and the section leader in particular. I had to learn all sorts of inflections on the instrument to blend not only with the reed section but also with the band as a whole.

"In the bands I'd played in before, everybody was on the same age level. When I had my own band, everybody was between the ages of fifteen and seventeen. Everybody was together, phrasewise and stylewise, and whatever other way you can think of. When I came into this band—it was a big break for me—the ages ranged from twenty-four to fifty-four.

"My original influences were Johnny Hodges and Benny Carter. I admired them a great deal and was conditioned to them. I was still in the lesson-taking stage when I was listening to them, but by the time

I really started playing, along came Charlie Parker on a record called *Swingmatism,* by Jay McShann. That was in 1941 and I was thirteen. It came like a natural thing to me, not revolutionary. Then, in 1945, I heard *Now's the Time* and *Billie's Bounce,* and that was the beginning, really, of a new era.

"A lot of fellows who switched from alto to tenor said the only way they could get away from Charlie Parker and go on their own was to switch instruments. I know that so long as I played alto I didn't try to sound like anything but Charlie Parker. But with me the change came out of necessity.

"When I was in college [Wilberforce University], they had two alto players in the band and needed a tenor. So I switched, and I liked it very much because it was different to what I'd been accustomed to for more than four years. It seemed to have more guts to it than the alto. It seemed like switching from a Chevrolet to a Cadillac, and I never got a chance to go back to alto.

"I should say that I started out on clarinet in a school band, a marching band, the football band. Then when I had my own band in my last year at high school, I still played clarinet. It's the best reed instrument to start out on, because it's harder than saxophone. After two years of clarinet lessons, I picked up an alto and played it in a few minutes. That's no unusual accomplishment, although it may sound like it.

"I will never completely escape the influence of Charlie Parker, because he played a little tenor himself and had a very pleasing style on it. I didn't hear him play much tenor, but some of the elements of his style that I absorbed are still evidenced in my tenor playing today. I loved Don Byas, and still do, but Sonny Stitt was the greatest influence. Strangely enough, I wasn't too much influenced by Prez. I didn't come to appreciate him until around 1954 or 1955. I got to know him during that period. He was already over the hill by then. His best playing was from the mid-thirties till the late forties. I was drawn to him through personal contact and on the basis of his early records with Basie. His tone, and the way of phrasing and execution had a lot to do with it, and even if he had lost a lot of what he had, he was always Prez up till the very end.

"But from 1949 to 1951, all I could hear on tenor saxophone was Sonny Stitt. I admired Wardell Gray's playing very much, but he could not penetrate too much because Sonny had me in his grips then.

"The next two years in the army were not a void, although there was not much association with the world of music as we know it. It was good experience and I don't regret it. I got to play quite a bit the last year and a half, in a combo and a large dance band. We played numbers Miles Davis, Charlie Parker, and Dizzy Gillespie had written, and we had a ball doing it.

"I joined Basie in 1953, a few months after Frank Wess. I didn't know how long I'd be there. All I knew was that I *wanted* to be there. Frank's style and tone resembled, say, Don Byas's, and perhaps Lucky Thompson's, whereas I brought to the band what was then referred to as the 'hard bop' style. It had been in the band before, because Wardell Gray played that style. Of course Basie had had Paul Gonsalves for a time, and then Eddie Davis, who gave him a contrast with Paul Quinichette.

"Whereas Wardell and others had fit the band very well, I didn't seem to fit too well with my style. I didn't think so, anyway. Frank Wess was smooth, and I had a little more drive, but there were certain tempos I couldn't fit into at all. I could only fit on the tempo of *Jumpin' at the Woodside*. The older men wouldn't let me do any ballads because I didn't seem to have the tone for them, and even on medium-tempo things I didn't seem to do too well. Much confusion resulted from this through '54, '55, '56, '57, and even maybe through '58. I was torn between styles and didn't consider myself as having one of my own at all. Sometimes I wanted to play like Ben Webster, and sometimes like Sonny Stitt.

"A grown man in his middle twenties is supposed to be going for himself so far as style is concerned. I had outgrown the Sonny Stitt influence and was trying to find something for myself, but what caused the confusion was my feeling that I didn't fit. I groped in the dark, practiced at home, and finally stumbled on a little technique. The end result was that I seemed—to myself—to emerge as a cross between several tenor players, namely, Ben Webster, Wardell Gray, Sonny Stitt, and some of myself. Sometimes I'd play like Ben Webster as a sort of burlesque on the bandstand, and Basie would like it and want me to keep on playing that way. But I couldn't keep it up because I'd always want to go for myself. Lockjaw can do it because that was his natural style. The natural style of Ben Webster and Lockjaw really appeals to Basie, and I guess I was too much from the new school. He called me 'Junior' all the time. I wanted to sound old, in one way of speaking, but I couldn't manage to sound old enough! I really did want to sound *something* like Ben Webster, but I still wanted to be myself! I liked the way he played, I liked that sound, I liked his way of getting over the instrument, and his tone was just beautiful. I've been striving for a beautiful tone for years and years, and it seems as though I'm only now on the threshold of acquiring a tone. I still don't consider myself adequate. I don't think a musician approaches his peak until he's around thirty years of age. He's arriving at maturity, acquiring better, smoother technique, better tone, and everything that goes with that. In his early twenties he's usually more conscious of technique than of anything else.

"The experience of playing with this band has been wonderful and very valuable. It's led me to sit down and try to figure out just what to do with myself. Had I played in small combos I would perhaps have emerged with a more definite style by now, but the mainstream-type influence of the Basie band helped me toward maturity. To a degree, style has to conform to the character of the band, unless you're such a great star that you can build it around yourself. I came to the band a very young man, relatively unknown, and I had to find my own way.

"What I think had a large bearing on the issue was the fact that much of my time was concentrated on arranging. Quite a few arrangers have had much trouble being good arrangers and instrumentalists at the same time. You'll find that most arrangers who play are not exceptional players. There are a few exceptions to that rule, too, but usually something somewhere is sacrificed by those who try to write *and* play. When you concentrate on the writing alone for a month or so, sometimes your playing will fall down, and vice versa.

"I met Tadd Dameron in the early fifties, but by the late forties I was influenced by his writing for ten-piece groups. He recorded a lot of things with a group that included Fats Navarro. What I admired about Tadd was not his unconventionality but the fact he wrote so pretty. His voicings were very beautiful. He wrote for Dizzy Gillespie's big band, and in recent years I've heard he had written things that were very adventurous.

"I wrote a couple of arrangements in the first two weeks I was with Basie. They didn't go too well. The first I wrote that did make it was *Blues Backstage*, and then another called *Down for the Count*. Both were written in the winter of 1953, and both were recorded for Verve.

"I maybe got too ambitious in my early arranging. I didn't want to change the style of the band but merely bring it some very original ideas of my own. Not all of 'em got across. I had had no tuition and was self-taught. My experience, in the beginning, was from playing in big bands around Cincinnati, Ohio, playing stocks and special arrangements by fellows in that area. I listened and analyzed what I was hearing. I had a pretty fair ear for chords and changes. I could pick up bits of knowledge here and there.

"My first arrangement was of *Stardust*, and it turned out pretty good. I wrote it for a big band in Cincinnati in '43 or '44. I didn't know what I was really doing, but they played it anyway. It was just hit or miss from then on, and I gradually developed. By the time I

had my own band, I could sit down and write out parts in block harmony and make it sound pretty good.

"During my entire eight years with Basie, I've found that whereas
one arrangement is accepted, the next one may not be. Basie himself
decides. I've had rejected and accepted arrangements over the whole
period! The unforgiveable sin so far as Basie arrangements are concerned is overloading. He will not accept an overloaded arrangement.
What he always says is, 'Give me the simple life, baby.'

"There is a new emphasis on fast tempos for showing off technique
and creating excitement. A fellow named A. K. Solomon wrote *Blee
Blop Blues* and it was exciting to play. It was short—not long or too
drawn out, and as a flag-waver it generated tremendous audience re-
sponse because of all the screaming. It would swing if we played it a
little slower, but we just keep it upstairs.

"But I have to say that Mr. Basie has not forgotten the groovy
tempos. He still likes them, and flag-wavers remain a minority so far
as the repertoire is concerned. The few flag-wavers we play *are* played
often, and maybe the book has been replenished with enough groovy
material.

"Of my own contributions, one of those I prefer is *In a Mellotone*,
although *not* all of the fellows dig it too much. If it's late and they're
tired, the trumpet players sort of drop in the closing chorus. But we
won't go into that! One of my favorites is *Discommotion*. It's named
on the new album, but that track actually is a flag-waver by Ernie
Wilkins called *Basie*. A very sad mistake, so far as I'm concerned! I
hope it's corrected soon. I don't like someone else to get credit for
mine! I want any royalties I receive to be my own, too.

"Others of mine in the book that I like are *Blues in Hoss' Flat*, and
then there's *Easin' It*. Basie likes both of those—the groove, the simplicity. There wasn't too much sweat writing *Easin' It* down, so as an
achievement it's not much.* It's in that easy *groove* and the performance actually means everything. Sometimes you get a poor performance of a good arrangement because the fellows don't interpret it the
way you wanted, or because you can't get across to them *how* you
wanted it interpreted.

"In general, our rehearsals are very tiresome because we rehearse
too many tunes at one rehearsal. By the time we get to the eighteenth

---

* The album entitled *Easin' It* (Roulette R 52106) makes an excellent introduction
to Frank Foster, all seven compositions and arrangements on it being his work. He
was also responsible for six of the arrangements on *Count Basie Swings, Joe
Williams Sings* (Verve V-8488). Among other valuable works not mentioned above
were *Who, Me?* and his most famous composition, *Shiny Stockings*.

arrangement that's been brought in, the fellows don't want to hear anything about how to interpret it! All they want to do is get out of there!

"We have a big turnover, but everything that gets in the book doesn't get played and some things in it get played too much. The turnover of arrangements comes from the fact that we have other arrangers in the band, like Thad Jones and Frank Wess, and Ernie Wilkins is still working for us. Then I like the whole album Benny Carter did for us (*Kansas City Suite,* Roulette 52056). Most of those are wonderful arrangements. He's a brass man as well as a saxophonist, but I think he used to use the trumpets more or less to punctuate the saxes.

"I feel I've neglected the trombone section quite a bit and I plan to do something about that in the future and make better use of the trombones. But three is a hard number to work with. There is so much more that could be done with four.* Ninety percent of the time I've used trombones as part of the brass section, and it doesn't give them enough exercise really. With one more trombone they could be an independent section, although you can get over that by using one or two saxophones with the trombones. No one section is a weak link in this band. Each section is excellent, and they should be featured more, as sections. I'm carrying on a personal campaign now to bring back the reed section, because I'd say in the past ten years reed sections have largely been neglected and brass has been heavily leaned on. I don't intend neglecting anybody in future, but I'm going to show off the reed section more in my arrangements. I don't think we could have a better section leader than we've got now in Marshall Royal.

"I know he plays great clarinet, but for one reason or another the instrument is neglected nowadays and is waning in popularity. In the heyday of the clarinet, of Goodman and Shaw, the flute was hardly ever heard except when Wayman Carver played it with Chick Webb. I guess that was long since forgotten, but in the fifties we had the return of the flute, which I think is a wonderful instrument. I have one. I don't play it well yet, but I shall one day. It seemed new on the scene, and I think the novelty of it appealed to the people.

"I would like to revive interest in the clarinet. There are several good clarinetists around, and it may still be more popular than I know it to be, because I don't keep up with trends unless they are very obvious and all over. I'm going to use clarinet more in the reed section. Whenever I can, I've been snatching a little practice on it, and I'm getting to the point where I can get over the instrument a little

---

* The section was expanded in 1963 and it has contained four trombones ever since.

bit now. I'm going to write a few little simple ditties—no real show-off music—on which the clarinet will be heard. You take *Blue and Sentimental,* on which Prez played clarinet. That is about the extent of what I play at this stage. You don't have to have all technique in the world to get a little color, and I think I can play enough clarinet to vary the shading.

"Neal Hefti, I think, gets more variety in the brass section than he does in the reed section. One nice effect was when he used flute and one trumpet in the harmony and one trumpet in the straight music. Other than that, he hasn't used the clarinet and he hasn't used any different voicings for the reed section other than the straight block harmony. Basie likes the simplicity, but I think you can still achieve a lot of effective color and have the simplicity he likes—and still have arrangements that will please the listeners. Simplicity has nothing to do with lack of color. You don't have to sacrifice one for the other. Color has just been omitted, and that's what we'll have to try to find.

"Perhaps for some listeners there are not enough holes left in the arrangements. If you listen well, you'll find quite a few arrangements we play in which there are some holes left. Basie himself would be mad if there weren't. It's a matter of taste, really. If I think the holes in an arrangement of mine are too filled up, I'll speak to the drummer about it and say, 'Leave it vacant here so the piano can tinkle, or something can happen, or the rhythm can just walk.' If it's too empty somewhere, I say, 'Fill this in.' I haven't really been displeased in this area, although sometimes I feel it could be done with more attention to shading, and a little softer at times. If it were done that way you wouldn't notice it as much as you do. In Birdland, I know, every mistake can be heard. In dance halls some of our mistakes go unnoticed, but in Birdland every mistake is right there, and noticed. Basie is not so fussy about it. We play the same everywhere, whether it's Birdland, the armory in Flint, Michigan, Carnegie Hall, or the Hollywood Bowl, which is for the most part, I guess I'll have to say, loud. But we do know how to shade, and we don't play loud *all* the time.

"Because of the intimate atmosphere in Birdland, if the fellow next to you laughs at you, the people at ringside will know what he's laughing at. I made a terrible mistake last night. I beeped when I should have bopped. I played a note that shouldn't have been there. I was all by myself, and I should have been arrested. Well, that happens. As long as there aren't too many of those to cause the boss to roll his eyes!

"A true jazz fan in Europe is one of the best that you can have sitting out there in front of you, but everybody who comes to listen isn't a true jazz fan. I've seen people bring their whole families, say three or four generations. Probably Grandma and Granddad came out of curiosity, as well as the little five-year-old child. They come and they sit and they clap—what you might call perfunctory applause. They don't always know what it is they're hearing, but they've heard about it and so they come to see what it's all about. Some are always converted.

"The *true* jazz fan in the United States is also an excellent listener, and in the past few years our listening audience has increased—and improved. That is, when we play a dance, there's a larger crowd gathered around the bandstand than before and a smaller crowd off at a distance dancing. Some stand there all night long. That picture has definitely changed from '55, '56, and '57. Jazz listening must have become more universal, because the outdoor jazz concert was something unheard of—by me, anyway—when I first joined the band. A lot of people come to the festival-type thing to listen, and a lot come to do other things."

(1961)

Joe Williams

"My Number One son!"

That is how Count Basie introduced Joe Williams at Basie's seventy-fifth birthday party in Disneyland in 1979. The tall, commanding singer sprang up on stage to a roar of spontaneous applause, and he proceeded to excite an experienced audience of Basie's well-wishers from within the profession.

Although Basie has featured many singers with his band, and has accompanied even more, most of his followers think in terms of two only—Jimmy Rushing and Joe Williams. Since Rushing was a year older than Basie, he could scarcely qualify as a "son," but he was a major factor in the band's success during its early years, just as Williams was in the period that followed the recording of *Every Day* in 1955. The impact of this record was enormous, and Williams was immediately established in the public's mind as a blues singer.

But he had never thought of himself as strictly a blues singer. Although he had gained experience with bands led by Jimmie Noone, Lionel Hampton, Coleman Hawkins, and Andy Kirk before he joined

Basie, his repertoire was the normal mixture of popular songs, ballads, and standards. Rushing's chief successes were the blues he sang, but he, too, featured such songs as *Pennies from Heaven, Exactly Like You, London Bridge Is Falling Down, You Can Depend on Me, I Can't Believe That You're in Love with Me, I Want a Little Girl*, and *Blue Skies*. In Basie's case, the proportion of vocal blues was certainly higher than in those of the other major bands. While most of them played a considerable number of blues, it is curious how few were sung as compared with those performed instrumentally. The biggest hits of some of the more important bands were often blues in one form or another, such as Duke Ellington's *Things Ain't What They Used to Be* and *Diminuendo and Crescendo in Blue*, Fletcher Henderson's *Sugar Foot Stomp*, Erskine Hawkin's *After Hours*, Jimmie Lunceford's *Uptown Blues*, and Earl Hines's *Boogie Woogie on St. Louis Blues*, And there was certainly a profitable lesson to be learned from *Jelly, Jelly*, the Hines hit on which Billy Eckstine sang the blues.

It is important to recognize that social mobility upward had led many urban blacks to regard the blues as low class, as speaking of times and conditions best forgotten. Instrumentally, the blues still meant good music for good times, but the lyrics too often reflected rural origins. References to mules, cotton, and cornbread were not very relevant to city dwellers, except in Chicago, where newly arrived immigrants from the South abounded. And it was in the South, of course, that blues-playing groups like Buddy Johnson's, Louis Jordan's, and Roy Milton's could still tour successfully after most of the established big bands had broken up.

The blues boom of the fifties was largely supported by young whites. They did not, of course, approve of the conditions and hardships that lent authenticity to the accents and delivery of singers from the South, but the grim and often sordid background to the music that they enjoyed undoubtedly gave it savor. In effect, the North preferred the blues of the South and measured authenticity by its Southern and rural characteristics.

Trombonist Quentin Jackson once described the Basie band of the fifties as "a sophisticated blues band." With Joe Williams, the leader added a sophisticated blues singer to it, and then launched him with a song by Memphis Slim, a veteran but not unsophisticated blues artist himself. So evident a success was *Every Day* that Basie's supporters promptly divided into two camps.

"I went ape," said Nat Pierce, recalling the first time he heard Williams at Birdland. "As I was leaving, I met John Hammond coming down the stairs.

" 'Basie got himself a singer,' I said.

" 'Ah, I like Jimmy Rushing,' John answered.

" 'Wait till you hear this cat!'

" 'Nobody like Jimmy. . . .' "

Hammond's preference was not merely a matter of loyalty to Rushing. There was a generation gap, a difference of approach, a different conception of what was or was not authentic, and Joe Williams was well aware of it.

"There were a lot of people like that," he said, "and a lot of critics in England and Europe who were hostile. After the posters went up and signs were stuck on them saying, 'All Seats Sold,' the reviewers would write, 'Most of the applause was reserved for a singer, and he is no Jimmy Rushing,' and so on, blah, blah, blah. It took 'em a long time. It took them years before they finally decided: 'So it isn't Jimmy Rushing. But wait a minute—he's got something to say, and not only that, he says it well.' Some people just have preconceived ideas about things like that. They don't want to hear the band without Prez and Buck Clayton. That's *their* band. It's like when Duke had Ben Webster. 'How can it possibly be as good now?' they'd be asking years later when he had Paul Gonsalves. That's an example, I think, of a closed mind. When Ben himself went in that band, he brought a new sound to it, and I went out and bought those records like *Cottontail* and *Koko* before I'd even got a record player!"

The union recording ban of 1943, a crucial year in jazz history, prevented the preservation of many important musical developments. It may also have delayed the arrival of Joe Williams at center stage by a dozen years.

"Lionel Hampton had a singer called Rubel Blakely, who left Hamp's band in 1943," Williams remembered. "The manager of the Regal Theatre called me and said, 'Hey, I want you to join Lionel Hampton. He's going to pay you eleven dollars a night.' So I went and joined him in Boston. Man, what a band! Oh, my God! He had Joe Morris, Joe Newman, and Lammar Wright, and Joe Wilder was playing lead trumpet. Milt Buckner was playing piano and arranging. He had Arnett Cobb on tenor, Eric Miller on guitar, and George Jenkins on drums. Man, that band was cooking! I was with Hamp two or three months, but didn't get a chance to record because of the ban. Then I went back to Chicago, and I didn't mind, because Chicago was still Chicago in those days. Good Lord, *every*body was making some money!"

It was in Chicago, in 1950, that Williams first sang with Basie, during the period he was fronting a small group.

"I worked with him at the Brass Rail," he continued, "when he had Clark Terry, Wardell Gray, Buddy De Franco, and in the rhythm section, Freddie Green, Jimmy Lewis, and Gus Johnson. Talk about swinging! They'd get into some things that would swing you into bad health! Clark would play *any*thing, and so could Wardell and Buddy. Basie, Freddie, Jimmy, and Gus would just lay it on 'em. That was a lot of fun, and that was where I found out about responding to musical cues. I'd be someplace out in the room, and he'd give me that *ding-ding-ding-ding*. That meant the number might run another five minutes, so go to the bathroom and do whatever you have to do, but be ready to hit the stage as soon as it is over.

"Later on, in the fifties with the big band, when we got those long introductions to tunes, we no longer needed signals like that. *Every Day* had a four-bar introduction plus two choruses—twenty-four bars—and another four-bar interval in front, so I had plenty of time to get on stage for it. That was how Ernie Wilkins conceived and wrote the arrangement, and that's the way it's been ever since. Nobody said, 'Let's have it this way, in case Joe is in the back of the room!' The same thing with *The Comeback*. Basie plays two choruses and then the trombones come in—ba-*ba*-ba-*ba*-ba-*ba*—with that old-time blues figure in the bass, and then it's *I know my baby. . . .*

"Working with musicians like Frank Wess, Joe Newman, Thad Jones, Marshall Royal, and Benny Powell, there was never a lull, and I don't think there ever was a time when we felt we were being put upon or anything like that. You take care of your *own* business, of course. I never had any big problems, because I never felt I needed much, and I used to arrange for money to go home. There wasn't one cat in that band who was a drag. There was real esprit de corps, pride in what we were doing, in getting it right.

"We made some long trips, but they were fun, too. I remember some of the Birdland tours, and one in particular in 1957 when we jumped from Los Angeles to Texas. That was a *looooong* trip! There were no facilities on the bus to relieve yourself, so the bus would make what we called a Pittsburgh stop. We have pictures of all the guys lined up beside the bus, and turned towards it to take a piss. We have pictures of Sarah Vaughan getting out of the bus and running across a field to some bushes for the same purpose. Sometimes, when we were on a tight schedule, the bus driver would just open the door a crack, and we'd stand there and wail and let it go. Because of the companionship, it was a lot of fun, and there were a lot of jokes."

As his association with Basie lengthened, Williams felt a need for new material.

"When I had something new I wanted to do," he said, "I'd go to Basie and tell him, and he'd be so cool all the time.

" 'You don't need more music,' he'd say. 'You've got our arrangements, and you're breaking it up every damn night everywhere we go. What do you need more for?'

" 'I just want some new music,' I'd say.

" 'Well, okay, talk to my guys then,' he'd answer.

"So I'd get with Frank Foster or Ernie Wilkins, have an arrangement made, and do it that very night. Basie would sit there at the piano, look at me, and give me that nod. What I got from that was the knowledge that you have to do what you believe in. Man, you sometimes have to fight the person that's closest to you. You have to fight your *mother* sometimes! And your father! I consider Basie a father, but I had to fight him every inch of the way to get what I wanted."

Nevertheless, there was a time when Basie provoked an addition to the singer's repertoire.

"We were in Boston," Williams resumed, "and we went to a theater where Buddy Johnson and his band were playing. Buddy's sister, Ella, was singing *Alright, Okay, You Win,* and I was just kidding with Basie, talking about the way she was singing it. Later that night we were in an after-hours joint. I always remember that, because it was the first time Sarah Vaughan and I did a duet together. We did *Teach Me Tonight,* just for kicks. We were still sitting there when they played Buddy Johnson's record of *Alright, Okay, You Win.* Sonny Payne and I were kidding about this chick singing her head off. 'She sure sounds funky, doesn't she?' he said. 'Yeah,' Basie said, turning to me, 'and you ought to sing that song.'

"I thought he was kidding me, but he knew how to get my goat and make me angry. 'You ought to sing it,' he added, 'but you probably can't sing it as well as that bitch can.' He has a way of doing things like that, and it works with most guys.

"So I got with Frank Foster and he made an arrangement. I wasn't going to do it the way Ella Johnson did it. It suited her with her little cutesy ways, but it wasn't ballsy, and so far as I was concerned it didn't suit a male vocalist. So I changed it. After I recorded it, the people who wrote the tune recalled the sheet music, rewrote it the way I did it, and now everybody does it that way."

By 1960 the urge to go out on his own and do something different had become compelling. Williams gave Basie six months' notice, and when he left the band early in 1961 he had six months of engagements already set.

"We closed at the Apollo on a Thursday, and Joe Newman and I left the same night," he recalled. "I was to open at the Storyville in Boston the following Monday. Basie was great. He took the time off, blocked the date out, and we rode up in the club car on the train together. We ate and drank all the way, and when we got out of our cab in front of the Bradford Hotel there was a sign which said *Count Basie Presents* in very small letters and *Joe Williams* in very big letters. Basie introduced me at both shows that night, and then went back to New York.

" 'I knew you'd be all right,' he said before he left. It was really beautiful. He's always been like my Number One fan."

Since then Joe Williams has become an international star in his own right, but the bond with Basie remains strong and there have been many happy reunions.

(1979)

Al Grey

(TROMBONE)

"I see a future in you, Al Grey, but you'll have to listen to me!"

Count Basie and Al Grey sauntered up the street from the club they were playing in Philadelphia.

"Well, okay, Chief," Grey replied.

"I can tell you, but you'll have to listen."

Grey listened, and continued to listen.

"Basie's been in the business so long," Grey said, "He *knows*, he really does know. He gives me ideas on how to play that plunger style. He mentions trombone players from so way back that I never heard of them, but he'll hum, and I'll listen, and when it strikes he'll say, 'That's it!' Like when we recorded *The Rare Butterfly*. He listened to the first playback and said, 'Yes, but I want a little more humor.' Other times he'll say, 'I want you to be more boisterous here,' or maybe 'a little more delicate.'

"I didn't have the feeling at first, but with him as an advisor to me, I do have it now. Trombone players ask me how to do it. It's a matter of how you move your fingers, moving them in and out on the plunger, letting the air leak to form different sounds. What I'm working on now is how to make words out of notes—more talking than 'yes,' 'what,' and 'no.' I think that can be developed quite a lot. The style can be very melodic, too. I listen to singers and often prefer to play more or less like a singer would sing."

Born in Aldie, Virginia, Al Grey came from a musical family. His father started him off on baritone horn when he was only four years old. In his high school band, he subsequently played and became very proficient on the E-flat tuba, but when he joined the navy and was sent to Great Lakes he realized there was no future on that instrument. Knowing bass clef, he decided trombone was the logical horn for him, so he took it up on his own, without regular instruction. "I used to have to get up early in the morning and practice," he said, "because I just couldn't make it." But two trombone players influenced him at that time. One he remembered only as Trombone Smitty from Detroit—"He could play!" The other was Rocks McConnell, who had been with Lucky Millinder. Osie Johnson, who was writing for the band then, also helped him greatly.

When he left the navy, he joined Benny Carter. Like everyone else who worked for him, Grey had the greatest respect for Carter: "He's an accomplished, finished musician, and the biggest thing about him from my point of view was that he taught me how to *phrase*. Then he played all of those instruments, and played all of them well. One day he decided to pick up the trombone. Though I was only a newcomer, I thought I sounded pretty good. So he played, and I was soon saying to myself, 'Well, well, you'd better take note here!' "

Jimmie Lunceford heard and hired Grey about the time Carter broke up his band and went to Hollywood. "I had to take Trummy's solos," Grey recalled, "and I even used to sing his numbers like *Margie* and *'T'ain't What You Do*. Trummy was one of my idols then. He was the first one I thought could really play trombone. I used to play his solos note for note and at that time he played so high I had to find another mouthpiece. I was the youngest in the band and they really had to hold me down. Bebop was popular at that time and they weren't going to have any bebop players in that band! But it wasn't bebop to me. It was just a difference in playing chord changes that had more notes in them, and being more familiar with them."

After Lunceford's death and a period with Lucky Millinder, Grey joined Lionel Hampton's band. Here he found quite a different atmosphere. "The fellows would sit up and clap their hands and pop their fingers, and Lionel would say, 'Gate, eh-eh-eh . . . pop your fingers, gate!' I couldn't see it at first, but it developed a different feeling, a stronger rhythmic feeling. It taught me the more human side of life, to be more jolly in music, something I didn't get with Benny and Lunceford. Theirs was more like the modern approach, more serious, where you concentrate on playing the music and nothing else, but somehow this gave me more feeling, more of what they call 'soul' today. The band had been together long enough to shake down, and there were great artists in it like Clifford Brown, Fats Navarro, Jerome Richardson, Jimmy Cleveland, Benny Powell, and Ellis Bartee. But I think everyone should have that experience, to be around someone who has as much rhythm as Hamp. Lucky Millinder had rhythm, too. He could clap his hands and get a beat that would make you stop and listen."

When he left, Grey went into studio work with Sy Oliver, an experience that reminded him somewhat of his period with Benny Carter. "Sy's was a brain made for music," he said, "and he made everyone stay up on their toes—no relaxing. That kind of work is more of a business matter, of taking care of music, and it can be kind of cold and impersonal, but it was good for me to be working alongside those studio musicians. They have finesse, but, you know, some of them believe Negroes can't play trombone. They say Negroes can play all the instruments *but* trombone. Of course, it's very different from a finger instrument, and I appreciate the difficulties violin players sometimes have, but . . ."

Next, Grey tried it with his own eight-piece group in the South. He accompanied singers like Bobby Blue Bland, Junior Parker, Willa Mae Thornton, Marie Adams, and Gatemouth Brown on Don Robey's record sessions and went out on tour with some of them. The band made good money but had little opportunity to play good music, and after three-and-a-half years he felt he was in a rut. He returned home to Philadelphia, where he at first found himself back in the same r. and b. groove. Then he worked with Arnett Cobb—"We had a nice little band, but we played good music, so we didn't get too much work."

After Cobb's automobile accident, the band dissolved and Grey joined Dizzy Gillespie's big band, in which he was very happy. "Dizzy," he said, "let everybody play, regardless of how well you could play—or how badly. He would give you a chance and let you blow. He brought me back to life really, because I had been hidden away down South so long. It was a family band—really together— and everybody just hated to see it break up." The spirit of gaiety and humor that emanated from Dizzy was something Grey carried with him when he joined Count Basie in 1957.

Grey has one of the biggest trombone sounds in jazz. He gratefully remembers his high school teacher, Harvey Leroy Wilson, who taught him the nonpressure system. ("It takes the pressure off your lips, but it is a process," he explained with a grin, "of building the stomach, which is why the stomach gets bigger all the time!") He feels the plunger style retains the true character of the trombone, which has tended to be lost. The production of the low notes at the bottom of the horn is a function of the instrument, whereas those musicians who think the idea is to play only high often sound like trumpet players and lose a lot of color. The plunger up against the bell makes more pressure and develops strength, which is why, Grey imagined, Cootie Williams has one of the biggest trumpet sounds.

Plunger trombone has, of course, a long tradition back of it, a fact acknowledged in the title of Grey's Argo album, *The Last of the Big Plungers*. How he feels about that tradition, and how he came to help extend it, he explained like this:

"When I was with Lionel Hampton, he had Sonny Parker singing. He could holler the blues and he used to make me want to express a happy humorous feeling. So sometimes I would get to play fill-ins with Sonny. After I got comfortable with Basie, Joe Williams was singing the blues one night at the Blue Note, and I was feeling pretty good, and he hollered something that reminded me of Sonny. So I just picked up the plunger and made a figuration. 'That's it,' Basie said, 'keep it in!'

"From there on, I started to develop the plunger. Some people think it's a freak thing, but it's not. It's a development, because you can find the same notes with the plunger as with the open horn. I think we need more humor in music today, too, and I try not to play the same note-for-note solo night after night, because that can become very boring for the fellows around you. Sometimes I crack 'em up with something quite different, and sometimes I know Joe Williams wishes I'd keep the same little things in there so as not to distract him. He'll turn around and look, but he'll keep on singing!

"I'm trying to set my mind on playing more of the true form of jazz. I know about the technical side of music, but if you take too much of jazz away you'll get back to something like symphony. Already some music they call jazz is so intricate it has no warmth, no personal feeling to the heart.

"Sometimes people say to me: 'You're hamming it up. You're enjoying life too much. It's out of place. That's something that belongs to the past.' Other times when I don't feel so jolly the music can be just as sad. Then they'll ask, 'What's the matter? You're so nasty tonight. Something bothering you?' Sometimes the difference comes from taking a little stimulant. A jazz musician is surrounded by drink all the time, and it can release the emotions and help him to convey a message. It's just not natural to feel and play in the same mood always."

(1960)

Sonny Cohn

"I was born in Chicago March 14, 1925. My father could sit down at the piano and play things by ear, but while he was working at Sears Roebuck, before he went into the Post Office, Omer Simeon persuaded him to buy a trumpet. I heard him tooting on the horn, but although he tried and tried and tried, he never really did anything with it. So he decided to put the horn up and wait till I was old enough to try it.

"When I was about eleven years old I started taking lessons with Charles Anderson, a guy who worked with my father. He used to come out to the house once a week, and I think he played trumpet in some local band that didn't amount to much of anything. Because they worked together, he and my father had a deal going and the charge was only fifty cents a lesson. I would more or less mess around and wouldn't practice, but I had a good ear. 'How does this go?' I'd ask him. He'd play it, and I'd cop my ear on him and play it right behind him. Gradually I got more and more interested. When I graduated from elementary school and went on into high school, I started playing with the little bands. I found out that little girls liked musicians and bands and everything, so I just went on from there.

"I have a brother and a sister, and I'm in between the two. My brother studied clarinet and saxophone, but he never did anything with it. My sister had piano, and she was pretty good. In fact, she can still play, can sit down and read anything she likes. She and I and a couple of other guys in the building where we were living got together and formed a quartet that we called Frances and Her Rhythm Kings. We used to play around at little social affairs on Saturday nights and make two or three dollars.

"One of the guys, Johnny Thompson, became pretty well known in Chicago. He played tenor and would have been a very, very good saxophonist, but he met with an unfortunate accident three or four years ago. I think he was on his way to work and tried to catch a subway train when something happened, and he was killed.

"Guys are funny about girls in a band, so eventually Johnny and I organized an eight-piece group with a piano player called King Fleming. (He has several albums out.) That's when I *really* started getting interested. We used to play a social dance every Wednesday at Union Park. We were still in school and this was indoors, like a field house. Admission was fifteen cents, and kids from all over the neighborhood would come. It started out with the band taking half and the park taking half, but it grew till we were each making about three dollars. That was good for lunch money and other stuff at school. The band began to get very popular, and some of the guys wanted to join the union and some didn't. That was where we came to the parting of the ways. It was still King Fleming's band, and it kept on going.

"At the time Roy Eldridge was working at the Three Deuces in Chicago. I was too young to hear him, but I always looked forward to a time when I would have the chance to work with guys like that. Then a couple of years ago he came into Basie's band and he inspired me very much. Of course, Johnny Thompson and I used to buy *all* his records when we were with King Fleming. I liked to listen to Buck Clayton, Sweets Edison, and Ed Lewis on the Basie records, to Tommy Stevenson, then Paul Webster, and then Snooky Young on Lunceford's. It's been almost like a fairy tale for me. It shows what time will do for you, because I've *played* with a lot of those guys. I've sat with Snooky for years, and I've played with Sweets. I've never played with Buck, but I've listened to him a lot, believe me. Of course, we listened to Duke Ellington's band, and Ray Nance. It's a funny thing, but Ray and I are both from Chicago and didn't really meet until I was in Basie's band, and then it was like we were old friends who'd been knowing each other all the time.

"Right after I graduated from high school, I started working with Richard Fox's band in Calumet City. That's when I got my first taste of playing for shows, and I learned an awful lot from Richard. He's still one of my dear, dear friends, and each time the Basie band comes into town I look up and see Richard Fox sitting in the audience.

"We started buying little stock arrangements when I was in King Fleming's band. There was quite a bit of reading to do with Richard, what with the pieces you had to play for the acts. That's when it really started coming for me. Along with this I was still practicing, but I seemed to spend most of my time getting to and from the job.

"I was still living on the West Side of Chicago, and I'd have to catch a bus at about six in the evening to get out on the South Side in time to meet the car at seven o'clock. We'd get to Calumet City about 8:30, hit at nine o'clock, and play till two or three. By the time I got home it would be six o'clock in the morning! This was seven nights a week. It was my first steady job, so I stood it for about five months, but then it got so I couldn't take it anymore and I had to leave Richard.

"Captain Walter Dyett of Du Sable High School, who taught some of today's great musicians, had a band of professionals who had been to the school. Even though I hadn't been to Du Sable, I worked in that band for over a year before I went in the service for eighteen months. When I came back, I worked with him again. It was like a club-date band. We'd play at the Parkway Ballroom, the Pershing Ballroom, Warwick Hall, and different clubs for social events, three or four nights a week. With this band, and by gigging steady as I did, you could make a nice little taste to live on. Captain Dyett's band was usually ten or twelve pieces—three trumpets, two trombones, three saxes, and rhythm. He made some of the arrangements himself, and he'd buy stocks. It was just a good, commercial band that worked all the time. A dollar was a dollar then, in '43–'45. I learned a lot in that band, and I think the fellow who influenced my playing more than anyone I worked with was Melvin Moore. He was a wonderful trumpet player. He lives in California and he's still active.

"I went in the army at the end of '43 and got out early in '45. They sent me to Fort Custer, MacDill Field, in Tampa and from there to Fort Myers. I was in the engineers, but I never got a chance to do anything because as soon as they found out I was a trumpet player they'd always make me the bugler! But I finally got in the 770th AEF band in Greenville, South Carolina. It was a good band, we stayed in one place, and there was comradeship among musicians. When the band was inactivated, I returned to Captain Dyett for six months and then went with Red Saunders.

"Red had just left the Club DeLisa and it looked like a step up and steady work. He had six pieces, and we worked at the Capitol Lounge for six weeks. Then we moved to the Garrick Lounge and the Downbeat Room, where Red Allen, Stuff Smith, and everybody had worked. We were at the Garrick Lounge for fourteen months, and it was one of the best jobs I ever had.

"Red was an excellent drummer. He had the reputation of being one of the greatest show drummers in the country, but with our six pieces we were more or less an act in ourselves. I guess the people just liked us, because we were drawing good. He had Leon Washington, a *very* good tenor saxophone player; Antonio Cosie was on alto; Mickey Sims on bass; Porter Derico on piano; and Red played the drums. When Cosie left, we got Nat Jones in his place. Nat plays a lot like Johnny Hodges and is just wonderful. He's still in Chicago. Why isn't he better known? Well, a lot of musicians in the Chicago area let music become their second means of income, because they get good jobs and don't want to travel. They have quite a few things coming, like commercials and that kind of stuff, so they can make it comfortably. But they're still good musicians! I think Nat has a good daytime job, but he's still active in the music business and works with one of the gig bands at weekends.

"After Nat came, we went to New York and played at Kelly's Stables for about six weeks in 1946. This was my first time in New York. We made some records that were quite successful, but after two years Red reorganized, formed a twelve-piece band, and went back to the DeLisa. I was there until it closed in 1958, and altogether I was with Red from 1945 to 1960.

"We played mostly show music at the DeLisa. Bill Davis was arranging for the ensembles then. Producers and choreographers are forever making changes up to the last minute, and you have to sit down and write arrangements right then and there. Bill would do that and they *always* came out beautiful. He had come to Chicago from Texas with Milt Larkins's band, and so had Illinois Jacquet. Another wonderful arranger was Marl Young. He wrote the arrangement for Miss Cornshucks's hit, *So Long*, and if I'm not mistaken he did some for Dinah Washington, too. We played things for a whole lot of different singers, like Lurlean Hunter. She's good looking, still sings, and I don't understand why she didn't break through, because everyone—including all the singers—knew how good she was. You could hear her voice on quite a few commercials, like those for White Rain, Campbell's soups, and the Jolly Green Giant.

"At the DeLisa, for her spots she would have arrangements by Osie Johnson and Pee Wee Jackson. They used to collaborate and they turned out some beautiful arrangements. Pee Wee was another excellent trumpet player. He and Freddie Webster worked together in the Lunceford band and were great friends. Pee Wee died too soon, but you can hear him on some of the old Dinah Washington records. One in particular I never forget is *I Can't Get Started*. Pee Wee and his big sound. . . . He and Freddie Webster could *play*. Another very good trumpet around Chicago was Shorts McConnell, who had been with Earl Hines. I think he had the misfortune to lose his mouthpiece. Anyway, something happened to him, because you never hear of him now.

"Chicago had its share of good musicians! You'd be surprised at the number of musicians and entertainers who have been working there for years and years, and you never hear about them. Harold Jones is from Chicago. I had heard of him but didn't meet him till he joined us on drums. I knew about Oscar Brashear because he was a pupil of Charlie Allen, a good friend of mine. Charlie's a very good teacher and makes all my mouthpieces. He was lead trumpet in the Earl Hines band, and right today he can still pick up the horn and hit those high notes.

"George Dixon, who was also with Earl, is another good friend of mine. We all belong to the same lodge. Because of my friendship with people like him, I know far more about the past than most musicians my age. I know more than just the contemporary styles. When the Red Saunders band started up again at the Club DeLisa, we had three trumpets, but for the last six years there was only one—me. We had good trumpet players in that band, like Charlie Gray and Nick Cooper, and I'm not ashamed to admit that I've learned something from everyone I've played with.

"I was working at a place called Robert's with Red Saunders before I joined Basie. They have a five-day law in Chicago—five days' work and two days off. Basie was in town, playing the Regal Theater, when John Anderson got sick. He had taken Wendell Culley's place. Someone called and asked if I'd be interested, so I went down, worked the rest of the engagement, and made a light rehearsal with them after they finished. 'Well, I'll see you,' I said, leaving. This was in November, and a couple of days later I got another call asking if I'd like to join the band on a permanent basis. I said I would, after the holidays. Something like that. Duke used to play the Blue Note before the holidays, and Basie would come in right after. I didn't have a wife then, because I'd been divorced a few years, and I felt I'd been living at home long enough, so I joined Basie on January 19, 1960.

"In the trumpet section then were Snooky Young, Thad Jones, and Joe Newman. I always thought of Joe as a human dynamo. He's always in there driving—always, never no letup. We got to be real close. Thad and I were friends even before he joined Basie, because whenever he came to Chicago he'd always come to the DeLisa. Every Sunday night– Monday morning, everybody would come to the breakfast show, which actually started at 6:30 in the morning. It was a huge place. You could get a thousand people in there. It was the first club with one of those hydraulic floors. When the show was on, the floor would go up, and when it was over it would go down and people could come out and dance. Show people knew it was a place where they could come after they finished work, see their friends, and have a good time. The DeLisa was important. After two of the brothers who ran it died, the other brothers tried to keep it going, but they had their problems. The club is still there under a different name, and it functions, but it's not like it was.

"How was it coming from a seven-piece band to Basie's? It didn't take long to adjust, and it was just the greatest. Especially with that dream section. Every now and then I had to pinch myself and ask, 'Is this really happening to me?'

"Snooky Young and I were friends, too, and we had something in common. We didn't volunteer, but if we were asked we could do it. I think I'm pretty well equipped, and if I'm asked I can cover it. Snooky, that son of a gun, *can* play everything. I sat beside him and was thrilled for two whole years. To me, he's the greatest, and I'll always sing his praises. He's got it! He plays the trumpet the way it *should be played*. We'd sit up there and he would make it just like it was *nothing*, those notes just ringing out of that horn! He thrilled me for two years. Some things trumpet players do, it looks like they're hard. Snooky does them like falling off a log—he makes it *look* so easy. He does everything right. You get out what you put into it, and he must put everything into it.

"When I joined this band, I was called on to do what Wendell Culley did—to play all the pretty things and play the lead on ballads. I inherited the solo on *Li'l Darlin'*, and off and on I would take the one on *April in Paris*. I alternated on *The Deacon*, and when we made the album with Benny Carter, I was assigned the plunger solo on *Meeting Time*. I was real happy about my role. In fact, I still enjoy it, and I've been here for nine years. It just doesn't seem like its's been that long!*

"Today, the trumpet section consists of Gene Coe, Al Aarons, Oscar Brashear, and myself, and it has been going well over a year. It's a good section and we all get along. There's a fine human relationship. Gene's a very good lead man. Oscar is new, but he's just like one of the guys

---

* Ten years later, Sonny Cohn is still there, still apparently happy, and clearly a much valued part of Count Basie's organization.

from the old school, and that's rare in up-and-coming trumpet players. As for Al, he really hasn't had the recognition he should have had. He had been in the band about eight years, and he's like me—another trumpet player who's not pushy. He does what he has to do, but that doesn't mean he can't do more. I don't think there's anything Al can't do on that horn. He's technically gifted and very versatile. In the last couple of years he picked up the flugelhorn, and it's just beautiful.

"All four of us in the section now have flugelhorns. I like the instrument. It's good for solos. You really need a special flugel mouthpiece. A flugelhorn with a trumpet mouthpiece doesn't get that sound. A flugelhorn mouthpiece is deeper and the throat a little bigger. Charlie Allen makes all our mouthpieces and makes the rims the same as our trumpets, so it's the same feel even though the flugel mouthpiece is deeper. That way, going from one to another doesn't present a problem.

"Home is still Chicago, and when we have a week off I can indulge in my hobby, photography. I have my own darkroom and quite an expensive collection of cameras. I like taking pictures of kids. I have a daughter of twenty-five and a granddaughter. There are nieces and nephews, too, who are still young, so I have plenty of subjects to practice on. You don't have to say 'Smile!' You just let them do what they want to do and catch them when they don't know they're being photographed."

(1969)

Eric Dixon

(TENOR SAXOPHONE, FLUTE, AND ARRANGER)

"When I was about eight, I got into a drum-and-bugle corps on Staten Island, where I was born. They had to lie about my age to get me in, because I was small then. I was always interested in the melodic side of music and I started in playing bugle rather than drums, and I stayed in that band until I was about sixteen. I used to get a big kick out of watching the street bands with all the different instruments, and when I was a kid I used to walk beside the saxophone players. The instrument had caught my eye right away and when I was twelve I insisted that my mother buy me a tenor saxophone. I found a teacher who taught me fingering and the rudiments, and I think I caught on pretty quick because I always had a good ear. After a few years, he felt he wasn't qualified to take me any further, so he recommended a teacher in New York and I went to him every week for another five years.

"Music was a kind of hobby for me then and I didn't give it a thought as a way of making money. So long as I was living at home and going to school, I was torn between music and sports. Sport was very strong with me until I went into the service in 1951, and then the fact that I was well up on my horn helped me get into the army band after my basic training. Of the twenty-four months I was in the army, I spent twenty-two in the band at Fort Dix. This was when I realized that if I had gone to a school with a band of more or less this kind, I would have grabbed on to music much quicker. In those two years I really got into it. Sport gradually drifted away and it became music, music, music. . . . So in a way the army made a big turning for me. We played military music, but we also played jazz in the service clubs. Andy McGhee, who was with Lionel Hampton, was in the band, and so was Lou Blackburn, the trombone player.

"It was jazz from the beginning with me. I was an 'old school' lover —the tenor saxophonists like Don Byas, Ben Webster, and Coleman Hawkins. It was their sound and technique I liked, but most of all their sound. Right away, when I hear good sound, I'm captured. I go to hear Duke Ellington for the band and particularly Paul Gonsalves. Sometimes, when he's playing, I just stand there with my mouth open. He has such a wonderful sound, and he maintains it all the time. You occasionally run into a good musician who substitutes technique when, for some reason, he can't get the sound together. I can listen to someone like that for the sake of his technique, but sound is just very important to me.

"When I was in the service, I didn't play with the type of sound I do now, but more like Stan Getz. There was a fellow in the band who had a Don Byas sound, and whenever we were jamming I would notice it. It would overshadow everybody, no matter how well they knew their instrument, and no matter how much they played. When he played and was done, a well-spoken story had been told. So I listened to him and realized he was really taking charge. He was Henry Durant, from Newark, but I haven't seen him for years. I think he would have gone a long way in music had he continued, but he got off the track.

"I thought about music seriously when I was in the service, but when I got out I didn't know of anything I could get into! I had had a job before in a factory, packing dresses up, and they had told me I could go back, but I had decided I'd take a little time off first. The day after I came out, a fellow called me on the telephone who didn't even know I'd been in the army two years. He wanted me for a job at Copa City, Long Island, and it lasted four or five months, six nights a week. Mal Waldron played piano in the group at first, and then Al Richardson (Wally's brother). That was in 1953, but the job kept on going and I worked another in 1954 with Mal, Peck Morrison, and Frankie Brown. Later that year, I started working with Cootie Williams at the Savoy Ballroom. He had six pieces and I was with him seven or eight months. Then in 1955 I went with Johnny Hodges for about his

last trip out—about three months—before he decided to go back to
Duke. The following year, I was with Benny Green's quintet for a
while.

"All this time I had wanted to go to Juilliard on the G.I. Bill, but
when I went to the school I found they only allowed about two weeks
off. This was at the time I was with Johnny Hodges, and he did a lot of
traveling. Although I had wanted to study composition, I figured it
was better to be out there, working, and getting myself a little
recognized—or hoping to—than being two years in school. Finally,
time ran out. You have only so long after you get out of the service.
Deep down in my heart I regret it, because though I love to blow, I
also want to write music. Although I haven't written for Basie's band
yet, I can do it, and I've written quite a few arrangements for big
bands, and I have them home. For a short while I used to rehearse a
band. Freddie Hubbard and Julian Priester used to come. There were a
lot of young fellows and they put the idea of writing to me. I was
satisfied with what I did, but although it wasn't hard, a lot of those
fellows hadn't had any experience of playing in a big band and they
weren't blending together. Then, too, the arrangements were written
for fourteen or fifteen pieces, and sometimes only ten guys would
come by. Other times, I could have had two orchestra rehearsals a
week. There are a couple of my big-band arrangements on Reuben
Phillips's U.A. album—*Two by Four, Eric's Flute.*

"Even without a Juilliard background, you can make progress, and I
found the biggest help was just listening to other arrangements. Some
of the most famous jazz arrangers didn't have much training, because
there weren't schools equipped to teach them in their day. Now you
have to risk embarrassment to get good. You may write something you
think is good, but when you hear it, it's awful. That sharpens you up,
makes you get on the ball. It might not be all wrong, but you have to
experiment, get laughed at, too, and everything else. My problem is
that when I write I need a piano, and I never did have one. You need
it when you're experimenting, just to strike a chord and see what it
sounds like to your ear. When you have a piano and play it all the
time, and you're familiar with the keyboard, you really know those
chords you want to play, the voicing and everything.

"With a lot of groups you hear today, the rhythm section starts playing and then a horn comes in, but there's no real togetherness. Anytime
there are six pieces and you have three horns, there can and should be
an awful lot going on. It's so much better, too, from the fact that if one
man has to be replaced you still have music. Of course, I've always
liked big bands, but today there aren't enough to give young players
experience. I was discussing alto players with some other musicians

recently and we came to the conclusion that we knew of no one in our own age bracket—thirty to thirty-two—who could sit down and lead a saxophone section. That doesn't mean there isn't anyone, but men like Marshall Royal, Russell Procope, and George Dorsey are older, and when they were coming up there were a whole lot of big bands. Jimmy Powell is another very experienced saxophone player. Once, when Marshall had to go home on emergency leave, Jimmy took his place for two weeks. He was with Basie in the forties, and he has worked with Machito, Bill Doggett, and Reuben Phillips.

"I like big bands because you can always have something going on. I've been on a lot of dates with arrangers like Oliver Nelson, and Oliver is one of the finest today. I was on those *Afro-American Sketches* sessions, and I thought he did a wonderful job. He keeps very busy now, but he always tries to keep up on his horn. He told me Johnny Hodges and Jimmy Forrest were two of his idols. Before he writes an arrangement, he always likes to hear the group, to see what style will suit it. He asks you what you want. How much do you want happening behind you? He's very capable, and he's always on time with his music, not like some arrangers. He's very sincere, too, and if he gets his foot in the door he'll call the musicians he really wants.

"I also like Billy Byers as an arranger. I was on that Mercury album he did—*Impressions of Duke Ellington*—and it was very good for a studio band, but there's nothing like a band that works regularly together. If I get a band of good musicians, and we work together for a time, and then you get a band of the best studio musicians, your band still won't sound as good as mine. When somebody brings a new arrangement to Basie's or Duke's band, they feel it so much better, because they're accustomed to playing together. When I first joined Basie, I found a lot of things in the music were not written, the different bends and stuff you hear the saxophone and brass sections playing. It was difficult for me at first, because I would go straight ahead when they were bending, but when a new arrangement is brought in now I know what they're going to do. It doesn't take you long, if you can think in that Basie vein.

"That's getting too far ahead of my story. After Benny Green, I free-lanced for years and years. I was in the Apollo band with Reuben Phillips four years, and I always managed to work. Quincy Jones asked me to join at a time when I was working pretty steadily, but before ever I went with him I had been to Europe with Curley Hamner, the Cooper brothers, and Lloyd Mayers. We were with the Josephine Baker show in 1959 and worked a whole year in Paris. When we came back, in the Topa Club on 125th Street, I played tenor, alto, and trumpet. I always played all the saxophone family, but I never studied trumpet. (My brother had one when we were younger—I'm the youngest of four brothers.) At the end of 1960, Quincy was going over to Europe when we were working at the Purple Manor, and that was the trip Jerome Richardson didn't make, so Budd Johnson and I played tenors. It was an enthusiastic band and the book was very interesting. Maybe Quincy tried to do it the hard way, without a singer. Yet the people didn't dance to that band. On the biggest dance floors, the crowd would be packed all around the stand. I enjoyed the group and I stayed with Quincy until it broke up in November, after we were at Basin Street East with Peggy Lee and Billy Eckstine. I joined Basie in December [1961] when Budd Johnson left.

"The difference between Basie's and Duke's band is the greater variety of music that Duke has, but I think Basie's is the more consistent band. I've heard people say they've heard Basie's band sound better, but they always add that it still sounds good. Everybody in that Ellington band has a mood, and they have such moods it amazes me how well they can play together. And nobody is going to sound as good as that band when they decide to play. Buster Cooper is in the trombone section now and I think it was the right move for him. He's a good trombone player and the experience will help him. He was in Lionel Hampton's band before he joined Curley Hamner, but that's different, altogether different, although just about everybody you ever heard of was in Hamp's band at some time or other.

"Basie's band is another I enjoy being in. Maybe we don't look so interested in what we're doing *every* night, because—you know, one night here, one night there—sometimes we're awfully tired. But it's always pleasing, even if you wouldn't believe it from the facial expressions. If it didn't sound good, we wouldn't enjoy it. And I think Basie has one of the finest reed sections. His and Duke's are opposites, but both are distinctive. Before I joined, I could always tell Basie's by Marshall Royal's lead and Duke's by Harry Carney's sound. Harry has a way of playing which dominates the section just enough to give it Duke's distinctive character. Frank Wess is a very valuable asset to Basie's band, too. Quite apart from the flute, he's a good alto and tenor player, and he does a lot for the blending in the section.

"The way I came to take up flute was when I was in Cleveland with Benny Green. James Moody was in town and he spoke to me about flute, told me he would be around the rest of the week, and that I could borrow his, because he wouldn't have time for it. He showed me the fingering and after a week I was sold on the idea. Back in New York, I bought a flute, just a flute, so that I had one, and I kept it for about a year before I really decided to play it. I would carry it around, practice all day, walk from room to room. I practiced so · much my mother would say, 'Will you please put that down and go *out!*' Even now I do it, when I'm sitting in my car at four or five in the morning on the ferry that carries you over to Staten Island.

"One night—this would be about 1956—I brought the flute out in Connie's, a little bar across the street from Smalls' Paradise. I was there several months, and, although all the musicians used to flock there, I don't think anybody ever wrote about it. I don't think it seated more than forty and weekends there would be lines of people waiting outside. Anyway, when I played the flute, the people applauded, which they shouldn't have done! I never studied the instrument, but I've learned one thing about it. There's a legitimate way of playing it, but you can't play jazz with a legitimate sound. I can get that legitimate sound—it's not the best in the world!—but it takes away on jazz solos. To get the jazz effect, you've got to bend notes in a way that isn't correct. A lot of things I play on flute now, such as the fingering, are wrong, but they get results and they sound right as jazz. If I went to a teacher, he would turn me all around, because he's naturally supposed to show you the correct method.

"I played clarinet on the Impulse album Basie made with the Kansas City Seven. I never studied that either, but I feel I could play much more if there was more opportunity. I think it's one of the most beautiful instruments in the world, and that's one of the things about Duke's band sound—he's always got those clarinets working. Basie's been using flutes, clarinet, and bass clarinet, too, and it's good, because it gives the band a whole new color. I don't know what it is about the clarinet—a mental block maybe—but it frightens me every time I pick it up. I can play a good enough clarinet solo to get by on, but it's not free the way I want it to be. There's always a tightness that gets me. It's one of the hardest instruments to play, much harder than flute, but the Boehm system is the easier. The fingering in some cases allows you two ways to make it, where on the Albert there's only one. I once talked to Barney Bigard, who has an Albert clarinet, and he showed me how there was only one way to make C-sharp, I think it was. It's difficult to make it on Albert, but after you've been playing as long as he has it comes to you. The way they make clarinets now with auxiliary fingerings and added keys, they've really simplified it.

"Quite apart from solos, the clarinet is so valuable in playing parts. You hear them come in in Duke's band and the whole mood changes. Duke has had a head start on everybody for years with the way he has used clarinets, and plungers, and his different muted effects. I think European audiences appreciate things like color in arrangements. I suppose people here do take jazz more for granted, but I would see the same people quite often in Paris while I was there with Curley

Hamner, and they were *always* interested. I've been over four times and those audiences made an impression on me. When Basie played all those folk parks in Sweden, you might have thought they were country people out there who hadn't heard much, but the funny thing is that they were calling every number we played. They'd call for *Segue in C*, and *Splanky,* and *Corner Pocket.* That *Segue* is a good number for listening or dancing.

"The flute has just been one of those things with me, but I'd like to get with that clarinet. We used to do a sort of life story of Josephine Baker in Paris, so we'd play some Dixieland, calypso, and so forth, and then I got to play clarinet. When we came back to New York, we added a saxophone and I used to write arrangements for the three horns. Curley still has the book. I'd very much like to do an album with four horns, and that's the kind of band I'd like to have one day, but where would we work? I know when I got into Basie's band, after being with Quincy, that I thought to myself, 'You know, you're pretty lucky working all the time like this!'

"I've always believed in being dependable, because I've been on gigs which were, shall we say, too cool. If a leader calls me and I accept it, then I'll be there, and usually ahead of time. I hate that being-late feeling. If I come in late, I can't do anything right. I feel wrong, even at a rehearsal. When I was working at the Apollo, I was nearly always the first one there, although the other fellows lived in New York and I came from Staten Island. I might be sitting there a whole hour, just doing nothing, but I was relaxed, which I wouldn't have been if I'd come running in at the last minute.

"And, yes, I have a nickname—'Big Daddy.' It began with my girl friend, and then the Cooper brothers started calling me by it. I always thought somebody told Quincy, but it just came to him, too, and now everybody calls me that. If ever I get a chance to make my own album, that will have to be the name of it!"

(1963)

Bobby Plater

(ALTO SAXOPHONE AND ARRANGER)

"In Newark, where I was born [in 1914], I started going to the theater when I was about twelve. I'd go three or four times a week—sometimes I'd sneak in—and usually I'd sit in the front row. I liked the sound of the saxophone and I used to get as close to the lead alto man as I could. They had only three saxophones in the band then, but I'd sit there all day and just listen to him. This was before I'd taken up an instrument, but I was there so much that it got so he knew me. His name was Clarence Adams, and he used to turn around and wink at me.

"A friend of mine had a brother who played saxophone, and I used to go to his place and listen to him practice. I told my father about it. (He used to play drums for what they called 'block' dances, when they roped off a portion of the street and had three or four musicians.) He got me a saxophone for a Christmas present, and my mother paid for the lessons.

"I studied and practiced regularly for about three years. After I found I could play a little bit, like most musicians I didn't want to practice any more. So I stopped taking lessons, but I discovered later I should have gone on. There are certain things I'd like to do that I'm not able to do. That is, in the technique department. Then I took up clarinet, but I didn't study it long. Just enough that I could play a little on it. After all, you had to double. You couldn't get into a big band unless you did.

"I started out professionally by playing what they called 'house rent parties' in those days. Sometimes they called them 'parlor socials.' If you were short of the rent, you'd have little cards printed up that announced you were having a house rent party Saturday night. You'd hand them around among all your friends and neighbors. Usually, they'd have about three pieces playing. I'd get about three dollars, and the money they made they used to pay the rent. This gave me experience, and I got into everything I could get into. I was around seventeen, but I didn't work any steady job, just gigs. Don Lambert, the piano player, used to play at those rent parties sometimes, all by himself. He was very good, in a class with James P. Johnson and Art Tatum. He'd go from one place to another and sit in. He stayed right in Newark. That's where he liked to be, where he liked to play.

"I first got into a professional band when I joined a nine-piece local group called the Savoy Dictators. It was a good band, ten years ahead of its time. We made some records for Herman Lubinsky's Savoy label right there in Newark [*Rhythm and Bugs*; *Tricks*; *Heyfuss, Geyfuss*; *Jam and Crackers*]. Count Hastings, who was later with Louis Jordan, was the tenor player. The trombone was Howard Scott, and he was very good. We had two trumpets, Harry Mitchell and Chippy Outcalt. Chippy plays trombone now. The piano player was Clem Moorman; Willie Johnson was on guitar; Al Henderson on bass; and Danny Gibson on drums. They were the best musicians in New Jersey at that time. Chippy Outcalt and Clem Moorman did most of the arrangements, but I learned to get my hand in there and once in a while I threw one in.

"I never had any schooling in writing but picked up things as I went along. I wish I had had some tuition. Another hindrance is the fact that I can't play piano. If I could play piano, I could write more. I can hit a few chords, of course, but when I write I don't know what it is going to sound like till I hear it. So I am limited, and there are only certain things I can do.

"The Savoy Dictators worked in Newark and the vicinity, and occasionally we played New York. When the Depression came along, some of the guys had to take other jobs to make it. For about a year we had a ballroom in Newark called the Savoy. We soon had a good following and were at least able to pay our expenses, but in the end the band folded because we just couldn't keep the guys together.

"I was more interested in playing lead than soloing, so the guys I listened to were Earle Warren and Willie Smith. When I first heard Benny Carter, he was playing trumpet in a band of his own. I had gone to audition with another band on Broadway, and it was not until later that I listened to Benny on alto. I heard a lot of Johnny Hodges, and I was influenced by him also, and in those days I was more active as a soloist.

"When our band broke up, Count Hastings, a couple of others, and I had an offer to join Tiny Bradshaw. He was a road man and he had a band of about thirteen pieces, his singing being the feature. It was a good band, but we sort of took over the style of it because he had our key men playing all the lead.

"We played mostly in the South, all the way out to Texas, and ended up in Chicago. I'd had offers before to go on the road, but I'd never had the nerve. I used to hear about fellows getting stranded, and things like that. I stayed with Tiny about three years, and then I went in the army from 1939 till 1942. I was attached to an infantry outfit for three months' basic training, and then they put me in a band. Usually in an army band you just play marches and things like that for parades, but with an infantry outfit you have other duties. They took the whole division out to Fort Huachuca in Arizona, where they put me in charge of what they called the B orchestra, and left me to do the best I could.

"We had fourteen pieces and I enjoyed it, because military life can become monotonous, especially if you've been accustomed to playing music. Every now and then we'd go out and play a dance, so this was a good outlet. We went overseas to Italy and the Mediterranean Theater.

"As soon as I got back, I received a wire from Lionel Hampton. I guess he'd heard of me from men in his band who had been with Tiny Bradshaw. Herbie Fields was leaving and he needed someone to take his place. I went in as lead alto. Arnett Cobb was straw boss then, but when he left, about two years later, I became straw boss. I stayed with Hamp eighteen years. He had a good band, and I was satisfied with him. I was never one to jump around and make changes so long as things were going right. I'm not hard to get along with.

"Apart from Billy Mackel, the guitar player from Baltimore, I guess I was the guy who stayed with Hamp longest. There's nothing but good you can say about Billy. I didn't play many solos in those days and I didn't worry about it. I was content to play the lead and try to make everything go right. I had taken up the flute in the army, and I was ahead of the fashion when I played it with Hamp. I didn't do too much with it, but I still played it with Basie. The only time I play clarinet now is when we're playing for singers. The band doesn't play the arrangements with clarinet parts anymore. I think one of the big reasons why clarinet went out is because it is such a difficult instrument, and saxophone players just didn't want to be bothered with it. Just to play it straight is difficult, so that discouraged them, because they all want to solo. Then, too, arrangers stopped writing for clarinet. The only band today that features them is Duke Ellington's.

"The arrangements I wrote while I was with Hamp were mostly vocal arrangements, like for Sonny Parker, who sang blues and ballads. Except for a couple Hamp wanted, I didn't get around to writing instrumentals.

"When I left, it was because we weren't working enough and I couldn't make ends meet. He still had a large band, but every weekend we went to work there would be different men. So then I had an offer from Basie and I've been with him ever since.

"Two of the arrangements I've written for him are *Happy House* and *Tidbit*, and both of them have been recorded. I solo on the first, Al Aarons and Basie on *Tidbit*, which was more of an experimental dance arrangement. I'd never written for the band, so I just thought I would like to see how it would sound. I had done *The Hour of Parting* for Charlie Fowlkes before I joined the band, and I gave it to him, but we haven't rehearsed it yet. There are so many we haven't rehearsed—a book full of arrangements that just lay there! I've got another one called *Laughing in the Sunshine*, a hillbilly tune that sounds so much like *Can't Stop Loving You* that I put it on a commercial kick. We ran over it once.

"The most writing I'd done in years was when Lockjaw [Davis] approached me and asked me to write for an album he was going to record for RCA [*The Fox and the Hounds*, LSP 3741]. It was a few weeks before he left Basie, and it's pretty hard for me to say no to people. The good part was that he told me at a time when I didn't have to rush. It's hard when you're on one-nighters, better when you're on location. But when I have something to do, I go ahead and do it. I don't fool around and wait till the last minute. So I started on his project right away and had it done in plenty of time. The tunes were mostly standards like *When Your Lover Has Gone*; *Out of Nowhere*; *Bye, Bye Blackbird*; and *People Will Say We're in Love*. He had seventeen pieces and I thought the dates came off pretty well.

"I always get a kick out of Benny Carter—anything he does, playing or writing. I like Quincy Jones and Billy Byers, too. Of Hamp's arrangements, I liked Milt Buckner's the most. He was a genius. Eric Dixon is doing most of the arrangements for Basie now, and he's very talented. So is Frank Foster, who did *In a Mellotone.* Anytime you want to write an arrangement, as often as you want to, it's all right with Basie, but I don't feel I'm really qualified. I don't have the knowledge and I never did really try to write anything original, but Basie finally got eight out of me! He asked for eight, but I said I couldn't do all that. 'Well, do two for me,' he said. I did those, and then he asked for two more. 'You better ask somebody else,' I said, but he got two at a time until he had eight altogether!

"For me, it's very difficult if you're writing a whole album. You start repeating yourself when you write consecutively. The same things keep coming back to you. The writer needs time to do something else in between. It's just like a guy who gets up to solo, takes four or five choruses, runs out of ideas, and starts repeating himself. You're in one bag and you can't get out of it.

"My future? Well, I don't ever expect to be a great writer. My style, of course, was formed before Charlie Parker, but I still like to play. I'd like to stay with Basie.* I like being with this band, and I've always liked his bands since way back in the thirties. I hope they can continue to do some great things and that I can be a part of them. Sweets [Edison] has been a big asset since he returned to the band. He fits. A man can be a great musician in his particular bag, but not everybody necessarily fits this band."

(1966)

---

* Still with the band in 1979, Bobby Plater had become one of its key men, an able deputy and musical director who would conduct the band as necessary when the leader was at the piano.

Richard Boone

(TROMBONE AND VOCAL)

Count Basie used to introduce Richard Boone as "a man of very few words." Before those familiar with Basie's own terse conversational style could laugh, he completed the introduction by saying, "He has a message he wants to lay on you!"

Boone's message, hip, sly, and very amusing, was delivered in English, in his personal Boone language. It was the wittiest form of scat singing heard in many a long day, and his versions of *I Got Rhythm* and *Boone's Blues* provoked a hilarious reaction. On the blues, to everyone's surprise, the mountain jacks of Booneland yodeled instead of hollering.

It seemed that in Boone Basie had discovered someone who could partly fill the void left by Joe Williams. The singer was also a very capable trombonist, both in solo and ensemble, but unfortunately he stayed with the band only three years. After he recorded an album in Hollywood for Nocturne in 1969, all too little was heard of this talented artist.

"I was born in Little Rock, Arkansas, on February 23 or 24, 1930. There were no hospital records, and for eighteen years I celebrated the 24th as my birthday, but when I went in the army I had to get a birth certificate and the certificate said the 23rd. My grandmother assures me they got it wrong, that it was a weekend and when the midwife reported the birth on Monday she got the dates mixed up.

"My mother and grandmother sang in church, the New Hope Baptist Church, and that's where I began singing spirituals and hymns when I was five or six. I don't know anything about being a prodigy or anything like that, but I was considered pretty good. Until I was ten or eleven, I would go from church to church to sing solos. Different churches used to visit each other in those days with their choirs and featured singers.

"When I got to be twelve, I went to a high school that covered from the seventh to the twelfth grades. I started in the seventh, and that's when I first got an instrument. If you wanted to take up music, there was a particular day to go to the band room. When I got there, everybody had been before me and all they had was a trumpet with keys that wouldn't work—and a trombone. The trombone had never come into my mind before. What I had really wanted to play was tenor saxophone. I was always the skinny type, and my arms were long enough, but trombone—that's a hard instrument!

"I had two teachers, the first a Mr. Bowie. He's still active in St. Louis at one of the high schools as a bandmaster. The second was a Mrs. Robinson, and she was good, too. But I think the best musical training came after I went into the army. I volunteered when I was eighteen, and I played in Special Service orchestras. I was there six years, from 1948. I went to Europe, not Korea, which was very lucky.

"But before that I had played in a band led by Grover Lofton. He was from Little Rock, and he'd been in Chicago with Red Saunders, but he came home and formed a big band. There were few trombone players around, so I got in to make up the section, although I was only fifteen. So I went out on the road with him in the summer of '45. The following year, when I was still in high school, Lucky Millinder came to town. He was sponsoring talent contests through the South, and I won for the city of Little Rock—as a singer. By then I knew all the old pop standards and I won as a sort of ballad singer.

"I was scatting, too, in my way. Around 1945 I started listening to Charlie Parker, Dizzy Gillespie, and bop musicians. I was a young cat then and I naturally went to left field, to the way that was supposed to be ahead of the times. Diz used to scat, and I'm sure I heard Ella, so they must have had some influence on me. I knew about Cab Calloway, but I didn't know it was done by anyone much in earlier times. Only last night I heard a record of *Sweet Sue* by Satchmo on which Budd Johnson was scatting in 'viper's language.'

"What I was doing as a teenager couldn't be considered professional. I guess nothing can be professional unless you're earning money at it, even if your *standard* is professional! What I was doing was really for kicks. But in that contest I won, guess who won second place? Ocie Smith, who sang with Basie a few years ago. I always kid him about that. His father was some kind of government man who worked a few years in one city and was then switched to another. Ocie went to school in Little Rock, but I know other guys who went to school with him in a different city at a different time.

"For the finals of the winners in Lucky Millinder's contests in the Southern states, I went to Atlanta and took second place there. The winner was a singer from Mississippi who had recorded and been around, but I can't remember his name now. My second prize was a month's tour with Lucky, and I was able to take it because it was summer. The song I had sung in the contest was *Embraceable You*, and I did it as a straight ballad. I sang that and other tunes during the month. Some people said I sounded like Nat Cole, but I think that was because I was into that soft-type thing and did some of the songs he'd made popular.

"That was the way it went up till the army. Two of my six years were overseas. Seldon Powell, the tenor player, was in that Special Services orchestra. Eddie Fisher was attached to the band, Vic Damone was in the company, and I first met Pearl Bailey there. Stars would come over to perform for the troops. They'd join us in Munich, fix up a schedule, and travel with the band. It was seventeen pieces, just like Basie, and we played no marches or anything like that. It was a crazy band. So far as the army was concerned, all the cats were like deadbeats. Good musicians, you know, but cats that wouldn't be soldiers!

"There was no real tuition, but you learned things continually out of experience. There were periods allotted for individual rehearsals, section rehearsals, and then band rehearsals. There was a lot I didn't know about changes, chords, and structure up until then, but I learned all about that from the piano player in the band, Art Simmons. He opened my eyes to a whole bunch of things. There were other fellows in the band who helped me, too. I had to learn to read music fast, because the stars were bringing their own special music over. I wouldn't have traded the experience for a semester in college, or whatever. I learned about the keys and the songs, and how to play them right on the spot. When I joined Basie, he kicked off *Jumpin' at the*

Woodside the first night. 'What number?' I asked, and the guys next to me said, 'There's no music, man. Just make up your part.' Now if I hadn't had that army experience I might not have been able to pick myself up a part!

"When I finished in the army, I went back home to Little Rock, to college. It was a small Methodist school that had come into prominence because Elijah Pitts, the football player, had gone there. They had a pretty good music staff and that is where I got formal tuition and training. They taught you how to teach, and that was the thing for many black musicians in the South. They had a good thing going there, but it was basically an education-type program, with courses in psychology and child study. I just took all the *music* courses I could take.

"I was sick of Little Rock and there was no outlet there. I didn't like New York, and I still don't, so I went to Los Angeles. This was 1958. I had no money to speak of, but I didn't meet too many problems. It took me about a year to get around to knowing 'most everybody. I worked at the post office for six months, and I had another job with Magnetic Recorders, who sell tape recorders and that kind of stuff. I finally got established with enough gigs coming in so that I didn't have to work in the daytime. There were recording dates, too. Besides recording in the big studios, there were others where anybody could go in and record. So, for instance, when I got a song together and wanted to record it for a demo, I'd have to pay musicians fifteen or twenty dollars for a forty-five side. There was a lot of that going on in L.A. Cats were always putting things together.

The first gig I had in L.A. was five nights a week and I was making ninety dollars, singing. It was a club where they had dancing and a small group that played old standards, not rhythm and blues or rock 'n' roll. I worked there six months before any of the guys knew I played trombone! But there were all kinds of gigs to keep me going, and in '62 I got a chance to work with Della Reese in Las Vegas. Although I went to Sydney, Australia, with her, I didn't normally travel with her, but I'd join her when she was on the West Coast to play in Vegas, Reno, San Francisco, and at the Grove in L.A. She carried her rhythm section with her everywhere and just picked up other guys in the area. She usually had three trombones and three trumpets, guys like Bud Brisbois and Buddy Childers. Buddy, who was first trumpet with Stan Kenton at one time, borrowed $5,000 from Stan to buy a plane and wrecked it next day. That was the kind of cat he was, always drinking.

"Streamline Ewing called me several times to take a job for him when he had so much work he couldn't make it. He'd got the studio thing in L.A. sewed up. There are a lot of guys there you don't hear much about, but they're working all the time in places like San Bernardino, Pasadena, Santa Monica, or Pomona. I don't think I would have left for anybody but Basie.

"He was in L.A. and they had a party for the band at Memory Lane. I went over and sat in with the group that was playing—I didn't sing. They got to hear me that way, and I met some of the guys. Jaws [Lockjaw Davis] was in charge of hiring and firing then, so I said to him, 'Well, look, man, if you're ever out on the West Coast and need a trombone player, give me a ring.' That was what happened when they were out there again about a year later. I think Jaws knew from Sweets that I sang, and some of the other guys had probably heard, because I often used to go around places and sing. But I was hired as a trombone player.

"We were still out in California a couple of months later when Basie started out one night with an elaborate concert-type intro and then went into the blues. Everybody wigged out, because it was the first time he had done it. Usually, when he plays his intro, all the guys know just about what the tune is to be, but they were sitting there wondering this time. It was a nightclub, the atmosphere was very nice, and he was playing the blues real slow.

" 'Hey, man, why don't you sing some blues?' Jaws suggested.

" 'I don't really know too many blues,' I said, 'but I know a whole bunch of standards.'

" 'Well, do like they did in the old days. Make up something.'

"That's how it began. I sang a few words and scatted a bit. And I got a laugh. We got going into it, and finally we took it out. The ending was also groovy. I had never worked on it at all, but I really started thinking about it when Basie called it again the next night. From then on he would call it almost every night, which finally got it around into some shape. I had sung tunes like *Bye, Bye Blackbird*, where I sang the words for a chorus and then scatted another, but never like this where the words and the scatting were all mixed in a format. I've got a thing going, I know, but I'm really getting tired of it now. I guess I've got as much ego as the next musician, but I very seldom push things too much, especially where I myself am concerned. I might tell you I can do such and such a thing, if you need me to do it sometime, but I probaby won't mention it to you anymore. If I didn't think I could do the thing good, or well enough to tell you, I wouldn't tell you. That's the way I am with my singing and playing. Like I can half play trombone, you know. But to go into a businesslike thing of selling it—well, that's something musicians don't seem to have, and they say they should have.

"Since I've been in the band, three or four vocalists have come and gone. I really feel that I can personally fill that spot, but at the same time I feel that Basie is the leader of the band and, if he doesn't hear it, I'm not going to bug him. After all, I was hired as a third trombone player. I didn't know they were getting rid of Bill Henderson till the night he was getting ready to leave. Sometimes the cat didn't get to sing but one set a night, depending on where we were playing. Maybe carrying a singer is like carrying one more guy than they need. That was what I thought.

"I've been singing that blues for eighteen months, as well as the up-tempo thing. I felt I had to get me something new, so I sat down and worked on *Some of These Days*, and wrote an arrangement. I've done quite a bit of arranging, but not much for a big band. Out on the Coast, when we were recording those demos, many of the guys were singers who got a tune in their heads but didn't know much about music and needed a musician to write it down. I'd ask them how many pieces they wanted, how much money they wanted to spend. Usually it would be a working sketch, the simplest form with some notes for the horns. I knew how to voice things and I feel if I were really serious, and took enough time, I could probably turn out a good arrangement. So, anyway, I intended making this one for *Some of These Days*, but there were a couple of hard spots in it, so it was kind of refused. I never got a chance to clean up those spots, because we didn't get around to rehearsing it again. The idea of it was okay, I was convinced of that. So I said to myself, 'The only way I can get this one in is to let Frank Foster or somebody else arrange it, and then when they try it again I at least have Frank's arrangement on my side!'

"Maybe things are different now from what they were in early jazz. I think there was more love going on between musicians than there is today. You have to be *known*, and it's difficult to be known unless you are recognized as a successful musician. That's how it is with arrangements, too, but I've heard arrangements by people who are accepted that I don't dig at all. They'll accept a cat who is a good musician but who is also a junky known to mess up on the bandstand. He might not show up at all, but still they'll accept him quicker than some guy they haven't heard who plays very well. And I think that's bad.

"Of course politics gets into everything today, and I think there's more politics than love. I don't think you can put seventeen musicians together now and have them come up with good head arrangements like they did in the old days. They don't have that much love for each other—everybody is competing. I really try to stay out of that bag!

"There were no trombone players that really influenced me. Every once in a while I get a compliment that substantiates this. Now I like all the good trombone players that everybody knows, but when I was coming up I used to listen to the tenor players. That's what I wanted to play. Sometimes a musician will tell me that when I solo my ideas aren't like trombone ideas, but have more of a tenor feel. I don't get to solo much here, but I figure that will come in the next couple of years, although I don't plan to stay with Basie as long as some of the guys have. You get to play more in a small combination.

"One of the guys I worked for in L.A. was Dexter Gordon. We were at the Zebra Lounge a couple of months and we made an album for Jazzland called *The Resurgence of Dexter Gordon.* I liked it, and not just because I was on it. I think Coltrane must have been influenced by Dexter. Coltrane was more modern, but Dexter was doing that screaming thing way back, when they were having the battles of tenors. He was one of the tenors I admired, and then there was Gene Ammons. For big-tone tenor on slow tunes and ballads, you can't beat him. He's been 'in' about five years now, and that should be enough to get a parole. I have a feeling Gene came up against the wrong person on the political scene in Chicago. A cat can not like you, and if he's big enough he can wipe you out, no matter what profession you're in. You can't make it anymore. And maybe for some little thing. Like you went out with his girlfriend, or something.

"Wardell Gray's case was much the same. Of course, it was supposed to be an overdose, but the talk before was that he'd burned the people in power, who supply the heroin. He'd done something wrong, not enough to kill somebody, but from their point of view they figured they'd snuff him out.

"Another tenor player I liked in the early days, when I was eighteen and up, was James Moody. I got really hung up on buying him. And I was really hung up on buying Bird, too, although he played alto. My age thing really starts with Bird.

"Now, I guess, my mind is more on singing than trombone, because of this scat thing, because it seems to be something profitable. Vocalists joining bands make more money than musicians. They jump up and do a couple of tunes, and they can dance all night. That was a nice thing Basie did for me on the Merv Griffin show. There was no mention of trombone. He just said, 'I got a singer I want you to hear.' I went over to thank Merv the next day, and he said it was a gas and hoped I'd be back. Like I said, I don't like to drag myself posing the business angle, running around trying to find out who got the money for my appearance. The night before the show, someone comes and says, 'Hey, you're on the show!' That's what makes me so mad with this business. The same thing happened when we went in the studio and recorded *St. Louis Blues* and *Frankie and Johnny.* Out of a clear blue sky they say, 'Hey, we're going to record your two songs.' Businesswise, you're supposed to discuss a contract price, but am I going to argue when I haven't been heard singing on a record? Am I going to hang up the whole bit while we go in the office? That album was produced by Teddy Reig, a kind of difficult guy to get along with, who likes to shout. So that's where it is.

"My position right now is something like it was eighteen months ago. I came as a trombone player, and if I wasn't discharging the job right I'd have been gone from there. I take solos on *Hitting Twelve* and *In a Mellotone*, but about the time I get up it's time to sit down. The whole thing is rough, making it as a singer *and* a trombone player.

"Like when I joined the band, I wasn't all that naive, but I had visions of the guys getting together when they weren't working. I really thought the kind of thing might go on like you see in the movie, where the guy is playing his guitar in the bus. But these guys never go out to jam. I can understand it to some degree, because they work so hard and never have too much time, but it's still difficult for me to grasp inasmuch as I still want to play. That's where jazz ideas are born, in jamming. They're not born in a pen. Not really with the writer or composer either."

(1967)

Nat Pierce

(BANDLEADER, PIANO, AND ARRANGER)

"I've been arranging for Count Basie, off and on, for twenty-nine years, ever since I first met him in Boston in 1950. He had given up the big band and was working with a small group made up of Clark Terry, Wardell Gray, Buddy De Franco, Freddie Green, Jimmy Lewis, and Gus Johnson. Each last set at the Hi Hat Club, Basie would ask me to sit in, and that was a great thrill for me! I was about twenty-five years old, and whether it was a small group or a big band made no difference. It was Count Basie's, and that was more than enough for me!

"Some producer had the brilliant idea of making an album called *Count Basie Plays the Melody,* so Neal Hefti sent up arrangements of 'Golden Oldies' like *Confessin'* and *Little White Lies.* I went to a rehearsal at the Hi Hat, and Basie was sitting there at the piano as they rehearsed and rehearsed and rehearsed. The parts had been made by a professional copyist, but they were obviously having trouble. After a while, Basie called a break and sat down at a table with me.

" 'I've just found out the bass player can't read,' he said, 'and he's been with me three years! I was playing the bass notes on the piano part, and he was playing different notes.'

"I couldn't believe it. Maybe he *felt* some different notes? Those guys were supposed to be professional musicians who could play whatever was put in front of them.

"Serge Chaloff became an added attraction with the group while they were in Boston, and I think he stayed with Basie about six months. So they had four horns and four rhythm. It was really a gorgeous band, and they had some beautiful arrangements. They did the tunes of the day, bebop tunes like Charlie Parker's *Donna Lee*. Basie would play *Indiana* in front, and then the horns would come in. They all had the so-called bebop thing down, but this group sounded different to all the other bebop bands in that the rhythm section was playing straight ahead. The drummer wasn't too outside, because Gus Johnson just swung, like Jo Jones and people of that kind.

"I had my big band in Boston at the time, so Wardell, Buddy, and Serge came over and helped me rehearse it. We were very into bebop then, and we knew all the hottest licks of the day. We had heard Dizzy Gillespie's big band and Billy Eckstine's, and it was a kick for all of us in the Boston area to hear their wonderful arrangements and marvelous soloists like Fats Navarro and Budd Johnson. But when Count Basie showed up with this small group, it was frightening. 'How come these guys are playing bebop with a swing-type rhythm section?' we asked one another.

"At that point, Clark Terry was one of the beboppinest trumpet players of all time, but he could also play *On the Sunny Side of the Street* and *Confessin'* like Louis Armstrong. Buddy De Franco could play like Benny Goodman and the way Jimmy Hamilton used to with Duke Ellington. Wardell Gray was simply one of our gods in those days. He kind of consumed the styles of Coleman Hawkins, Lester Young, and Charlie Parker, and came out with one of his own. His nickname was 'Waistline,' because he weighed about ninety-eight pounds. I wrote an original for him called *Mosquito Knees*. And then Serge Chaloff was one of the masters of the baritone, and he has not been credited with all he could do. He could play fully as well as Harry Carney in the section, and a more fluid, or more modern type of solo than Harry. He was the first breakaway on baritone, and he spawned people we have today like Gerry Mulligan, Art Pepper, and Nick Brignola. When you hear sensational musicians like these as a young man, they make an indelible impression on you.

"Basie told me he was going to start another big band in a little while, and he said he wanted me to write some arrangements. Charlie

Mariano, Sonny Truitt, and I wrote some, gave them to him, and never thought anything more about 'em. Soon after that I went with Woody Herman's orchestra, and towards the end of 1951 we heard that Basie had gotten his band together one more time, with Marshall Royal, Joe Newman, Paul Quinichette, Gus Johnson, and people like that. When I went to hear them, they were playing my arrangements, and I said, 'Oh, wow, that sounds great!' Then a record came out called *New Basie Blues*, which I recognized as my tune. I went to see Jack Bregman of Bregman, Vocco and Conn, the publishers, and after some discussion I got my first composer credit on a big-time record with a big-time orchestra.

"As the years went by, and we floated around the East Coast, I'd go and see Basie and he'd ask me to write this or that. But he had Neal Hefti, Ernie Wilkins, Frank Wess, and Frank Foster writing for him, so he didn't really need my things and they tended to get phased out. It was maybe ten years later, after I'd left Woody's band the second time, that Basie asked me to write arrangements for a whole album of tunes by pianists. I wrote them for some of Horace Silver's numbers, for Willie 'The Lion' Smith's *I Want to Ride the Rest of the Way*, for Jelly Roll Morton's *King Porter Stomp*, and for Fats Waller's *Squeeze Me* and *Handful of Keys*. When I showed up where they were playing, Basie said, 'Oh, Nat is here. We must play his arrangement of *Handful of Keys*.' And he played the shit out of it! Then he said, 'I got to tell you something about the modulation into the second strain,' and other things like that. He was thinking of *Handful of Keys* as he had learned it when he was a young man and a disciple of Fats Waller.

"Around this time, too, I wrote *Willow, Weep for Me* for Roy Eldridge, and a tune called *Mr. Softee*, but Roy never played them, because he had left Basie before I turned them in. When Harry Edison came back in the sixties, he played them. I also wrote a number called *Open All Night*, which opened that show, *The Sound of Jazz*, in 1957 when Basie had an all-star band. I had written all the music on that show—the arrangements, that is—and much later the band Frankie Capp and I lead recorded the arrangement of *Dickie's Dream* for Concord. During the fifties, I also made a lot of records with idols of mine like Freddie Green, Joe Newman, Milt Hinton, Shadow Wilson, and Jo Jones. We were trying to get the old Kansas City kind of rhythm section.

"When I'd go to see Basie's band, I often used to sit by the piano and watch him play. On one occasion I noticed that he suddenly laid out on a certain chord.

" 'Why did you do that?' I asked him.

" 'I'm going to murder that chord,' he answered.

"To be technical about it, let's say the chord was a C-minor seventh with a flatted fifth. He didn't know that chord. But if I had written an E-flat-minor sixth, which has the same notes in it, he would have played it. So I decided that was the way to go.

"I wrote a few more arrangements and went to his recording sessions. Once, when he was called to the telephone, Marshall Royal said, 'Nat, sit in here and play this tune.' So I played it, and from the booth they said, 'Okay, next tune.' But Count Basie wasn't even in the room. In the same way, I recorded *There Are Such Things*—an old tune from the Tommy Dorsey time—with Sarah Vaughan for Roulette Records, and a number that happened to be in six flats, *Tell Me Your Troubles*, with Joe Williams, but my name was not on the records. To me, it just remained a thrill to be involved with the band over the years.

"It seems that every time Basie blinks his eye, cocks his head, or something, I end up playing the piano. It's exciting, because to play piano in a piano player's band is something that doesn't normally happen.

"I had the opportunity to go out in 1972 with Stan Kenton's band. It was not exactly my cup of tea, but I was not trying to do my Woody Herman or Count Basie act there, and somehow it jelled. It was a marvelous experience to have. On a few occasions during my time, I even sat in with the Ellington orchestra. These are things that don't pay the rent, and the landlord couldn't care less, but they are very important in my life.

"I found out that even today, in 1979, Count Basie's orchestra will play only a certain type of material. In other words, if you write an original tune, you must frame it on a sequence of chords Basie already knows, because he is not going to sit down and learn a lot of strange things. He'd rather sit outside and listen to the band play through the arrangement, and then jump in if he feels comfortable. Way down deep he hears something that is very important. If it doesn't fit with his band, he'll stop the arrangement in the middle and call another. I've seen arrangements by Sam Nestico, Billy Byers, and Quincy Jones stopped right after the introduction, because they didn't suit the way he felt at the time. It's a strange thing, but after being with Woody Herman for many years, I know he feels the same way. And I presume Duke felt that way, too. There are a lot of rejects from the Basie and Herman orchestras out here, arrangements they *knew* were not going to happen. Maybe five or ten years later, with a different sound, the arrangement might happen. Maybe it was written too late and they had bypassed it, or maybe it was too soon. Everybody has

his own conception of arranging, but although Basie and Woody
were not arrangers, and never wrote anything down on paper, they
knew how to edit. They were the greatest editors of all time!

"Many of Duke's arrangements, of course, were written in sections.
If he didn't like one section, he threw it out and wrote another, and
added that to what was already acceptable. So he edited in his own
way, just as Basie and Woody do in theirs.

"I feel very privileged to be Basie's Number One substitute pianist.
That's what *he* told me I was. We have a special thing between us.
We don't talk about it or publicize it. But there's no way I could ever
play the amount of piano he's played in all his years in the music
business. There's no way I could play *Prince of Wales* and all the
things he did with the original Bennie Moten band. It would be
absolutely impossible. People think Basie just goes *ding . . . ding . . .
ding*, but I've heard him really play that piano.

"Back in my Boston days, I had a little upright piano in my humble
apartment near the Hi Hat Club. One night he came over and played
Handful of Keys in a direct copy of Fats Waller's version. Fats was
his man, and later he watered Fat's style down to where it became the
Count Basie style, but on a lot of the earlier records he played with
two hands. Today he is seventy-five, God bless him, with maybe a
problem that he calls arthritis, and I'm twenty years younger, but
sometimes when he really wants to play . . . then it's like a spark, or
when you get your car tuned up. He may not be the most accurate
piano player of all time, but for rhythm, time, and swing, he is one of
the greatest in the history of jazz piano. There have been some great
ones, too, like Mr. Earl Hines, Mr. Art Tatum, and my very favorite,
Mr. Nat 'King' Cole. They may know or have known more tunes than
Basie knows, and all kinds of other things he doesn't know, but don't
let anyone try to outswing him! I think there's only man left in this
day and age who could, and that's Jay McShann. He's a monster!
Erroll Garner was one of the great swing giants, but I wouldn't want
him in a contest with Fats Waller, Jay McShann, and Art Tatum.
Pete Johnson was regarded as a boogie-woogie pianist, but I wouldn't
want to put him in the same room with Jay McShann and Basie and
tell the three of them to just go ahead and play piano, because there
would be a terrible mess and no way of deciding who did the most
swinging.

"Of course, jazz critics—not so much jazz historians as jazz critics—
always say, 'I like this,' or 'I like that,' and that's anybody's prerogative.
But I think that if you had to show up in the same room as those
three piano players, and decide who blew away whom, it would be
quite impossible. Nobody could really say who was best or better

of three such individuals such as they. But today, who could tell the difference between Keith Jarrett, Chick Corea, and Herbie Hancock? That is what the alleged or so-called jazz music has come to. And to Cecil Taylor, who was thrown out of Boston for playing thirteen-bar blues. He should be in the country-and-western bag, down in Nashville. But there are still giants out there, like Barry Harris and Al Haig. Barry Harris is like a disciple of Hank Jones and Tommy Flanagan, and he puts it all together. He's some kind of piano player! I can never approach the kind of thing he does, nor can Count Basie.

"Nobody much ever gave Nat Cole any great credit. He was a disciple of Earl Hines, and Earl came out of nowhere in the twenties, and there was no one before him who did what he did. After him came Erroll Garner, another true genius. I know that word is used very loosely nowadays, but I was on a record date with him when he said something very important. The red light went on and he started to play. The red light went off and he kept on playing. Everybody waved to him from the booth, and when he eventually finished they said, 'Erroll, we turned off the light. You were supposed to stop.' He looked at them and said, 'I couldn't stop. I wanted to find out how *it* would come out.'

"Now whether you believe in God or not, 'it' implies that there is some higher power upstairs. That's heavy stuff, I know. But *how would it come out?* In other words, he had no control over what he was playing at the time. Maybe he hit a couple of strange notes here and there, but there was no doubt he would work his way out *through none of his own effort.* 'It' came from another place. 'It' worked itself out.

"I'm sure that was how it was with the great musicians like Louis Armstrong, Lester Young, Bix Beiderbecke, Charlie Parker, and George Gershwin. And Gershwin was a great *pianist*, a favorite of Fats Waller and Art Tatum. They sat down and improvised to the point of no return. I'm sure Duke Ellington had the same feeling on certain occasions. Billy Strayhorn was also a great pianist in my opinion, of the same kind that people considered Gershwin to be. He could play up and down that piano! So many to remember! And I've hardly mentioned that happy-go-lucky guy with the strongest left hand anybody ever had. Nobody could smooth out the rhythm like Fats Waller.

"I go back to William James Basie. He knew those other guys were playing pretty good, and he knew he couldn't challenge Fats Waller or Earl Hines. He didn't have the same kind of gift from above, but he did have a very nice rhythm section. So he decided on something original and said to himself, 'Once I start off and play a bit, I'll just let them roll, and then I'll throw in a note or two here and there.' All of a sudden the world changed! They already had Benny Goodman, the King of Swing. Now they had Count Basie, the Jump King of Swing. What did 'jump' mean? There were a lot of tunes written with 'jump' on the end of the title. The jump was Kansas City, although Count Basie was never a Kansas City pianist in the way that Pete Johnson, Jay McShann, Mary Lou Williams, or Julia Lee were. They lived and grew up in that area. Count Basie was from New Jersey, but he walked in there like a renegade and ended up with the whole thing, so that writers made him the epitome of Kansas City jazz. When he became famous, they made all the other bands try to play in his fashion, and it didn't work. The feeling was different. Even today, they make records of Jay McShann playing *Jumpin' at the Woodside* and whatever, but that's not the way Jay goes. He goes with the blues and Pete Johnson. He's the only one left who can play that certain type of blues piano. Ray Charles has tried to for the last fifteen or twenty years. He started out like a poor man's Nat Cole and then became a 'genius.' I've never believed he was a genius. If you went into a corner saloon and listened to him play the piano and sing, you'd walk out in five minutes, or earlier. It would be that horrible. But if Jay McShann were in there, playing and singing the blues, you might stay all night.

"When Basie showed up at the Grand Terrace in Chicago in 1936, he had some little-known head arrangements like *Moten Swing* and *One O'Clock Jump*, and a few blues. Fletcher Henderson had been in the Grand Terrace while Earl Hines was out on the road, and he gave some arrangements to the young Basie orchestra, because he knew that if they didn't make it on this gig it would all be over, and they'd have to go back to Kansas City and the Reno Club. So now Basie and his guys took the same arrangements Fletcher Henderson and Benny Goodman had played, but how different they made them sound! The notes were the same and maybe even the conception was the same, but the *individuals* in the band made that difference in the sound. Duke had found that out years before with Johnny Hodges, Harry Carney, Cootie Williams, and Lawrence Brown, but now Basie arrived with his impeccable rhythm section, with a type of rhythm never heard before. You might almost say that Swing was born then, because they swung in the *true* sense of the word.

"Changing, but bringing some of the roots with you, is what it's all about. But who is swinging now? We have all kinds of combos playing all kinds of atonal groups of notes, but what would they do if they had to go in a country club and play a dance? We've got great musicians today, but they don't play any music to get those feet going out there! It's impossible to explain, but something happens between an audience and a band, a kind of electricity. It's one to one, you and me, and that's the way it goes down. That's the reason the big-band era happened. Later on it died, because it got too strange and many of the groups refused to play dances. It had nothing to do with rock 'n' roll, rhythm and blues, punk rock, or the Beatles. When you get up on that stand, you've got to have the right tempo and the right music to tear up the world!"

(1979)

PART 2

Jay McShann

(BANDLEADER, PIANO, AND VOCAL)

"Look. I'll be frank with you," Earl Hines said. "I want to hire that guy Bird, Charlie Parker. You don't know what to do with him. Let me have him and I'll make a man of him."

Jay McShann was remembering the night Hines had come out to hear his band in Washington, D.C. "He wanted one or two of my trumpet players, too," he said. "Bird owed me so much by then that I told Earl he could take him if he paid me the money, made a man of him, and let me have him back. Bird didn't want to leave, but I told him to try it for a few weeks. 'If you like it, just stay on,' I told him, 'and if you want to come on back home, come on back home.' Eventually he left, because for one thing he was going to get more bread than I could afford to pay him. Later on, I saw Earl at a Sunday afternoon jam session on 52nd Street in New York. He threw up his hands when he saw me and said, 'That's the worst man I ever met in my life! He owes everybody money. Come get him!' Earl had bought Bird a saxophone worth four or five hundred dollars, and Bird really had him crying the blues! It was true, too, that he owed quite a bit. In those days

he would take another cat's horn, pawn it, and then take the ticket to
him and say, 'Man, you want your horn? Here's the ticket!' "

McShann is a pianist and bandleader whose reputation has been
overshadowed by the immense legend surrounding Parker, whom he
brought to New York in his band in 1942. With his ally Dizzy Gillespie, the saxophonist was chiefly responsible for the idiom known as
bebop that radically transformed the character jazz had assumed
during the Swing Era of the thirties. The importance subsequently
attached to their innovations by critics and musicians helped obscure
the fact that McShann was—and remains—one of the great players
in the swing tradition. That he is modest, retiring, even shy partly
accounts for the lack of recognition. But a long documentary film on
Kansas City jazz now in preparation, *The Last of the Blue Devils*,
should do much to rectify this. When he found himself billed by the
film's title during his last New York appearance, he was mystified,
because he had never played with the legendary Blue Devils band in
Oklahoma. The title, nevertheless, was not inappropriate. Ralph
Ellison has explained in *Grackle* that "blue devils" was the name given
to those who cut wire fences during range wars in the West, and it is
not hard to hear in McShann's music a love of the loose, loping freedom of yesterday.

When his band first arrived in New York, it was to play at the
famous Savoy Ballroom in Harlem opposite Lucky Millinder, an established leader with a band full of experienced musicians. They took
one look at the "ragged" band from Kansas City, listened to its
"ragged" ensemble work, and decided they had nothing to fear.

"During the first two or three sets we came up with some stocks and
sort of played around," McShann recalled. "So then Lucky said to his
guys, 'We're going to get ready to blow those Western dogs off the
stand!' My cats saw his musicians going into their books [of arrange-
ments] and asked me, 'What're *we* going to reach?' I told them we'd
hold off another set, but after Lucky's guys had really carried on, mine
began to get restless. Now we had a number called *Roll 'Em* that we
used to play for about twenty-five minutes, and if we got it going,
moving right, we would extend it to thirty minutes or more. This particular night my cats—mostly young and wild—were so eager that we
just turned them loose and played that number ten minutes into
Lucky's time. That broke the house up! Lucky came back on the
stand and fired seven of his guys right there. I guess it was just a
gesture, but he did it. He took me out afterwards to some night spots,
and we hung around for a while and had a little taste. 'Man,' he
kept saying, 'you cats came and blew me out tonight.' He wanted to
know where he could get the music of some of the tunes we played.

'We don't have any music to lots of 'em,' I told him. 'We just put them together out of our heads.'"

This encounter was not untypical of what were known as "battles of bands," and it was not the first time Western groups had humbled some of New York's best. Earl Hines and his Chicago-based band had done it on several occasions, and Count Basie's had set a precedent for McShann when he came from Kansas City in 1936. Basie's was not then notable for polish and precision, but it had a superior rhythm section and a great gift for swinging. Like McShann's, it's outstanding innovative personality was a saxophonist, Lester Young, whose reputation in retrospect has also tended in some quarters to diminish that of the band. Yet no matter how great his sidemen, Basie himself was always the rhythmic heart of the group, just as McShann was of his. And it is significant that so many of the period's best bands were led by pianists, such as Duke Ellington, Earl Hines, Claude Hopkins, Fletcher and Horace Henderson.

McShann's career as a bandleader, so full of promise in 1942, was cut short by World War II. He was drafted in 1944 right from the bandstand in Kansas City.

"We had a marvelous crowd that night," he said with a wry smile, "about six or seven thousand people. An FBI guy came up about 11:30 and served papers on me. There were two red letters on them—two 'I's—and when I asked what they stood for, he said, 'Immediate Induction, and that means we go right now to Leavenworth!' I asked my manager to take care of the band's book, but we lost the whole of it that night. Two guys came in and told the caretaker of the auditorium that they were to pick up the band's things, and I never did find out what happened to that trunk of music.

"I was in antiaircraft for thirteen months. When I got out of the service, I still had the big-band sound on my mind, and I tried it again, but it had become too expensive. Most of the dance halls were using combos of five or six pieces, so I had to cut down, and I went out to California. Since then it has been small groups for me nearly all the time."

Jay McShann was born in Muskogee, Oklahoma, in 1916. Although a small town, it is the birthplace of such notable jazz musicians as Don Byas, Barney Kessel, Walter "Foots" Thomas, and the Ellington bassist, Aaron Bell. McShann was nearly twelve years old when Bell's mother began teaching his older sister piano. The family could not afford lessons for both children, but after singing and whistling the melodies his sister played, McShann found out how to reproduce them on the piano. The same thing happened when she began to play organ at their church, but there he had to be careful to open the hymn book at the right place and pretend to read the music. He also began to listen to the piano players on blue records, and to bands on the radio like Earl Hines's from Chicago. ("I would tell the folks I was going to do some studying, so I could stay up and listen to Fatha Hines, but I wouldn't be studying at all. When Fatha went off the air, I went to bed.") He heard the famous Kansas City band of Bennie Moten at local dances, but it was one led by Clarence Love that really fired an ambition in him to play jazz. He still could not read a note when he finished high school and went off to Fisk University in Nashville.

"I was trying to play football there," he said, "but it didn't work out too well because I went out on that field and got my fingers hurt. Then some fraternity was having a party and couldn't find anybody to play for it. A friend of mine told them about me, and they came and asked me. I told them I knew only three or four tunes. 'That's okay,' they said. 'You just keep going from one to another.' That was how the gig went. After I'd played my four tunes, I'd go back to the first and on down to the second, third, and fourth—all night.

"Then things got a little rough. We had tried to get jobs to help us through school, but I got despondent and decided to hobo back home with a buddy. After a week in Muskogee again, everything seemed so dull that I told my dad I thought I would go to Tulsa. He said if things didn't work out to contact him, and he'd get me back.

"Soon after I got to Tulsa, I was passing a hall where I heard some guys rehearsing. It was Al Denny's band—about twelve pieces—and they had no piano player! I went in, sat and listened to them, and memorized the tunes they played. When they started talking about what they were going to do for a piano player, I went up to see one of them and said, 'Look, man, I think I can play those tunes.' He said, 'You can? Well, come on up then!' They put the music in front of me and they thought I was reading it. 'Man,' they said, 'we've got a cat here who can read, and fake, and everything!' I had a good ear, but they soon found out I couldn't read. Then they helped me, and I learned fast.

"That was really how I got into music. I was fifteen years old. I stayed in Tulsa with Al Denny until I got a chance to go to Arkansas City with a small group. I worked there a year or so and then decided to get a little more education at Arkansas City Junior College. I fooled around until my money ran out. I used to raid the landlady's icebox at night after everybody had gone to sleep. When she got smart and emptied it, I realized I was going to have to get out, and I went to Oklahoma City."

There he joined Eddie Hill and His Bostonians. They worked at a ballroom in Shawnee and then went to a resort in the mountains twenty miles outside of Albuquerque. The band broke up in 1934 and McShann returned to Arkansas City, working for the first time in a duo with a drummer. Eventually the club closed and he set out for Omaha, where he had an uncle. When his bus made an hour-long stop in Kansas City, he visited the Reno Club, and bassist Billy Hadnott persuaded him to stay. He got a job in a trio with Elmer Hopkins on drums and Ed Lewis, who later made his name with Count Basie, on trumpet. After that he was in Dee Stewart's band in a downtown club, and in another piano-and-drums duo at Wolfe's Buffet, where blues singer Joe Turner sometimes joined him. Turner and boogie-woogie pianist Pete Johnson were two of his greatest pleasures in Kansas City, which soon became McShann's second home. It was there that drummer Jesse Price gave him his nickname of "Hootie." Some connected this with his liking for hootch, or "ignorant oil," but his close friend, bassist Gene Ramey, also related it to his habit of staying up at night with the hoot owls.

"After I got through where I was playing," McShann recalled, "the joints were still going till five or six in the morning, and I'd go around and hear everybody. It was so exciting I'd not want to go to sleep, because I was afraid I'd miss something! I heard Mary Lou Williams with Andy Kirk at Fairyland Park; and when Basie came back to Kansas City I finally had the chance to hear his band."

He worked around the city from 1937 to 1940 and had a long engagement at Martin's-on-the-Plaza with a seven-piece group that included Earl Jackson, Willie Scott, and Bob Mabane on saxophones, Orville Minor on trumpet, Gene Ramey on bass, and Gus Johnson on drums. This was to be the nucleus of his big band, and it was enthusiastically reported on by Dave Dexter, a young writer on the Kansas City *Journal-Post* who later became editor of the influential *Down Beat* and was much responsible for focusing attention on McShann.

"Charlie Parker worked with us for a time then, too," the pianist continued. "He had joined George Lee's band and gone down to the Ozarks for two or three months. There's nothing to do in the Ozarks, but he said he went there to 'woodshed.' I'd say he went through a quick transition there, because when I was walking along the street one day I heard this unfamiliar saxophone sound. 'Who could that be?' I asked myself. I figured I knew everybody's sound then, but I'd never heard one like this. So I went up and there was this cat, back in town, blowing altogether different. He was soon upsetting all the musicians around, and anyone who was in Kansas City in those days just loved to see Bird come in with his horn in that sack under his arm. They liked what he did, even if they didn't understand it. He

asked to join our group, and he was with us five or six months before
he decided to go to New York. That's when he went on his own, just
standing around, looking and seeing. He told me how thrilled he was
to stand across the street and see the Apollo Theatre. He looked New
York over, came back, and joined Harlan Leonard's band.

"This was in '39, and I was just beginning to organize a big band.
Dave Dexter begged me to keep the small group and let everything
stay as it was, but I always wanted a big band. When I got a job at
the Century Room, I had to get me some more musicians, so I went
to Omaha and got some of Nat Towles's men. It was Mr. Bales, an
insurance executive who had helped me before, who gave me the
money to do that. All the other monies, for uniforms and everything,
came out of the band. A lot of people think that Johnny Tumino, who
was booking us, did that, but the band carried itself, particularly
when we had hit records later. Unfortunately, I didn't improve as a
businessman. I lost the value of money with that big band. If a guy
told me he badly wanted a new horn, I'd tell him, 'Okay, go get it!'
We hadn't been together long when we had a battle with Harlan
Leonard. Charlie Parker made up his mind where he wanted to be
that night, put his notice in, and joined us two weeks later.

"He was an *interested* cat in those days, and I could depend on him
to take care of the reed section. He'd be mad at the guys if they were
late for rehearsal. Then one night we had played a couple of numbers
before he showed, and I knew he was 'messing around.' But he was
strong mentally and physically, and it was some years before he
started deteriorating, before his habit really began wearing on him.

"He got his nickname when we were driving through Texas. The
car we were in hit a chicken and he made us stop. He got out, picked
it up, and had it cooked that night at the hotel where we were staying.
And he insisted we eat what he called 'that yardbird' for dinner. From
then on he was known as 'Yardbird' or 'Bird.'

"Tadd Dameron heard us play an arrangement he'd written for Harlan Leonard, and he liked the way we played it better. The difference
was in the phrasing. We played it long and singing. That's where the
'first' man is so important. If he's singing, everybody sings along with
him. Our first man was either Charlie or John Jackson. So long as we
were playing from a written arrangement, I had John phrase it, but
when it was a 'head' tune, then Bird phrased it. He set most of the
riffs on the heads, too. Bird didn't have the tone John had, but he had
so much feeling. Some people used to think I was crazy when I told
them he was the greatest blues player in the world. Everything he
played, even when he played a sweet tune, it was the blues. As compared with Johnny Hodges, he'd play a dozen notes where Johnny

played one, but he'd make you like 'em, so that made up for the difference in tone.

"I always say his *peak* was when he was with my band. He played *more* then. If anything, he *lost* when he got involved with the 'stuff' and got so far out. No one who heard it ever forgets the time we were broadcasting from the Savoy Ballroom and playing *Cherokee*. The engineer on that broadcast must have been a musician, because he told me to keep right on, and we played right through the theme. Bird was straight then and he really had his chops. I knew how remarkable it was and I tried to get John Tumino to record him, but Bird was ahead of his time. When we went to New York we had a heck of an arrangement on *Body and Soul*, and Bird would blow that *Body and Soul* till there wasn't anything else to blow, but the people wouldn't even clap their hands. Then Jimmy Forrest would take over, and the house would break up when he got through. It used to make me so mad! I know that was an audience of dancers, but believe me our rhythm section was giving them a solid beat.

"We had a lot of music, but we had twice as many head arrangements that had been put together on the stand or in rehearsal. The guys were young and they could remember where we were going if we wanted to stretch a number out for twenty or thirty minutes. That was how our style was shaped. Sometimes the rhythm section would play three or four choruses by itself in front. That set the band up, and by the time the horns came in they were rarin' to go. We used to play *Willow, Weep for Me*, and the way we did it made people ask what it was. '*Sport 'Em Up*,' we'd tell them. We'd be playing the same chords, but with all different riffs. And when we came to the out chorus, the reeds would be doing one thing, the trumpets would be doing one thing, and the trombones another— but not clashing! Some of the written arrangements may have been more stiff and formal to begin with, but by the time our cats were through with them we were back to playing our way!

"Bird was with me four years, but he changed in that time. His heart wasn't like it was at the beginning of our big band. He had got into the habit of going to places like Monroe's in New York with his horn under his arm. There he might blow just a couple of tunes and then step off the stand for a taste. With me, too, his time had been going bad—showing up late, and so on. Gene Ramey would say to me, 'Let me handle it. I'll get him here on time.' They were very close, and Gene would go by and check him out. He tried, and I went with it for a time, until it began to have a bad effect on the other guys.

"I let him go at the Paradise Theater in Detroit. I'd been warning him, because those pushers would be hanging around, standing in the wings and wherever they could get to him. This time, I think he had an overdose. Now he used to have bad feet, and when it came time for him to solo he went out to the mike in his stocking feet. I was sitting at the piano, wondering what all the people were laughing at, and there he was with his big toe showing! He went back to New York with Andy Kirk, and then joined Earl Hines.

"He and Dizzy Gillespie were responsible for launching bebop, but there was a big difference between them. Both of them could run up and down the horn and play a lot of notes, but nobody could play a whole bunch of notes and swing like Bird. Swing is strange. I put it this way: some people have to walk the chalk line, while others walk the same distance but don't have to walk the chalk line. You either swing or you don't. Swing is free. Blues is free. Latin rhythm is a structured thing. That guitar player, George Benson, can play Latin rhythms—and swing. There are plenty of good musicians in jazz who can't swing, and it's often because they get too technical to swing.

"One night a band swings more than another night. My theory is that if the guys have a full dinner thirty minutes before they go on the stand, they're not going to do anything because they can't coordinate. One's fuller than another! Another's overstuffed. Catch them when they've just got off the bus and haven't had anything to eat if you want to hear what they can really do. They play better and coordinate better.

"At one point, we were short of bookings, so we took some dates with Don Redman, who would stand out front of the band with his baton. Some of the cats had been griping, saying if things didn't pick up they'd have to go home. What was funny was that they played so well one night that Don said to me, 'Man, listen, don't worry about nothing. The way those cats played tonight, ain't nobody going nowhere! Don't you believe what they're saying."

Records played a curious trick on the McShann band and its potential audience. When the band recorded for Decca in Dallas, the producer was less interested in its jazz repertoire than in blues. *Confessin' the Blues* and *Hootie Blues* were made by just the rhythm section with vocals by Walter Brown, who sang in a nasal, rather uneventful manner. It was a manner, however, with which people could clearly identify. Not everyone wanted dramatics. When the two titles were issued back to back on a seventy-eight, they proved a smash hit, reputedly selling half a million copies. This unexpected success dictated a pattern, and very few of the band's best arrangements, written or oral, were ever recorded. In later years, having also been responsible for the discovery of singers like Al Hibbler and Jimmy Witherspoon, McShann would answer requests for Walter Brown's blues by singing them himself, and singing them very much better.

After cutting down to a small group again, McShann enjoyed considerable success in California, and it was there that he met the renowned pianist, Art Tatum.

"Art could really play the blues," he insisted. "To me, he was the world's greatest blues player, and I think few people realized that. The way I found out was when we used to hang out together, around about '47. I'd do his driving when we went out, because he couldn't see well, and when he stayed out late I had to do the explaining to his wife, too. We'd go to Hollywood and listen to Duke Ellington when he was in town, and then we'd go to our hideout, an after-hours place where they had a piano and sold booze. He thought I could play the blues, and after he got to feeling pretty good he'd tell me, 'Go play the blues!' So I'd play, and he'd sit and listen. If I did something he liked, he'd start popping his fingers. I'd keep it going strong, because I'd want him to play. After a while he might get up and go in the kitchen, and then come back to where the piano was. I'd finish up right quick then, and sit down. He never did want anyone to ask him to play. It took something out of him. You had to prime him a little and wait until he got ready. As a rule, he'd play all that old technique stuff first, but when he settled down he played blues. He was a great piano player, a great technician, and he felt the blues and could play the blues."

McShann reflects the importance of this friendship in the way he plays the blues today. He will close his eyes, shake his head from side to side, rock on the piano stool, and deliver the blues with unrivaled authority. Although he plays with tremendous rhythmic vitality, it is not with the heavy, pounding touch associated with many blues pianists. His is much lighter, more akin to Tatum's, and he is by no means limited to blues and boogie-woogie as some suppose. He plays ballads and standards with refreshing originality, his knowledge of harmonics being much in evidence. This results in part from his decision to "go back to school" in 1952, to Kansas City Conservatory, where he studied under Dr. Francis Boubendork and Dr. Herb Six.

"I knew that sooner or later I would have to settle somewhere," he said. "I looked Chicago over, but I thought I could maybe do a better job of raising the three kids, and seeing they got their schooling, in Kansas City. I worked around there five years or more, sometimes with a six-piece group, sometimes with a quartet or trio. We went with the punches. As the kids grew up, I started moving out more. We often played three months of the year in Lincoln, Nebraska, and we also went into Iowa, Michigan, Minnesota, and the Dakotas—cold country!"

Since a first visit in 1968, he has toured Europe several times and is as much appreciated there as in his natural habitat, the Great Plains. New York doesn't see him often. The city is probably too abrasive for one of his genial, unassuming personality. But in 1977 he was finally presented with an appropriate group at Michael's Pub, where for three weeks the swinging was as intense, and the values as fresh and undated, as any experienced in Manhattan for many a long night. Then he was gone to Kansas City again, unconsciously fulfilling the kind of blues lyrics he delivers with such droll nonchalance: *Sorry, baybay, but I can't take you!*

(1970 and 1977)

17. *Count Basie's Orchestra, featuring Jimmy Rushing. Preston Love is third saxophonist from the right.* (Stanley Dance collection)

18. *Jo Jones.*
(Stanley Dance collection)

19. *Helen Humes at the Oceanic Hotel, Sydney, Australia, 1964.* (Courtesy Helen Humes)

20. *Dicky Wells and Benny Morton.* (Stanley Dance collection)

21. *Buddy Tate.* (Courtesy Jean Pierre Tahmazian)

22. *Count Basie's Orchestra, 1958. Eddie Jones (bass); Freddie Green (guitar); Sonny Payne (drums); (left to right) Thad Jones, Snooky Young, Wendell Culley, Joe Newman (trumpets); Henry Coker, Al Grey, Benny Powell (trombones); Billy Mitchell, Frank Wess, Marshall Royal, Frank Foster, Charlie Fowlkes (reeds); Count Basie (piano).* (Courtesy Willard Alexander, Inc.)

23. *Frank Foster.*
(Courtesy Jack Bradley)

24. *Billie Holiday and Snooky Young.* (Courtesy Snooky Young)

25. *Eric Dixon* (left) *and Frank Wess* (right). (Courtesy Impulse Records)

26. *Harry Edison* (left) *and Earl Hines* (right). (Courtesy Georges Braunschweig)

27. *Carnegie Hall reunion, January 15, 1966. At microphone: Ed Hall (clarinet) and Joe Turner (vocal). At side of piano: Harry Edison, Buck Clayton (trumpets), Buddy Tate (saxophone). First row,* left to right: *Eric Dixon, Bobby Plater, Marshall Royal, Billy Mitchell, Charlie Fowlkes. Second row: Norman Keenan (bass); Freddie Green, Harlan Floyd, Grover Mitchell, Richard Boone, Bill Hughes. Third row: Jo Jones (drums); Gene Goe, Sonny Cohn, Al Aarons.* (Courtesy Columbia Records)

28. *Count Basie and Lockjaw Davis.* (Courtesy Jack Bradley)

29. *Catherine and Count Basie at Basie's seventieth birthday party, New York, August 21, 1974.* (Courtesy Jack Bradley)

30. *Nat Pierce and Count Basie at Disneyland, 1977.* (Photo by Mal Levin, courtesy Nat Pierce)

31. *Joe Williams.*
(Courtesy Red Saunders)

32. *Sonny Cohn.*
(Courtesy Red Saunders)

Gene Ramey

(BASS)

"Where I was born in Austin, Texas, April 4, 1913, is now Brecken-ridge Hospital, so I call that a personal monument to myself. Austin was a very small city then. There had been an oil boom thirty miles away, and there were great ranches around. A lot of cotton was grown in those days, but now the government has limited how much they grow.

"On my birth certificate it says my father was a teamster. He was a horse trainer. He'd take colts and train them to pace, train them for saddling, for the wagon, and for working. When he died, he was a regular farmhand and did all the plowing and everything. He worked for General Hamby, one of the baddest men Texas ever had. He was one of those men who would ride his horse into the saloon and shoot out the clock and all the lights. Anyone who wanted to protest was shot, too. On Sunday afternoons, he and his wife would ride in the gig and my father would drive. General Hamby had two black and white .45 revolvers and he could shoot birds off the telephone wire as they were riding along. Pow! There goes another bird! In the fifties, he killed three men and was put in a home. He must have been in his nineties, but he wrecked that home. He couldn't get that wildness out of his blood.

"My mother was a housewife, but she also did laundry. She'd take her three boys and my baby sister when she went to wash in people's backyards. My sister would have some toys to play with, my mother was on the wash, my older brother was on the old black pot you boil clothes in, and my other brother and I were on the two rinses. I was on the pot nearest my mother, which always gave her a chance to pop me when I didn't do right. But I took advantage of the fact that I was the baby boy! I was more or less a midget and kind of sickly, so when she told me to bring an armload of wood I'd grab my stomach and say, 'My stomach feels bad.'

"There were eight sisters and three brothers on my mother's side, and five of the sisters were good piano players. Somebody loaned my mother one of those old foot organs, and today I know how difficult some of the songs she played were, like, *He Married Another . . . O Dee . . . Three Little Babes Lost in the Woods . . .* and *Ball and Cabbage.* That last one was more like a reel in the South, and the people would be doing their dance to it.

"My grandfather, John Glasco, was half Comanche Indian. My grandmother came from Madagascar at the age of four or five. All she remembered was being put on a sailing ship that howled like a monster. She owned a restaurant right in the heart of downtown Austin, and my father's half brother owned another a couple of blocks down the street. Everybody called my grandmother Mother Glasco, and she managed to give her kids a good education. She brought them up in the church, and they must have done lots of singing and playing. My only surviving aunt recently retired as organist for Ebenezer, the largest black Baptist church in Austin. She had the number one choir there for years.

"My Uncle John married a lady named Leila Johnson, who was a first cousin of Jack Johnson the prizefighter. Their daughter, Nannie Mae, played classical music, was a featured artist with the Chicago Symphony, and became president of some kind of music society. She travels all over the country. There was a younger daughter, whose name was Bunch—we called her 'Dootsie'—and she also made her way in music. She played piano and sang. After I left Texas, she joined a trio and they became pretty prominent. She was Ivy of Ivy, Verne, and Von, who sang with Floyd Ray's band. She was the one who sang the solos, and she visited me when they were passing through Kansas City. When the band broke up, the trio continued successfully with one playing guitar, another piano, and Ivy the bass. They played bits in a couple of movies, too.

"Another cousin of mine was Louise Jones. She and her husband were both great musicians. Her son, Parrish Jones, was the one Kenny Dorham learned from. He played trumpet, and he was one of the greatest in the country, but he wouldn't leave Texas. He took up teaching, but he played jazz and Diz [Gillespie] and them were afraid of him. He passed away, very young, last year.

"There was music on the Ramey side of the family as well. Grandfather Jack Ramey was a whiz on violin. They said I took after him, the way he'd have his foot patting the ground. I can't play unless I pat my feet. My father played banjo and sang in a quartet, but he was more of an athlete. He died before I was four, in his early forties. I remember how my sister and I would be waiting at the front gate when he came home, and he'd take us down to the store and buy us candy. And I remember somebody picking me up to see him in that old, brown, wooden casket, and I kept saying, 'Why doesn't he wake up and take me to get some candy?'

"The Glasco children would go out with us to pick cotton where my father had worked. When we finished picking, we'd sit outside the cabin singing and telling stories until maybe midnight. We'd harmonize and sing all those old, good church songs—and some funny songs, too. That was where I composed my first song:

> *I went down the street and saw some pretty women,*
> *Don't nobody care about me?*
> *I went down the street, and I had patches in my pants,*
> *Don't nobody care about me?*
> *I woke up one morning, and I had cornbread and beans,*
> *Don't nobody care about me?*
> *I woke up this morning, and I had wet in the bed,*
> *My mother beat my back so bad, it sure did hurt.*

"They used to ask me to sing that song, and I'd sing it all over. Then I'd get out there and preach. I could roar, and get down there and say, 'Oh, brother, don't you want to go to Heaven?' Everybody knew I was going to be a preacher, because I could preach when I was five years old. I could tell ghost stories, too, and scare them all, but I'd scare myself more.

"I got some of the preaching from going to church, and also from all the camp meetings around us. The St. John's Association had one every summer, and so did a Holiness church about a block from our house. My brothers used to help park the cars of the white people who came to watch and listen to the singing, shouting, and speaking in unknown tongues. It used to be in a great big pasture, and the church appreciated the white people because they'd get a good collection, but there was always that color line. The whites would stand *outside* the tent, and the blacks would stay out of the way so they could see.

"Now the funny thing about Texas is that it's such a *plains* country. When we stopped singing outside our cabin, we could often hear another family singing three miles away! Sometimes we'd all get together and sing. My brothers and cousins would form a ring and start clapping their hands. Then one at a time they would get out in the middle and do a buck dance. They called that 'getting off the puppy's tail.' They danced flat-footed and my brothers got very good at it. They also had little team things where they would all do some particular step together, and they formed vocal quartets. Ira Glasco went to sing in the Deluxe Melody Boys Band, which played around Austin and did some touring. They started about 1926 and went up to '30 or '31. They were all local musicians.

"When George Corley took the band over, it became George Corley and His Royal Aces. There were three Corley brothers. George played trombone, Reginald trumpet, and Wilfred some other instrument. I started working in that band at the end of '31, and I stayed till I went to college. I borrowed some things called timber blocks—not *temple* blocks. They were like a xylophone, like the African ones, and I started to try to play them, picking up things as I went along.

"At school, I'd played field drums in the Boy Scouts, and I'd sung in a quartet. We had a Sergeant Willis there who was really terrific on drums and the ukulele. He interested me in getting a trumpet, and I learned to play ukulele. My brothers and sister used to get every record that came on the market with jazz on it. I'd be sitting on the floor just like the dog on the record that was listening to his master's voice! Everyone in our family could sing, and we could hum and scat every note of Louis Armstrong's. My cousin Duke became like the Texas Cab Calloway. He had long hair like the white man has, and he'd throw it over his eyes and do all those contortions.

"I got most of my music fundamentals in Anderson High School from the lady who was the choir leader. She also taught the quartet I sang in. Trumpet was my first instrument, but I found I could never get the pressure to play more than an octave. When I was thirteen I began playing tuba. Austin was known as the Friendly City, and we were very blessed. We had a lot of help from the old people and ex-soldiers, and from whites who bought us uniforms. Every Friday night during the summer there was a band concert in the park by a black brass band of about twenty pieces. Mr. Timmons, a barber in town, played bass horn in that group, and he was my teacher.

"After the trumpet I went to baritone horn but found that was too much in between, so then I got a tuba, an E-flat helicon. You don't have to squeeze your lips so tightly as with a trumpet, because you get more support from the mouthpiece. Now I belonged to a social club called the Moonlight Serenaders. Others I remember were the Wild Fire Sheiks and the Mystic Knights. They'd take it in turns giving dances for us teenage kids, and they'd have three or four pieces to play. Somebody got the idea we were paying too much for musicians, so they took money to buy instruments and we organized our own band. We became very popular because we had six pieces where the other groups could only afford three.

"I didn't really know how to apply what I'd learned in high school, but we'd practice all night. The neighbors would complain about us boys playing all out of tune. Eugene Love, who later played piano with Sammy Holmes's band, took an interest in our group and had the patience to make us go over the music till we got it right. We soon had enough showmanship to fool the people. Then Sammy Holmes and his La Palm Orchestra came in. Herschel Evans played in that band, and Buddy Tate says he did, too. Sammy used to hire me for jobs when I wasn't busy. I couldn't play much, but that was how I first met Herschel. He came from a little town not far away. At that time there were a lot of road shows and carnivals. They'd hire musicians, get them so far, and drop 'em. Maybe they'd get up in the middle of the night and leave them. Herschel may not have been stranded like that, but there were many cases of musicians who were.

"Now when I got with George Corley's Royal Aces, I took the place of a learned sousaphone player who was also the coach on the school football team. That's when they started calling me 'Warm-up Ramey.' That coach always gave me pants that were too big for me, and about two minutes before the game would end he'd holler, 'Ramey, warm up!' And I'd be running down the sideline, and never get in the game. But my cousin's husband was the basketball coach, and I got to be like a star on his team.

"When my schooldays were over, I got a kind of musical scholarship to Western University in a suburb of Kansas City. I left Austin August 18, 1932. I had to work my way through. I'd had experience in Texas picking cotton, picking turkeys, shining dirty cowboy boots on the street, and working as a dishwasher, but an uncle, who was a house painter by trade, had also taught me painting. So when I got to Western a friend of mine and I took over the furnace room and those big boilers. We also painted all seven buildings on the outside. Everybody was afraid of those scaffolds, but we'd get up there, three stories high, and do the whole thing, windows and everything.

"I started getting music jobs right away on the side. I remember going to the music store and getting stocks of Jimmie Lunceford's *White Heat* and something by Duke Ellington, after I had organized a fifteen-piece band. Buddy Anderson [trumpet] was in it, and Lawrence 'Frog' Anderson played trombone. We mostly rehearsed. It was a kind of outlet for us, but when Alf Landon had his political campaigns some of us got on a flat-bottomed truck and played for him.

"On Labor Day that first year they had a Battle of Bands in Kansas City. I think they had eight bands and they started about seven o'clock and played till three in the morning. It was very exciting. Bennie Moten was usually the boss in those days. After Bennie died, Andy Kirk ran away with it, but the Blue Devils were always bad and the Southern Serenaders were a powerful group. Then there was George E. Lee with that mighty voice, and later on they had Thamon Hayes. Sometimes Alphonso Trent would come up from Dallas, when he was available. Incidentally, an uncle of mine was head bellboy at the Adolphus Hotel where Trent mostly worked.

"I went to Western University to study electrical engineering, but after the first year the school lost its credit rating. So then I thought I was going into a journalism course, and ended up getting a certificate in printing. I didn't get a chance to write anything, but I learned how to run a printing press! I took a course in arranging and public school music with Marie Little—what you'd *teach* in the elementary grades. But Little Jack Washington was a graduate of Western University and I used to go over to his house. He showed me everything about reading.

"I was still a tuba player when I got to Kansas City, but I made the switch to string bass in 1933. I didn't have nerve enough to go out in the open with it, but I played it with my band until late '34. They'd had a real big band at Western at one time and there was a storeroom full of instruments. Guy O'Taylor was director of the band and he just told me to get what I wanted. I took a bass, and then I went back and asked if I could have a saxophone as well. So I was learning both instruments at the same time. O'Taylor was a good violin player who worked with Basie at the Eblon Theater where Basie played organ and accompanied the silent movies. We had an eighteen-piece marching band, and eight of us played for assembly every morning.

"I've had guys ask me why I didn't learn to play the bass properly, because they sometimes see me with two fingers on one note. That's because I was born double-jointed. I have no pressure in the balls of my fingers. When they talk of my 'long' notes, it's partly due to that, but I never gave up the big-band style until about three years ago. In fact, guys ask me do I still have my strings a half-inch off the finger board. You had to do that, had to keep it up high, because you didn't have a mike in those days. But I never appreciate the guys who wanted the bass fiddle to stand out all alone in the rhythm section. I like an *even* rhythm section, not the bass dominating. You listen to Basie's rhythm section—it was all balanced, the drums didn't sound any louder than the guitar, the piano, or the bass. Then all of a sudden, around '47 or '48, they started making the bass dominant and noisy with all those amplifications. It was wrong. The *drummer* is hired to carry the tempo. He can decorate, but it's up to him to hold the tempo. Back when bop came in, Curly Russell and I were the most hired guys on 52nd Street, because that was when drummers began to put their foot in their pockets. It didn't matter how fast the tempo was, or how ragged it got. So they had to have a strong bass player to carry that beat while the drummer was decorating and actually stealing the solo in places from the horns. It became an exciting thing and it was accepted.

"But the man I adore most, Walter Page, saw things differently when he created the Basie rhythm section. When they were first playing together after Jo Jones came, he would constantly tell them to remember that that drum is not supposed to sound any louder than the piano or the unamplified guitar. 'Now come on down,' he'd say. 'See if you can do all that stuff and come on down.'

"If you think back to the days of King Oliver, it was the drummer who swung the band. They had to have a bass horn, because the bass fiddle could not compete with that one-man rhythm section. All you could hear was the *pop-wop-wop-wop* of the bass drum, although the drummer was also playing the snare drum. I call that New Orleans style. Baby Lovett's a good example, and he's still a genius on those snares although he doesn't play with that heavy foot. Zutty Singleton played the snare and the rims, but later, in Chicago, he started playing the cymbals. In the Chicago style, the drummer not only used his foot, but played some on the cymbals. Of course the sousaphone could play as loud as the drummer, but he couldn't play those fast tempos. Happy Jackson, who lived outside Kansas City in Liberty, Missouri, was the baddest bass horn player in the world, and when it was played the way he did, the sousaphone could be felt as well as heard, even at those big battles of bands. But even before amplification, they started changing to bass fiddle because the bass horn would take up a whole truck bed. You couldn't unscrew that bell and fold it into a compact little thing. It was three times as big as a bass fiddle.

"Pops Foster and those guys in New Orleans had shown how the bass fiddle could be used if the drummer would come down a little bit. It could not be heard with that big foot. How splendid Sonny Greer and Wellman Braud sounded on Duke's early records. Sonny still has a heavier foot than Jo Jones, but the way they blended and swung showed that the rhythm section was *teaming*. Braud was strong. He might get close to the mike when they were recording, but there was no such thing as a mike in most little towns. And yet you could hear them. Lunceford's bass player, Moses Allen, mostly played two-beat, but he and ol' Crawford cut right through. They blended. I say no band was great unless it had a strong rhythm section. It had to have a motor.

"With the exception of Duke's, there weren't many that were great. Earl Hines had fine arrangements and sounded so beautiful on piano. He had a good rhythm section but it wasn't *even* till he got Alvin Burroughs. Neither Cab Calloway nor Fletcher Henderson had good rhythm sections at the time Walter Page was sitting down and telling the guys, 'Now listen, we gotta get the balance! You gotta stay out of the way, or we'll have to get rid of either the piano or the guitar.' This was right in Basie's lot, because when he came to Texas with Bennie Moten they would play places with only one piano. Moten would sit there and play the bass part, and Basie would play the treble. They learned how to stay out of each other's way, so there was no problem at all for Basie to stay out of the way of the guitar.

"Freddie Green, that famous guitarist in Basie's band, does not flirt with the chords. Chords can follow progressions. Or chords can just stay on rudiments, and that way people know where you are and don't have to clash with you. Why Freddie's so great is that he plays that fundamental chord and doesn't get in the way of the piano. When bop came in, they eliminated the guitar player because he was clashing with the piano. Then when amplified guitar arrived, not only did the piano player have trouble, but the bass player as well!

"I first met Walter Page at the battle of bands in 1932. He was there with his own Blue Devils, and a week or two later I saw him with Bennie Moten. I didn't learn any technical things about playing the bass from him, but I learned from him how to construct, how to support a soloist, and how to work with a rhythm section. What he showed me most of all was restraint. I'd stand next to him, next to the door leading out to the alleyway, and he'd tell me things. 'There's a whole lot I could do here,' he'd say, 'but what you must do is play a straight line, because that man out there's waiting for food from you. You could run changes on every chord that's going on. You've got time to do it. But if you do, you're interfering with that guy [the soloist]. So run a straight line.'

"He told me that, generally speaking, when you've got a slow tune and the melody goes up, the bass should ordinarily run his line down. If the melody is coming down, the bass should go up to put body in it. He taught me such things as building the second chorus and how to avoid a drummer that's gotten on the wrong beat—how to stay out there, and let him catch up, so that you find each other without showing him up.

"I valued what he told me very much, because I didn't have too much real music training. I bought a Frank Skinner book and pasted the chart from the middle of it on the bass fiddle. It showed the names of each note, and where your fingers should be, but I couldn't finger them like I should because of my fingers being double-jointed. It was a handicap, especially for speed and endurance, and when you're bowing you should really play on the ball of your fingers. With those fingers, I should have joined a carnival instead of a band!

"The bass player who preceded Jimmy Blanton with Duke for a short time was from Kansas City. His name was Adolphus Allbrooks, and I used to see him walking across the viaduct from Kansas City, Kansas, to Kansas City, Missouri, with his bass on his back. He was a great bass player, but he complained that Duke was using all the wrong chords. He was a great arranger, too, but he didn't want to consider that Duke was creating a new sound in music. He became a professor up at the University of Minnesota, but I guess he was too legitimate in his thinking because I believe he's the only guy who quit Duke. Everybody else wanted to get with him.

"Kansas was dry in the days I'm talking of, but Missouri was wide open. People who lived in Kansas went over to Missouri and raised hell. It was like some people say of New York—a place to go and have fun in, and then you get on out. But Kansas was a 'northern' state. Western University was right where John Brown brought the slaves across the Missouri River into Kansas. The schools were integrated in Kansas, too, but on the Missouri side you couldn't sit with the white people in a club unless the boss fell over backwards and said, 'Come over here and talk.' Like in the Reno Club, they would get Basie, Jo Jones, or somebody, and bring them over to the table.

"We'd go over from Western and have our little jam sessions. We heard Joe Turner at the Hawaiian Gardens, and then we'd go down to the Sunset Club. That was really something—about twelve feet wide and maybe sixty feet long. It was just like going down a hallway. They hired a piano player and a drummer to come on at midnight, but we'd get over there before that and sometimes there'd maybe be ten musicians up on the stand. That was where I first met Prez and Ben Webster. They took a liking to me, so they had me going over there every night. They'd fight it out till daylight, sometimes to ten o'clock in the morning. They were both three or four years older than me, but they noticed I wasn't a heckler. I'd just stand and listen to them, and not keep asking why or how they did this or that. Around nine o'clock in the morning, we'd go across to the Sawdust Trail, a dining room with sawdust on the floor, where all the musicians met. The Lone Star, where Pete Johnson was playing, was directly across from the Sunset. It was a nightclub, a little like Ryan's in New York, a little less crowded than the Sunset. The Sunset was not a bucket of blood, but you might see some fighting in it, and you'd have to break out of there. Anyway, after breakfast at the Sawdust Trail they'd get us back to college.

"Another place where we had after-hours jam sessions was the Subway, over on 18th Street. Piney Brown ran it and he was a big man in all that black neighborhood, although Felix Payne was actually the boss. Piney was a friend to the musicians and in with the politicians, because he could get you out of jail. Felix Payne had an open lottery right on the street, with a roulette wheel and everything. You could go right in there and gamble, and there was always peace, although that was the area where you found the hustlers and good restaurants. The only place that's still there is Matlow's Clothing Store. There isn't much musical life there now. It's scattered way out to the suburbs, but even in our time the clubs weren't all in one locality.

"Lester had a very spacey sound at the end of '33. In fact, I still try to play like that now. He would play a phrase and maybe lay out three beats before he'd come in with another phrase. You know, instead of more continuous staying on style, like Bird would play. Prez had kind of loosened up, but Ben Webster had not developed his style at all. I don't think he had really developed it even when he was with Teddy Wilson. I think Duke Ellington brought that out of Ben—he and Johnny Hodges. At that time, everybody thought Dick Wilson was next to Prez in Kansas City. I didn't know Dick Wilson that much, but one thing they held against him was that he liked to play the higher part of the saxophone. I liked the way Prez played tenor with an alto style, but everybody seemed to be a Coleman Hawkins fan then.

"I slipped away from school the night Hawk played at the Cherry

Blossom. Ben, Herschel, Dick Wilson, and three or four other local tenors were there, and Hawk was cutting everybody out. Until Prez got him. He tore Hawk apart. He tore Hawk up so bad he missed a date in St. Louis. Hawk was still trying to get him at twelve o'clock next day. Seemed like the longer Prez played, the longer that head-cutting session went on, the better Prez got. He played more creative things. The adage in Kansas City was—and still is—*say something on your horn*, not just show off your versatility and ability to execute. *Tell us a story, and don't let it be a lie.* Let it *mean* something, if it's only one note, like Louis Armstrong or Duke would do.

"Prez tore up Hawk, Herschel, and everybody else, and then got the job with Fletcher Henderson, but Fletcher fired him right away because of his tone. Everybody put him down, but he wasn't too proud to come on back to Basie. He was always nice and considerate. In fact, he was like my big brother. That tenor saxophone, that silver Conn he had in New York, was one I gave him, the same one they had given me at the university. He liked it best of all.

"He was going with the Countess, Margaret Johnson, at that time. She took Mary Lou Williams's place with Andy Kirk. She was very good, and everybody said she was better than Mary Lou. In 1935, I had been working with Oliver Todd's band at Frankie and Johnny's, where we played with our overcoats on because the man couldn't pay for the heat. Five of us then got a job in a club on 12th Street, and we persuaded her to play piano and act as leader. Countess Johnson and Her Band—the name made us a good draw. We had Orville 'Piggy' Minor on trumpet, Earl Jackson and William Scott on saxes, Bill Nolan as singer and drummer. In those days Earl Jackson was better than Bird or John Jackson. After we played a couple of places, we opened the State Line Tavern. I was still at Western University, but I'd graduated and taken a job as assistant engineer in charge of the generators and transformers that fed the laundry they had there. It paid only sixty dollars a month, but it was a kind of security. I was married and had a child, so that was why I had to have the other job with Countess Johnson.

"Those clubs on 12th Street ran from eight to four o'clock, sometimes to five, and I was getting very little sleep, not more than two or three hours. But being as talented and honorable as I am, I had found a very nice thing to do. I'd get down in the boiler room at Western University, stuff that thing full with coal, and go to sleep. Sometimes I could sleep five hours in the day, until somebody came running down saying, 'Listen, all the buildings are cold!'

"Countess Johnson didn't show any effort when she played. Her style was different, between Earl Hines's and Basie's but nearer to

Earl's. She was fast and powerful, and she said something. Of course, Earl was a strong influence not only in Kansas City but in Texas, too. All the gang at home used to make it to the radio when he came on from Chicago. We couldn't get New York too easily on those radios. We'd sit there all night listening to *Deep Forest, Rosetta,* and all that stuff. Earl was really a big influence all over the United States, bigger than anyone else since maybe Jelly Roll Morton. Some magazine had shown how he could stretch those tenths, and guys were saying he had had the webs cut between his fingers. He hadn't, but everybody was patterning after him and trying to stretch tenths!

"There was another band came on from noon to one from the Gunter Hotel in San Antonio, playing the nearest thing to nice, soft society swing. It was Herman Waldman's band* and at noon we would make it to a Chinese restaurant where they had the radio on. Sometimes, too, we'd hear Alphonso Trent's band from the Adolphus Hotel. Its success could be due to musical ability, but socializing ability was important, too.

"Basie's band built up their popularity on socializing. I mean the big following they had in and around Kansas City. But that whole band didn't believe in going out with steady black people. They'd head straight for the pimps and prostitutes and hang out with them. Those people were like a great advertisement for Basie. They didn't dig Andy Kirk. They said he was too uppity. But Basie was down there, lying in the gutter, getting drunk with them. He'd have patches in his pants and everything. All of his band was like that.

"The job with Countess Johnson lasted till she went with Andy Kirk's band. They went to New York, but she didn't live long after that. They brought her back home and she died shortly afterwards of what people thought was tuberculosis. She had made one record, with Billie Holiday. Prez was crazy about her, and I believe he got her on that date. Her brother, Roy Johnson, played bass with Lionel Hampton, but last I heard he was playing piano in Kansas City.

"Everett Johnson was another good piano player, and one of the cats who could stretch out Pete Johnson. They'd battle all night. He could really play barrelhouse and eight-to-the-bar blues, and at the time I'm talking of he was a little more popular than Pete. A whole lot has to do with who chooses whom. Andy Kirk was winning all the battles, but he didn't have the right people to give him a build-up. His was the most popular band in Kansas City, but Basie ended up with Benny Goodman and John Hammond behind him. You think Kirk's band didn't have the drive of Basie's, but I'd put it a different

---

* Not Herman Walder's, Gene Ramey insists.

way. Some bands—and I could name others in Kansas City—had too much orchestration. When you listen to the original Basie records, they sound so exciting. Sometimes it wasn't really the solo that made it exciting, but the riff backing it up that Buster Smith, Herschel, Jack Washington, or any of the four guys in the sax section set. That also left the soloist free. The horns weren't fighting to make that note on time, like in those real experienced bands of Duke, Lunceford, and Andy Kirk. One band that went to New York and didn't really make it, because it didn't do enough ad lib playing, was Harlan Leonard's. That was why Jay McShann's band outblew them every time. Jay would give us the first chorus and then turn us a-loose.

"After the job with Countess Johnson, I played in a band for a walkathon at the Pla-Mor Ballroom. No Negroes had been allowed there before that, and we just went in the back door, got up on the stand, and played while the people walked around so many hours a day, trying to outlast each other. It was more or less an offshoot of the carnivals and shows the bands used to do. When the medicine man came through town, they'd build a tent and have a band to go with the two-headed man and the billy goat with a dog's head. The Pla-Mor had brought in all the good white bands, but they canceled the other engagements of the company that had rented the hall and brought in the black band!

"Some people seem to think the Cherry Blossom was a ballroom, but it was the old Eblon Theater turned into a huge nightclub. It was on Vine Street, between 18th and 19th, directly across the street from the Booker T. Washington Hotel, which had become the most popular one for musicians. Next door to it, on the right, was the Kentucky Tavern, where jam sessions would usually start around two o'clock in the afternoon. 'Spook breakfasts,' we called them in Kansas City! Anybody who'd stay up all night we called spooks or ghosts. Jay McShann got the name of 'Hootie' because he'd stay up so late he was up with the hoot owls. They also used to say that he would hoot like an owl when he'd drunk some whiskey!

"I keep sidetracking, but after the walkathon I went with Bus Moten. His brother had died, and he was trying to get the Reno Club job after Basie had gone to New York. There was never all that much work in Kansas City. Bennie used to play places like Fairyland Park and then go out on the road. None of the bands stayed in Kansas City that long. They had a regular circuit, whether they were booking themselves or not. That's why we used to see them all in Texas. Not only Bennie Moten and George E. Lee—with those long, beautiful cars—but King Oliver, Louis Armstrong, and Cab Calloway, too. Earl Hines was so much in demand because of the broadcasts they'd have taken him on a Monday morning if they could have gotten him. Every time they came down, they'd steal musicians out of Texas and Oklahoma. That's how they got Lips Page and others.

"Bus Moten played piano *and* accordion, so he could take jobs where there was no piano. I wasn't too keen on his playing of either instrument. There are two kinds of piano players: one is a soloist, a single, and the other plays with the band. Buster would start a tune and then just go for himself. You had a better chance with the accordion when you were playing bass, because he was playing on the treble side. When he was playing both hands on the piano, it was kind of rough! I think Bennie may have been a better player, although I never heard him solo, but apart from his musicianship he was a good organizer and a good manager. He kept his bands together better than anyone else, even though he was robbed by eastern bands like Blanche Calloway's.

"I first met Jay McShann at one of the jam sessions in the Taproom on 12th and Paseo. It was an all-black club, one of those walk-in-off-the-street places. When they had spook breakfasts there'd be a houseful there, but normally they had three pieces. So far as a rhythm section was concerned, McShann's gang then was Billy Hadnott on bass and Jesse Price on drums, but I joined him on either the 18th or 28th of April, 1938, for a job at Martin's-on-the-Plaza. We had seven pieces—trumpet, alto, tenor, baritone, and rhythm. Pete McShann, Jay's cousin, played drums the first two weeks, because Gus Johnson, who had come back from Omaha, had to give two weeks' notice where he was working. Hadnott didn't want to join till Gus came in, but at the end of the two weeks McShann called him and said he liked what he got, meaning me. We became like bosom friends.

"We immediately began to get trouble from the white local in Kansas City. They started saying we were out of our territory according to a zoning law they made up quickly. The Plaza was a real ritzy part of the city, with beautiful homes, trees in the yards, gardens, and everything. There was a real estate man, a Mr. Bales, who was a good friend of Jay's, and he may have had some interest in Martin's. We played soft music from eight to ten o'clock. Then the waiters moved the chairs and tables in the restaurant and we played dance music—twenty minutes on and forty minutes off. We had a dressing room where we played cards, but none of us did much drinking because we wanted to protect the job. Jay started taking care of business there, too, but after we were through we'd get down on 18th Street and Vine, where the gang was, and he'd get tore up. And I'd have to take him home.

"They loved him at Martin's. They were promoting their chicken-in-the-basket then, and I made up a song about it to the melody of *Pennies from Heaven*. We'd sing it there and on the radio, and it turned out to be a great thing. Society people would come from all over to order this chicken that would 'knock you out.' Then McShann became so popular that we got on what they called *The Vine Street Varieties* at the Lincoln Theater, a show for black people that started about 12:30 at night and went on till around four in the morning. Besides our group, they'd have a comedian, a couple of singers, and maybe a shake dancer. People down at the radio show were trying to get McShann, and some afternoons we'd have to go down to the big music store where Thamon Hayes was by this time working as a salesman. Then Dave Dexter, a newspaperman, met him and fell in love with him. From then on, McShann was on his way.

"It was partly Jay's personality, but he was really playing the piano and he was appreciated by all sorts of people. When we were at Martin's, we played numbers like *Hawaiian Paradise*, *Over the Rainbow*, and *Sierra Sue*. We only played what you might call 'hot' tunes at certain times. So those who thought of McShann and Bird as only playing bluesy and jazz were wrong, but he didn't get a chance to record ballads until years later [for Master Jazz]. I can see improvement and a lot more variety in his playing, but it's a different kind of piano when you play with a rhythm section and when you play as a single. But back in those days he was really cooking, and I'd say he was as much of an influence on Bird as the other guys who supposedly taught him.

"By his own personality McShann created a happy band. The guys were like a family. Often I'd pick up *all* the guys, and after work we'd go back home or to some restaurant in town. You knew he was the boss, but you could sit down and talk with him or cuss him out. It was a real good feeling like that.

"McShann would hit some phrase at the piano and the others would pick up on it. Long before we came to New York he created a tune he never finished, called *The Master's in His Solitude Today*. He'd get half tore up and say, 'I'm the master, you know.' Then he'd play this thing, and that's where the flatted fifth started coming in. He didn't let it show, but it kind of hurt him when his own ability wasn't recognized. He mentioned it to me a couple of times. 'Everybody's introducing me as the man who discovered Charlie Parker,' he said. I tried to console him by telling him, 'It's coming. Twelve years ago they would hardly let you back in New York.' But he thinks it's the jokers in his life. When he went on that tour behind the Iron Curtain with the Charlie Parker package, he said those guys played him down so low that it was just getting to him. One guy was talking nightly as the authority on Bird, on how he learned to play, and McShann was treated as just another man in the band.

"When we went to Europe recently, we had the same kind of thing going, and I threatened to come home. Fiddler [Claude Williams] brought both his violin and his guitar, and he played them at the highest pitch he could get them. I spoke to McShann first, and then to Fiddler, and I said, 'You don't really have to play that loud. I think we are supposed to be a team, and one guy is not supposed to walk off as the individual god of this thing!' McShann was in charge of the show and he'd run it, but this guy was telling him how to play it and what he wanted played.

"McShann is a very easygoing person until he fills up, and then he blows up. I used to tell him, 'You can nip it in the bud, stop it before it goes too far. Do it easy, rather than wait till you get really mad and don't know what you're saying.'

"To go back to Martin's-on-the-Plaza. . . . We stayed there maybe three months and then switched over to the Continental. It was there in 1938 that McShann had an offer from Charlie Barnet, who wanted to hire me. I didn't know about it, but instead of telling me, 'Go ahead, be happy,' McShann hid me, stuck me off in the corner somewhere. I wouldn't have gone, anyway, because McShann had established a beachhead in Wichita and, thanks to Dave Dexter, we'd been voted promising new players in a *Down Beat* poll. Jay and I were brought to Chicago along with George Barnes, Anita O'Day, and a drummer who had won in his category. We were supposed to go for two weeks, but we stayed six.

"While we were away, we left the band under the control of Willie Scott, a tenor player who had that real business manner about him. Bird and Earl Jackson had been in and out of the band before, but when we got back we found Bird had hoboed to New York. It was then that McShann began organizing a big band with John Tumino, our booking agent. Tumino leased a club called the Century Room, and bought us fine uniforms—black coats with striped pants, like evening dress. We did pretty good there, and then Don Robey in Houston booked us on a tour down there in the latter part of 1939 or beginning of 1940. McShann just tore it up all over the country. Most of what we did were heads. Willie Scott was doing some arranging, but we used the same things we'd done with seven pieces, voiced them out for the other horns, and fixed little riffs. The only thing I remember Bird writing was *What Price Love?*—which we recorded as *Yardbird Suite*. We recorded it in Dallas for Decca, but we never heard anymore of it. 'This is a little far from the picture we have of

Jay McShann,' they said. 'We want some blues.' Each time we played it, they told us to go back to the blues, and a lot of things we did were made up as we went along. Walter Brown had the words for them.

"I never knew too much about Brown, except that he'd been in a federal CCC camp up around Topeka. The lyrics were different, but he sang more or less the same melody to everything he did. He even had a bad talking voice—completely nasal. He didn't have good diction, and people could misunderstand when he sang, 'Baby, here I stand before you with my heart in my hand.' Jay can sing in a nasal way, too, but you can hear the different tunes. Before Brown, we'd mostly had ballad singers. There were quite a few blues singers around Kansas City, but to us they all seemed like poor imitations of Jimmy Rushing and Joe Turner. After the record of *Confessin' the Blues* was such a big hit, it began to go over good wherever we played. The whole band played it, although on the record there was only a trio back of Brown. There was never one note written on it. In fact, Bird and I were supposed to have written *The Jumpin' Blues*. We sat down and started humming riffs that would fit. I got the first eight bars and he got the last four. Then Brown came in and sang, and as we rehearsed we fitted other riffs. Not a note was written on that, either, but it became McShann's theme song. Before that he used that mournful blues theme as on the Wichita recording.* That kind of thing may have typed us as a blues band. We used to reminisce about old tunes as we rode home in the bus. One somebody sang was *My Mama's Dead and My Papa's Across the Sea*. Sometimes in their solos guys would go back to something sad like that that had got to them.

"I have to say that when I first met Bird in 1934 he was a terrible saxophone player, but I could always get him to jam with me. Even when he was with McShann, and he was getting ready to get himself some drugs, I could always ask him to give me fifteen minutes to get our fingers together. Then he'd start playing and forget all about the other things.

"In the McShann years, Bird was generally in control of his habit. He wasn't scratching his face, which was always an obvious sign. It was very rarely you would see him nodding and that sort of thing, but you could tell. The other guys who were trying to be like him by using it were the ones who showed it worse. He was wise enough in his way, and while we were playing at Tutty's Mayfair in Kansas City he got all the guys who were following him to take a teaspoon

---

* *Early Bird,* Spotlite 120.

of nutmeg and a drink of water. You don't get high that same day, but for two or three days afterwards you'll be walking like a sick duck. The grocery store where Tutty bought his supplies told him, 'You sure must be baking a lot of cakes and pies!' But when Bird got to New York and was hanging out with Tadd Dameron, they were experimenting with everything. He was even soaking the reed in his mouthpiece in Benzedrine water. That was a waker-upper. The drug was a go-to-sleeper.

"I think Jay first heard him when he came back from working with George E. Lee. Basie's 'Jones-Smith' record had come out and Bird startled everybody by playing Lester Young's solo on *Lady Be Good* note for note. 'Here comes this guy,' the cats used to say. 'He's a drag!' They couldn't believe it, because six months before he had been like a crying saxophone player. Although one famous writer says Bird was not influenced by Lester Young, if you listen to him you can tell he was *completely* influenced by Prez.

"Buster Smith's influence was not so direct. At spook breakfasts, Buster would set the riffs. There might be one trumpet and ten saxophone players. Usually, when one horn sets a riff, the other guys play in unison with him, but with Buster the other horns had to harmonize. Then it would sound like a written chorus, and that's what you hear on records when Basie's band was jumping so good. Buster was noted for that, and for eliminating those who didn't get the harmonic notes right in the riffs. You may have played your solo well, but you had to get out and not play for a while. Buster would always do that at jam sessions where there were too many horns. The guys would take their horns to a table and listen to the heavy riffs he set. It made them think, yes, but it also showed the young guys that they had to learn to team as well as play a solo. The sections, too, had to learn to breathe at the same time. All this was inspiring to Bird, who learned many tricky riffs that way.

"Buster was also a great improviser. He didn't have the strong sound of Johnny Hodges, Bird, or Benny Carter. He had a soft alto sound, more like Charlie Holmes's when he was with Luis Russell, or Johnny Hodges's in the early days with Duke. But though it was soft, he was very good playing lead. And when Benny Goodman or any other clarinet players came into a spook breakfast, Buster would get his clarinet out and clean everybody up, including Benny.

"He was a nice, easygoing man, and still is. The last time I heard from him he was playing piano in Dallas. He told me once he was sorry in a way that he didn't go with Basie, yet I think it was Buster who really made the Basie band what it was, a riff band with very little music. They were so well organized that Benny Goodman and

John Hammond couldn't believe a small band like that could sound so big.

"In the McShann band most of the sax riffs were set by the two alto players, Bird and John Jackson. Buddy Anderson or Piggy Minor set the riffs for the brass. So we were really picking up on what Buster Smith had done. Then, of course, the simple blues is *it*. When I was talking about the different phases of jazz, I meant to say that we looked upon Kansas City jazz as like a camp meeting, completely imitated from one of those revival meetings, where the preacher is singing and the people are replying. It's something you're bound to feel.

"I have to admit that all bands had things they riffed by the time Moten came out with *Toby* and *Lafayette*. If we were rehearsing a stock at a McShann rehearsal, someone in the reed section might find a phrase that didn't swing. 'We're going to play it this way,' they'd say, 'to make it swing more.' Then, too, McShann built his band and his solos playing behind the beat. He would try to arrange it so that the melodic line was played just a fraction behind the beat, but so that we would catch up just before we got to the end of the phrase. If you listen to *Hootie Blues,* you'll notice how far behind the real tempo the horns come in. That gave it a lazy image and a bluesy sound.

"They riffed in the East, but the rhythm sections there until very recently had a metronomic beat. It didn't accent like the western beat with the sock cymbal. The eastern drummer would drive you crazy—*tick, tick, tick, tick,* like a metronome. The western beat gave you a chance to relax—and that came from those camp meetings again. That's why I said the rhythm section makes the band. Remember how the rhythm sections in Basie's band and Duke's band were beating the heck out of a song. Those horns *had* to play! Lunceford's rhythm section was very good, too, and with their two-beat rhythm they were the first movement towards the churchy feeling. The horns were playing in a unique style from the arrangements, and it was so relaxed you'd still be patting your feet in your sleep. Lunceford played a ballroom on Woodland in 1934. It was an old building, the Masonic auditorium. He had the whole house jumping. The people were dancing and swinging so hard the floor went down about six inches, and they had to cancel the dance! I used to hear Claude Hopkins's band from Roseland, too, and they *moved.* I remember when Don Redman came out to Kansas City with McKinney's Cotton Pickers. He had Cuba Austin on drums and they tore it *up.* I only heard Fletcher Henderson once, right after they introduced Israel Crosby, that great little bass player, and made *Chistopher Columbus.* Probably because I was so prejudiced in favor of Kansas City bands, I just wasn't impressed. There wasn't the same sort of looseness. The remnants of the Kansas City thing were slowly taken away from Basie's band as all those changes were made. Most of the guys were saying the looseness was going, but the powerful rhythm section held it together.

"To go back, it was the same way with Duke when he had Wellman Braud, Sonny Greer, and Freddy Guy. I remember when *Ring Dem Bells* came out. That was a totally different kind of rhythm section. For the first time you could hear the bass player coming through, and Sonny Greer knew how to team with that bass fiddle, because it wasn't as strong and couldn't cut through like the bass horn had been doing.

"Now when McShann, Gus Johnson, and I got together, we were slightly influenced by Basie, and I was definitely influenced by Walter Page. We used to talk and I would explain to them what Page had told me, about how we should team, how the drummers' foot should not be too heavy, and how the bass player should get a straight line where he could *push*. McShann was naturally talented in how to play with a band, and we began to find each other. During that first year, the horns would lay out lots of times and the rhythm section would just walk for five or ten minutes. We got a guitar player in 1940, but I think it was a fill-up because back in those days certain halls had to have a certain number of musicians.

"Before we went to New York to play at the Savoy Ballroom, we got a postcard from Lucky Millinder which said, 'We're going to send you hicks back to the sticks.' McShann had one of those big old long Buicks, and I was driving, with about five or six guys in it. I took what I thought was the shortest route to New York, up and over the mountains, instead of taking the Pennsylvania Turnpike. We struggled and struggled, but we finally got to New York, raggedy and tired. When we got up on the bandstand where the Savoy Sultans used to play, the people were looking at us like we were nothing. Lucky Millinder was on the main bandstand.

"Everything we had was shabby-looking, including our cardboard stands, and we only had one uniform—a blue coat and brown pants. But from the time we hit that first note until the time we got off the bandstand, we didn't let up. We heated it so hot for Lucky Millinder that during his set he got up on top of the piano and directed his band from there. Then he jumped off and almost broke his leg. Well, that opening was on Friday, the thirteenth of February, 1942. That Sunday we had to do a matinee at four o'clock. In fifteen minutes we played only two tunes, *Moten's Swing*, I think, and *Cherokee*. Bird started blowing on *Cherokee* at that extremely fast tempo. It was way up there. The program was going out on the radio and somebody in the studio called the man with the earset and said, 'Let them go ahead.

Don't stop them!' We played about forty-five minutes more, just the rhythm section and Bird, with the horns setting riffs from time to time. That night you couldn't get near the bandstand for musicians who had heard the broadcast. 'Who was that saxophone player?' they all wanted to know.

"From the Savoy we went to the Apollo, and then back to the Savoy, where we had an incident on a Sunday afternoon. Bird had gone over to Walter Brown's wife and gotten Brown's last five dollars! Brown came over while Bird was on the bandstand and they got into a fight. Each of them was so high, they never made contact. It was like a slow motion picture of a fight. They'd swing at each other and fall down. As a result, a guy came from Joe Glaser's office, gave us a lecture, and demanded that Charlie Parker be fired immediately. McShann had to let him go, but after a couple of weeks we were getting so many complaints that we got him back. I persuaded McShann to let me hire Bird, act as his agent, and look after him. He'd been working at Monroe's Uptown House, an after-hours joint, but not making any money.

"Then we went on a tour down South and had a lot of trouble. In Augusta the operator left with the money at half-time and the cops said we had to pay the rent of the hall, as well as the bouncers and people on the door, or go to jail. In Martinsville, Virginia, the same thing happened, and this time they were not only going to take us to jail but they were going to take our instruments and the bus as well. In Natchez, Mississippi, they put Walter Brown and Bird in jail for smoking cigarettes in a screened porch of the rooming house where they were staying. If they'd been smoking pot, they'd have been there forever, but Johnny Tumino had to go and pay twenty-five dollars each to get them out. When they joined us in Little Rock, they had knots on their heads big enough to hang a hat on. They had really taken a beating. Not that Bird had sassed the cops. He got us out of trouble many a time. I remember once we'd just got through Baton Rouge when the cops caught us. 'You Yankee niggers, huh?' they asked. Bird got up, turned out nice in well-fitting clothes, and started to tell them how his father had worked in Louisiana, all the while giving them a 'Yes, sir' or 'No, sir.' His father had never been there, but they ended up escorting us to the next town. He was talented at that sort of thing. With them, it was all a matter of making an example to keep blacks frightened. Like in Texas, when we were kids, they'd get some guy, tar him, lynch him, and drag him through the black neighborhood.

"By the time we got back to Kansas City, McShann and the band were mad and disgusted. Bird, Buddy Anderson, Orville Minor, Freddie Culliver, and several of them quit. Gus Johnson and I were among the few that stuck with McShann, but that was when Bird officially left. When we went out again, we picked up Paul Quinichette in Denver, and about that time Bird rejoined us. When we got to San Antonio, Paul and Walter Brown were arrested. They were out in a field picking that stuff! Bird was lucky that time and slick enough to get away.

"We picked up Al Hibbler in San Antonio, and when we came on back to New York we had three singers—Bill Nolan, Walter Brown, and Hibbler. Nolan sang the blues before Walter Brown, but he didn't have a nasty voice and was really a great ballad singer. Eventually McShann had to tell him it was too expensive carrying three singers, so Bill went back to Kansas City. Bird left permanently in the fall of '42 to join Earl Hines. I went by the Apollo Theatre in February 1943, when Earl was there. I had just left McShann's band, and Bird bought me a secondhand bearskin coat. 'Now I got some money,' he said, 'the first thing I'm going to do is buy you a coat!'

"I'd had a fight with Bob Merrill in McShann's band when we were in Boston with Don Redman fronting. Bob was supposed to have torn up a difficult piece of music, and came in the dressing room and said, 'What are you going to do about it, so-and-so?' He had a pitcher in his hand ready to hit me and I got my knife and cut him in front of his ear all the way down to the chin. From that day, I've never carried a knife. I was so ashamed and disgusted with myself, I went back to Kansas City and got a job, first in a packing house and then in a railroad station.

"McShann kept calling me to come back, and I joined him in Chicago. I was with him till he went in the service, but there were guys I had helped get in the band who hated my guts because Jay liked to show me off and have me take solos. When he went away in the army, we were supposed to be billed as *Jay McShann and His Orchestra, featuring Walter Brown, under the direction of Gene Ramey*, but somebody came from the agency and said they'd decided we were taking too much of a chance that way. Until Jay came back, it was to be Walter Brown and His Band, under the direction of Gene Ramey. So I told them I was not going with that. The guys got mad, too, because nobody wanted to work under Walter Brown, who was very hard to get along with and a far worse dope addict than Bird. I understand six men got to Cincinnati, but the music had been lost and that was the end of that band.

"I worked about six weeks with Oliver Todd at the new Reno Club, out on Independence, going towards [Harry] Truman's home. Then the Luis Russell band came through, with Lil Green, the singer. He had lost his bass player, Ted Sturgis, and they asked me to go with him. Razz Mitchell was on drums, so we had a swinging rhythm section. Most of the guys were amateurs, excepting Charlie Holmes on alto and Howard Callender on trumpet. It was really a band put together to accompany singers, in a package. We also had Gatemouth Moore, a great blues singer, who became a pastor down in Memphis. Later on we had the Ink Spots and Ella Fitzgerald. They were all working out of Moe Gale's office, and we played the Apollo three times. I left them in October 1944. Barney Richmond, from Galveston, Texas, took my place.

"I saw Lips Page and he wanted me to stay in New York. I applied for my union card, which meant that I couldn't play with guys who weren't 802 members for six months. When McShann got out of the army, I explained what I was doing, and he understood. Lips Page gave me plenty of work, and I played with Ike Quebec and Noble Sissle, too. Then I worked steady with Ben Webster, and for a time with Tiny Grimes. It got so I was one of the most wanted bass players in New York.

"While I was working with Ben at the Onyx, Prez was across the street at the Spotlight. He was living in the Chesterfield, and I'd walk around there and we'd have breakfast together. He kept asking me to go with him, and when a job at Minton's with Ben folded, I joined him. This was in 1948, and Moe Gale sent us out on tours with six or eight pieces. We had Jo Jones, and Junior Mance on piano. While Prez was out with Jazz at the Philharmonic, I joined Miles Davis and we opened in Birdland opposite Lips Page. Then Prez came back and we had a quartet with Jo Jones and John Lewis.

"We worked at Birdland a long time, and whenever John Hammond came in Prez would say, 'Lady Ramey and Lady Jones, Tommy Tucker's in the house!' John Hammond would sit there with a smile on his face, and on many occasions he really made efforts to regain Prez's friendship, but he never did. Prez used to tell me things, because we were close. I was best man at his wedding and like the father of his children for a long time. He said he left Basie because he wanted a hundred-and-twenty-five dollars a week, and he [Hammond] said he wasn't worth it, or something like that. When Prez and Billie Holiday got together, all they'd talk about was John, and how he tore that band asunder when it was on its way to make it.

"Prez would go out for Norman Granz, but whenever he came back I would go work with him unless I was already committed. We renewed our old, tight relationship, and if I was working for somebody else and got off early I'd wait for him and take him home to his hotel, the Mark, on 43rd Street. He always talked about his cat. He called her Philharmonic. He said something one day that the cat didn't like, insulted her, and the cat jumped out the window from the eighth floor. He said it hurt him so badly.

"Prez, Ben Webster, and Roy Eldridge were the only people who were really vocal about the new rhythm sections. The other guys would say, 'Well, man, there's something new. I ain't going to put it down. I might have to go with it.' But Prez, Roy, and Ben played their solo in phrases, and when a guy dropped a bomb in the middle it killed the phrase. Prez would turn around and say, 'Just give me some tinkdee-doo.' He got rid of one drummer who was back there *soloing* behind him.

"In Kansas City, the rhythm section stayed straight, but in New York, we ran across this new thing Max Roach and them developed. That's how I managed to stay in there as long as I did, with Monk and Dizzy and all of them. They needed a strong bass to carry the beat while the drummer was carrying on. Oscar Pettiford was on 52nd Street and he did lots of work with those guys. He wasn't strong in the rhythm section, but it didn't bother him what they were doing. He could walk right on through it, too.

"Ben and Prez were vocal specifically about the drums. They didn't like what was going on in the rhythm section, and they didn't like the flatted fifths and that stuff. The fact that the piano player sounded like he was one-handed wasn't too bad, so far as the bass player was concerned. They couldn't play like Basie, who could play with both hands and still stay out of the way of the bass.

"Another thing that happened at that time was that the guys who drank whiskey were condemned by the guys on the other side of the street who used dope. They'd see Ben or Prez or Hawk half-drunk and say, 'Man, you a drag. You a damned drunkard.' You couldn't turn around and tell a guy who was high and bent all out that he was a dope addict, because that would be squealing! Drinkers like Ben and Roy used to talk about this. 'Man, this guy's hitting me,' they'd say, 'and I can't fight back.'

"One night the cops came and arrested twenty-four guys on 52nd Street. Sid Catlett and I often used to talk about it. We were hanging in the White Rose at intermission when it happened. 'Man, isn't it amazing,' he said, 'how those federal guys knew exactly who to pick up?'

"When the heroin users started coming out on the Street, it ended the career of lots of trumpet players who could have kept on working. With heroin came the idea that guys had to play with a straight sound, a symphonic sound. They put everybody down who was playing the other way. Ben Webster had always used a buzz, but he just eased out of it.

"I stayed with Prez, off and on, until 1957. He was married to a white girl named Mary and he had sent for her when he was in the army, in some town in Alabama, I think. He told me they put him in their disciplinary barracks, and every night the guards would get drunk and have target practice on his head. He named that *D B Blues* after his experience—*Disciplinary Barracks Blues.* His style of music changed after he got out. I think he'd had lots of blows on his skull. He lost coordination of his speed. He still had the feel and everything, but you'd see him finding a way to shortcut and get out of holes in his solos. I think he had a *bruised* membrane in his head. He made a record called *Up 'n' Adam* and it was like someday he was going to find those guys who did it to him and knock them down. Later, I made *Down 'n' Adam* with him, and that was where he'd got them down.

"His favorite phrase was, 'Nice eyes, no evil spirits,' but I think the effect of that experience was lasting, at least until he married another Mary, a colored girl, who gave him two kids, a boy and a girl. That helped him pull out of it for a while, but then he started getting back on the bottle and drank so much he lost his taste for food.

"In 1952 I was at Birdland when I had a call from Denver to join Basie. 'You make the price right, I'll come,' I told them. When I got there, it was a pleasure working with Gus Johnson again, and we had a good time. I stayed there several months until I found different ones in the band had formed a clique to get Gus out. I don't know what was back of it, except that Gus had had a couple of run-ins with members of the band, but I made up my mind I wasn't going to be a part of it. Basie brought a fifth of whiskey up to my room in a hotel in Detroit, and we talked and talked practically all night. He begged me, but I said, 'Man, I'm leaving. I know what you're going to do. You're going to get pressures on you, and you're going to let Gus go.' He kept Gus until Gus got sick, and when he came back he didn't have a job. Sonny Payne had it.

"I always kid Gus about the time when we were both singing in the Trinity A.M.E. [African Methodist Episcopal] Church choir. His voice is as light as mine, but I was singing tenor and he was singing the bass line. When we were with McShann, I was the only one with a car, but I never had it in the daytime because Gus would be over first thing in the morning. In fact, I had a key made for him. He was having a ball, but so long as he put gas in it and brought it back in time, I just let him have it.

"A big duty of the big-band drummer is to make those dynamics with the brass, while the bass player has to play along with the reeds unless the arrangement is written so that he marks those dynamics with the brass, too. Gus and I worked on that.

"With the big-band drummers, we'd have to say Sonny Greer and Jo Jones were the original bosses. Gene Krupa wasn't bad, and Buddy Rich is good but more or less an individualist. Shadow Wilson was one of my favorite drummers, an expert. He came in to cut a show while I was with Basie. In fact, I think the best solo I ever took was with Shadow, on *Audubon*, on Sonny Rollins's first recording date. Osie Johnson was a great drummer in a small band. Walter Johnson was good, but I wouldn't say he was a take-command drummer. Sidney Catlett was *the* boss.

"Sidney and I finally started working together in 1946 on 52nd Street. We played many jobs together, especially on Sunday afternoons where they featured 'All Stars.' Usually, we'd have Marlowe Morris on piano, but sometimes Sir Charles Thompson. Sidney was a man who could play anything, in the big band and the small. So could Kenny Clarke—'Klook'—who lives over in Paris.

"But I go back to Sonny Greer, Jo Jones, and Jimmy Crawford, because those cats made the rhythm section pop. They heard everything the brass was doing and they knew how to bring the band up. A rhythm section is not going to play the second chorus like the first chorus. In the first chorus they play more or less easy, and give the soloist especially a chance to find himself and relax, but in the second they're supposed to blow them out of the building!

"After Prez, I went with Roy Eldridge, Sol Yaged, and Cozy Cole at the Metropole for two years. Then I went to Europe with Buck Clayton, came back, and played with Cootie Williams at the Roundtable. After working with, first, Teddy Wilson, and then, Earl Hines, I got a job with Chase Manhattan Bank. I'd no sooner got it than I had a call from Louis Armstrong! But I decided to stay with the bank, although I continued to play weekends, mostly with Buck Clayton and Buddy Tate.

"I'd gone to school again, to the American Institute of Banking, and they gave me a job as a kind of teacher. Altogether, I worked in about forty different Chase banks. I went back to Europe in 1963 and took off in 1969 to go over with Jay for about a month. I retired from the bank at the end of 1975. Although I had a good record and many commendations from them, those people at Chase Manhattan didn't allow me any chance for promotion. I think it was more due to the race than my age.

"As soon as I got my release from them, I shipped my furniture, got in my car, and tore out for Texas. I didn't even have a chance to tell the guys good-bye. I bought a little farm and a home, so you might say I'm a farmer now, but I still play concerts and go to Europe with Jay McShann from time to time."

(1976)

Gus Johnson, Jr.

(DRUMS)

Gus Johnson was born November 15, 1913, in Tyler, Texas, the only son of churchgoing parents. They separated after a few years of married life, and his father went into the army during the First World War.

"We lived right by the tracks," Johnson said, "and I remember when his train passed by the house. He was hanging out the window, waving, and crying. I was about four then."

When his mother married again, he went with her and his stepfather to Beaumont, in southern Texas, close to Louisiana. He had already been drawn to the music he heard on the street or in the circus, and particularly to that of the drums. A drummer, Joe Bonham, lived next door in Beaumont, and when he found how interested his young neighbor was, he persuaded his mother to let him take him to rehearsal every other night.

"I learned everything they played," Johnson recalled, "just by listening. I couldn't read music then. One night the guy who played the bass drum couldn't make it, so Joe showed me the notes the bass drum played and the notes he played on the snare drum. I sat down and played the bass drum that night. I knew how the songs went. Of course, I was very excited, and my mother didn't want to believe my story till Joe Bonham came over and told her. Later, they had a parade and I played the bass drum again, walking down the street. They had the drum mounted on a little bitty wagon, which someone else dragged along."

Meanwhile, Johnson, Sr., had also married again. His new wife was an entertainer, and when the show in which she was dancing went to Beaumont, she took her stepson to see a performance. He was most impressed by the drummer who traveled with the show: "He played a solo that really knocked me out. He had a big bass drum with little Japanese tom-toms on the side. I was right there in front, and it was a great experience for me."

From Beaumont the family moved to Houston. A Dr. McDavid lived nearby, and his two sons had a jazz band that rehearsed in his house. They allowed Johnson to be present, and here again, a good listener, he added to his fund of musical knowledge. He went downtown and bought himself a little drum at the five-and-ten-cent store, and he used to play on this at home, humming to himself. Sometimes, too, he would accompany an accomplished pianist who was living in the same rooming house. He was also lucky enough to make friends with Holden DeWalt, whose father was head of the NAACP in the city and owner of the Lincoln Theater on Prairie. The theater mostly showed movies, but occasionally it presented a show, and it always had a six-piece pit band. Because he could get in free, Johnson went every day and sat down front where he could watch the drummer, Abner Jones. They eventually struck up an acquaintanceship.

"I see you in here all the time," Jones said. "You just watch. Can you play drums?"

"A little bit," Johnson answered.

"You want to sit in and play?"

Johnson was now twelve years old and, although he had practiced assiduously on a snare drum his mother had recently bought him, he was understandably nervous. Nevertheless, when the band played a "medium-slow" number he sat in and "kept time."

"Joe Bonham had shown me how to hold the sticks and everything," he said, "and anytime I came in the theater Abner would get up and just go out and talk to somebody he knew, while I took his place. As long as I kept good time, the band didn't mind. All I wanted to do was to play right along with them, and that's what I did—nothing fancy. And one day when I was playing they flashed my name on the screen as 'Abner Jones's protégé.' That really got to me.

"The DeWalts knew how much I liked the drums, and their son

and I were such close friends that they would take me when they went on vacation. With them, too, I was listening to good music all the time, because they had lots of records. Holden was taking violin lessons with one of the best teachers, a German. I'd see this teacher hollering at him—'Do this, do that!'—and eventually he gave up. My mother wanted me to take violin, too, but I couldn't stand that screeching. I took lessons in music and learned to read with a teacher in the Fifth Ward, a Mr. McMillan. I had to ride a streetcar over there, with my drum under my arm. We were living in Fourth Ward, and they didn't allow Fourth Ward guys in Fifth Ward. They asked me where I was going, and I'd say 'to take my music lesson'; but they didn't ask where I lived, so I never had any trouble.

"The DeWalts were the richest black people in Houston, but Mr. DeWalt was doing too much for the blacks in the city. The operator of the theater shot and killed him. He was paid to do that. That happened in 1929 after I left Houston. Mrs. DeWalt tried to run the theater, but it didn't last long. They opened a barbecue place and did very well for a time. When I went back in 1930, Holden and I plotted to get even with the man who killed his father, but his mother got wind of it and stopped us. We would have got him, too. They had caught him and put him in jail, but he got out very fast. Everybody knew exactly what had happened. The man is dead now; but that messed up things for Holden, upset him altogether, and later on I lost touch with him.

"When we went to Dallas, I went to the Booker T. Washington High School in north Dallas, and I got into everything there, although I didn't meet many of the well-known musicians from there till years later. T-Bone Walker was in much faster company, a rougher kid, always with his guitar, and already mature. Booker Pittman, the saxophone player, was at a dance hall, but he left Dallas and went to South America, where I met him years later. Buddy Tate was from Sherman, Texas, and I never saw him in Dallas. Illinois Jacquet lived in Houston's Fifth Ward, and I didn't meet him till I was with Jay McShann. Budd Johnson's from Dallas, but he's older than I am and I didn't know him. Same thing with Tyree Glenn, from Corsicana. I met and worked with him later in New York.

"I was in the glee club at high school, and we had a very good teacher—Professor A. S. Jackson, Jr. With him, you had to know the music first. He would have you stand up at the blackboard with your back to him, and when he hit a note you had to tell him what it was. I got so I could tell every note he hit. I have almost perfect pitch, like Henry Coker, the trombone player, who was in the same music class. Long and lanky, he had the trombone that had been his daddy's.

"After I finished school, I went to Kansas City to live with my dad.

That was the first time I'd seen him since he and my mother separated. He found out I was in Dallas and asked if I would come and stay with him a while. I had my mind on more schooling, and I went to Southern Junior College in Kansas City, Kansas. My father's brother, Uncle Charles, used to go to all the dances, and he would take me. I heard all the big bands there—Bennie Moten, Andy Kirk, George E. Lee . . . Joe Turner wasn't singing when I got to Kansas City. He was the janitor, cleaning up the place at the Lone Star. Later on, he tended bar, and after he had learned all the blues they started letting him sit in and sing. Pete Johnson was playing piano there, and I was sitting in with him the night I met Jo Jones.

"'That's Jo Jones just walked in,' Pete said. 'He just joined Basie's band.'

"'Oh, yeah?' I said. 'See if you can get him to sit in and play.'

"Jo had met Pete before. 'Oh, I'll be over after a while,' he said. He sat down at a table and was talking to different ones, and listening. Finally he came over and said, 'You play a nice drum. I'll take over now.' I think we were playing *I Got Rhythm,* and the way he played was something else. I never saw anything like it, the way he was with those brushes. It was as smooth as you'd want to hear anybody play; and it was just right easy. He was smiling, doing little bitty things, and he wasn't *working.* The personality and everything just knocked me *out!* I was standing there with a grin from one ear to the other. All I was doing was chin-chin-chin-chin, just rhythm, but he came on with all this flash and I was just petrified. I had seen Sonny Greer with Duke Ellington's band, with his chimes and everything, and he had been one of my idols; but for me it was Jo Jones from now on. Nobody else. He was it!

"'Have you ever been to Omaha?' he asked afterwards. 'I'm sending a band there. Would you like to go?'

"It was a good six-piece band—piano, bass, Floyd Smith on guitar, Jimmy Keith on tenor sax, Paul King on trumpet, and myself. It was the first time I really left home and was out on my own. Jo Jones had told us where we could stay. A fellow named Henderson, a barber, had a house and we all had rooms there. After three months I left that band and joined Lloyd Hunter's. I had bought myself a set of drums from Wurlitzer in Kansas City, what they called a pony set. I loved that little old set and hated to turn it in when I bought a new, sparkling gold set in Omaha.

"I was twenty or twenty-one, and I was all tied up in the music. You could get cigarettes for five or ten cents then, but I wasn't messing with anything like that. I always liked straight bourbon, but I would drink only just so much. Lloyd Hunter's guys would get so drunk, I said I didn't know what I was going to do. Then the bass player left and they couldn't get another. I told Lloyd if he'd buy a bass I'd try to play it. He got his old drummer back, Debo Mills, and he got me a German teacher. I took two lessons. What I wanted to know was how to slap the bass, but he wanted to teach me how to *play* the bass.

"Before this, while I was going to college in Kansas City, I had a vocal quartet called Four Rhythm Aces. Roy Johnson played guitar and could chord on piano. His sister was Countess Johnson, who took Mary Lou Williams's place with Andy Kirk. She was *very* good. Our big thing was imitating the Mills Brothers, and the group was *together*. When beer first came in after Prohibition, we'd sing at places where they had little stands, and guys would throw us money. Then we got a program on the radio station for The Store Without a Name, a fifteen-minute thing every morning at seven o'clock. We had to be at school at eight, so we had to get down there real fast, but we got twenty-five dollars per man each week, and that was good then. I'm mentioning this because in the Four Rhythm Aces I had played some simple bass.

"When I left Omaha with Lloyd Hunter's band, the first thing they threw at me was *White Heat*, a fast number with a bass solo! In no time I had blisters on my fingers, and soon they were bleeding. So I had to wrap my fingers in tape; and then I began to notice that I didn't feel any pain. Eventually, I left the tape off. I enjoyed playing bass, but I didn't really learn how to play it properly. I could hit the right notes, but I was moving the whole hand, sliding up and down, instead of using the fingers.

"I stayed with Lloyd Hunter all of 1936, and when he got another bass player, a fellow we called Bassy, I went back to playing drums. It was a twelve-piece band, with Jimmy Coe on trumpet, Little Jimmy Byron on trombone, a fellow named McKinley on guitar, and Jimmy Bikewood was the tenor player. Lloyd was a good trumpet player, and he wrote a lot of the arrangements. Nat Towles had a good band, good musicians and arrangements that sounded like Jimmie Lunceford's, but we cut him one night at the Greenland Ballroom in Omaha because his drummer was the weakest guy in the band, one who didn't cut the mustard, as they said. Buddy Tate and Henry Coker were with Towles, and it was a really sharp band. They even had a sleeper bus; but they didn't swing like Lloyd's band. The dancers knew what was happening.

"Lloyd Hunter had good musicians, but they were kind of raggedy-like. They could play—until they drank too much. I remember we were playing off in some field near Pipestone, Minnesota. Everybody came from different little towns around, and it was *hot*! A guy brought a bucket of water with ice and then poured a whole gallon of straight alcohol into it. Lloyd's guys began drinking this and soon the band began to sound bad. They were missing notes and couldn't play their horns. I got mad and started cussing out Lloyd and all the guys who were drunk. I told him and everybody else they were fired. I fired the leader of the band that night!

"'Okay, I'll just take my horn and go,' Lloyd said. He packed his horn up and walked out the door; but then it struck him that it was *his* band, so he came back in.

"'You can't fire me,' he said. 'I'm the leader of this band!'

"After we finished the gig, he started talking about it: 'I've never had nobody to fire me out of my band before.' It didn't help that I was the youngest man in it.

"They just got on my nerves. I couldn't take it, but I got even one night in Nebraska. 'They going to get drunk,' I said to myself, 'I'm going to get drunk with 'em!' So I got drunk before I got to work. When we started playing, the whiskey hit me and I just threw up all behind the stand. The white guy giving the dance came up and asked, 'What's wrong, Gus?'

"'Oh, my stomach,' I said, 'it's about to kill me!'

"'Where'd you eat?'

"'That little place down the street.'

"'Don't you know better than to go down there? That place will kill you. Go out there in the bus and get some sleep.'

"I went out and slept for about half an hour, and then went back and finished the gig. It was my first time for anything like that. I never got drunk on the job after that. If I got drunk, it would be after I finished my work.

"I was with Lloyd about a year and a half. One night in Nebraska with him I always remember. There was a blizzard and it was thirty-two below zero. We used to switch about with the driving, and I was driving when I saw a snowdrift right across the road. I stepped on the gas to go through it, but it was like hitting a brick wall and I got stuck. We couldn't move any further, and it was lucky we couldn't because there were about twelve cars ahead of us. I had one of those big camel's hair coats they were wearing then, so I got out and walked about two miles looking for a house where we could get help. The baritone player put a second coat over his own and went looking, too. When he saw a light way across the fields, he started walking towards where he thought he saw it, and he found a house. A white guy came out with a wagon on a sled—no wheels—and took us to his house, and kept us there and fed us for a whole week before we could get out. There were thirteen of us altogether, and we just cuddled up and slept on the floor. The man didn't charge us a penny, but when we got to Omaha we sent him some money. They were real great out west then!

"'Oh, Lord, help me,' I said as I was getting into that wagon, because I could barely move my feet.

"'Ain't nothin' *I* can do for you,' Lloyd Hunter said.

"'Oh, Lloyd, shut up!'

"'Aren't you talking to me?'

"Lloyd was a funny cat, but a very nice cat!

"Anna Mae Winburn was singing with the band then and she had less clothes on than we did, but she didn't get frostbitten or anything. I think women can stand cold better than men.

"After a year and a half with Lloyd, I got a letter from Ernest Redd, or 'Speck' Redd, as they called him. He was a cousin of Red Perkins and had played piano in his band, which was another 'territory' band out of Omaha, like Lloyd Hunter's. Ernest was a very good pianist who could imitate Earl Hines and play a lot in Art Tatum's style. He had gone to Ottumwa, Iowa, and formed a little band. He had a couple of his brothers in it, John on tenor and Little Johnny Redd. Little Johnny played piano, too, and he could imitate everybody, but he was very young and still going to school. For his age, he was a genius. Later, he went to California and changed his name to Yolando Coloponto, or something like that. Francis Bates was on bass, Leonard Chadwick on trumpet, and my buddy Raymond Fields played alto, tenor, and clarinet.

"Ottumwa was only a small town, but we had a lot of fun. Leonard Chadwick and I had day jobs at Hart's Furniture Store, and I also acted as busboy at the only hotel in town. John Redd worked at a filling station, and Bates worked at a garage. We had all the jobs sewed up! I had been paying a dollar a week for a room in Omaha, but in Ottumwa I had to pay $1.35, with one meal a day included. I shared an attic room with Raymond Fields. It was in a sporting house, and we—the madam and the girls—all ate around one big table.

"I was making so much money, I sent for my mother to come to Ottumwa. I had been sending her money all along, but when I met her at the train station I found she had married again and had her husband with her. She'd kept that a secret, and I was as mad as I could be; but I found them a place to stay and got her a job at the club where we were playing. I was salty with *him*, but he turned out to be an A-1 guy. He's always been in my corner; and they're still together.

"Eventually I went back to Kansas City to visit my father. He worked for the Santa Fe Railroad and was always on the go. While I was there I saw Bill Hadnott, the bass player, who told me about Jay McShann starting a band. He said he was going to join it, and I said I would, too. I had never met Jay before, but they sent for me and Bill introduced us. Jay impressed me as a fine, jolly guy, and we soon opened at Martin's-on-the-Plaza, a swank place, but with Gene Ramey on bass, not Bill Hadnott. We had Orville Minor on trumpet, William Scott and Bob Mabane on tenors, and Earl Jackson on alto. Little Joe Coleman was the singer, and William Scott did the arrangements. Oh, it was a swinging little band!

"We used to have jam sessions at the house where Jay and I stayed on Park Avenue—Park Avenue, Kansas City. We'd rehearse first and then jam. Earl Jackson would get pretty juiced at times, but not enough to mess up. Jay was the only one that really drank a lot. Because we were in the same house, I often made him go to sleep. Then I'd wake him and put him in the shower and get him so he could play his job. He never did throw his weight around as a leader. He's always been an easygoing guy. You couldn't find anyone better than he is, and I don't say that because I played with him. But sometimes after work he'd get drunk, go home, and start raising hell with his wife.

" 'I'm going in and cook her head this morning,' he'd say.

" 'You want me to throw your hat in for you?'

" 'Oh, stop that, W.W.,' he'd say. 'You know good and well she's not going to do anything.'

" 'W.W.' was the nickname he gave me, but I don't know how he dreamed that one up. He had different little names for different guys.

"I had a Model A Ford and we would drive up and down the streets, doing about ten miles an hour, and he would speak to everybody we passed. That was his thing!

" 'Howdedo! How're you? You're looking so *beautiful* today!'

"I'm sitting up there behind the wheel, and people would think we were the nicest fellows in town. Then one day I had just turned my head to look at something and hit the back of a car in front. The bumpers hit each other, that was all, but the guy jumped out and came around.

" 'What the hell's wrong with you? Cain't you drive that car? Don't you have any brakes?'

" 'Yeah,' I said, 'don't you see the marks where I slid after I used them?'

"There was nothing more for him to say, so he got in his car and left. Then Jay turned to me and said, 'W., you drunk?'

"Charlie Parker joined us when we started the big band in 1939 at the Century Room. Before he got to be good, they wouldn't let him play anyplace, wouldn't even let him get up on the stand. But he went in the woodshed and after he came out he blew everybody off the stand! He didn't care nothin' about nobody! When we had our jam sessions, we would play a number in five or six different keys—what we call chromatics. We'd start in B-flat and then take just a half step to C, to C-sharp . . . Even McShann himself had to figure out these keys. Charlie would just run all through 'em. All the guys in the band would do the same, trying to keep up with him. He liked fast tempos, but sweet numbers, too, and he could play those if he wanted. He played altogether different then than he did later. When he went to New York he changed his style, but I liked the way he played his alto better when he was with Jay. His tone was different, and he knew what he was doing. When he got to New York he got on this bop kick.

"Everybody was mad with us when we came into New York, because we were late. The cars had broken down. Johnny Tumino had retreads on one car and they all blew off, so we had to buy new tires. We were supposed to have been at the Savoy at five that evening, but it was almost nine when we got there. We didn't have time to change clothes, so we just got up and played in what we were wearing. Lucky Millinder was on the stand and he had stayed there, playing, because he didn't know whether we were going to show or not. Charlie Buchanan, the boss, was mad and rolling his eyes, but when we started playing the floor started jumping. The jitterbugs were there and they were swinging back. We stayed in one tempo nearly all night long and at intermission Buchanan just ate us *out!* Lucky Millinder and his guys called us the Western Dogs, but we swung 'em off the stage! Lucky was a good front man and he was playing all types of tunes, fast and slow, but when we finally played some fast ones—that was it! Everybody came over to us and was glad to meet us.

"I was with Jay till 1943, when I was inducted at Fort Sheridan. They sent me down to Camp Rucker, Alabama, where I got in the 250th Army Band. My first sergeant was Joe Comfort, the bass player who worked with Harry James, Ella Fitzgerald, and Charlie Barnet. After I got out of the army I was with McShann's big band again at the Famous Door in New York, but then he wasn't getting the right money. I don't think it was so much a matter of the times being bad for big bands. The managers would tell the bandleaders they could get the same money for a smaller band. I think that was what happened to Earl Hines.

"Being in New York was always good for me to hear other famous drummers. I had seen Chick Webb in Kansas City when I was at the College Inn with Prince Stewart. He was a thrill, not only for his bass drum but for everything he did—his accents, beats, and all that. He was strong, and he had his drums tuned the way he wanted them. Then I met Sid Catlett at the Onyx Club, with Stuff Smith. He was real cool with his brush work—very fine, and a very nice guy. I was *very* happy to meet him, and he acted the same way, like he was happy to meet me, a little old western dog from Kansas City. When I came back after the army, everybody was talking about Hal West, another good drummer.

"I was staying with my mother in Chicago when I found out they needed a drummer at the Club DeLisa. Red Saunders was going on vacation and Jesse Miller was taking a band in to replace him for two months. It was a very good show band, with a lot of guys who had played with Earl Hines. This would be in 1945. After that Eddie Vinson sent for me. I met him at the Savoy when Cootie Williams was playing opposite us. Now Eddie was putting his own big band together. Dinah Washington was the singer, but he had to replace her when she got pregnant. It was a good band. We played the Apollo and the Savoy, and then we went out on the road in a package with the Ink Spots. When we came back, we went out again, playing dance halls. I quit in St. Louis, because Eddie was drinking and gambling a lot then and messing up with the money.

"I was back in New York in 1947 when Earl Hines wired me, and I joined him in Chicago. I knew some of the guys in the band, like Budd Johnson and Scoops Carry. Soon after I joined, we made some records that never came out.* He had three violins on the date, but it was a good session. The band soon broke up, and then I worked with Cootie Williams's small band at the Savoy. It was a fine group. Cootie had Arnold Jarvis on piano and Leonard Swain on bass, and we got Willis Jackson from Florida. I gave him the name of 'Gatortail,' because they say all that the people down there eat is alligator tail and rice!

"I went with Basie at the very end of '47 for an engagement at the Strand Theater, but while we were there Shadow Wilson returned and the office wanted him back in the band. Basie insisted I stay till the Strand job was finished, but Shadow took his former place again when the band went into the Royal Roost across the street for about a month. Then they went out on the road, and Shadow put his notice in and joined Woody Herman. So now Basie was without a drummer and he told Jimmy Rushing to call me.

" 'No, I ain't going to call him,' Rushing said. 'You didn't treat him right when he was here.'

"They got Butch Ballard in the meantime, but later on Basie came to see me himself at the Savoy, where I was back with Cootie. He said he was going to start a small band and wanted me in it. I asked how

---

* Several titles appeared on Bravo K 134 many years later.

much, and he offered $125 a week. When I said, 'No thanks,' he raised it to $135. I told him I'd let him know, and when he called me up later I said, 'Okay, I'll make it with you.'

"When we did the first job at the Brass Rail in Chicago, Freddie Green wasn't with us. There were just Clark Terry, Buddy De Franco, Bob Graf on tenor, Jimmy Lewis on bass, Basie, and myself. We were there about a month and we sounded good, but I missed Freddie because we were pals. I saw him when we got back to New York.

" 'Man,' he said, 'tell Basie to hire me back in the band!'

" 'Yeah,' I said, 'I told him already.'

" 'You kidding? All I do is dream about that band,' Freddie told me.

"I'm quite sure he meant it, too, and when we went out again he was in. We had Wardell Gray on tenor in place of Graf. Clark Terry was with us, and he was so versatile. He even played like Louis Armstrong on four or five numbers and just knocked Basie out. He used to sing *Mumbles* on the bus just like he did on his hit record, many years later. This was in 1950, and during 1951 we traveled all over from Boston to Seattle. It was a good little band; but Basie missed the sound of the rest of the brass just as I did, so he decided on a big band and reorganized.* I was in that band until December 22, 1954. On the 23rd I was in the hospital with appendicitis. I was there ten days or so when Basie wrote me to say he had got Sonny Payne and that he was doing a good job. Basie liked a lot of flash, and some of the fellows in the band thought Sonny was better than me because he was more of a showman. Charlie Fowlkes told me that later on he [Charlie] fell and broke his kneecap and Basie didn't hire him back either. The same thing happened to Marshall Royal when he had to go into the hospital. Moral: don't get sick!

"But it was okay with me, because right after that I went to work with Lena Horne and stayed quite a little while, and the money was good. But she had a kind of snarl when she was singing, and I thought I wasn't doing my job and that she was snarling at me! It was really just her way of putting a song over, but it used to worry me. I began to get pains, and the doctor told me I had heart trouble and couldn't play tennis. When I went to another, he took my blood pressure and asked what I was so uptight about. It registered then, right in my

* The band that opened at the Savoy in October 1951, opposite Jimmy Rushing's group, consisted of Basie, Freddie Green, Jimmy Lewis, Gus Johnson, rhythm; Idres Sulieman, Johnny Letman, Gydner Campbell, Tommy Turrentine, trumpets; Matthew Gee, Benny Powell, Jimmy Wilkins, trombones; Marshall Royal, Floyd Johnson, Paul Quinichette, Ernie Wilkins, Charlie Fowlkes, reeds; Bixie Crawford, vocal. Most of the arrangements were by Neal Hefti, Nat Pierce, and Buster Harding.

head, that what I was uptight about was the thought that I wasn't doing my job well enough. Lena had never said anything to me, and Lennie Hayton, her husband, had told me I was playing her numbers fine, but I went right back then and put my notice in at the Coconut Grove in Los Angeles.

"After that, I went to work with Ella Fitzgerald. She had her little ways, too, you know. She's self-conscious, which she shouldn't be at all, because she's so great. But she knew she wasn't as pretty as Lena, although she sounded better. Nobody's going to sound like Ella! Still, she's very sensitive, and if she saw you talking she might think you were talking bad things about her. I used to tell her all the time, 'Go ahead and sing. Nobody's talking bad about you. They love you!' She wanted people to love her, and she's beautiful, to me, but she was always trying to improve herself in everything she did. When Tommy Flanagan came with the group, we were playing some club in Cleveland, and the first night he was doing the best he could when she turned around and like to scared him to death. I saw it happen and just told her, 'Turn around!' I believe that pretty well shocked her, so afterwards I walked right behind her, waiting to hear 'You're fired!' But she had evidently gotten over it. 'This is his first night,' I told her. 'He doesn't know the numbers, and he's nervous.' It worked pretty good, because Tommy stayed on with her for years.

"I joined Ella in 1956 and I was with her nine years, till 1965. I really loved working with her. Norman Granz, her manager, is a great cat, too. Everybody's got their ways, but I like him. He knows what he's listening to and he knows his business. I never had any trouble with him—no problems whatsoever. Norman used to have dinners for the guys, and when I was in Boston with Ella his show featured Oscar Peterson, Count Basie's band, and Louis Bellson. He took everybody on the concert down to a Chinese place for an eating contest! Guess who won the contest? Eddie Jones, the bass player, couldn't eat any more. Basie couldn't eat any more. Oscar Peterson—he couldn't eat any more. But there was Louis Bellson, still eating up! He's terrific on drums, too. He plays so clean, till it sounds to me like he is reading it out of a book. And he can swing. Buddy Rich can, too. The first time I heard Buddy Rich was when I was with Jay's seven-piece band. He was with Artie Shaw, and the manager at the club suggested we try to get him to sit in. Well, he came over, and right then and there he was terrific. This was the first time I heard him, and I knew he outplayed Gene Krupa. We became friends, and later on, when I was with Basie's small group in Chicago, he came by.

" 'How'd you like a new set of drums?' he asked.

" 'Fine,' I said.

" 'Okay, go to Ludwig and tell 'em I sent you over.'

"I went next day, and the guy said, 'Oh, yeah—you're Gus Johnson. We've been looking for you. Pick out what you want!' Just like that. And that was the first set of drums *given* to me that way.

"As for Tommy Flanagan, I 'hate' him like I do Buddy Tate. That's our little thing together. We love each other, actually. Same with George Duvivier. He's another of my worst 'enemies.' If he walked into a record studio and somebody told him Gus Johnson was playing drums, he'd holler, 'Give me my bass and let me get the hell out of here!' I'd do the same if I saw him first and say, 'I can't play with *him*. Get somebody else or I don't make the gig!' Another time, I remember, we were going to California. I was driving his car and we had to stop for a light in downtown Denver. He was arguing about my driving, so I told him to get the hell out of my car—*his* Cadillac. He got out, slammed the door, and I drove off around the block. When I came back by where he was standing, I called, 'Hey, what do you know? You want to ride?' People looking on were amazed when he said, 'I don't mind if I do,' and then got back in the car.

"It's a different thing with Buddy Tate. I call him the Texas Pimp and he's always saying I'm 'messing with his women.' He has a very pretty daughter, and one night she came out to listen to the band. They were sitting together when I went over and said, 'My goodness! Won't you introduce me to the young lady?'

" 'Never mind that,' Buddy said. 'This is my daughter and I don't want to catch you hanging around *her!*' Then he turned to her and added, 'Honey, see that guy? Don't say nothing to him. Don't trust him. Don't turn your back on him! He's a dirty guy!' Then Buddy looked up at me and laughed."

By the time his engagement with Ella Fitzgerald ended, Gus Johnson was well known and well liked wherever jazz was heard. He subsequently worked with Woody Herman, Ralph Sutton, Zoot Sims, Gerry Mulligan, Al Cohn, and Stan Getz.

"The only somebody I had any worries with was Bob Brookmeyer. He would keep calling me 'Gussie.' So while we were in Europe I had to straighten him out." After an engagement with Peanuts Hucko in Denver, Johnson took Morey Feld's place in The World's Greatest Jazz Band during the period when its fortunes were directed by Dick Gibson. He also appeared at many of Gibson's famous jazz parties, and when he brought his wife and children along from New York in 1973, they liked Colorado so much that they moved out to Denver and have since made it their home.

Looking back over his long career, he named Ben Webster, Coleman

Hawkins, Chu Berry, Lester Young, and Dick Wilson as his "top" tenor players; Roy Eldridge, Buck Clayton, Clark Terry, Hot Lips Page, and Sweets Edison as his top trumpet players. "Cootie Williams was something else; and then there was Freddie Webster, with Lunceford, who had Snooky Young sitting right beside him, and they both could blow."

"My top alto man was Johnny Hodges," Johnson stated. "Nobody had his sound; and you know who loved him? Charlie Parker. Johnny had me on a lot of record dates, and I loved playing with him. 'You're just the guy I want to see,' he said a while back when I went by where they were playing. 'I'm making a date three weeks from now.' But he died before ever the three weeks were up!

"I played with Duke Ellington, too. Every time Sam Woodyard didn't show up, they'd call me. I think the reason was because I had played in Mercer Ellington's band four or five times, and he'd told Duke about me.

"Back in those days there were a lot of good bands. Things change suddenly in this country and big bands just might make a comeback again. I know a lot of kids around here [Denver] who like that sound."

(1979)

Paul Quinichette

(TENOR SAXOPHONE)

"My father was French, a kind of lend-lease surgeon. They brought him over to Denver, Colorado, to consult about something. He saw my mother, and they fell in love and got married. Because she was a Negro, his parents didn't want him to marry her, but that only made him mad. His surname was Quinichet, and he continued to pronounce it that way, although he added 'te' to make it look different.

"My parents weren't musical, but by the time I was ten my dad had me in a beret and knickers, with a clarinet on my arm. All I could do was Beethoven and Bartók—classical music. I had regular tuition and I could read around the corner. I went to Denver University and then for two years to Tennessee State College. They wanted me to play in the band and they told my mother they'd give me my tuition and everything free. So Mom took me down to Nashville, and she didn't know anything about that southern thing! I studied hard and then went back to Denver U. and graduated from there, a music major. I was burning the midnight oil a lot of the time, and asking myself, 'Why in heck do I have to study history, when I'm trying to be a good *musician?*'

" 'Listen,' they used to tell me, 'if you're a musician you've got to know history, art, and everything. It's not all just notes. When you are out there talking to the public, you can't just look stupid. You've got to be accomplished, educated, in other things, too.'

"I went for it, but my parents were disappointed when I turned to jazz. My mother wanted me to be a surgeon like my father. So when I rebelled, she didn't speak to me for years. But I bought her her first mink coat, and after that it was okay!

"I learned jazz from the oldtimers. They taught me, and then I kept going. I could read, but improvisation is another story. Yehudi Menuhin once said he wished he could improvise. He's a genius, but he can only play from the music. I think you learn to improvise by listening and practicing. You make a lot of mistakes, but you proceed by trial and error. You acquire stock phrases and riffs. That's a beginning, then you have to have a knowledge of the basic harmonic changes in the songs you're going to play. I was so frustrated at first that sometimes I'd go home crying, because I couldn't improvise like I wanted to. I guess it's really a matter of innate ability, or a bent to do it, and if you have it sooner or later it comes out. With me, it was a matter of experience. Then it all seemed to come suddenly to me.

"When I was coming up through the ranks, Lester Willis Young was living in Denver, working with a fellow named Art Bronson. He liked me and helped me as best he could. We used to practice together and everything. 'What do you think about this passage?' he'd ask. Or he might say, 'I don't like the way you played that passage. This way, see?'

"One time when I was playing at the Village Vanguard in New York, Mary Lou Williams and Ben Webster came down and tried to insult me. They were going to carve me. So Lester heard about it, and he had actually taught Ben how to play. 'You leave my man alone,' he told him, 'or I'll get up there and tear you up!' See, Ben was all bark and no bite. He wanted to show off, but he'd give you the shirt off his back. He insulted Joe Louis once in Sugar Ray's bar uptown, so Joe punched him right in the stomach. Pow! He didn't do that anymore! He was such a belligerent character, but he played wonderful saxophone.

"You know that Lester's father had like a carnival band? Irma Young played fantastic alto saxophone and Lee Young played drums. Louis Jordan's father had a carnival called The Rabbit Foot Minstrels, but Lester's father's band was more sophisticated and beat 'em up all the time. It was no contest.

"I started professionally with territory bands during the summer semester. Then I'd go back to school again. I played with Nat Towles and Lloyd Hunter out of Omaha, and I did some things with Bojangles

and Ernie Fields out of Tulsa, Oklahoma. The first time I met Charlie
Christian was during one of these summer 'vacations.' He was working
with a girl named Anna Mae Winburn, who ended up as leader of the
International Sweethearts of Rhythm. Those girls were good! They
made Phil Spitalny look like a fool, and they messed up Ina Ray Hutton
when she had a band, too. They came from all over, those girls, and
they were playing! Some were Chinese, some were Jewish, and some
were colored. When they went down south, they'd put dark makeup on
so as not to run into trouble, and they had a big old matron, like a
warden, and she'd lock those girls up at night!

"Sir Charles Thompson was with Nat Towles, and Neal Hefti used
to bring his arrangements around. Jimmy Mundy was writing heavy
arrangements in those days, and Neal used to say, 'Well, listen. It's
gotta be light!' So even then he was doing those light and nimble
things like he did for Basie years later. That must have been around
1938.

"When I finished college, I started traveling with bands like Lucky
Millinder's and Shorty Sherock's. I was the only non-Caucasian in
Shorty's band, and he was an Irishman drinking Bushmill's whiskey.
One time, we were on the North Side of Chicago and he was hanging
out with Jack Teagarden and Jimmy Dorsey. They got so juiced, he
didn't show up for a week, so I had to take over the group until he
sobered up and dried out. It was only a quintet, but they were very
prejudiced on the North Side.

"I dropped the clarinet entirely because I couldn't make any money
playing it, and I was a clarinetist first, but it was tenor people wanted
to hear. I always liked Artie Shaw better than Benny Goodman. Buster
Bailey could outplay Benny, too. Benny had Gene Krupa, Harry James,
and Toots Mondello to back him up, but Artie Shaw had only Georgie
Auld, out of Bunny Berigan's old band, behind him. My aunt had a
record of Benny Goodman trying to play alto saxophone, and it used to
crack me up. Now Rudy Rutherford, who has been playing with Earl
Hines, is an excellent clarinetist, but he can't play the saxophone. Old
Omer Simeon sure could play clarinet, but it went out of favor. The
flute came in and it's not a good jazz instrument—too sticky, too tight.
I never liked the soprano either—too raucous and brash a sound. When
you look at the pictures of the old bands, all the sax players had
several instruments in front of them, but they could only play one good.

"The old-timers, like Buster Bailey, played the Albert system. So
did Artie Shaw. The Albert system was simpler, more like a saxophone,
but when the Boehm system came in the old-timers couldn't get conditioned with it. That's why they say, 'Put the blame on Boehm.' But

the Boehm has more range, three octaves, and that's why I chose it. I figured the Albert system was going to be obsolete.

"Josephine Baker came over here once when I was with Basie, and I had to pick up the clarinet again to play her arrangements. It was the same backing Valaida Snow. When Lester Young and I were practicing, we didn't have a Selmer or Leblanc from France, but an old metal clarinet. We called it 'the gas pipe.' It sounds just as good as the other kind if you know what to do with your embouchure and how to 'imaginate.'

"I don't play a Selmer saxophone to this day. I call my horn Matilda and I've had eight of them. This one, the eighth, is a collector's item, a Conn. I can get up over the brass section with it, even when I'm with Basie.

" 'How can you get up over those brass riffs behind you?' fans and young musicians ask me.

" 'I've got Matilda here,' I tell them. 'That's how.'

"When Prez came back from Paris, another company had given him a couple of horns and he gave me one of them.

" 'Prez,' I said, 'this ain't doing nothing!' He put his down, too.

"Kansas City was only five or six hundred miles from Denver, and I just *had* to go there during the summer, to learn about this music. Mother would be sending the police out to haul me back to Denver, and she would be screaming at me when I got back, but I wasn't that dumb and nobody hurt me. Even the underworld people would take up for us musicians. So I met all the people like Joe Turner, Sammy Price, Charlie Parker, Al Hibbler, and Jay McShann. I ended up in Jay's band and in 1942 we went to the Savoy Ballroom, playing opposite Al Cooper's Savoy Sultans. We were so goddamned raggedy, the uniforms would whistle when the wind blew! But we blew those Sultans right off the stand!

"Jay McShann plays good piano, more than Basie actually. He's got that Kansas City shit! And when he plays boogie-woogie, even Sammy Price can't beat him. In fact, Sam is scared of him.

"Jay was always an easygoing guy. Of course, during the war we had transportation problems. If we were traveling by train to the next gig, and officers came aboard, we might have to stand up all the way. One time, when we were down in Tulsa, Jay hired two station wagons. 'Paul,' he said, 'I want you to drive this one. I'll sit in the back.' So I drove all the way from Tulsa to San Francisco, because we had a dead-line to meet. I was taking no-doze tablets to keep me awake. We were using retreads, because you couldn't get new tires then. They kept

blowing and we'd pull into a gas station, have them jack the wagon
up, and put another retread on. The guy driving the other car kept as
close behind us as he could. A sixteen-piece band and all the horns in
two station wagons! Can you imagine that?

"I stayed with McShann until he went in the army. I was straw boss
for the band. I had a portable typewriter and I had to write his letters
for him, because he stayed juiced. That's why they nicknamed him
Hootie. (It's a western term—gimme a drink of that hoot, gimme a
shot of that red-eye.) I got so mad with him in San Francisco—he
wouldn't buy the right uniforms—that I quit and joined Johnny Otis.

"Johnny had a full sixteen-piece band and Little Esther, who was
about eleven years old. Preston Love was playing first alto and we were
getting some of Basie's arrangements and recording them before Basie
did. I was with Johnny Otis about two years. World War II was over
and the bottom seemed to drop out of everything. I remember working
on Sunset Boulevard with Benny Carter and Big Sid Catlett, and I
remember being in a hotel room next to Sammy Davis, Jr.'s. We were
so broke we were eating mustard sandwiches.

" 'Hey, man,' he says, whenever he sees me, 'how about them mustard
sandwiches?'

"About this time Louis Jordan came to get me. He really wanted
Wardell Gray, but Wardell had told him, 'Fuck you, you Uncle Tom, I
ain't going to work for you!' But by this time Louis had his Tympany
Five and he was a big shot. He told me once about when he was playing first alto with Chick Webb. Chick would let him go out and sing
a couple of tunes. Apparently he was in the wings with grease and
a stocking cap on his head. When he went out on stage, all the people
laughed and he looked like a fool. I guess that started something, but
he was considerable of a blues singer and in the year I was with him
we made a whole lot of records.

"Next I went to Lucky Millinder at the Savoy Ballroom, which
was owned by the Metropolitan Life Insurance Company. A lot of
people don't know that. Ed Wilcox, who took over the band when
Jimmie Lunceford died, had hired me, but Lucky had a good band and
was paying his musicians more than Basie. Andy Gibson was writing
most of the arrangements and they were good, never too ponderous. I
always told Lucky he missed his calling, that he should have been a
producer, like Ziggy Joe Johnson or Larry Steele, but he liked fronting
a band and he'd stand out there on big old dice at the Apollo. When
we were there, Mr. Schiffman wouldn't show the movie, but he'd
show previews of what was coming and cartoons. There were no
elevators backstage, so we'd hardly have time to run upstairs and
change uniforms between shows. Remind me not to go there no more!

"I did go back again with Joe Thomas when he had a sixteen-piece band. He had been the tenor star with Lunceford.

" 'Come on, Paul,' he said, 'work with me. There won't be any solos for you, because I'm the feature.'

" 'That's all right,' I said. 'Just give me the money.'

"Now he's a funeral director in Kansas City, burying people, and he's got Cadillacs and all the money.

"Around this time I worked with J. C. Heard at the Village Vanguard. Sometimes I did dates with Lips Page and Red Allen playing those old Dixieland tunes I can't stand, but which are part of the game. That's where the money was at that particular time, and they'd help me and tell me where to go if I got screwed up. But Hot Lips Page stranded us up in Canada. I couldn't get out, couldn't pay my hotel bill. He had been juicing and gambling at those after-hours joints, and he'd gambled our money away. His wife worked for the First National City Bank and she bailed us out, but when he got home she wouldn't let him in the door! The next thing my doorbell was ringing.

" 'It's me,' Lips was hollering. 'Move over, move over!'

" 'Well look, Lips,' I said, 'I can't do this no more. To hell with ya. I'm going to Basie.'

"Basie sent Wardell Gray to get me. He was mad with Lucky Thompson, and Lester had told him, 'Paul will play my chair, not Lucky Thompson.'

"Wardell was a good saxophone player, but a junkie. Wardell disliked me, because like Stan Getz, Zoot Sims, and Al Cohn, he didn't really know Lester. Lester paid them no attention, but he and I were together, and he showed *me* how to do this and that. I think the others resented this and may even have been jealous of my good luck, especially when people started calling me the 'Vice-Prez.'

"Basie was doing the Kate Smith show then and everything was fine. He had Freddie Green—'Green Bay' or 'Pepperhead', as we used to call him—and I think he'd be lost without him. If you put the tempo too fast, Freddie kept it down there, always controlled. He's got it right there, in his wrist. And Basie listens to Freddie Green, one reason why he's still successful to this day. He might not listen to me, but he's going to listen to Freddie, because he knows that's where it is. Basie would stomp off the tune two or three times, getting it right, what I call the right slot, the right tempo. When Walter Page died, the only one he had left was Freddie, the only one he could rely on to keep tempo. After Gus Johnson left, he got Sonny Payne, who did all that trickerating like Lionel Hampton used to do before he started playing vibes.

"The reason I left Basie was because of the records I was making for

Mercury in 1952. There were no big hits, but they were fairly successful, so Basie said, 'All right, get out of the band. I'm going to be your
manager.' But James C. Petrillo, the boss of the union, sent Basie and
me a telegram which said in effect, 'You cannot have a monopoly on
a sideman.' So then Basie thought he would put it in his wife's name,
but Petrillo sent her a telegram, too! Meanwhile, Basie had hired Lockjaw and others for the band. They had families, too, and he couldn't
turn them down just because this caper of ours hadn't worked.

"Soon after that I got a call from Ralph Watkins to go into Basin
Street East with Benny Goodman. We had a lot of trouble. 'Benny
only plays fifteen minutes,' Ralph said, 'because when you guys start
swinging the people don't buy booze.' At any other joint, Benny had to
play forty minutes. Previous to this, Gene Krupa had said to me, 'Listen,
if you're going to work for him, get your money, because he's like a
horse trader. He's going to get you at the lowest price he can.' That's
the way he is, too. Gene also told me how when he did the concert
with Louis Armstrong, Benny was so mad because Louis had top
billing that he took a whole bottle of scotch and threw it up against
the wall!

"After the Basin Street engagement, he called me for some concerts.
I went to Montreal with him and I got a big write-up all on the front
page. Coming back on the plane he started screaming at me.

" 'Everybody thought it was *your* band,' he said.

" 'Well, thank you, Fletcher Henderson,' I answered.

"That was bad. So I told the truth on him and he didn't want to
hear it. He didn't hire me again.

"After that I got out of music, because they seemed to be booking
only rock 'n' rollers. Moe Gale was trying to talk me into being a
rock 'n' roll saxophone player, but I felt it was so wrong I couldn't
do it. I got a little poor then, until an investigator for the welfare department got me a grant from Nelson Rockefeller in Albany which
enabled me to take a three-year course as an electronics technician at
RCA. He knew I had been a ham operator at one time. I had got so
discouraged, I had to do something. If I had had a pistol, I would have
shot Elvis Presley right in the face! That's how I felt about it. I
figured I'd go to school and know two trades instead of one, but I fully
intended picking up my horn again. After I graduated from RCA in
1971, I gradually started back.

"Catherine Basie sent me a telegram asking me to take a group into
Basie's lounge uptown. There was no organ in the room, but she wanted
one. In a Harlem garage, all covered with cobwebs, I found her one
and I fixed it up. All went well till Arlene Francis, who had a television
show, went up there. Some woman took her white mink coat and left

a rotten old fox coat in its place. So now Basie was mad. He had to replace the coat, and he was saying, 'You shut this damn place up! If it won't be her, it will be someone else again. I can't keep paying for a lot of mink coats!'

"Later, I started working at a place downtown called Churchill's with Brooks Kerr and Sam Woodyard. The manager wouldn't let us play any slow ballads. So it was *Jumpin' at the Woodside* all night. I had two heart attacks down there, on the stand, working too hard, seven nights a week. I was tired, but I went to the West End Café and got a little attention. Then I went into Michael's Pub with Jay McShann, and made a few records. Now Matilda and I are looking for something good to show up."

(1977)

Jimmy Witherspoon

(VOCALIST)

"I was born in Gordon, Arkansas, August 18, 1923. My dad was named Leonard Witherspoon, and my mother's name is Eva. She's still living, in Stockton, California. My brother Leonard lives in San Francisco, and my sister Jimmie lives here in Los Angeles. Everybody in the family was musical, really. My mother and sister both played piano. My mother played in the Baptist church, and my daddy sang there, too. That's where I started singing, in the choir. I was singing a solo in the church when I was five years old, a song called *I'm Goin' Through*. I did it nearly every Sunday, and my mother played piano for me.

"My father was a brakeman on the Missouri Pacific Railroad for twenty some years, and we could ride a pass anywhere in America and Canada. He died when I was about six years old. I went to school in Arkansas, but when I was sixteen I forged my mother's name and got a pass and came out to California, because I figured in Hollywood I'd be able to get a start singing. But it was hard to get a job here in 1939 if you were black. Not to be paranoid about it, the only jobs blacks could get in California were as chauffeurs, busboys, or maids. It was hard. I used to walk all the way from 42nd and Central to 5th Street downtown, just to try to get a job. Finally, I got a job washing dishes at the Owl Drugstore, 8th and Broadway, for seventeen dollars a week. I worked there for a long time and worked up from dishwasher to cook.

"While I was working at the Owl Drugstore, everybody used to think I was a singer. I used to go to Little Harlem, and that was the first place they let me sing. T-Bone Walker had a white drummer from Texas, named Jimmy, Big Six playing tenor saxophone, and Norman Bouton on trumpet. Bouton was going with a girl from my hometown, and he asked them to let me sing. 'Let Toots sing,' he said; and I might as well confess that 'Toots' was my nickname then. From then on, whenever T-Bone would call me, I'd get up and sing.

"I was too young to run around with T-Bone at that time. He was the biggest thing on the West Coast, the biggest name in the black area. He used to do a radio show with Al Jarvis, one of the first blacks to do that. He had recorded with Les Hite by then, and also with Freddie Slack on a tune called *Riffette*. Not too many people seem to know about that, but I know it, and I remember it. A lot of people recognized T-Bone's great talent, but they didn't give him the chance he should have had. He never had it, even until his death. But T-Bone didn't have regrets. He lived a good life, and he made a lot of money. He had a lot of hits and he gambled. He also gave plenty of money away. He never did say no, even when he wasn't doing too good at the end. He helped everybody, but he was an artist who could never get stranded anywhere in America, because there'd always be somebody to help T-Bone.

"Besides Little Harlem, I also used to go to Lovejoy's and stay up all night long with Slam Stewart and Art Tatum, who played in the hallway there. They all thought I was entertaining, even Tatum. Lovejoy's was a big after-hours joint, a chicken place upstairs at Vernon and Central Avenue. Ivie Anderson's Chicken Shack was right across the street.

"For a time I was also a cook on the Union Pacific, and when I was in Omaha I used to sing with Johnny Otis. I always claim that I'm the one responsible for him coming to California. I used to hang out with Jesse Price and Harlan Weatherford, and I told Jesse about Johnny. So when Jesse was getting ready to leave, he told Harlan what I had said, and Harlan told me that when I went back to Omaha I was to tell Johnny Otis that if he came here he could have Jesse Price's job.

"What Johnny loved in those days was Basie and big-band stuff, and when he came out here he got a good big band himself. He dug musicians, but he didn't dig blues then. It was later that he saw the way the wind was blowing with rhythm and blues and found out how popular the blues were in Europe and Japan.

"I was still at the Owl Drugstore when war broke out, and they wanted me to go in the army. When they sent me job papers, I had my landlady tell 'em I'd gone to Richmond to see my mother. When I got there, I went over to the Maritime Commission, told 'em I was a cook, and they gave me a bar and a half as chief steward and cook in the Merchant Marine. I just didn't want to go in the army!

"I was in the Merchant Marine when I sang with Teddy Weatherford (the pianist) in Calcutta. That was the first blues I ever sang in my life! We were unloading ammunition and stuff for the CBI theater—China, Burma, India—where they were fighting the Japanese.

"Teddy Weatherford had gone to China with Buck Clayton. When war broke out there, they all went home except him, but he couldn't stay in China so he went to India and married an Indian lady. He had a family, and he died in 1945; but when I was there he had a big band in the Winter Gardens and was doing well. He played great jazz piano, and also violin. He had Caughey Roberts, who Lester Young had brought to Count Basie. He's a good alto player, and he's still playing in town. Teddy also had a tenor saxophone player out of Chicago. Anyway, when they asked me to sing, I sang with 'em!

"When I got back to California, my mother was living in Vallejo, and that's where I joined Jay McShann. Walter Brown had left Jay in San Francisco, and then he had a little light fellow who used to pattern after Wynonie Harris, but he quit, too. Anyway, everybody in Vallejo was asking Jay to let me sing. Eventually, I sang a Joe Turner tune, *Wee Baby Blues*, and Jay McShann hired me that night. I was about twenty; and I really never had to scuffle like a lot of people did.

"I liked Jay right away. We went to Stockton next day, and then on up to Seattle. We had to ride trains at that time because of the gas shortage, and on the way he told me he wanted me to sing conventional blues, as close to Walter Brown as I could. For the rest of the tunes, he said for me to go for myself. I admired him for that. Where so many other bandleaders would have been telling you, 'You got to do what I tell you,' he said, 'Go for yourself!'

"Jay taught me a lot, and I stayed with him. I would ask what to do, and he told me. He took a liking to me because I would listen. He's only about a couple of years older than I am, and he's not as old as a lot of people think he is. He came to Kansas City *young*. He taught me a lot of moral things. Drinking was his worst enemy at that time, but contrary to what a lot of people thought, Hootie was one of the most wonderful persons. He was much misused at that period. He was just starting to make money, and a lot of people got to him. Managers are a necessary evil, but there was no protection in those days. The army had taken him right in the prime of his career, but with his flat feet he couldn't stand around in the army long. When he got out, he put another big band together, and that was when I joined him. He was carrying sixteen pieces, and he had great musicians like Paul Quinichette, Jesse Price, and Benny Bailey during '44, '45, and '46.

"I never forget the first theater date I played. I had been looking forward to it for a year and a half. It was at the Regal Theater in Chicago, and Dinah Washington and the Ravens were also on the bill. They went to the manager and said there was too much singing, so they cut me off the show. That hurt me worse than anything in my whole life. It was the biggest disappointment, and Jay couldn't do anything about it. All I'd been doing was opening the show; and Dinah was the star.

"Years later, when I'd gone out on my own, I had the pleasure of working on the same bill with her in Chicago. I called Jay McShann in Kansas City and said, 'Jay, this is the first time I ever had any vindictive thoughts about an entertainer, and I'm going to stop this show cold if I have to crawl on my knees!'

" 'Who is the entertainer?' he asked.

" 'Dinah, and I'm opening up in front of her.'

" 'Good,' he said. 'Go ahead.'

"She was a great talent, and I never did mention that she'd been responsible for one of the biggest hurts I ever had; but I think she sensed how I felt. She introduced me in the second show by saying, 'Ladies and gentlemen, now the male star of our show . . . !'

"McShann had taught me how to go on the stage. He had also taught me never to worry about where they put you on the bill. I still use that knowledge today, and it pays. It may be a big responsibility closing a show, but I don't want it. I'd as soon open as close; because I know whoever's following me is going to have to be good, and that makes the whole show good.

"I guess I was with McShann about three years. We used to drive everywhere together, and he took me into his confidence. He was married then and living in South Bend, and I knew a lot of his private, personal business. It was all *great* experience. You could be mad at

Jay, but he'd have you laughing twenty minutes after you hit the bandstand because he'd be so involved in his music. After a while, he had to reduce the band from sixteen pieces to five or six. Times were rough for big bands then. We kept Benny Bailey. We had Addison Farmer on bass, and Pete McShann, Jay's cousin, was on drums. On alto we had a guy we called Floatin' Booty, but his real name was Bill Barnet. We played all over, including here in Hollywood. I asked Jay to play on the session with me when I made *Ain't Nobody's Business*, the one that sold all the records. A lot of people didn't know he was on it.

"Art Tatum loved Jay McShann, idolized him. He said he was the greatest blues player he ever heard in his life. One day I never forget, we were down at Mike Jackson's, a bar on Central Avenue, and Tatum was drinking a beer.

" 'Would you like to sing one?' he asked.

" 'Yeah,' I said.

" 'What key?'

" 'Put it in B-flat.'

"He started in B-flat, but after that he went to every key in the ladder, and I didn't know what key he was in. Jay had told me what he would do, so I paid no attention to Art and his chord structures, kept my mind on B-flat, and sang right through.

" 'Spoon,' he said, hitting me on the shoulder and laughing, 'nobody in the world can do that. I put you through so many keys.'

"He had a sense of mischief and loved to do things like that.

"Jay and I never had a falling out—*never!* People like to tell how he'll go in his pocket and pull out a dollar if somebody needs money. He's the greatest in the world for that. He can have $5,000 in his pocket, but out will come a one-dollar bill! He pleads poverty all the time, but if you press him he'll say, 'You're about to kill the old man,' and out will come two dollars! I don't know, but I guess when you're hiring sixteen men you have to use tactics like that.

"At the time I'm speaking of, we were staying at the Mom's Hotel on 5th and Central, here in Los Angeles. All the bands stayed there— Lionel Hampton's, everybody's. The manager of the hotel took a liking to me and said I should stay out here in California and further my career. I didn't think much about it until we went to Omaha and some of my things were stolen out of the truck. From there we went on to Chicago, where I told Jay I was thinking of going back to California to try something on my own.

" 'Aw, he just had a nightmare!' was what Jay's manager, Johnny Tumino, said when he heard I was leaving. But I did quit, because I knew I could stay at the hotel. That kept me going till I got straightened out; but I had it rough for a time."

(1978)

Jimmy Witherspoon was much more versatile than the average blues singer, and his career subsequently burgeoned. He toured frequently in Europe, where records had made him popular. He had his own radio show in Los Angeles, starred in a film entitled *Black Godfather*, appeared often on television, scored a big success at the Monterey Jazz Festival, went to Japan in 1973, and sang in clubs throughout the United States.

Eddie Barefield

(ALTO AND TENOR SAXOPHONES AND CLARINET)

"I was born in a little coal town called Skandia, right out of Des Moines, Iowa. All my people were coal miners—my father, his father, and grandfather's father. They all worked in the pits, and they'd go from one town to another in the Des Moines area. My father died when he was thirty-five. They had to bring him out of the mine for an emergency appendix operation. I was eleven.

"My mother played some piano and my father played guitar around the neighborhood. They used to sing in two-part harmony, songs like *Sweet Adeline*, and I'd join in with third harmony when I was just a little tyke. I was the first child born in the family [December 12, 1909], and I used to spend half my time with my grandparents and half with my father and mother. I always wanted to be a fighter, and my father taught me. I had a punching bag in a barn in my backyard, and I'd be out there punching and training myself to be a fighter all day. When I started school, the big boys used to put pennies in a hat to see me box older kids 'cause I was very good with my dukes. I had a hundred and twenty amateur contests, fighting for the Des Moines newsboys at Tommy Ryan's.

"A friend of mine, Merle Williams, lived across the street and was learning to play piano with a lady named Josephine Guy. 'Boxing's a rough game,' he said. 'Why don't you learn to play music?' So I started studying with his teacher, and practicing on his piano. After about a year I quit, because the fellows thought Merle was a sissy and they began to call me one, too. I didn't want to be a sissy, so I went back to boxing! But Merle was persistent, and one day he came over and persuaded me to go to a rehearsal of a community band they were organizing. 'The girls will like you better if you go to music,' he said. When we got to the rehearsal, an old man was playing tenor saxophone. I had never seen one before, and I immediately decided that that was what I wanted. I found out that with the C-melody sax you didn't have to transpose, and I begged my mother to get me one. When Christmas morning came, there was a York alto saxophone under the tree. 'Santa Claus didn't have any C-melody saxophones left,' my mother said.

"The first thing I did was to get a screwdriver and take that alto apart! I wanted to see how it worked, but when I couldn't put it together again, my mother put all the pieces in a bag and took it back to the store. She wouldn't let me have it again until she found a teacher for me, a fellow named Charles Bushman. I took one lesson from him and he taught me the preliminary scale. From then on, when my mother gave me a dollar for a lesson, I put my horn in a drugstore and went to the movie. But I was practicing every day, practicing with records. We always had records in the house—Fletcher Henderson's, Sidney Bechet's, Boyd Senter's, and Rudy Wiedoeft's. In those days, even Senter wasn't *too* corny. I learned all Coleman Hawkins's solos, all Sidney Bechet's, and some of them I still play, like *Wild Cat Blues*. I used to listen to Joe Smith's trumpet, too, on the records by the blues singers.

"Merle Williams and I got a little group together, the Jimtown Rounders, with Melvin Saunders on drums—just a trio. We used to rehearse, and people got to like what we were doing. My mother always believed in lodges and social groups, and she had joined me to a junior lodge. We used to have a turnout on a certain day of the year, and we'd all be dressed up with red socks and everything. I was standing watching the parade when a lanky kid came running by, and he yelled, 'Look at the sissy with the red socks on!' I couldn't break the line, but as soon as the parade stopped I was going to go out and punch him in the nose. We started fighting, but after they pulled us apart he told me he was a trumpet player. 'Well, I'm a saxophone player,' I said. His family lived in Perry, Iowa, and his father knew mine and was a coal miner, too. That's how I met Leroy White, later known as 'Snake' White.

"He joined the Jimtown Rounders, but he and Merle didn't get along. Snake was a tall, handsome guy and he had all the girls, but Merle was short and jealous of him. However, we started playing little school dances for kids and we became quite popular and began to get all the jobs around. Older musicians would come down and turn up their noses at us, and I guess we made some pretty horrible sounds.

, "One day I was downtown buying the music of *Aggravatin' Papa*. (Snake was the only guy in our group who could really read. Merle could read a little, but all pianists did in those days was *oompahs*. I was playing by ear, although I was like the star.) They were building the Capitol Theater on 6th and Grand Avenue in Des Moines at that time, and as I passed by a guy way up on the scaffolding hollered down to me.

" 'Hey, kid, where you going?'

" 'I'm going home.'

"He came down and saw the music in my hand.

" 'What you got there?'

" 'Some music.'

" 'Let me look at it.'

"Then he wanted the trumpet part, but I told him we already had a trumpet player. He came and heard the group, said he would play tuba, and got him an E-flat. His name was Edgar Pillows, and he was in his twenties, while we were all under fifteen. He took over and we became the Edgar Pillows Night Owls. He started booking us and we began to play homecomings, country clubs, and all kinds of dances. In 1926, he got a job in Omaha for us to go to Galveston, Texas, on a train with Miss Nebraska for a beauty contest. They took the seats out of one coach so people could dance, and we played the whole trip. We stopped off in Hot Springs and several places in Arkansas, and stayed ten days in New Orleans. Alphonso Trent's band was playing at the Hotel Galveston. That was when he had Snub Mosely on trombone, James Jeter on sax, Lester Clark on trumpet, and A. G. Godley on drums. When we were not playing, we hung out with them and had a good time. We were in Galveston nearly a couple of weeks and it was great experience for a boy of sixteen!"

This was the real beginning of Barefield's extraordinarily varied professional career. Pillows next got the band work with a carnival, where they played for a minstrel show led by Rastus Jones. After traveling through Missouri, Arkansas, and Texas, Barefield arrived in

Kansas City on Labor Day, 1926, when he should have been home and getting ready for school. He heard all the bands in the area, including those of Bennie Moten and George E. Lee, and was preparing to go to California with a bunch of youngsters from Pittsburgh led by Syd Valentine, when detectives, acting on his mother's behalf, found and returned him to Des Moines—and school.

After playing with pianist Ace Oliver and groups in the Des Moines area, he went to Chicago by train at the instigation of his friend, Bill Fulton, riding the blinds hobo fashion. "I soon found out," he said, "that I wasn't as great a player as I thought I was." While looking for jobs, he went to work in the Hammond stockyards so that he could send money each week to his mother. He lived with Fulton, a chef, who always kept a big pot cooking for friends from Des Moines. In return, Barefield taught him saxophone.

Barefield met Louis Armstrong for the first time on Easter Sunday at the Warwick Ballroom. "He didn't mean too much to *any*body then," he recalled. "People used to laugh and make fun of him. 'What does he think he's doing, singing?' In those days, if you didn't sound like Caruso you weren't singing! But when those records like *Heebie Jeebies* and *Cornet Shop Suey* came out, musicians began to take notice."

After Barefield was hired by a group called the Society Syncopators, the leader soon discovered he could not read and recommended him to Bill Frye, a pianist who played house-rent parties and chitterling struts on weekends. Working with Frye, Barefield made a living until a telegram came from a group called the Virginia Ravens, who had heard of him in Des Moines. He joined them in Genesco, Illinois, playing tenor saxophone, and soon became an attraction with his slap-tonguing and antics modeled on those of Slim Freeman, "a big, long, tall guy" who was featured with the Midnight Ramblers. The Virginia Ravens were led by Lee Lancaster, a singer and something of a disciplinarian. When he in turn found out that Barefield could not read, he fired him, but the band's sponsors, a Mr. and Mrs. Fath, insisted that Barefield remain. Ill feeling ensued, and the saxophonist scornfully rejected Lancaster's offer to teach him to read. Then one day he realized that he was being foolish, so he went to Lancaster and apologized. The singer thereupon taught him for an hour a day, and in a few weeks he was able to switch from tenor to alto and play lead saxophone. This led to a job at the Broadway Gardens in Madison, Wisconsin, with a band led by pianist Don Pilips. The pay was sixty dollars a week, very good for the time, and he enjoyed his stay in Madison, but the engagement ended with the summer. He went to stay with a cousin in Milwaukee, where he again encountered the Virginia Ravens. The group was reorganized with the addition of Merle Williams on piano, Edgar Pillows on bass, Snake White on trumpet, and Joe Thomas [Walter 'Foots' Thomas's brother] on alto saxophone. They worked the Wisconsin territory sucessfully until one night at a resort on Sharon Lake, Barefield had too much applejack and took out his .38 automatic on stage and fired it off, scaring everybody in the ballroom. ("Most of the musicians who went on the road had guns," Barefield said, "because we were carrying money and needed protection.") This incident provoked a split in the band. Five of the musicians elected to stay with Barefield, among them Pillows, White, and a "terrific" piano player named Frank Hines, who had replaced Merle Williams.

On their way to Minneapolis, they ran into Red Curry, a gangster from St. Louis. He got them to play on the train, collected money for them, and then took them in a truck to a gangsters' convention on Grandview Island. It was late when they arrived and the hotel was dark, but Curry had them open up from the truck with *Hail, Hail, the Gang's All Here.* Lights went on and startled heads popped out of windows.

In Minneapolis, the musicians organized a group they called the Ethiopian Symphonians, and it was here that Barefield taught himself to write arrangements, copying from Fletcher Henderson records. "Everything was written from the alto saxophone," he said, "and after I'd learned the part I'd write the harmony parts. Frank Hines got me interested in chord progressions, so I got a McNeil banjo book and really started studying chords."

That winter of 1927–1928 was a hard one and work was scarce, but Minneapolis was then a wide-open city with a flourishing red-light district. Barefield used to play at Royal Langford's, where the prostitutes congregated after work, and often he would end up with a saxophone bell full of money. Eventually, pianist Clarence Johnson— "known as Mr. Five by Five, because he was short and wide"— secured a job at the Spencer Hotel in Bismarck, North Dakota, and Barefield and Snake White went with him.

The Young Family Band was in Bismarck and it was there Barefield first met Lester Young, who was playing alto saxophone. Their hotel rooms were near together, and one day Young knocked on the door and introduced himself. He had heard the records Barefield was playing, among them *Singin' the Blues* and others by Frankie Trumbauer, whom he always referred to as a strong early influence.

After they had all returned to Minneapolis, the Fletcher Henderson band came to town. Barefield remembered that Benny Carter heard Young jamming there "and flipped over his playing." The Trumbauer style was translated to tenor saxophone when Young changed to that instrument in Minneapolis, and he became "the first tenor player to play different from Coleman Hawkins." Barefield himself cited Coleman Hawkins as a major influence, along with Sidney Bechet and Johnny Hodges. The latter's soloing on Ellington's *It's a Glory* made a powerful impression on him.

"The Do Dads from Diddy Wa Diddy" was the picturesque name, derived from a comic strip, of a seven-piece group Barefield and his friends, Snake White and Merle Williams, formed to play at the Nest Club. When bandleader Eli Rice came through the city, he heard and liked the group and persuaded Barefield to join him in Milwaukee, where he was required to play clarinet for the first time. Ed Inge, who was there with Bernie Young's band, gave him his first lesson. Earl Keith was more responsible for his subsequent proficiency. "Earl was one of the finest musicians, on saxophone and clarinet, I ever played with in my life," Barefield said warmly. "He had a great ear, he could sight-read, and he played a little piano too, but he never went far away from Minneapolis. His parents were good to him, and I think he had a bunch of kids. He was a better jazz man than Chauncey Haughton, another underrated musician. Chauncey could have been a virtuoso, but he was out of place in Duke Ellington's band." Keith played lead in the Rice band, Willard Brown tenor, and Barefield third saxophone. Others in the band who were to make big names in jazz were Joe Thomas and Eddie Tompkins on trumpet, and Keg Johnson on trombone.

After a short period with Grant Moore's ten-piece band, Barefield took Ed Inge's place with Bernie Young, whose group went into Chicago's Savoy Ballroom in the fall of 1929 for the winter. Young's group featured Barefield as the "Child Wonder" (he was nineteen) and trumpet player Raymond "Syd" Valentine as the "Patent Leather Kid." Valentine was "a very tall, handsome fellow, and vain, but he'd amaze you when he played. He was very fast and didn't care nothing about Louis Armstrong or anybody. Louis and his band played opposite us at the Savoy in 1930 when he was doing his fifty high Cs, but Raymond still stood them on their ears." Also in the band was Cassino Simpson, the one pianist in the city who could challenge Earl Hines. Unfortunately, he became addicted to heroin and ended his days in a mental home. Omer Simeon was playing in the Metropolitan Theater with Erskine Tate's band. "I used to go over just to hear him," Barefield remembered. "He was a great saxophone player as well as a clarinetist, but he never had the credit he deserved. His record of *Beau-Koo Jack* had just come out."

At the beginning of the summer, 1930, the Bernie Young band went to Tulsa, where Barefield met the Alphonso Trent band again, this time with violinist Stuff Smith in its ranks. Tulsa, an oil town, he recalled as being full of "pavilions and dance halls" at that time. Returning to Chicago, he rejoined Grant Moore and went to Sioux City, Iowa. When he was late getting to the bus one day, Moore drove off and left him.

Next he went back to Eli Rice and Minneapolis, where he found Lester Young again, playing at the Nest Club with Frank Hines. After a short stay with Rice, Barefield joined Frank Terry's Chicago Nightingales in Toledo for an engagement at the Recreation Ballroom, where he heard Art Tatum for the first time. "Somebody led this little blind guy up on the bandstand, and Frank Terry said we ought to hear him play at intermission," Barefield said. "Well, I'd heard Earl Hines and Frank Hines, and I was on my way out of the hall when I heard this *Brrrrrrmmmm!* on the piano. That was Art, and he stood me on my ear. He lived across the street from me with his parents, and we became friends. Teddy Wilson was in Toledo, too, so we had a little gang that used to hang out together—Art, Teddy, George White [a saxophone player], and me. We'd go around to the houses and jam in the barns. Art played at a club called Noble's, and he also had a job on the radio, so he got a chauffeur. One night we were down at Noble's wondering where he was. We found out that he went out for juice, got in his new Ford, and ran into a telephone pole. I don't think he could see so well then as he did later."

From Toledo, Barefield returned to Minneapolis, where Ralph Cooper, "a promoting type of character," sent for him to join the band at the Regal Theater in Chicago. But the union intervened and took the whole band off the job because Cooper had imported an out-of-town musician. "So there I was," Barefield said, "stuck in the Hotel Trenier with Ralph Cooper and Reginald Foresythe as roommates. Reginald was from England and he was writing arrangements for Earl Hines at the Grand Terrace. Earl told me to bring some of mine over, but I had only written for one trombone and when I added another trombone part I wrote it wrong. It sounded horrible, so then Reginald showed me how to voice for the brass.

"Luckily for me, Bennie Moten's band came to work at a theater on the North Side, and they stayed at the Trenier, too. Ben Webster had left Blanche Calloway and was with them, because they were planning to reorganize the band. I was always jamming in those days, and my reputation had gotten around. So Ben took me out to the theater and I jammed with Basie and all of them. The result was that they took me back to Kansas City with them. We had three saxes, two altos, and a tenor, because Jack Washington was playing alto then.

They got Hot Lips Page and Joe Smith—Pops Smith's brother—on trumpets. Joe had married a Kansas City girl and wanted to live there, but he didn't stay too long. He drank a little, but nobody could play like him. He had been in that show, *Shuffle Along*, and everybody knew him through his records. He was a quiet, moody guy, and I liked him, but he was quite independent, too. They got Dee Stewart in his place, so we had Dee, Lips, and Joe Keyes for a trumpet section.

"I was the lead man in the reed section and we cooked up a lot of 'head' arrangements. If somebody knew the melody, we'd play that first. Then Ben would take a solo, and I might take one. Lips Page would come down next and play ten, fifteen, or twenty choruses, while we set up riffs behind, a different riff for each chorus. That's how riffing started. Lester Young and I used to play a dance for kids in Minneapolis, just two alto saxophones, no piano, bass, or drums. We'd pat our feet, take solos, and riff together. Of course, it could get repetitious, but the reason the Moten band was so much looser was because it had so little written material. The playing was freer, but we didn't just grab a bunch of notes and play 'em without any division. No matter how many notes you play, you divide them into some kind of form. The music has to be divided and accented. Hawk started double-timing, but he still swung, even on a slow tune. Parker, Dizzy, and all of 'em double-timed, but when you start getting away from that and playing a group of five or a group of seven, then the swing leaves. When we were playing by ear, jazz was limited by what the ear could hear. Then we utilized chords, up and down, and Dizzy and the boppers embellished it a bit more by using the scales. But I never did go along with all the talk about a Kansas City style, a Chicago style, a West Coast style. Styles are individual things, and at one time everybody had his own different, distinguishing style.

"We played around Kansas City and down in Oklahoma. Sometimes, to make ends meet, I had to play with other bands, but then Moten decided to go east once more. He was established, but it was a hazardous trip, especially since someone was stealing the money. It was quite a band we had, with Lips, Dee, and Joe Keyes on trumpet; Eddie Durham and Dan Minor on trombone; Jack Washington, Ben Webster, and myself on saxophones; Basie and Walter Page in the rhythm section, with Leroy Berry on guitar and Pete McWashington on drums; and Jimmy Rushing as vocalist. Bennie Moten played piano, too, but Basie played most of the time and Buster Moten conducted.

"We were stranded in nearly every city on our way to New York—in Columbus, Ohio, in Zanesville, Ohio, and in Cincinnati. In Zanesville I stayed in Sy Oliver's mother's house. I didn't know Sy then, but I met his mother, his sister, and his little brother. We were all young in the Moten band and we didn't care. We just hung around the town until they got another raggedy bus. And those buses were always breaking down! One time in Virginia we were coming down one of those steep hills and the brakes refused to work. The hand-brake came out in the driver's hand, and the bus went careening down through a town at about sixty miles an hour. We were frightened to death and we were just lucky we didn't run into anybody.

"Being stranded meant that you were in a town without work or money. You had to eat and sleep, but you couldn't get out. Bennie might hustle up enough to get us a meal ticket. We would eat *any-thing*. Mostly it was hot dogs and chili, with booze. We weren't alarmed, because it was a common thing, and finally, somehow, we got to the Pearl Theater in Philadelphia. We knew we were going to work for a week and get a week's salary, so everybody could have some money in his pocket. We were all whooping it up, juicing, and taking the chorus girls out. When payday came, we all lined up to get our money. When I saw Bennie send a guy out to get a plate of beans and some whiskey, I felt something was wrong. Then he told us that the bus and the box office receipts had been attached to pay for uni-forms he'd bought on his previous engagement at the theater, when he borrowed the money from Mr. Steiffel, the theater owner. So there we were, standing out in front of the theater with our bags and horns—and no bus! The man had booked us for a whole week only to get his money back. Now we couldn't pay our rent, our tabs, or anything. But Bennie finally met a little, fat colored guy named Archie Robinson, who was an agent, and they went off together in Archie's car. They came back with a great big old raggedy bus, and we all piled in to go to Camden to record for Victor, something they'd cooked up at the last minute.

"Now we were all very hungry, but somewhere or other Archie found a rabbit. We pulled off the highway to a pool hall, where they made a big tub of stew with this one rabbit. I always figured it was a cat, because I couldn't understand where he'd find a rabbit in Philadelphia or Camden. Take the head off and you wouldn't be able to tell the difference. I always made a joke of it and kidded Basie about having had some cat stew. Anyway, it tasted very good. We stood around the pool table sopping up the gravy and stuff with bread until the tub was empty, and then we got in the bus again and went over to the church they used as a studio. That was my first record date.

"We recorded ten sides: *Toby, Moten Swing, The Blue Room, Imagination, New Orleans, The Only Girl I Ever Loved, Milenberg Joys,*

Lafayette, Prince of Wales, and Two Times. We never got paid for them to this day. *Toby* was a tune I wrote, and when I later signed a new release on it a woman gave me fifty dollars and said I'd be getting further checks. But I never got any more checks, and in '41 or '42 I instituted a suit against Victor. Ben Webster talked to my lawyer and they advised me to drop it, because Victor might one day be able to help me. I never got any help nor any money, not even when *Toby* was reissued. I don't know whether Moten originally got money. We were just young, stupid kids at the time.

"The way we played on those records, with those fast tempos, was the way we used to play every night. We didn't have any music, but we sure used to swing! The people used to do the Peabody to those fast numbers. In the old days they called it the one-step. It was white dancers who named it the Peabody.

"I think the secret of swinging comes from the drummer's foot. Why don't drum teachers teach the drummers now to play the bass drum today? They all have fast hands, but no foot. Buddy Rich can swing because he's got a good foot, but most of them can't keep the beat going without rushing the tempo. Willie McWashington didn't do anything on those Moten records but just keep time. In those days that was *important*. Of course, Walter Page's bass was the big thing, and working with him was the making of Freddie Green. He's not an outstanding soloist, but for time. . . . The different sections of the band rehearsed separately, so the piano, guitar, bass, and drums were *together*, but today everybody has his own time. Even the horn players played in time in the old days, but nowadays guys think they're too good to pat their feet! When I teach now, I encourage guys to do that, because it helps get a body rhythm that helps their playing.

"After the Camden session, we set out again and were stranded in Newport News, Virginia. Eventually we got back to Kansas City. There were a lot of musicians there, but not much *regular* work, despite what they say. The work was around, out on the road, and K.C. served as a center. There were jam sessions, but they were nearly all freebies. Piney Brown was like a numbers man and he owned the Subway Gardens. He liked musicians and took care of them, so all the guys hung out in his place. Hot Lips Page's man was Ellis Burton, who ran the Yellow Front Café. But there were no places where a big band could keep working steady except Fairyland Park, where Thamon Hayes had the band.

"So I left and joined Zack Whyte's band in Columbus. Sy Oliver, Snake White, Ben Richardson, Vic Dickenson, Eli Robinson, and a boy named Benson on drums were in it. So was Gus Wilson, who played trombone and was Teddy's brother. He was writing, too. He made fifty arrangements on the same tune, *Clementine.* Every night he would come in with a new one and tear up the old one! I was playing lead alto and I often wish I hadn't. I'd have gotten more solos and more recognition if I'd been a tenor player. Hawk was the cause of that. His work from the early twenties onwards meant that the arrangers favored the tenor. Basie was a tenor freak, not only for Lester Young but for Herschel Evans, too. I first heard Herschel when I was in San Anton' with Bennie Moten. I got him to come up from Texas to Milwaukee once. He didn't stay long. He hadn't seen snow before, and the first day it snowed he went back to Texas!

"I stayed with Zack Whyte till I got pneumonia in Chattanooga, and I had to spend a couple of months there recuperating. Then I got an offer to join McKinney's Cotton Pickers in Erie, Pennsylvania. We went out on the road from there with Billy Bowen conducting, and they finally fired McKinney! We went down to Carlin Park in Baltimore and played there all summer. Roy Eldridge and his brother Joe joined us there. We already had Buddy Lee on trumpet, Prince Robinson on tenor and clarinet, Ed Cuffee on trombone, and Cuba Austin on drums, but the band was really going downhill then and we were making only thirty dollars a week.

"In the fall of 1933, the Cab Calloway band came to the Hippodrome Theater in Baltimore. We used to go out jamming every night till daybreak in our red Eton jackets, and one night Cab was out drinking and heard me blowing in some little club. He invited me down to the theater to hear his band, but I thought he was drunk and didn't go. Then I ran into Doc Cheatham and Walter 'Foots' Thomas, who knew me by reputation, and they said Cab had looked for me to go by.

"I went down the next day and went backstage. Baltimore was segregated then and the doorman stopped me and said Mr. Calloway was busy. (The Hippodrome was for whites, but the Royal was a black theater.) Cab was just coming downstairs and saw me. 'Yeah, let him in,' he said. So I stood backstage and watched the show. Afterwards, I borrowed an alto and we had a little jam session. Cab called Irving Mills and told him to come on down from New York. 'I've got Johnny Hodges and Benny Carter all wrapped up in one guy!' he said.

"Cab hired me as an addition to the three saxes he already had, but I went back to the Cotton Pickers that night. It was payday, and when I said I was leaving they said I couldn't without giving two weeks' notice. They refused to pay me and we had a big fight right on the bandstand. I had been using Billy Bowen's clarinet and I said, 'If you don't pay me, I'll keep it.' When he grabbed at it, I hit him. Then three or four of them jumped on my back, and I threw all of them up against the wall. The only guys that didn't jump on me were Roy Eldridge and Prince Robinson. We fought all the way to the hotel, but I didn't get my money, and when I went down to Cab the next day I had a black eye. He asked what had happened, and after I explained he put a hundred dollars in my hand right away so I could go and pay all my bills.

"Right after that, we played a week at the Capitol Theater in New York, and then we went into the Cotton Club. The following year we went to Europe, but before we left we had a record session where I was featured on an instrumental version of *Moonglow*. Cab always sang on his records, but after we'd made three titles that day he found he hadn't any lyrics for a fourth, so we made *Moonglow* in one take to complete the date. After we got back from Europe, we were playing a dance in Texas and heard this record on a jukebox. I was always crazy about Benny Carter, and when I heard the saxophone chorus I thought it was him. I asked the manager of the place who it was playing, and he said, 'Don't you know your own record?'

"Cab was one of the best bandleaders I ever worked with. One thing I specially liked was that he would always let bygones be bygones. He periodically threw a party for the fellows, and he always gave lavish Christmas presents. When payday came, you never had to go and ask for your money. The road manager was there to hand it to you. Everything was done first-class—traveling, playing, and accommodations. He wouldn't work unless the accommodations were suitable for all the men. He was so hot then he could dictate his terms. The kids used to come to the theater, bring their lunches, dance in the aisles, and pull his clothes off him. Often, when I dream in my sleep, it's about Cab, and I'm always rushing, trying to get to the job on time, but I never get there.

"I left Cab in California in 1936, not that I was dissatisfied, but I was always a bit of a vagabond and this was the first time I'd been in such a beautiful climate. Also, I was sick with ulcers and I decided I'd settle there. I thought I was a pretty carefree guy, but later I found out I was a worrier. I still am, although I think I'm more relaxed now. I worry about not being able to play like I want to play, and I still practice two or three hours a day."

Barefield formed a band of his own that included such musicians as Don Byas, Tyree Glenn, Dudley Brooks, and Lee Young. His old friend, Snake White, came out to join him. The union raised the customary objections to out-of-town musicians, but Barefield got around this by adding the secretary of the union to his personnel. He also wrote a book of arrangements for the band, which soon secured a coveted engagement, at Frank Sebastian's Cotton Club. The band was a success, played up and down the West Coast, and appeared in a movie called *Every Day's a Holiday* with Louis Armstrong.

When the attractions of Los Angeles began to pall, Barefield disbanded and took the opportunity of going back east as a member of Fletcher Henderson's band for an engagement at the Grand Terrace in Chicago. Because Hilton Jefferson was playing first alto, Barefield played third and inherited the role of clarinetist, previously the responsibility of first Buster Bailey and then Jerry Blake. The keys of Henderson's arrangements made the clarinet solos difficult, and after a week he indicated his intention of quitting. "Aw, man, don't worry," Henderson said. "I'm satisfied. Just stay in there." Barefield did that, took his parts home each night, practiced, and after a while got them under his fingers.

From Chicago he went to Don Redman's band at the Savoy Ballroom in New York. (*"Down Beat* credited the alto solo on the record we made of *Milenberg Joys* to Don, but it was me.") From that time on, New York was Barefield's base. He had more bands of his own. After Chick Webb's death, he led the Webb band for Ella Fitzgerald. He auditioned for a job on ABC's Blue network, got it, and stayed four years, working with leaders like Paul Whiteman and Paul Laval. For two years he conducted the band in *A Streetcar Named Desire*. After touring South America with Cab Calloway in 1951, he became involved, like so many musicians of his generation, in the Dixieland revival and often played with Sidney Bechet at Ryan's. ("When Sidney got drunk he'd say, 'You got it the rest of the night!.' Then he'd go home.") The big-band business had deteriorated as a result of wartime taxes and other restrictions.

"For about ten years," Barefield said, "people forgot to dance. The music became listening music, and the bands began to stop swinging. When you have to get the people to dance, you have to swing!

"For me, the greatest alto player who ever lived is Benny Carter. Charlie Parker brought a whole new and fresh thing to saxophone playing, but there was no comparison in terms of sound. Benny's fitted him for playing lead *and* solo work. Charlie's led to solo work only. It wasn't right for a lead sax, but he was one of the most talented musicians. Today, all these young white kids have got a Charlie Parker school going. And not all the bop tones were bad. For instance, Clifford Brown, the trumpet player, played all the stuff and had a big, fat sound with it.

"I think there is a misunderstanding among the younger musicians.

There's a time for a straight sound and a time for vibrato. A musician like Benny Carter can play with or without vibrato, as all good saxophone players can. When you play in harmony together, and everybody has a different part, vibrato should be used, but when you play in unison and everybody's playing the same thing, then you need the straight tone. People who rehearse bands, and a lot of musicians, don't always know this.

"Basie's band *sounds* better rehearsed than all the other bands I know of today. I give the credit to one man, Marshall Royal. He's a thorough, trained musician, good on both alto and clarinet, and he turned out to be one of the greatest lead men. He and Bobby Plater are both from the Benny Carter school. I don't agree with people who said Marshall played too loud. Benny played strong like that, too, and he could take a bunch of mediocre saxophone players and make them sound good. When Marshall wanted to come down, he'd bring that whole section to a whisper, but when he came on strong, I don't think the rest of 'em had the technique to come up with him, especially on fast numbers."

A hardy survivor, Barefield continues to play with enthusiasm and conviction in all kinds of contexts, but he is not blind to the realities of his profession: "The record companies have played God and changed the whole trend. The first thing they ask is, 'What's your gimmick?' There's no gimmick in just playing good music."

(1972)

Leo "Snub" Mosley

"I was born in Little Rock, Arkansas, December 29, 1910. I used to be a clown in school, and that's where I got my nickname, after a popular comedian called Snub Pollard. The high school band was my first step. My parents weren't musical and I had no tuition at all. I got different trombone books and just studied and practiced. The books tell you the positions, and you go from there to chords and things like that. The first real lessons I ever had were years later in New York with David Gornston.

"I was inspired by a trombone player in Little Rock called Slats. He played with Sterling Todd and His Rose City Orchestra. Todd played piano and had about ten pieces. Alphonso Trent got his inspiration from that band.

"Trent formed a band in Fort Smith and came down to Little Rock. He had James Peter and Hayes Pillars playing saxophones. They looked a bit like Mexicans, and so did Trent. He was a beautiful piano player, and he always kept the style he started out with. His band could swing, but it also played pretty music. I was fifteen when I joined, and my father, who was a drayman with wagons and trucks, didn't want me to leave home.

"There wasn't much work around Little Rock, apart from hotels one or two nights a week. Sometimes we'd go to Brinkley or Memphis, for a short engagement. Eventually we decided we were going into Texas. That's why I believe in predestination. It was one of those things that determined our destiny.

"We called Trent 'Foney,' short for Alphonso. He was wealthy and his parents were considered to be among the few Negro millionaires at that time. Real estate was their game. Trent didn't need to worry. He was Grand Master of a couple of lodges, and he really got into music for kicks, but nevertheless we found out about hunger on our travels.

"We played three or four towns on the way to Texas. I remember we played a show right in front of Sale's Drugstore in Helena. One day we made only six dollars, out of which we had to buy sandwiches and pay for our night's lodging. We were nine pieces and we traveled in three cars. The great A. G. Godley was on drums and Britt Sparks on tuba. A bit later we got Peanuts Holland on trumpet.

"The section we went into was very bad, racially speaking. We played a place called McKinney and they advertised us on the front page of the newspaper: FAMOUS NIGGER BAND HERE TONIGHT. Nigger, not Negro! I kept that paper for years. It was insulting talk, but a lot of them had used the term for years and forgotten its significance. There were intelligent and quite nice white people in Texas who had become so accustomed to using it that they wouldn't think of apologizing.

"When we got to Dallas, we played a curb dance out at a park. We didn't have many people, but the guys just felt like playing. In the meantime, a bellhop at the Adolphus Hotel had told the manager about our band, and at intermission he took Trent over and introduced him to Mr. Ellifritz and a bunch of people sitting over on the side.

" 'I think we might just try you fellows out for a couple of weeks at the hotel,' they said.

"In the Southwest, where I was born, it was not unusual to play in big hotels for white dances, but we were the first colored band to play for a white audience in the state of Texas. Not only that, we were playing in the Adolphus Hotel, *the* biggest hotel in Texas at that time. The Goulds, the Rockefellers, they all came to that hotel. I never forget when Paul Whiteman came and stayed there in 1926. His band was nationally famous, and when Henry Busse, his trumpet player, came up to me and said, 'Young fellow, I like what you're doing,' I thought it was a heck of a compliment.

"We went in there for two weeks and stayed a year and two months.

The difference between then and now was that we had to go in and out by the back elevator, although inside we had every compliment and respect. No such thing as using the front door, even though we were artists! Management couldn't do anything about that then, and they took a big gamble when they got us in there. It was a big step forward, and the Ku Klux Klan planned to tar and feather us, just because we were playing for the white people. That wasn't the feeling of the majority, especially not of the big, rich people, but only of the lower element, the crackers.

"There was some opposition, too, from the biggest white band around there, the Jimmy Joy band that played hotels in Dallas and the Muehlebach Hotel in Kansas City. Later on, we played the Muehlebach, too.

"After we left the Adolphus, we were at the Gunter Hotel in San Antonio for six or eight months. I met Buddy Rogers and Clara Bow there. It was big time! When we started broadcasting over one of the biggest stations in the nation, WFFA in Dallas, we used to get an enormous number of letters from all over, even from Canada. We became so famous in Texas, Arkansas, and Oklahoma that we used to make even more money when we went on tour than at the hotel engagements. To make ten dollars then was like making fifty nowadays, and often we'd make as much as seventy-five apiece a night. If it had all been organized with agents as in New York, we wouldn't have made as much, but we didn't have agents to contend with. Everybody was writing about the band in those days, because it had done what they called the impossible. All the men were upright guys. They dressed beautifully, carried themselves and behaved well—and they played! I really got my schooling in that band.

"Trent was a happy-go-lucky guy, but he knew what he wanted. As I said, we used stocks, but we also had great head arrangements. When he brought Sy Oliver in, Sy changed the band somewhat, but we didn't let him change it too much! He was a better arranger than he was a trumpet player, but he was only in the band, I would say, about six months.

"I did the writing on *I Found a New Baby*, and it was a hit when the record came out. I think Gus Wilson did *Clementine*, which was on the back. He was Teddy Wilson's brother and a very good arranger. I'll tell you why *Clementine* sounds like Lunceford to you. Trent was Lunceford's inspiration.

"When we first got famous, we went to Memphis to play a dance, and Jimmie Lunceford came to it. In fact, I gave him his first arrangement. I don't remember what it was, but I sneaked it out of our book and let him copy it, and then put it back. Willie Smith was playing in a local school band that Jimmie was teaching, and Sy Oliver was still with Zach Whyte. By the time Sy joined us, we had three trumpets, two trombones, and four saxophones. He was quite enthused about the band and the fine musicians in it, and we were quite enthused about his arranging.

"I took most of the trombone solos, but Gus Wilson took some. I never have been influenced by other trombone players, and I always had my own style. Sometimes people say, 'Doggone, you sound like Tyree Glenn!' That's because I gave him his first lessons. He used to come to Dallas when he was a little boy, and I used to slip him into the dances.

"The guy that impressed me most was Jack Teagarden. He was with Mal Hallett when we played a battle of music in a restaurant in Cleveland. He impressed me greatly and we exchanged compliments. Jimmy Harrison I heard only on records, but I don't believe what people say about Teagarden getting his stuff from Jimmy.

"Tommy Dorsey wasn't a jazz soloist, but he could play beautiful, melodic music. I like both Dicky Wells and J. C. Higginbotham, as friends and trombonists. They came up about the same time as I did, but they didn't influence me. I always stressed tone, and no matter how fast I played I always tried to keep my tone going.

"Going back to the Trent band, I should say that a lot of the time Sy Oliver stood up and conducted. It was when he left that we got George Hudson. We also got Stuff Smith. We'd heard of him, and he used to stand in front of a little group and direct it. He played a helluva jazz violin, as you know. He was one of the greatest I ever heard. I've heard other guys who were sweeter, but for swing and all-round band work, jazz, and everything, he was *it*. He sang and danced, too, and so did I. We made a record for Gennett where Stuff, Hayes Pillars, and I were the vocal trio. It was on *Gilded Kisses*, the first number I ever wrote.

"We played in different sections of the Adolphus. One day we'd be in a place called The Spa, where there was no dancing at all. Bambooland was another place that was just for listening. In both of them, besides jazz and sweet, we'd play silly classics like *William Tell*, but not in the Junior Ballroom. Besides Stuff on violin, we had Wendell Hayman, who doubled on alto and violin.

"We went back to the Adolphus Hotel twice, each time for three or four weeks. It's still a fine hotel, and my biggest ambition is to go back there with my own group. It's owned by the Busch family, and money is no object.

"The second time we played San Antonio, we were at the Plaza Hotel for six months. It was in San Antonio that I picked up the slide saxophone. I heard a guy there who had something that was almost like mine, but more like a whistle. Anyway, it gave me the idea. It's altogether different from the trombone. The positions are smaller, and it slides up and down, which was awkward for me at first. It's not a real complicated instrument, but you've got to play the exact positions because they're close together. Nobody who set his mind on it would have much trouble. Very few of these instruments have been made, because there has never been any promotion. But I've had mine stolen twice. The second time I had to buy my own instrument back! I used to use a trombone mouthpiece, but now I use a sax mouthpiece on what is basically a soprano sax.

"The Trent band broke up in Albany, in 1932, I think. We'd just finished playing the Kenmore Hotel there. That's when the original Ink Spots came into being. Charlie Fuqua was singing with Trent, and the guitar player was up in front of the band. We'd picked them up in Indianapolis where they had an act. When we broke up, we decided to drive to Cleveland, and there I introduced them to Deek Watson, the original owner of the Ink Spots. The three of them got together in the Majestic Hotel, and then they went to Cincinnati and got Hoppy, the fourth Ink Spot.

"I started working around Cleveland in little dumps with small groups. I worked in one place where I made about twelve dollars a week. With tips, you might end up with thirty dollars. You couldn't save any money, but you could live fairly well on that. Then Claude Hopkins told me they needed a band in St. Louis, and I turned that over to Jeter and Pillars. I went down and played with them about a week, until they got straight, and then I came back and joined Claude Hopkins.

"I was with Claude about a year. That was some rhythm section he had—Claude on piano, Henry Turner on bass, Pete Jacobs on drums. They were really swinging.

"Ethel Waters came to Little Rock with Johnny Dunn and His Jazz Hounds when I was still in school. That was when I first became aware of jazz and a lover of it. Back in the early thirties, when we said a guy took a 'hot' solo, we meant he was jumping and swinging. Of course, Louis Armstrong started a lot of that. I think we were all influenced by him, no matter what instrument we played. When I went with him after I left Claude Hopkins, that was the biggest thrill of all.

"I joined without a rehearsal, but I'd had my schooling with Trent and could sight-read anything, so I had no trouble at all. Although I hadn't had a teacher, all the studying, practicing, and playing with first-class musicians—that paid off. I guess if I had had teachers they

would have told me not to get my tone the way I did. But to my mind
the best way for a man to get his tone or notes is the way he knows
how to get 'em. You take Dizzy Gillespie—I don't see how he does it.
I was always determined to play my horn right, and I tried to be
original. My chops are as strong today as when I was twenty-five. I
massage my gums, all my teeth are strong, and I practice as much
today as I ever did.

"Louis Armstrong had taken over Luis Russell's band. It was just a
background for Louis, really, but there were musicians in it, like Louis
Bacon, Harry White, J. C. Higginbotham, Charlie Holmes, Pops
Foster, and Paul Barbarin. I wrote a song called *Man with a Funny
Horn*, meaning my slide saxophone, and they did it on just one show
at the Earle Theater in Philly. It wasn't very good, so they took it out
and I never got a chance to do much of anything after that.

"I was with Louis a bit over a year, and it made headlines in the
Amsterdam News when I left: *Mosley Quits Armstrong*. I quit because I didn't get a chance to play anything of my own. I went out on
a tour with Fletcher Henderson for a few weeks, playing a lot of
college dates in New England at places like Yale and Harvard. Chu
Berry was in the band. They had some of the damnedest music, in
keys like B-natural. You're supposed to be able to play in any key,
but . . .

"Then I went with Fats Waller's big band for a few months. The
first engagement was at the Howard Theater in Washington, and after
that we had a lot more theater dates. It was better, but I still couldn't
play like I wanted to play.

"When I left Fats I organized my own band of six pieces. We used
to broadcast on that '*Round the Town* program over WNEW. My first
job as a bandleader was at Maury's Tavern up in the Bronx. I had
Sheets Tolbert on alto and he was very good. He's teaching down in
Texas now. Freddie Jefferson was on piano, Carl Smith on trumpet.
We went from the Bronx to the Famous Door on 52nd Street for about
three months, in 1938, and then over to the Onyx. I was at Leon and
Eddie's for a couple of weeks, singing and entertaining. Then we went
to the Queens Terrace on Long Island, in 1939, when Alan King and
Jackie Gleason worked downstairs. I was with the William Morris
Agency by this time, and they put me in the roof garden of the
Wisconsin Hotel in Boston in 1940. From there we went to Hollywood,
playing places in between like the Beachcomber in Omaha. We were in
Billy Berg's Swing Club a couple of months, broadcasting coast to
coast. Ken Murray heard us, came down and caught us one night,
and put us into his show, *Ken Murray's Blackout*, a great hit. That

would be about 1942. We started recording for Decca in 1940. *Amen* was really improvised at a 1941 session. It sold well, but Woody Herman's version sold even better.

"In 1945, I went overseas on a USO tour. It was during the war and they needed entertainment. We were gone nearly a year, in New Guinea, the Philippines, the East Indies, the Bismarck Sea—all those areas. I had Bill Johnson, who used to be with Erskine Hawkins, on alto, Bob Carroll on trumpet, and A. G. Godley on drums. He's still around, in Seattle. He used to drink very heavily, but he was one of the greatest drummers I ever listened to. I think Jo Jones would agree with me about him, although their styles are different. I think A.G. may have started that bit where everybody jumps off the bandstand and leaves the drummer to work out by himself up there.

"It's been small groups for me since then, all the time. Around 1945 I got Keg Purnell, a big asset, on drums. We were at the Hundred Club in New York for about eight months, and on the ABC network. I went in the Follies on Broadway in 1955 or 1956 and stayed until 1961, all the time playing both instruments. Then I was out at The Sands at Needle Beach for six seasons, and The Sands in Las Vegas isn't any finer.

"I keep thinking the trend is away from rock toward jazz and melody, but you know the guys promoting rock are not going to take that lying down. So they call it the 'now' sound. When I went back to visit my father in Little Rock, I was going to play with a rock group there until one guy began screaming at the top of his lungs over a powerful mike. The group knew three chords, but not very well. Times sure do change."

(1971)

Sir Charles Thompson

"Hey, Chase," Illinois Jacquet called, "ain't you got one of those tunes, man?"

"Yes, here's one!" Sir Charles Thompson answered.

It was May 21, 1947, and the record session had not been fruitful until that moment, when Thompson took charge. "I want you to play this soft, fellows," he said. "Joe, I want you to use a mute. You play the melody. I'll answer on the piano. Illinois, you take the middle." There were two takes and a new jazz standard was born.

"So far as I was concerned," Thompson said, "I didn't care if they called it *Mud in the Hole,* but Fred Robbins was a big disc jockey then and I could see the possibilities when they named it *Robbins' Nest.* Jacquet's managers were under the impression it was his tune and they arranged for all kinds of people to record it. Claude Thornhill made one of the best versions, a classic, and I think he and I have a similar conception of piano playing. Later on, after Ella Fitzgerald had made her record of it, they brought in someone else to write words, so

now there are three names on the song and it is no longer *Robbins'*
Nest but *Why Have a Falling Out Just When We're Falling In Love?*

"It's surprising how many ditties come out of the backgrounds of
arrangements. The riffs you set behind ad lib solos can often become
songs, and that was just what happened with *Robbins' Nest*. It was one
of many tunes I had in my head, and I had been writing music and
lyrics since I was sixteen. Singers, for instance, have always been crazy
about a song called *Wishing Well* I wrote on a bus between Philly and
Washington, but, like a lot of others, it has never been published or
recorded. After *Robbins' Nest*, I wore out many pairs of shoes going
up and down Broadway trying to place my songs. They would want to
change the words to make them sound like other songs, and they had
all kinds of other unoriginal ideas. So many of these guys in the publishing business imagine they are in a position to say what will or will not
be a hit. If they are such geniuses, why don't they write hits themselves? I never would go in with my hat in my hand and one knee on
the floor, so some doors were closed in my face because of that, and
word got around that I was pretty hard to deal with. Well, I had spent
a lot of time learning to play, but I had also picked up some ideas about
music.

"Today, you may have talent, but it isn't necessarily accepted, because you have competition from rock 'n' roll and what is known as
'progressive' music, a term which in my opinion is just a lot of
baloney. It's not progressive music. It's just another style. I don't know
anyone in the world who plays more alto than Buster Smith, and he's
thirty years older than Vaseline. When they start telling me someone
like Ornette Coleman is a genius, I don't go along with that at all. What
word are they going to use for musicians like Coleman Hawkins, Duke
Ellington, and Art Tatum? Music is made by musicians and singers,
but critics and a. and r. men have taken the front seat instead of the
back seat. Rock 'n' roll is nothing but a manufactured product. They
take the very least of jazz and build it up to where people accept it.
Anyone can play it, if he has the nerve—and very little pride! The
musicians who play rock 'n' roll *best* are musicians who can't play anything else. When I talk about rock 'n' roll I'm mad, and I don't try to
hide the fact.

"As far as I'm concerned, the guys who made big-band jazz too
complicated are as bad as those responsible for rock 'n' roll. I remember
when you could hear 'progressive' musicians along the street saying,
'Count Basie isn't playing anything,' because he wasn't playing what
they were playing. If you're too far over the people's heads, no one
understands it. If it's beneath the people, you're underestimating their
intelligence. I hope the day will soon come when we musicians can

play as we feel, as we did when I started in the game. And if you didn't play well, you couldn't get on the same bandstand with those who could. You have to have qualifications. But the way rock 'n' roll has it now, it makes a man with no qualifications stand up and fill his chest out, just as though he were a real artist. That isn't fair to musicians or the public."

The son of a Methodist minister, Thompson was born in Springfield, Ohio. The whole family was musical. Although his mother played piano, and his sister, a schoolteacher, taught the same instrument, he began his musical career at school on violin. He took instruction for three years and found it interesting until he realized how few were the opportunities in classical music. "There was," he said, "even less opportunity for violin in jazz. I don't think I heard any jazz on the fiddle until well into the thirties, and that was by a guy who played around Chicago.

"I became interested in jazz because it was a way of expressing myself freely. I understand nonmusicians who say they envy us, because we have this way of expressing moods and emotion that they haven't. I can be very disgusted with life and the business, but if I can play piano, I can lose myself in the music completely. It's like medicine to me, or golf.

"Golf was my real first love, and indirectly it led me back to music. You have many interests as a child, but from the age of twelve on I've been very definitely interested in golf. I caddied for Jimmy Thompson at that time in Broadmoor, Colorado. We were only allowed to play in the early hours of Monday, but I soon became good at the game. We used to practice with one club, a niblick, back and forth in a field, a hole at each end. Now I'm lucky if I shoot under ninety. But it's surprising how much a child sees, and hears. I didn't like the tone of voice or the names some of those players would use when I was shagging balls for them, and the restricted opportunities for playing made me think about music again. Everybody wanted to hear music, no matter who you were or what you looked like. They would accept you if you played good jazz, because there were not too many who could.

"Very few people recognize the similarity between golf and jazz. There are almost identical conditions in both. There's a fundamental way of playing, but there's no set pattern for doing it the same way twice. You're always trying to improve your game and there's always a challenge. It's the challenge that makes you lose yourself and give off your emotions. You can get mad, you can explode, or you can be happy because you made a terrific shot. Even if your ball falls in the exact spot it fell in yesterday, your shot isn't going to be the same. To get that ball on the green depends on how the wind is blowing, and you have to consider how damp it is, or how the ball's going to roll when it hits the green.

"When you play piano or organ, you're thinking all the time of the chord changes that go with the piece, but simultaneously you disregard the chords to an extent to play what you feel. In golf, there are certain ways you make a shot, to make it go high or low, or maybe curve to the left or right, and it requires quick thinking as in music, because you can never stand around long figuring what kind of shot to make. For instance, when you make a shot out of the trap, you're taught to 'explode' it, which means hitting the sand about a couple of inches behind the ball and following through, but plenty of times the shot requires you to hit the ball itself. You have to size this up in a moment. Sometimes you play music softly for expression, sometimes loudly. Sometimes you hit a golf ball soft and easy, sometimes hard. You look the course over like a map, and what's more like a map than an arrangement?"

"My family wasn't poor, but there was always a certain economic strain. So I've done many things, none of which I'm ashamed of. I've shined shoes and washed cars; I've been a bellhop, an elevator operator, and a hotel clerk; but as a caddy I learnt lessons in psychology that have been invaluable.

"The very Christian background I had didn't fit jazz, but my father wasn't critical. In fact, he always told me the important thing was to do *well* whatever I was interested in, but I knew it wasn't too good for him to have a son playing jazz in nightclubs when he might be in the pulpit preaching against that kind of life. So I joined a Franklin D. Roosevelt project, the Civilian Conservation Corps, which had to do with clearing land and forest. I was sixteen, but I put my age up to eighteen to get in, and I went to Cape Girardeau, Missouri, near St. Louis. It was from there I branched out into bands. I had gone through two or three piano books while learning violin, and I had had good teachers. I became the company clerk, played piano in the mess and then with local bands. They were not very good, but I was *heard*.

"I got an administrative discharge to better myself and joined Cecil Scott, who had one of the best bands in the Midwest then. This wasn't the same Cecil who came to New York in the twenties, but the band included the late Eddy Byrd, an outstanding drummer from my hometown. The other great band in St. Louis at that time was Jeter-Pilars's. Alphonso Trent's was another fine outfit operating in the area which included St. Louis, Memphis, Dallas, Oklahoma City, and Kansas City.

"I was too young and inexperienced to keep up the pace with Scott. Eventually, I was stranded and had to return to my family, which was then in Parsons, Kansas. That was the hometown of Buck Clayton, whose father was also a minister, although of another denomination. It was then I really got my inspiration to stay in the music field. Buck had just returned from China and was about to join Count Basie. In a small town like that, he was a kind of idol. He paid me a couple of compliments which encouraged me to believe I might make it some day. So I went off again with the first band that came along, a small one, what you might call a carnival band, and this time against my father's wishes. He didn't like the look of the little ragged bus we traveled in. I left that band in Omaha, Nebraska, because they weren't making any money at all. The guy would give you thirty-five cents for food, and though you take chances when you're young, I got tired of eating only one meal a day.

"Lloyd Hunter had had a good band long before I joined him and I was very happy when he came after me with a job. Gus Johnson was in that band, but he was playing bass fiddle. I remember one time it was so cold in North and South Dakota that he played with his gloves on! Debo Mills was on drums and he was compared with Jo Jones, they were so much alike. Debo was with Horace Henderson for a while later on, but he never got a chance to branch out in the East.

"As a pianist, I had originally been influenced by Claude Hopkins. I heard him in broadcasts from New York while we were living in Columbia, Missouri. Then I heard Fats Waller, and he influenced me, too. Another real inspiration was Duke Ellington. I was impressed not only by his music, but by his diction, his choice of words, his manner of dressing, and his suave personality. I'm sure he gets a bang out of words and it's original in our field. There are plenty of people who dress themselves up in tails, but then when they speak the words don't coincide with the clothes they're wearing. Of course, Art Tatum had the greatest of all influences on me, as he had on most pianists of his time, because of his ingenious imagination, his creativity, his speed, and his flawless performances. He's a subject I could talk about all night.

"By the time I left Lloyd Hunter to join Nat Towles, I was reading music well enough for a jazz pianist. In the normal stock arrangement you can cut a corner, because the chords are written above the notes in the staff. I had remained limited for a time through reading the chords and ignoring the notes. You hardly ever got to read sheet

music, but I had been doing that, working over popular songs, out
of my own ambition. Now I began to study arranging, for the men
in the Towles band were an inspired bunch and very competitive in
their thinking. They felt they were waiting for the chance to get to
New York to compete with Basie, Lunceford, and Duke Ellington.
John Hammond tried his best to get them there, but Nat couldn't see
where it would be to his advantage, and he was afraid of big offers
attracting his men away. Buddy Tate was a spark in the tenor department. On trombone we had the late Fred Beckett, and Henry Coker,
who, in my estimation, is unrecognized as one of the greatest trombones in the world. There was C. Q. Price on alto, a fine musician and
arranger. 'Little Nat,' a cousin of Nat Towles, was on drums. He kept
good time and wasn't in the way.

"C.Q. and a couple of the other fellows had had more experience
in arranging and I got quite a few tips from them. I studied all the
great bands and when I wanted further information I would take a
regular lesson. I was influenced by what I heard, but I often didn't
know who had written the arrangements I liked. I became aware of
what Andy Gibson was doing for Count Basie and Charlie Barnet,
realized he was a great arranger, and grew very interested in the
way he voiced. Then I was attracted to Fletcher Henderson. He was
so very valuable to Benny Goodman because he would write those
swinging ideas with simple voicing that could be played and understood easily. Until Nat Towles broke up the big band a few years ago,
he still used some of the arrangements we wrote then. I believe Neal
Hefti played in that band after I left and picked up quite a few ideas
about arranging from the book.

"I drifted to California in another very good band, Floyd Ray's, but
it was having booking troubles and was on the verge of breaking up.
It had one of the greatest trumpets of the day in Charlie Jacobs. He
played the same as Dizzy Gillespie, but he was killed in a freakish
case of mistaken identity. Eddy Byrd was on drums. Count Basie's
band was in California at the time and Buddy Tate—a good friend
of mine—and all its members seemed very congenial people, and they
were very inspiring to young musicians who were trying, as far as
possible, to stay within the realm of normalcy. I played in some
pictures while I was in Hollywood and eventually joined Lionel
Hampton's first big band.

"I came East with Lionel and I have respect for him as a person
and an artist, but the music wasn't to my taste and I felt uncomfort-
able. He wanted the drummers to play a back beat all the time, and
that was bad for a pianist. Shadow Wilson joined and he wouldn't be
influenced. He had a lot of will power. One time there was a move to

fire him, but all the fellows liked Shadow so well and their sentiment was so strong that Lionel had to keep him. After Shadow left, there were never any great drummers with Lionel.

"I quit the band in Chicago and worked with George Clark in Buffalo until John Hammond persuaded me to come to New York in 1940 to join the Lee and Lester Young band at Café Society Downtown. That was where I got my title. There was an Earl, a Duke, and a Count, so I guess they thought they'd have a knight as well. It was a great little group. Besides Lee and Lester, there was Paul Campbell on trumpet, Bumps Myers on tenor, Red Callender on bass, and a wonderful guitar player, Louis Gonzales. After that, Red, Gonzales, and I played a little stint as the Red Callender Trio. Red's a terrific musician, a strongly built, soft-spoken man with a gentle personality. He has a big warm sound and he's one of the very few I ever heard play with Art Tatum and meld with him perfectly.

"I was with Lucky Millinder a couple of years, and although he wasn't a musician he was good to work for. He had a natural ability for directing music and he knew every part of the arrangements. He was a great favorite at the Savoy, but unfortunately the best bands he ever had never recorded owing to some recording ban. He had an alto player called William Swindell who was one of the greatest I ever heard. I wrote one or two arrangements for Lucky. By this time I had also contributed to Basie's book (did you ever hear *My, What a Fry?*), to Hampton's, Horace Henderson's, and Jimmy Dorsey's, but now I was concentrating on playing. You have to play to play well, but writing is something you can pick up as long as you can hold a pencil in your hand.

"Next, I decided I wanted to participate in the 52nd Street scene. This was the time when Roy Eldridge and Lips Page were supreme, before Dizzy Gillespie became famous. I played with them, with Don Byas, and Coleman Hawkins. I went to California in 1944 with Hawk and made some records and a picture. He was another great inspiration to me and I found the recording very exciting. My solo on *Stuffy* was the first that ever sounded good to me. When the group broke up, I ran into Illinois Jacquet. We had been in Hamp's band together and had remained friends. Knowing his Texas background, and what he and I have both been subjected to, makes me understand him. He, his brother Russell, and I became partners in a band, but it didn't do too well until we started recording in the East. Illinois was suddenly hot, and it was because he had the opportunity to showcase songs that I made him co-composer of *Robbins' Nest. Strange Hour* was in a similar vein, but it was in a key similar to *Body and Soul* and I think the middle changes were a little too complicated for the average ear.

"Jacquet had made a lot of noise with Jazz at the Philharmonic, but he made the greatest impression with that little band he had in 1947. I remember once we played a battle of music against Dizzy's big band over in Jersey. When we got through it sounded as though we had fourteen pieces and he had eight. We were Shadow Wilson, Al Lucas, Joe Newman, Russell Jacquet, J. J. Johnson, Leo Parker, Illinois, and myself, so that gives an idea of what was happening musically. Leo Parker had great talent. He had a tone like Harry Carney—and there are very few baritone players who have that full sound—and he played fast with all the modern figures and designs of Charlie Parker, and he knew his instrument.

"Eventually, I got discouraged and went back to California. I was away from music for quite a time. Jobs out there were very scarce and the only pianist working regularly was one of my favorites, Hampton Hawes, a terrific musician. He's an improvement on Bud Powell, plays as fast and intricate as anybody, but has a very beautiful and soft approach to ballads. What brought me back to music was a shortage of organ players. I never cared too much for organ. Although it was a novelty, and I liked to hear Fats Waller play it, I didn't care for the sound. A fellow hired me because he couldn't get anyone else to play it. So I studied the organ, stayed out there three years, decided to give New York another chance, and have been here ever since."

During this period, Thompson played at Count Basie's Bar on Seventh Avenue, and recorded for Columbia, Prestige, and the British Lansdowne Series. He went to Europe for the first time as pianist with Buck Clayton's band in 1961. "If my mother had not fallen sick," he said, "I'd still be in Europe. I enjoyed playing over there more than I enjoyed playing any time in my life, because the people were receptive and so sincere in their liking for music."

(1961)

33. *Richard Boone at the Newport Jazz Festival, 1968.* (Stanley Dance collection)

34. *Bobby Plater.* (Courtesy RCA Records)

35. *Basie backstage in England, 1977.* (Courtesy Valerie Wilmer)

36. *Count Basie and Jay McShann.* (Stanley Dance collection)

37. *Jay McShann at the piano.* (Courtesy Jay McShann)

38. *Jay McShann's Orchestra, McShann at the piano.* Left to right: *Bill Nolan, Walter Brown, Charlie Parker, Bob Mabane, Bernard Anderson, Harold Bruce, John Jackson, Harold Ferguson, Orville Minor, Joe Baird, Gus Johnson, Gene Ramey.* (Courtesy Gene Ramey)

39. *Jay McShann's Orchestra, early 1940.* Left to right: (*front*) *McShann* (*standing*), *Bob Mabane, Earl Jackson, Lester Taylor, William Scott, Joe Coleman;* (*rear*) *Gus Johnson, Lucky Enois, Gene Ramey, Orville Minor, Harold Bruce, Buddy Anderson, unknown.* (Courtesy Gene Ramey)

40. *Jay McShann's Orchestra at the Savoy Ballroom, 1941.* Left to right: (*front*) *McShann, Lucky Enois, Gene Ramey, Walter Brown, Bob Mabane, Charlie Parker, John Jackson, Freddie Culliver, Lawrence Anderson, Joe Taswell;* (*rear*) *Gus Johnson, Harold Bruce, Bernard Anderson, Orville Minor.* (Courtesy Gene Ramey)

41. Gene Ramey and Count Basie. (Courtesy Jack Bradley)

42. Left to right: *Earle Warren, Teddy Wilson, Jimmy Rushing, and Sir Charles Thompson.* (Courtesy Earle Warren)

43. *Gus Johnson sings at Colorado Springs.* Left to right: *Milt Hinton (bass; partially hidden), Clark Terry, Johnson, Zoot Sims, Frank Rosolino, Benny Carter.* (Courtesy Gus Johnson)

44. *Alphonso Trent's Orchestra.* Left to right: *A. G. Godley, T. Holder, Chester Clark, Snub Mosley, Gene Crook, Alphonso Trent, James Jeter, Brent Sparks, John Fielding (vocal), Bill Holloway.* (Courtesy Gene Crook)

45. Left to right: *Joe Newman, Paul Quinichette, and Buddy Tate recording.* (Courtesy Atlantic Records)

46. *Jimmy Witherspoon* (left) *and Chico Hamilton* (right) *at a Los Angeles concert.* (Stanley Dance collection)

47. *The Virginia Ravens on tour. Eddie Barefield, tenor saxophone, is at left center.* (Courtesy Eddie Barefield)

48. *Eddie Barefield's California Band—Barefield, alto saxophone, conducting. Pianist unknown; Buddy Harper (guitar); Al Morgan (bass); Lee Young (drums); "Country," Tyree Glenn (trombones); (left to right, front) Jack McVea, Hugo Dandridge, Paul Howard, Don Byas (reeds); (rear) Red Mack, Freddie Traynor, "Pee Wee" (trumpets).* (Courtesy Eddie Barefield)

Melvin Moore

(VOCALIST)

"Nobody in the family, so far back as I can remember, was musical, but although she didn't sing professionally, my mom had a marvelous voice. I was born in Oklahoma City and I got my formal training in high school there—cantatas, operettas, and so forth. I think Miss Zelia M. Brough was one of the great music teachers of all time, and she turned out some wonderful musicians. But Charlie Christian was like Peck's bad boy then. He wouldn't go to school, although he used to be on the school grounds sometimes with his banjo-uke. Charlie would be swinging and Professor Page, the principal, would have a hard time running the kids inside.

"I played valve trombone in the school band, and our music was mostly standard pieces. When I found out I could make four or five dollars a night singing, that was the end of the instrument. I had started in the church, of course, where all black people who sing start with spirituals and gospel songs. Then at school I began singing things like *Trees* and *Jeannie with the Light Brown Hair*, but I actually got known around Oklahoma City first as a blues singer, because

Jimmy Rushing was a dear friend of mine. Only my voice was more mellow than his, and I *liked* ballads, and eventually I became known as a ballad singer.

"I started out with Charlie Christian's brother, Eddie. He played piano and bass, and he was a good musician. The whole family was musical and they had a family band like Oscar Pettiford's people had. Eddie's father played bass, his mother piano, and another brother played a little fiddle. This brother's real name was Clarence, but we called him 'It.'

"The first date with Eddie was what we called a 'pig stand,' one where his little group and bandstand were set up in the middle of a barbecue. After I'd sung my song, I'd take my box and go out and collect some money! I enjoyed that first night, and from then on that's where we'd be weekends. The five of us would make sixteen or seventeen dollars a night. Then Charlie got so it was a case of three-for-me-and-one-for-you, and everybody got mad. So we broke it up for a time, but we got together again and worked in a little place called the Rhythm Club. That's where I became like the toast of Oklahoma City and everybody was talking about Melvin Moore.

"I first heard T-Bone Walker at the Boga ballroom in 1935. He was in tails, playing the guitar behind his neck, and doing the splits! He was out of Dallas, Texas, and he was the only black guy in a band led by Count Balaski. He was the star, and he used to set the people on fire. There was even a big write-up about him in the white paper. He was about four years older than me, and I was sixty at Halloween [1977]. Being a musician, he came down to Second Street, where Charlie Christian and everybody hung out. He and Charlie used to cut heads. The guy that taught Charlie everything on guitar was Chuck Richardson. He was a big man with big hands, and he could read music. He used to show Charlie things, and I think he showed T-Bone about chords, too. Charlie was nearly a genius and it seemed as though he could do whatever he wanted to do. He was one of the best pool players around, and he could dance as good as anybody.

"Andy Kirk's band came to town and played and broadcast from the same Boga Ballroom. His singer, Pha Terrell, came in the club where we were playing, and I was into my big song. Everybody turned around immediately, telling each other, 'Pha Terrell's in the house!' I died. That was my first feeling of the green thing, so I slipped out the back door. But Pha had heard about me, and two weeks later he came by my house with Willie Perry, a friend of mine and a saxophonist.

" 'I know how you felt, man,' Pha said, laying it on, ' 'cause the same thing happened to me.'

"He ran it down, and from then we were the best of friends. He was a jack-of-all-trades and, like Charlie Christian, it seemed he could do whatever he wanted to do. He'd been a boxer. Then he was a dancer, and when his feet went bad on him, he just started singing. He taught me everything I know about shortcuts in singing and how to do things. He was a sweetheart. After he left Andy Kirk, he went out to California about 1944, and died. When I heard about it, it just tore me up, because he was such a good friend.

"Andy Kirk's band stayed in Oklahoma City a long time, and that was when Mary Lou Williams heard Charlie Christian, who was playing so good and so differently from everyone else. Just on Mary Lou's say-so, Benny Goodman had to hear him. When Charlie first came to New York, he came by train. I was living at the Woodside Hotel at that time, and I went down to meet him. Gigs were very, very short then, but my hometown boy arrived with six or seven hundred dollars in his pocket. He gave me a hundred, and I was rich! Charlie went all over town cutting heads. I remember that Fred Waring was in New York and he had Les Paul, the guitar player, with him. Les used to come uptown and cut everybody's head—until he ran into Charlie, and Charlie dusted it.

"I had first left Oklahoma City in 1936. I ran away from home! I needed about three credits to finish high school. What happened was that Don Albert and his band—out of New Orleans—heard me sing when they came through, and they wanted me to join them. I couldn't wait to do that! They were based on San Antonio, Texas, and in October, right before my birthday, I got on a bus and went down there. My old man like to died about that: 'Three credits and don't want to finish high school, blah, blah, blah.'

"Don had one of the best bands in the Southwest. I stayed with him about a year and a half. Sometimes we worked right on the Mexican line in towns like McAllen, Harlingen, and Brownsville, where it was always nice and warm. I remember once we came out of Amarillo through a howling snowstorm in the panhandle, and the next day we were pulling oranges off the trees in McAllen. It was gorgeous, and I'd never seen anything like that before. I also made my first trip to New York with Don. I was doing mostly ballads with him, but when they made the records in San Antonio for Vocalion, they had a wonderful singer named Merle Turner, so I didn't get to record till I joined Ernie Fields.

"Don Albert's and Alphonso Trent's bands were about the best in that area, although there was a bunch of nothing-but-good, fifteen-piece bands around. Every city had one. There was Eli Rice's out of Minneapolis. Clarence Love had a nice little band. And there were

about five good bands in Kansas City alone. Nearly all of them were
trying to sound like Jimmie Lunceford's. They couldn't get to Duke,
but they would get as close as they could to Lunceford. To come to
New York was *everybody's* dream then. That was *it!* Some of 'em
made it and some of 'em didn't. And there were *some* musicians out
there! Henry Bridges, a saxophone player out in Oklahoma, could play
as good as anybody. There was John Hardee out of Texas. Arnett
Cobb, Buddy Tate, Illinois Jacquet, and Budd Johnson—they all came
out of Texas, and good bands. Milton Larkins had one of those bands
and I just heard he's left New York, bag and baggage, and gone back
home to Houston, to some kind of music job on the radio.

"I left Don Albert because of my dad. He kept leaning on it: 'Why
don't you come home and finish high school?' So I went back and did
that, and during the Christmas holidays I was talking to Ernie Fields.
He had a band in Tulsa, which was about a hundred-and-twenty miles
away. He'd heard about me, because my name got around when I
was traveling with Don Albert, and he wanted me to work with him.
I was supposed to go to Langston University, but I told my dad, 'Man,
I've been out, I've seen what life's about, and you'd only be throwing your money away, because I don't think I could stand that school.'
He understood how I felt, and I played some good gigs with Ernie
during those Christmas holidays, and joined his band right afterwards.

"I was with Ernie Fields from 1938 to 1949. We were all over the
country, coast to coast. We played the Apollo every year. In fact,
Ernie's band was the only one Frank Schiffman allowed in there
twice a year at that time. We played the Savoy, we played everywhere. One of the outstanding musicians in the band was René Hall,
who played guitar and trombone, and was the arranger. Another was
Luther West, a very good saxophonist who had gone to school in
Tulsa with Earl Bostic. Tulsa was where we were established, our
base. We even had a little old hit called *T-Town Blues*, and I sang on
it: '*Goin' back to Tulsa to get my women in line . . .*' I'll tell you who
produced that record—Ahmet Ertegun, who went on to much bigger
things with Atlantic. We were successful, but we didn't really get the
breaks. John Hammond was the key to the whole thing then. He
brought a bunch of good bands into New York, but Basie's was his
preference, and he put all his energy behind it.

"I had offers from other leaders while I was with Ernie, but I stayed
because it was like home, and comfortable. Everybody thought I was
making a lot of money with him, but I was barely living. All I wanted
to do was sing, and maybe I never knew how good I was. But after
being ten years with one guy, other leaders thought they couldn't
afford me! When I did leave, I was supposed to work with Louis Jor-

dan. I had given Ernie a couple of weeks' notice in advance at the Apollo, and I went to Louis in Philadelphia.

"'Come on in, man,' Louis said. 'I've got some bad news.'

"'What's happened?'

"'Ernie's got a contract on you that can't be broken.'

"'I know better. There's no contract like that!'

"'Well, I'd rather not go through this thing.'

"He gave me a hundred dollars to go back to New York and rejoin Ernie, but I'd made my commitment and I wasn't going to do that. I spent a couple of weeks in New York, went to Chicago to see my mother's people, and then went back to Tulsa where my family was. (I was married by this time.) I got a little five-piece band together and started rehearsing. A man in the numbers business had some nice money, so he backed me and we worked for ourselves for a while. Then Diz [Gillespie] came through and played a dance in Tulsa.

"'Man, why don't you come on with the band,' he said, 'because Johnny Hartman's leaving?'

"'I'll think about it,' I said.

"That was in 1949. He kept bugging me, and finally he called and said, 'We're going in the Howard Theatre in two weeks. Come on! And that was my first gig with them, along with Sammy Davis and the Will Mastin Trio. *Everybody* was in that band! The piano player was John Lewis. Al McKibbon was on bass. Paul Gonsalves and John Coltrane were in the reed section. Melba Liston was on trombone. It was just a super band, but it broke up after I'd been with them about six months. I decided I was going to stay in New York and not go back to Tulsa.

"One day I was walking the streets and ran into René Hall. He had been writing for Earl Hines, but now he had also come to New York to stay.

"'Hey, man, what're you doing?'

"'Nothing too much,' I said.

"'Look, they're having a rehearsal at the Savoy with Fletcher Henderson.'

"So I went up there. Lee Richardson and a lot of others were trying to get the gig. Lucky Thompson was on the band, and when he saw me he walked me over to Smack [Henderson].

"'Hey, Smack,' he said, 'here's your singer!'

"I worked with Fletcher at the Savoy about six months. It was really a pick-up band. I remember Joe Benjamin and Don Lamond were in it. That must have been about 1950, and thanks to Joe Benjamin I next got a job with Lucky Millinder. Lee Richardson was with Lucky at the time. He had been with Luis Russell and *The Very*

Thought of You was his big song. He got in trouble, got a habit, and Lucky couldn't deal with it. So then I worked with Lucky nearly two years, and we made some pretty nice sides, too. Anisteen Allen and I were the singers and I had to do some of the songs Trevor Bacon had done earlier on. Trevor had gone with Bull Moose Jackson and His Buffalo Bearcats, and he was killed in an automobile accident down South.

"Lucky kept a good book and he always had good bands. Everybody liked him because he paid everybody well. Jimmy Mundy was writing for him at the time, and although I sang mostly ballads, I did a little bit of everything, whatever they wanted me to do, even things like *Chew Tobacco Rag*, which we recorded for King. Lucky and I would also go and make those big transcription records for the army, which is how I came to record with people like Earl Hines and Erroll Garner. I don't know what they ever did with some of those things.

"After Lucky, it was tough going till I ran into Billy Bowen, who was with the Ink Spots. Bill Kenny had just given up the quartet, and we were like the second Ink Spots group, because Charlie Fuqua had one, too. I worked with Billy Bowen for fourteen years. He played sax and flute, and another guy played guitar. Besides singing, I played drums. I had done a little of that at school. We went to Europe, to the South Pacific, all over the world. In fact, we were on a round-the-world tour when we broke up. We were in Bangkok, three months on the way, and everybody got homesick. We were all married, we had money in our pockets, and we were just tired of being away from home. Billy was crying the blues then!

"I was going to get me a little trio and work around New York, because I was tired of the road. Then I ran into Joe Medlin, a good friend of mine from way back. He used to sing with Buddy Johnson's band. Joe put me in the record business, where I've been ever since. He introduced me to the boss at Decca and we got successful over there with Jackie Wilson and a few others. The first time I ever recorded had been in the Decca studio where they had that Indian on the wall with his arms stretched out, asking the question, 'Where's the melody?' What I got into was more or less promotion, not a. and r. work. All my life I'd been communicating with people, and I felt I was very lucky to come out of one phase into another that was related to it. Music has been my whole life, and I was just telling a fellow today how it all revolves around the thirteen notes to a scale, the chromatics and the majors. In forty years, I've heard it all, and the same notes are still there. The only thing that really changes in the music is the rhythms. But so much of the music today you wouldn't even have listened to when I was a kid. Everybody would have said it was junk!

"What they call 'soul' now is nothing but a word. It's been there all the time. The blues, all the music, is based on the gospel thing. Basically, all of it comes from the church. Soul is nothing but blacks singing the way they feel. Some guys sing now so you can see their veins standing out! James Brown, for example, hollering and screaming with no inhibitions—I guess that's soul. But the people I sang to enjoyed the way I did my songs. The first time I heard B. B. King, he was a ballad singer, singing pretty songs, and scuffling with a little four-piece band. It took the white college kids about thirty-five years to discover him!

"Now I'm with Prelude Records, but I'm not optimistic about the record business. The way the big companies are combining, they're going to put all the little ones out of business. If you're not part of a conglomerate, forget it! They're into everything—shoes, food, films, clothing, books, everything. I just don't understand what's happening, or why it's allowed to happen."

(1977)

Melvin Moore returned to his old role briefly when drummer Panama Francis organized the presentation of "Music of the Savoy Ballroom" at Carnegie Hall in 1975. The bands of Lucky Millinder and the Savoy Sultans were recreated by musicians of the New York Jazz Repertory Company, and Moore's vocals with the "Millinder" band, in which Panama Francis had also played, impressed with their professional authority.

APPENDICES

Some Basie Itineraries

There are repeated references in this book to arduous tours of one-nighters back and forth across the country. These tours became a necessity in prolonging the existence of big bands. In the beginning, each band would travel in several automobiles, but as buses became more comfortable and reliable, the rented bus became the primary means of transportation. Fuel shortages compelled the use of trains during World War II, and after the war the proliferation of airlines opened up the possibility of international one-nighters—particularly in Europe and Latin America—but today the bus remains the most common and economical form of band transportation within the United States.

The following itineraries of Count Basie and his orchestra will give some idea of what is involved in terms of travel and distances covered. But besides traveling, to perform at night, the musicians of course have to check in and out of hotels each day, pack and unpack bags, get meals as and when they can. It is a way of life with which men like Count Basie and Freddie Green have been familiar for over forty years—and that says much for their temperament and physical durability.

Right into the 1960s, there were clubs where big bands could occasionally sit down for engagements of two or more weeks, but these places have almost become a thing of the past. Clubs such as Birdland, Basin Street East, the Cotton Club, and Grand Terrace, and Connie's Inn are long gone, and so are ballrooms such as the Savoy. Theaters that once employed bands as part of their stage shows no longer do so. What remain for big bands, essentially, are single concert and dance dates, usually in a different venue—when not in a different city—each night. An agent's commission for such bookings is customarily 15 percent, instead of the 10 percent for longer engagements. Transportation costs continually rise, as do the musicians' hotel and living expenses, and these together lead to higher salaries. . . . All of which attests to a measure of the heroic in the way Count Basie has for so long maintained a band of superior quality.

Itinerary for the period March 1–30, 1965

March   1   University of South Florida, Tampa, Florida
          2   Schrafft's Carriage House, Cocoa Beach, Florida
          3   Officers' Club, Charleston Air Force Base, Charleston, South Carolina
          4   Bennett College, Greensboro, North Carolina
          5   Rutgers University, New Brunswick, New Jersey
          6   Aronimink Country Club, Newtown Square, Pennsylvania
          7   NCO Club, Bolling Air Force Base, Washington, D.C.
          8   Frostburg State College, Frostburg, Maryland
          9   Downtown Motor Lodge, Mansfield, Ohio
        10   Meldwood Lounge, Brynon, Pennsylvania
        11   Macero's Tavern, Glens Falls, New York
        12   Gouverneur Morris Hotel, Morristown, New Jersey
        13   Open date
        14   Academy of Music, Philadelphia, Pennsylvania
        15   E. M. Club, Navy Training Station, Bainbridge, Maryland
        16   Hammond High School, Alexandria, Virginia
        17   Palace Theatre, Lorain, Ohio
        18   Open date
        19   Kiel Auditorium, St. Louis, Missouri
        20   Sheraton-Chicago Hotel, Chicago, Illinois

21 Holiday Ballroom, Chicago, Illinois
22 IBCW Hall, Local 1031, 5247 W. Madison, Chicago, Illinois
23 Club Laurel, Chicago, Illinois
24 Prom Ballroom, St. Paul, Minnesota
25 Civic Auditorium, Fargo, North Dakota
26 Open date
27 Sioux City, Iowa
28 Municipal Auditorium, Kansas City, Missouri
29 Hotel Savory, Des Moines, Iowa
30 WGN-TV, Chicago, Illinois

Itinerary for the period August 30–October 12, 1968

August 30 Century Plaza Hotel, Los Angeles, California
31 Recording date, Los Angeles, California
September 1 Factory Nite Club, North Hollywood, California
2 Jazz Suite, Beverly Hills, California
3–4 Recording dates, Los Angeles, California
5–14 Basin Street West, San Francisco, California
15 Friars Club, Beverly Hills, California
16 Hollywood, California
17–18 Sebastian's Hotel Eldorado, Sacramento, California
19 Chabot College, Hayward, California
20 Monterey Jazz Festival, Monterey, California
21 High Chapperal Ballroom, Chicago, Illinois
22 Laurel Club, Chicago Illinois
23 Miami Club, Miamiville, Ohio
24 Elks Lodge, Rochester, Michigan
25 Central Michigan College, Mt. Pleasant, Michigan
26 Rooser Tail, Detroit, Michigan
27 Chase Park Plaza Hotel, St. Louis, Missouri
28 St. Louis, Missouri
29 Orchestra Hall, Chicago, Illinois
30 Chicago, Illinois
October 1 Norfolk, Virginia
2 Jolly Roger, Brookfield, Connecticut
3 Steak Pit, Route 4, Paramus, New Jersey
4 Huntington Town House, Huntington, New York
5 Riviera, Port Washington, New York
6 Shannopinn Country Club, Pittsburgh, Pennsylvania

          7 Royal York Hotel, Canadian Room, Toronto, Ontario,
             Canada
          8 Coda Restaurant, Syracuse, New York
       9–11 Paul's Mall, Boston, Massachusetts
         12 Providence, Rhode Island

Itinerary for the period June 18–August 26, 1973

   June 18 Steamer Admiral, St. Louis, Missouri
         19 Pfister Hotel, Grand Ballroom, Milwaukee, Wisconsin
         20 Place des Arts, Montreal, Quebec, Canada
         21 Crossroads, Moira, New York
         22 Leisure Lodge, Preston, Ontario, Canada
         23 Richmond Hill Arena, Richmond Hill, Ontario,
             Canada
         24 Centennial Hall, London, Ontario, Canada
         25 The Grand Theatre, Kingston, Ontario, Canada
         26 Eduardo's Supper Club, Buffalo, New York
         27 Off
      28–29 Ramada Inn, Louisville, Kentucky
         30 Indianapolis Museum of Art, Indianapolis, Indiana
   July 1 Parkway Ramada Inn, Ballroom, Niagara Falls,
             New York
          2 Roseland Ballroom, New York, New York
          3 Carnegie Hall, Newport Jazz Festival, New York,
             New York
          4 Hopkins Plaza, Baltimore, Maryland
          5 Baynard Stadium, Wilmington, Delaware
          6 Stokesay Castle, Reading, Pennsylvania
          7 York Country Club, York, Pennsylvania
          8 Sheraton-Cleveland Hotel, Cleveland, Ohio
          9 Edinboro State College, Edinboro, Pennsylvania
      10–26 Off
         27 Eisenhower Park, East Meadow, New York
         28 St. Regis Hotel, New York, New York
         29 Watchung View Inn, Somerville, New Jersey
         30 Off
         31 Bethlehem, Pennsylvania
 August 1 High School Stadium, Clarkston, New York
          2 Ole Barn, Inlet, New York
          3 Brockton High School, Brockton, Massachsetts

   4 Off
   5 Jug End Resort, South Egremont, Massachusetts
   6 Brothers Two, Smithtown, New York
   7 Robin Hood Dell, North Philadelphia, Pennsylvania
   8 Rain date for August 7
9–11 Colonie Hill, Hauppage, New York
  12 Wisconsin State Fair, Milwaukee, Wisconsin
  13 Eastland Shopping Center, Harper Woods, Michigan
  14 River Oaks Shopping Center, Calumet City, Illinois
  16 Denver, Colorado
  17 Los Angeles, California
  18 Vancouver, British Columbia, Canada
  19 Seattle, Washington
20–26 Mr. Kelley's, Chicago, Illinois

Selected Discography

Many of the records in this discography, although no longer in catalog, can be found in specialist stores or on the mailing lists of secondhand dealers who advertise in such magazines as *Cadence* and *Coda*. The designation (E) after the record's number indicates an English release, (F) a French.

Count Basie
All records in this section are by Count Basie and His Orchestra unless otherwise noted.

BENNIE MOTEN'S KANSAS CITY ORCHESTRA, 1929–32	Victor LPV-514
THE BEST OF COUNT BASIE, 1937–39 (two discs)	Decca DXSB-7170
GOOD MORNING BLUES, 1937–39 (two discs)	MCA 2-4108
THE COUNT AT THE CHATTERBOX, 1937	Jazz Archives 16

COUNT BASIE AT THE FAMOUS DOOR, 1938–39	Jazz Archives 41
THE COMPLETE COUNT BASIE, VOLS. I to X, 1936–41 (ten discs)	CBS 66101 (F)
THE COMPLETE COUNT BASIE, VOLS. XI to XX, 1941–51 (ten discs)	CBS 66102 (F)

(The above two sets contain everything Basie recorded for the company, including previously unissued titles and alternative takes.)

SUPER CHIEF, 1936–42 (two discs)	Columbia G-31224
THE COUNT, 1939	Columbia P-14355

(The two comprehensive French sets contain everything on these U.S. releases, although SUPER CHIEF includes, oddly enough, several items on which Basie does not play! THE COUNT complements Columbia's Lester Young albums, q.v., and is notable for the total absence of Young as a soloist—despite which it remains a valuable collection.)

ONE O'CLOCK JUMP, 1942–50	Columbia JCL-997
THE V-DISCS, VOLS. I and II, 1943–45	Jazz Society (Sweden) AA-505, AA-506
COUNT BASIE, 1947–49 (three discs)	RCA FXM 3-7053 (F)

(All the essentials from Basie's underrated Victor period are included in this handsomely boxed set. Illogical groupings on single Victor and Camden LPs have been made from time to time. They may still be obtained occasionally, from specialist dealers.)

BASIE JAZZ (Count Basie Sextet), 1952	Clef 633
DANCE SESSION, 1953	Clef 626
DANCE SESSION #2, 1954	Clef 647
SIXTEEN MEN SWINGING, 1953–54 (two discs)	Verve 2-2517

(Many titles from the two DANCE SESSION albums are included in this reissue.)

BASIE, 1954	Clef 666
COUNT BASIE SWINGS, JOE WILLIAMS SINGS, 1955	Clef 678
APRIL IN PARIS, 1955	Verve 8012

HALL OF FAME, 1956	Verve 8291
AT NEWPORT, 1957	Verve 8243
THE ATOMIC MR. BASIE, 1957	Roulette 52003
BASIE PLAYS HEFTI, 1958	Roulette 52011
EVERY DAY I HAVE THE BLUES, 1959	Roulette 52033
BREAKFAST DANCE & BARBECUE, 1959	Roulette 52028
ONE MORE TIME, 1959	Roulette 52024
CHAIRMAN OF THE BOARD, 1959	Roulette 52032
NOT NOW, I'LL TELL YOU WHEN, 1960	Roulette 52064
KANSAS CITY SUITE, 1960	Roulette 52056
JUST THE BLUES, 1960	Roulette 52054
EASIN' IT, 1960–62	Roulette 52106
THE COUNT BASIE STORY, 1960 (two discs)	Roulette RB-1

(This is an interesting collection of Basie's hits from the thirties and forties as remade by the 1960 band, the soloists chiefly featured being Frank Foster, Billy Mitchell, Frank Wess, and Joe Newman. An excellent accompanying booklet by Leonard Feather is illustrated with a number of rare photographs, some from Mrs. Basie's personal collection.)

THE LEGEND, 1961	Roulette 52086
BASIE AT BIRDLAND, 1961	Roulette 52065
FIRST TIME (The Count Basie and Duke Ellington Orchestras together), 1961	Columbia CL 1715
ON MY WAY AND SHOUTIN' AGAIN, 1962	Verve V6-8511
COUNT BASIE & HIS KANSAS CITY SEVEN, 1962	Impulse AS-15
LI'L OLD GROOVEMAKER, 1963	Verve V6-8549
BASIE'S BEAT, 1967	Verve V6-8687
STRAIGHT AHEAD, 1969	Dot 25902
STANDING OVATION, 1969	Dot 25938
BASIE JAM (nonet), 1973	Pablo 2310-718
FOR THE FIRST TIME (trio), 1974	Pablo 2310-712
BASIE JAM, #2 (octet), 1976	Pablo 2310-786

BASIE JAM, #3 (octet), 1976   Pablo 2310-840
A PERFECT MATCH (with   Pablo D2312110
  Ella Fitzgerald), 1979
ON THE ROAD, 1979   Pablo D2312112

Several of the Roulette sets listed above have been incorporated in a
two-record series entitled ECHOES OF AN ERA, the relevant numbers being RE-102, RE-118, and RE-124. The Impulse album by the
Kansas City Seven and STANDING OVATION on Dot have been
united in another two-record set, Impulse IA-9351/2.

The Basie band has provided expert accompaniment to most of the
popular singers of the past three decades, such as Ella Fitzgerald,
Billy Eckstine, Frank Sinatra, Sarah Vaughan, Tony Bennett, Sammy
Davis, Jr., Arthur Prysock, Jackie Wilson, Kay Starr, Teresa Brewer,
and the Mills Brothers. Generally, these do not fall within the scope of
this book, but details of those records still available can be found
readily in the Schwann Catalog.

Jimmy Rushing

GOIN' TO CHICAGO, 1954   Vanguard 8518
LISTEN TO THE BLUES, 1955   Vanguard 8505
THE JAZZ ODYSSEY OF   Columbia CL 1152
  JAMES RUSHING, ESQ.,
  1956
IF THIS AIN'T THE BLUES,   Vanguard 8513
  1957
LITTLE JIMMY RUSHING &   Columbia CL 1152
  THE BIG BRASS, 1958
RUSHING LULLABIES, 1959   Columbia CL 1401
THE SMITH GIRLS, 1960   Columbia CL 1605
FIVE FEET OF SOUL, 1963   Colpix 446
BLUES & THINGS (with Earl   Master Jazz 8101
  Hines), 1967
GEE, BABY, AIN'T I GOOD   Master Jazz 8104
  TO YOU?, 1967
WHO WAS IT SANG THAT   Master Jazz 8120
  SONG?, 1967
EVERY DAY I HAVE THE   Bluesway 6005
  BLUES, 1967
LIVIN' THE BLUES, 1968   Bluesway 6017

THE YOU AND ME THAT USED TO BE, 1970	Victor LSP 4566

Lester "Prez" Young

THE LESTER YOUNG STORY, VOL. I, 1936–37, (two discs)	Columbia CG 33502
THE LESTER YOUNG STORY, VOL. II, 1937–38 (two discs)	Columbia JG 34837
THE LESTER YOUNG STORY, VOL. III, 1938–39 (two discs)	Columbia JG 34840
THE LESTER YOUNG STORY, VOL. IV, 1939–40 (two discs)	Columbia JG 34843
LESTER YOUNG & CHARLIE CHRISTIAN, 1939–40	Jazz Archives 42
PREZ AT HIS VERY BEST, 1943–44	Trip 5509
LESTER YOUNG & THE KANSAS CITY SIX, 1944	Commodore 15352
THE COMPLETE SAVOY SESSIONS, 1944–49 (two discs)	Savoy 2202
THE ALADDIN SESSIONS, 1945–48 (two discs)	Blue Note LA456-H2
LESTER SWINGS, 1945, 1950, 1951 (two discs)	Verve 2-2516
MEAN TO ME, 1954 & 1955 (two discs)	Verve 2-2538
PREZ & TEDDY & OSCAR, 1952 & 1956 (two discs)	Verve 2-2502
THE JAZZ GIANTS '56, 1956	Verve 1-2527
LAUGHIN' TO KEEP FROM CRYIN' 1956	Verve 8316
LESTER YOUNG AT OLIVIA DAVIS' PATIO LOUNGE, 1956	Pablo 2308-219

Buck Clayton

CLASSIC SWING OF BUCK CLAYTON, 1946	Riverside 142
JAM SESSION: THE HUCKLE BUCK & ROBBINS' NEST, 1953	Columbia CL 546

HOW HI THE FI, 1953–54	Columbia CL 567
ALL THE CATS JOIN IN, 1953–55	Columbia CL 882
BUCK CLAYTON JAMS BENNY GOODMAN FAVORITES, 1953–54	Columbia CL 614
BUCK MEETS RUBY, 1954	Vanguard 8517
JUMPIN' AT THE WOODSIDE, 1954	Columbia CL 701
CAT MEETS CHICK, 1955	Columbia CL 778
BUCK CLAYTON SPECIAL, 1957	Philips BBL 7217
BUCKIN' THE BLUES, 1957	Vanguard 8514
SONGS FOR SWINGERS, 1958	Columbia CL 1320
COPENHAGEN CONCERT, 1959 (two discs)	Steeple Chase 6006/7
BUCK & BUDDY, 1960	Swingville 2017
ONE FOR BUCK, 1961	English Columbia 33SX1390
ALL STAR PERFORMANCE, 1961	French Vogue LD 544-30
PASSPORT TO PARADISE, 1961	Inner City 7009
BUCK & BUDDY BLOW THE BLUES, 1961	Swingville 2030
ME & BUCK (with Humphrey Lyttelton), 1963	World Record Club T324
LE VRAI BUCK CLAYTON, VOLS. I & II, 1964	77 LEU 12/11 & LEU 12/18
JAM SESSION, VOL. I, 1974	Chiaroscuro 132
JAM SESSION, VOL. II, 1975	Chiaroscuro 143
JAM SESSION, VOL. III, JAZZ PARTY TIME, 1976	Chiaroscuro 152
JAM SESSION, VOL. IV, JAY HAWK, 1974–75	Chiaroscuro 163

Swingville 2017 and 2030 have been reissued together as KANSAS CITY NIGHTS, Prestige 24040. Similarly, THE GOLDEN DAYS OF JAZZ, CBS JC2L-614, contains Columbia CL 614 and CL 701.

Jo Jones

THE ESSENTIAL JO JONES, 1955–58 (two discs)	Vanguard VSD 101/02

JO JONES TRIO, 1958	Everest 5023
VAMP 'TIL READY, 1960	Everest 5099
PERCUSSION & BASS (with Milt Hinton), 1960	Everest 5110
DRUMS ODYSSEY, 1972	Jazz Odyssey 010 (F)
THE DRUMS, 1973 (two discs)	Jazz Odyssey 008 (F)
THE MAIN MAN, 1976	Pablo 2310-799

Eddie Durham

EDDIE DURHAM, 1973–74	RCA LPLI 5029 (E)

Earle Warren

EARLE WARREN, 1974	RCA LPLI 5066 (E)

Dicky Wells

DICKY WELLS IN PARIS, 1937	Prestige 7593
BONES FOR THE KING, 1958	Felsted 2006
TROMBONE FOUR-IN-HAND, 1959	Master Jazz 8118

Harry "Sweets" Edison

SWEETS AT THE HAIG, 1953	Pacific Jazz 11
SWEETS, 1956	American Record Society 430
GEE, BABY, AIN'T I GOOD TO YOU?, 1957	Verve 8211
THE SWINGER, 1958	Verve 8295
HARRY EDISON SWINGS BUCK CLAYTON, 1958	Verve 8293
MR. SWING, 1958	Verve 8353
SWEETENINGS, 1958	Roulette R-52023
JAWBREAKERS (with Lockjaw Davis), 1962	Riverside RLP 430
OSCAR PETERSON & HARRY EDISON, 1974	Pablo 2310.741
JUST FRIENDS, 1975	Black & Blue 33.106 (F)
EDISON'S LIGHTS, 1976	Pablo 2310.780
SIMPLY SWEETS (with Lockjaw Davis), 1977	Pablo 2310.806
EARL MEETS HARRY (with Earl Hines), 1978	Black & Blue 33.131 (F)

Buddy Tate

JUMPIN' ON THE WEST COAST, 1947	Black Lion 172 (E)
ROCK 'N' ROLL, 1954	Baton 1201
BUDDY TATE & HIS CELEBRITY CLUB ORCHESTRA, VOL. I, 1954	Black & Blue 33.006 (F)
ALL STAR JAZZ, 1955–56	Allegro 1741
SWINGING LIKE TATE, 1958	Bittersweet 827
TATE'S DATE, 1960	Swingville 2003
TATE-A-TATE with Clark Terry, 1960	Swingville 2014
GROOVIN', 1961	Swingville, 2029
BUDDY TATE (with Milt Buckner), 1967	Black & Blue 33.014 (F)
BUDDY TATE & HIS CELEBRITY CLUB ORCHESTRA, VOL. II, 1968	Black & Blue 33.020 (F)
UNBROKEN, 1970	Pausa 7030
BUDDY TATE (with Wild Bill Davis), 1972	Black & Blue 33.045 (F)
BUDDY TATE & EARLE WARREN, 1973	RCA LFLI 5034 (E)
MIDNIGHT SLOWS (with Wild Bill Davis), 1973	Black & Blue 33.054 (F)
KANSAS CITY WOMAN (with Humphrey Lyttelton), 1974	Black Lion 312 (E)
THE TEXAS TWISTER, 1975	Master Jazz 8128
JIVE AT FIVE, 1975	Mahogany 558.103 (F)
LOVE AND SLOWS (with Harry Edison), 1976	Barclay 900.550 (F)
BACK TO BACK (with Scott Hamilton), 1979	Concord CJ. 85

Helen Humes

HELEN HUMES, 1947–48	Trip 5588
HELEN HUMES, 1959	Contemporary 3571
SONGS I LIKE TO SING, 1960	Contemporary 3582
SWINGIN' WITH HUMES, 1961	Contemporary 3598
HELEN COMES BACK, 1973	Black & Blue 33.050 (F)

SNEAKIN' AROUND, 1974   Black & Blue 33.083 (F)
THE TALK OF THE TOWN,   Columbia PC 33488
  1975
ON THE SUNNY SIDE OF   Black Lion 30167 (E)
  THE STREET, 1975
HELEN HUMES & THE   Muse MR 5217
  MUSE ALL STARS, 1979

Snooky Young

THE BOYS FROM DAYTON,   Master Jazz 8130
  1971
SNOOKY & MARSHALL'S   Concord CJ-55
  ALBUM, 1978
HORN OF PLENTY, 1979   Concord CJ-91

Joe Newman

JOE NEWMAN & HIS BAND,   Vanguard VRS 8007
  1954
JOE NEWMAN & THE BOYS   Storyville 318
  IN THE BAND, 1954
THE COUNT'S MEN, 1955   Jazztone 1220
LOCKING HORNS, 1957   Roulette R-52009
JIVE AT FIVE (with Frank   Swingville 2011
  Wess), 1960
JOE NEWMAN'S QUINTET   Trip 5546
  AT COUNT BASIE'S, 1961
GOOD 'N' GROOVY, 1961   Swingville 2019

Marshall Royal

ALTO ALTITUDE (three   EmArcy 36018
  tracks), 1953
BLUE PRELUDE (Gordon   Sunset 50011
  Jenkins Orchestra), 1960
FIRST CHAIR, 1978   Concord CJ-88

Lockjaw Davis

KICKIN' & WAILIN', 1947–48   Continental 16001
MODERN JAZZ   King 506
  EXPRESSIONS, 1955–56
BIG BEAT JAZZ, 1955–57   King 599
UPTOWN, 1955–57   King 606

JAZZ WITH A HORN, 1956	King 526
EDDIE'S FUNCTION, 1956–57	Bethlehem 6035
COUNT BASIE PRESENTS (with Joe Newman), 1957	Roulette 52007
THE COOKBOOK, 1958 (two discs)	Prestige 24039

(The above set contains albums originally issued as Prestige 7141 and 7161.)

VERY SAXY (with Coleman Hawkins, Arnett Cobb, and Buddy Tate), 1959	Prestige 7167
HAWK EYES (with Coleman Hawkins), 1960	Swingville 2016
STOLEN MOMENTS, 1960	Prestige 7834
TRACKIN', 1962	Prestige 7271
LOCK THE FOX, 1966	Victor LSP-3652
THE FOX AND THE HOUNDS, 1967	Victor LSP-3741
LOVE CALLS (with Paul Gonsalves), 1967	Victor LSP-3882
LEAPIN' ON LENOX, 1974	Black & Blue 33.072 (F)
CHEWIN' THE FAT (with George Arvanitas), 1975	Spotlite 15 (E)
SWEET & LOVELY, 1976	Classic Jazz 116
EDDIE "LOCKJAW" DAVIS & HARRY "SWEETS" EDISON, 1976	Storyville 4004
STRAIGHT AHEAD, 1976	Pablo 2310-778

Frank Wess

THE AWARD WINNER, 1954	Mainstream 56033
KENNY CLARKE (with Kenny Clarke), 1955	Savoy 12006
NORTH, SOUTH, EAST . . . WESS, 1956	Savoy 12072
FRANK WESS QUARTET, 1960	Moodsville 8
WHEELIN' & DEALIN', 1962	Prestige 7231

Frank Foster

JAZZ STUDIO ONE (studio group), 1953	Decca DL 8058

FRANK FOSTER QUARTET (with Henri Renaud), 1954	Vogue 209 (F)
NO COUNT, 1956	Savoy 12078
BASIE IS OUR BOSS, 1963	Argo 717

Joe Williams

TOGETHER (with Harry "Sweets" Edison), 1961	Roulette 52069
JOE WILLIAMS AT NEWPORT, 1963	Victor LSP-2762
ME & THE BLUES, 1963	Victor LSP-2879
PRESENTING JOE WILLIAMS (with the Thad Jones–Mel Lewis Orchestra), 1966	Solid State SS 18008
JAZZ GALA '79 (with the Claude Bolling Orchestra), 1979 (two discs)	Personal Choice PC 51001
PREZ & JOE, 1979	GNP/Crescendo 2124

Al Grey

THE LAST OF THE BIG PLUNGERS, 1959	Argo 653
THE THINKING MAN'S TROMBONE, 1960	Argo 677
AL GREY–BILLY MITCHELL SEXTET, 1961	Argo 689
SNAP YOUR FINGERS (with Billy Mitchell), 1962	Argo 700
NIGHT SONG, 1962	Argo 711
SHADES OF GREY, 1965	Tangerine 1504
GREY'S MOOD, 1973–75	Classic Jazz 118
LIVE AT RICK'S (with Jimmy Forrest), 1978	Aviva 6002

Eric Dixon

ERIC'S EDGE (with Sonny Cohn), 1974	Master Jazz 8124

Richard Boone

I'VE GOT A RIGHT TO SING, 1969	Nocturne 703

Nat Pierce

KANSAS CITY MEMORIES (with Joe Newman & Jo Jones), 1956	Coral 57091
BIG BAND AT THE SAVOY BALLROOM (with Buck Clayton), 1957	Victor LPM 2543
JUGGERNAUT (Frankie Capp & Nat Pierce Orchestra), 1977	Concord CJ 40
LIVE AT THE CENTURY PLAZA (Frankie Capp & Nat Pierce Orchestra), 1978	Concord CJ 72

Jay McShann

EARLY BIRD (with Charlie Parker), 1940–43	Spotlite 120 (E)
KANSAS CITY PIANO (three tracks), 1941	Decca DL 9226
NEW YORK—1208 MILES, 1941–43	Decca DL 9236
K.C. IN THE '30s (McShann, Julia Lee, and other K.C. favorites), 1944–47	Capitol T1057
KANSAS CITY JUMP, 1947	Fontana SFJL-917 (E)
JAY McSHANN, 1947–49	Polydor 423.245 (E)
THE BAND THAT JUMPS THE BLUES, 1947–49	Black Lion 2460.201 (E)
McSHANN'S PIANO, 1966	Capitol T.2645
CONFESSIN' THE BLUES, 1969	Black & Blue 33.022 (F)
JUMPIN' THE BLUES, 1970	Black & Blue 33.039 (F)
GOIN' TO KANSAS CITY, 1972	Master Jazz 8113
THE MAN FROM MUSKOGEE, 1972	Sackville 3005
KANSAS CITY MEMORIES, 1973	Black & Blue 33.057 (F)
KANSAS CITY JOYS (with Buddy Tate and Paul Quinichette), 1976	Sonet 716
CRAZY LEGS & FRIDAY STRUT (with Buddy Tate), 1976	Sackville 3011

THE LAST OF THE BLUE DEVILS, 1977	Atlantic SD 8800
A TRIBUTE TO FATS WALLER, 1978	Sackville 3019
KANSAS CITY HUSTLE, 1978	Sackville 3021

Paul Quinichette

THE VICE PRESIDENT, 1952–53	Trip 5542
MOODS, 1954	Trip 5579
BORDERLINE (with Mel Powell), 1954	Vanguard VRS 8501
ON THE SUNNY SIDE, 1957	Prestige 7103
FOR BASIE, 1957	Prestige 7127
THE KID FROM DENVER, 1958	Biograph 12066
BASIE REUNION, 1958	Prestige 7147
LIKE BASIE, 1959	United Artists 4024
PREVUE (with Brooks Kerr), 1974	Famous Door HL-106

Jimmy Witherspoon

SPOON CALLS HOOTIE (with Jay McShann), 1947–48	Polydor 423.241 (E)
JIMMY WITHERSPOON, 1948–49	Crown CLP 5156
JIMMY WITHERSPOON SINGS THE BLUES, 1952	Crown CLP 5192
GOIN' TO KANSAS CITY BLUES (with Jay McShann), 1957	Victor LPM 1639
THERE'S GOOD ROCKIN' TONIGHT (with Harry Edison), 1958	World Pacific 1402
THE 'SPOON CONCERTS (with Roy Eldridge, Ben Webster, and Earl Hines), 1959 (two discs)	Fantasy 24701
IN PERSON (with Buck Clayton, Dicky Wells, and Buddy Tate), 1961	Vogue 456-30 (F)

ROOTS (with Ben Webster),   Reprise 6057
   1962
EVENIN' BLUES (with T-Bone   Prestige 7300
   Walker), 1963

Eddie Barefield
EDDIE BAREFIELD PLAYS   Cosmopolitan 500
   THE WORKS OF EDGAR
   BATTLE, 1962
EDDIE BAREFIELD, 1973–74   RCA LFLI 5035 (E)
THE INDESTRUCTIBLE   Famous Door HL 113
   E.B., 1977

Leo "Snub" Mosley
CASCADE OF QUARTETS,   Columbia 33sx1191/1218 (E)
   VOLS. I & II (one track in
   each), 1959

Sir Charles Thompson
SIR CHARLES THOMPSON   Apollo 103
   ALL STARS (with Charlie
   Parker), 1945–47
SIR CHARLES THOMPSON   Vanguard VRS 8003
   SEXTET, 1953
SIR CHARLES THOMPSON   Vanguard VRS 8006
   QUARTET, 1954
SIR CHARLES THOMPSON   Vanguard VRS 8009
   & HIS BAND (with Coleman
   Hawkins), 1954
SIR CHARLES THOMPSON   Vanguard VRS 8018
   TRIO, 1955
SIR CHARLES & THE SWING   Columbia CL 1364
   ORGAN, 1960
ROCKIN' RHYTHM, 1961   Columbia CS 8463
HEY, THERE!, 1973   Black & Blue 33.073 (F)

Bibliography

Books

Panassié, Hugues. *The Real Jazz*. New York: Smith & Durrell, 1942.

Ellison, Ralph. *Shadow and Act*. New York: Random House, 1953. (See Part II, "Sound and the Mainstream.")

Shapiro, Nat, and Nat Hentoff, eds. *Hear Me Talkin' to You*. New York: Rinehart, 1955.

Horricks, Raymond. *Count Basie and His Orchestra*. London: Gollancz, 1957.

Shapiro, Nat, and Nat Hentoff, eds. *The Jazz Makers*. New York: Rinehart, 1957. (See Nat Shapiro on "William 'Count' Basie.")

Hentoff, Nat, and Albert McCarthy, eds. *Jazz*. New York: Rinehart, 1959. (See Frank Driggs on "Kansas City and the Southwest.")

Williams, Martin, ed. *The Art of Jazz*. New York: Oxford University, 1959. (See "The Parent Style and Lester Young," by Ross Russell.)

Traill, Sinclair, and the Hon. Gerald Lascelles, eds. *Just Jazz, Volume IV*. London: Souvenir Press, 1960. (See Count Basie on "This Band.")

Hentoff, Nat. *The Jazz Life*. New York: Dial, 1961. (See "Count Basie.")

Hodeir, André. *Toward Jazz*. New York: Grove Press, 1962.

James, Burnett. *Essays on Jazz*. London: Sidgwick & Jackson, 1962. (See "Lester Young.")

Reisner, Robert George. *Bird*. Secaucus, N.J.: Citadel, 1962.

Green, Benny. *The Reluctant Art*. New York: Horizon Press, 1963. (See "Lester Young.")

Dexter, Dave. *The Jazz Story*. Englewood Cliffs, N.J.: Prentice-Hall, 1964.

Simon, George T. *The Big Bands*. New York: Macmillan, 1967.

Schuller, Gunther. *Early Jazz*. New York: Oxford University, 1968. (See "The Southwest.")

Dance, Stanley. *The World of Duke Ellington*. New York: Scribners, 1970. (See "Paul Gonsalves," "Clark Terry," and "Booty Wood.")

Williams, Martin. *The Jazz Tradition*. New York: Oxford University, 1970.

Wilmer, Valerie. *Jazz People*. London: Allison & Busby, 1970. (See "Lock the Fox" and "Buck Clayton.")

Blesh, Rudi. *Combo U.S.A*. Philadelphia: Chilton, 1971. (See "The Prez.")

Russell, Ross. *Jazz Style in Kansas City and the Southwest*. Berkeley and Los Angeles: University of California Press, 1971.

Simon, George T. *Simon Says*. New Rochelle, N.Y.: Arlington, 1971.

Wells, Dicky (with Stanley Dance). *The Night People*. Boston: Crescendo, 1971.

Feather, Leonard. *From Satchmo to Miles*. Briarcliff Manor, N.Y.: Stein & Day, 1972. (See "Swing and Basie" and "Prez.")

Russell, Ross. *Bird Lives!* New York: Charterhouse, 1973.

Dance, Stanley. *The World of Swing*. New York: Scribners, 1974. (See "Andy Gibson," "Vic Dickenson," "Quentin Jackson," and "Benny Morton.")

McCarthy, Albert. *Big Band Jazz*. New York: Putnam's, 1974.

Morgenstern, Dan, and Jack Bradley, eds. *Count Basie and His Bands*. New York: New York Jazz Museum, 1975.

Brask, Ole, and Dan Morgenstern. *Jazz People*. New York: Abrams, 1976.

Dexter, Dave. *Playback*. New York: Billboard Publications, 1976.

Murray, Albert. *Stomping the Blues*. New York: McGraw-Hill, 1976.

Dance, Stanley. *The World of Earl Hines*. New York: Scribners, 1977. (See "Budd Johnson," "Dicky Wells," and "Charlie Carpenter.")

Hammond, John (with Irving Townsend). *John Hammond on Record*. New York: Ridge Press, 1977.

Gridley, Mark C. *Jazz Styles*. Englewood Cliffs, N.J.: Prentice-Hall, 1978. (See "The Count Basie Bands.")

Giddins, Gary. *Riding on a Blue Note*. New York: Oxford University, 1981.

Besides the standard references by John Chilton, Hugues Panassié, and Leonard Feather, and the general discographies of Brian Rust and Jorgen Grunnet Jepsen, the following are particularly relevant:

Count Basie, 1929–1950. A discography compiled by Bo Scherman and Carl A. Hallstrom. Copenhagen: Knudsen, 1969.
Count Basie, 1951–1968. A discography compiled by Jorgen Grunnet Jepsen. Copenhagen: Knudsen, 1969.

Magazines

The best and most detailed research on jazz in the Southwest has been done by Frank Driggs, whose own book on the subject is long overdue. His many interviews include:

"Jay McShann." *Jazz Monthly*, March 1958.
"Elmer Crumbley." *Coda*, August 1958.
"Walter Page." *Jazz Review*, November 1958.
"Buddy Tate." *Jazz Review*, December 1958.
"Milt Larkins." *Jazz Monthly*, December 1958.
"Andy Kirk." *Jazz Review*, February 1959.
"Ed Lewis, I and II." *Jazz Review*, May and October, 1959.
"Don Albert." *Jazz Monthly*, July 1959.
"Clarence Love." *Jazz Monthly*, December 1959.
"Ben Smith." *Record Research*, March 1960.
"Tommy Douglas." *Jazz Monthly*, April 1960.
"Eddie Barefield." *Jazz Review*, July 1960.
"Budd Johnson, I and II." *Jazz Review*, November 1960 and January 1961.
"Harlan Leonard." *Jazz Journal*, October 1963.
"Red Perkins, I and II." *Jazz Journal*, November and December 1964.

Other articles that can be profitably consulted are:

Dance, Stanley. "New York Impressions." *Jazz Hot*, no. 17, 1937.
Simon, George. "Up for the Count." *Metronome*, November 1948.
Gleason, Ralph. "Count Basie: Bouquets for the Living." *Down Beat*, November 17, 1950.
Williams, Mary Lou, with Max Jones. "Mary Lou Williams: Life Story." *Melody Maker*, April 3 to June 12, 1954 (eleven consecutive issues).
Hammond, John. "Count Basie: A 20th Anniversary." *Down Beat*, November 2, 1955.
Freeman, Don. "Count Basie" (interview). *Down Beat*, May 16, 1956.
Panassié, Hugues. "Reminiscing About the Count." *Jazz Journal*, April 1957.

Dance, Stanley. "The Conquering Count." *Jazz Journal,* December 1957.

Dance, Stanley. "Skip Hall and Eli Robinson." *Jazz Monthly,* September 1958.

"Relaxin' with the Count." *Down Beat,* September 18, 1958.

Hodeir, André. "Du Côte de Chez Basie." *Jazz Review,* December 1958.

Panassié, Hugues. "Lester Young." *Bulletin H.C.F.,* April 1959.

Panassié, Hugues. "Lips Page." *Bulletin H.C.F.,* December 1959.

Gazzaway, Don. "Conversations with Buster Smith." *Jazz Review,* December 1959, January and February, 1960.

Gazzaway, Don. "Before Bird—Buster." *Jazz Monthly,* January 1962.

Feather, Leonard. "Basie." *Swank,* May 1963.

Gelly, Dave. "The Count Basie Octet." *Jazz Monthly,* July 1963.

Lambert, G. E. "Count Basie: The Middle Years." *Jazz Monthly,* September 1963.

Panassié, Hugues. "Herschel Evans." *Bulletin H.C.F.,* April 1964.

"Why Count Basie Keeps Swinging." *Sepia,* May 1965.

Holroyd, Steve. "Four Decades of Basie, I and II." *Melody Maker,* August 17 and August 24, 1968.

"Count Basie: Press Conference." *Asbury Park Evening Press,* August 17, 1969.

Giddins, Gary. "On the Road with the Super Chief." *New York,* May 12, 1975.

Postif, François. "Goodbye, Pork Pie Hat." *Jazz Hot,* nos. 362 and 363, 1979.

Index

Song titles are in *italics*.

DATE DUE	BORROWER'S NAME	ROOM NUMBER